PRINCIPLES AND VALUES IN CRIMINAL LAW AND CRIMINAL JUSTICE: ESSAYS IN HONOUR OF ANDREW ASHWORTH

Principles and Values in Criminal Law and Criminal Justice: Essays in honour of Andrew Ashworth

Edited by
LUCIA ZEDNER
and
JULIAN V ROBERTS

OXFORD
UNIVERSITY PRESS

OXFORD
UNIVERSITY PRESS

Great Clarendon Street, Oxford OX2 6DP,
United Kingdom

Oxford University Press is a department of the University of Oxford.
It furthers the University's objective of excellence in research, scholarship,
and education by publishing worldwide. Oxford is a registered trade mark of
Oxford University Press in the UK and in certain other countries

First Edition published in 2012
Impression: 2

British Library Cataloguing in Publication Data
Data available

Library of Congress Cataloging in Publication Data
Data available

ISBN 978–0–19–969679–6

Printed in Great Britain by
CPI Group (UK) Ltd, Croydon, CR0 4YY

Andrew Ashworth: A Tribute

Roger Hood

I am honoured to have been asked to introduce this Festschrift to mark Andrew Ashworth's retirement from the Vinerian Professorship of English Law at Oxford University and his Fellowship of All Souls College Oxford, posts that he has held with great distinction since 1997. We have been friends and colleagues since 1978 when he came to Oxford at the age of 31 (having been since the age of 23 a Lecturer, then Senior Lecturer in Law at Manchester University) to take up a fellowship and tutorship in Law at Worcester College, where his great supporter Sir Rupert Cross, then Vinerian Professor, had begun his outstanding career as an undergraduate. It was Rupert who had alerted me to Andrew's talents, declaring that 'Ashworth has become by far the best young criminal lawyer in the country'. That was certainly true at the time, but beyond that it proved to be a truly positive prediction of where his abilities would carry him.

It is not for me to try to review or assess his contributions: that will be done by the editors in the light of the essays contributed by Andrew's admirers. But a simple tally of them will show why he is now recognized as one of the most influential lawyers in Britain. Andrew Ashworth is renowned for his textbooks on criminal law, criminal procedure, sentencing, and human rights. He had begun by collaborating with Rupert Cross on the third edition of *The English Sentencing System*[1] but within two years had taken a fresh approach in his own *Sentencing and Penal Policy*,[2] later to become the much admired and influential *Sentencing and Criminal Justice*.[3] Likewise, his other textbooks have authoritatively defined their respective fields, being meticulously researched, written with great clarity, and kept up-to-date with unfailing regularity. His extraordinary tenure over almost a quarter of a century until 1999 of the editorship of the monthly published *Criminal Law Review,* each edition containing an informative, critically acute editorial, is legendary. In addition he has published many first-rate articles on key aspects of criminal law, criminal procedure, penal theory, sentencing, human rights, and other aspects of the operation of the system of criminal justice. He is greatly admired as a trenchant critic of anything that smacks of injustice or the unprincipled or disproportionate use of criminal sanctions. Andrew's promotion of reform in the field of sentencing and the application generally of criminal sanctions and the distinctive part he has played in forging links between criminal law, human rights, and criminological enquiry are outstanding features of his scholarship. Through his

[1] R Cross and A Ashworth, *The English Sentencing System* (London: Butterworths, 1981).

[2] A Ashworth, *Sentencing and Penal Policy* (London: Weidenfeld and Nicolson, 1983).

[3] A Ashworth, *Sentencing and Criminal Justice* (4th edn, Cambridge: Cambridge University Press, 2005).

teaching and very effective supervision of many graduate students—he has never been known to turn down a request to help a younger scholar—he has made a marvellous contribution to the careers of his doctoral candidates. Furthermore, he is very approachable and generous with his time in advising, assisting, befriending, and supporting colleagues. His unwavering and active support of the Oxford Centre for Criminology, including taking responsibility as Acting Director, first in 1982–83 and again in 2003 and 2004–05, has been vital to the Centre's success.

Not only has Andrew been a worthy successor to the great lawyers (such as Dicey, Holdsworth, Cheshire, Cross, and Treitel) that have held the Vinerian Professorship since William Blackstone at the end of the 18th century, he has in many ways developed the study of criminal law and broadened its perspective well beyond the subject he inherited.

He was appointed to the Edmund-Davies Chair of Criminal Law and Criminal Justice at King's College London at age 41 and five years later, in 1993, elected to a Fellowship of the British Academy and awarded an Oxford DCL. Appointments to an honorary Queen's Council, Honorary Bencher of the Inner Temple, and to the Vinerian Chair followed as he celebrated his 50th birthday. His work earned him Honorary LLDs from De Montfort and Uppsala Universities. There will be more to come. He has visited and lectured, as far as I am aware, at universities in Australia, Canada, Cyprus, Denmark, Finland, France, Germany, Ireland, Italy, New Zealand, Norway, South Africa, Spain, Sweden, and the United States—where his scholarship and fresh approach to well-worn themes have been greatly appreciated. His sterling work for the Council of Europe, for which characteristically he made sure that his ability to communicate in French was up to speed, on 'Disparity in Sentencing: Causes and Solutions'[4] in 1989, followed by being Chairman of the Council's Committee on Consistency which produced Recommendation R (92) 17, added to his international reputation. His international standing was further marked when the newly formed Association of Commonwealth Criminal Lawyers elected him as its first President in 2011.

Andrew has been named by The Times as 'Britain's most influential criminologist' particularly in the fields of criminal justice and human rights, and his contribution to British public life was marked in 2010 by the award of the CBE. He has made major contributions as a member of the Criminal Law Revision Committee between 1980 and its last reference in 1985; to the Council of Justice since 1997; to the Criminal Committee of the Judicial Studies Board between 2002 and 2008; and especially since 1998 to the Sentencing Advisory Panel, which he chaired between 2007 (along with membership of the Sentencing Guidelines Council), and 2010 when these bodies were replaced by the Sentencing Council.

His influence on sentencing policy has been profound. Between 1988 and 1996, all aspiring barristers in the country would have attended his course on Sentencing at the Inns of Court School of Law in London, and no doubt came away imbued with the principles of proportionality and penal restraint that Andrew has

[4] Council of Europe, 1989.

championed so effectively. Indeed, it was Andrew Ashworth, in a widely noted speech to NACRO in 1982 on 'Reducing the Prison Population in the 1980s: the Need for Sentencing Reform', who was the first in recent times to argue vigorously for the establishment of a Sentencing Council to bring greater proportionality, equity, and a principled approach to sentencing policy. Also, as far as magistrates' courts were concerned, Andrew was in the vanguard when in 1985 he promoted the formulation of 'structured decision-making' and worked effectively with Rosemary Thompson of the Magistrates' Association to get this idea accepted by the Judicial Studies Board. This led subsequently to the adoption by the Magistrates' Association of national guidelines for many common offences. As far as the higher judiciary were concerned, his proposal for a Sentencing Council was at first dismissed as a 'foreign' idea, aimed at unduly limiting the discretion of judges, but his determined persistence in championing his proposal led first to the establishment of the Sentencing Advisory Panel and then to the independent Sentencing Guidelines Council in 1998 and 2003 respectively by the New Labour Government, and finally to the present Sentencing Council in 2010.

How has all this and much more besides been achieved? Those who know Andrew well will have observed a quiet, rather reserved side to his nature. He is anything but showy, self-important, or superior. His modesty is matched by self-confidence, a wry sense of humour, and an ability to organize and carry through his heavy work schedule at a pace and within a strict schedule that amazes anyone who has collaborated with him. There are no signs of the panic that may invade most of us as deadlines approach: quite the opposite. The midnight oil is not for him. Each day he will arrive at his office at around 8.30am and leave with the day's tasks completed at around 5pm. As far as I am aware he does not usually undertake academic work at weekends. Rather, he enjoys exercising his many other talents. Formerly a keen golfer and long-distance runner (he still jogs daily), Andrew plays bridge every Tuesday evening to a high standard, he loves travel and his bolt-hole in southern France, is very knowledgeable about classical music, greatly enjoys fine wine and food, and has found time over the past ten years to take responsibility, alongside the Head Chef, for the choice of menus at All Souls.

It is only a remarkable person who could have achieved so much, and so serenely. Order, discipline, determination, clarity of mind, an exceptional 'legal mind', and an unerring ability to present ideas without unnecessary jargon or pretension, have all made this possible. He is the living embodiment of the adage 'If you want something done ask a busy person.' We salute Andrew on his retirement from his academic post knowing that we can expect many more distinguished contributions from him in the years to come.

Editors' Introduction

Lucia Zedner and Julian V Roberts

This Festschrift is first and foremost a celebration of its honorand—Professor Andrew Ashworth CBE, QC, DCL, FBA, the Vinerian Professor of English Law in the Law Faculty, Fellow of All Souls College, and member of the Centre for Criminology at the University of Oxford. His many publications and distinguished public lectures have had a hugely important impact on the development of criminal law and criminal justice in Britain and indeed throughout the common law world. Ashworth's scholarship is extraordinary in its range, extent, and, not least, its sophistication. Among the most important of Ashworth's contributions is the development and articulation of a body of principles and values in respect of the criminal law, the criminal process, and sentencing. This development of a principled approach has been an abiding theme throughout his work. His enduring achievement has been to inform the ways in which criminal lawyers and criminal justice scholars think about their subject, and to raise that thinking to new levels, not least by rendering normative considerations a vital companion to analytical enquiry.

Ashworth is unusual among academics in having made important contributions to the development of doctrinal law and legal theory, at the same time as having had a major influence over the development of criminal justice policy. The essays in this volume engage directly with Ashworth's work to date and seek to further his ambitions for criminal law and criminal justice scholarship. To this end, we asked leading academics in cognate fields to engage directly with some of the most important principles and values articulated in Ashworth's writings; to reflect upon their import, their applications, and their possible limitations in specific domains. Collectively, the essays in this book thus seek to build upon the extraordinary contribution to criminal law, criminal justice, and penal theory that Ashworth has made so far and to take forward his principled approach to these important areas of scholarship.

The essays that follow are written by distinguished and internationally renowned academics from Britain, Germany, America, Canada, Australia, South Africa, and Singapore, all of whom have been associated with Andrew Ashworth and his scholarship over the course of his career. Each contributor has responded to our invitation to engage in a critical appreciation and advancement of the principles articulated by Ashworth in quite distinct domains—criminal law, criminal process, human rights, penal theory, and sentencing. As the essays that follow make clear, the contributors took their remit very seriously. Not only do they engage closely with many of the principles and values set out in Ashworth's own work, they seek to elaborate upon and to develop these principles according to their respective interests and areas of expertise. We are delighted that the essays so amply accomplish our aim of producing a volume that both honours Andrew Ashworth and makes a substantial contribution to academic debates about normative questions in criminal law and criminal justice. Together they take the 'Ashworthian' project forward and, in so doing, we hope they will stimulate new debates and attract new audiences for them.

The Honorand

'Not every honorand wants a trumpet blown' observes Michael Taggart in his analysis of the role of Festschriften in the legal academy.[5] Of no one is this observation more likely to be true than Andrew Ashworth, whose natural modesty is remarkable in a field often characterized by self-promotion. Happily the need for trumpet blowing scarcely arises for, in Ashworth's case, further fanfare is quite unnecessary—the intense, positive academic and judicial attention that his scholarship has attracted serves as its own ample salute.

Ashworth's scholarship spans over 40 years and his publications have appeared at a rate that is humbling, especially given his many other academic responsibilities, his editorial roles, and policy-related duties. For example, as longstanding editor of the *Criminal Law Review,* Ashworth played a vital role in ensuring the reputation, high academic standards, currency, and value of the journal for practitioners. His successor as Editor, Ian Dennis, observed of Ashworth's tenure: 'few articles emerge entirely unscathed from the close, but sympathetic scrutiny to which they are always subjected by the editor' and he attributed to Ashworth the 'greatest credit' for attaining the 'worldwide reputation and influence' of the journal through his 'great editorial care and skill'.[6]

If the enduring quality of that journal serves as testimony to Ashworth's influence, another must surely be the Oxford University Press series *Oxford Monographs on Criminal Law and Justice.* Under Ashworth's sole editorship this series has published some of the most important and insightful contributions to the fields of criminal law, criminal procedure, and evidence of the past decades. It is not by chance that several contributors to that series appear also in this volume, including Duff, Horder, Lazarus, Mitchell, Redmayne, Shute, Simester, Tadros, von Hirsch, and Wasik. These major editorial undertakings are symptomatic of Ashworth's good citizenship as a leading member of the academic community and of his quietly effective stewardship of legal scholarship at the highest level. No less important has been his solicitous encouragement of generations of students, his supervision of dozens of research students, often writing in fields remote from his immediate area of interest or direct expertise, to whom he nonetheless offers inspiration, patient instruction, and sound guidance. Ashworth has long played an important role in

[5] M Taggart, 'Gardens or Graveyards of Scholarship? Festschriften in the Literature of the Common Law' (2002) 22 OJLS 227, 230.

[6] 'Editorial' [1999] Crim LR 181.

mentoring, appraising, and advising emerging and established scholars, both at Oxford and, in this increasingly globalized age, around the world.

The momentous task of bringing up to date his hugely important textbooks such as *Principles of Criminal Law*, *Sentencing and Criminal Justice*, and *The Criminal Process*,[7] all of which have run to multiple editions, to say nothing of his compendious *Human Rights and Criminal Justice*[8] would daunt most scholars. For Ashworth, however, the almost annual task of revising and updating new editions of his textbooks is accomplished alongside a steady outpouring of new articles in peer-reviewed journals and invited contributions to edited volumes. It would probably be unwise to see these activities as distinct. Ashworth's mastery of the cognate but separate domains of the criminal law, criminal process, human rights, and sentencing furnish him with an encyclopaedic knowledge, and the regular task of updating new editions sees him fully abreast of developments in each field. As a consequence, Ashworth is singularly adept at identifying new trends, responding to governmental consultations, analysing and critiquing legal reforms, and, in so doing, provoking and leading debates about legal developments as they occur. Little wonder that his scholarship often addresses issues at the very forefront of change. But Ashworth is no mere commentator on legal developments. His writings are often eerily prescient in foretelling or warning of changes before they occur. They have also played an important role in generating new legal forms and in inspiring new legal institutions—not least in respect of sentencing, a field in which Ashworth has played a prominent role for decades in pressing for more structured sentencing guidelines.

It is no exaggeration to say that it seems unlikely that England and Wales would have developed a sentencing guidelines scheme had it not been for the scholarship of Andrew Ashworth. He has advocated repeatedly the creation of such a scheme over the past 25 years, and has published many articles in which he adumbrates the form and structure that sentencing guidelines might assume. And of course once a statutory authority was established to generate guidance (the Sentencing Advisory Panel), Ashworth played a vital role in developing the guidelines. He served as a member (1999–2007) and then Chairman (2007–2010) of the Sentencing Advisory Panel and as a member of the Sentencing Guidelines Council (2007–2010). The Sentencing Advisory Panel and the Sentencing Guidelines Council were both replaced in 2010 by the Sentencing Council of England and Wales. Ashworth continues to contribute by his submissions to the Council's consultations and in his publications dealing with the guidelines.[9]

During a period in which the dominant penal environment has been a toxic mix of over-criminalization and popular punitiveness, Ashworth's scholarship has consistently made the quietly authoritative case for principled restraint in criminalization, and parsimony and proportionality in sentencing. Above all, it is his unusual

[7] Later editions of *The Criminal Process* are co-authored with Mike Redmayne.

[8] Co-authored with Ben Emmerson and Alison Macdonald.

[9] See <http://sentencingcouncil.judiciary.gov.uk/> accessed 22 March 2012. See eg A Ashworth, 'Departures from the Sentencing Guidelines' [2012] Crim LR 81.

combination of theoretical sophistication, exhaustive knowledge, and pragmatism that marks Ashworth's scholarship out as such a powerful source of intellectual stimulation within the academy and a potent source of guidance for policy-makers and practitioners.

The Essays

The contributions to this volume surely meet Taggart's prescription for the ideal Festschrift as comprising: 'the best current work... from the workbenches of handpicked lawyers honouring distinguished jurists'.[10] The essays that follow address many of the key substantive areas of Ashworth's scholarship: criminal law, criminal process and criminal justice, human rights, sentencing and punishment, although no attempt was made to cover all the substantive issues to which Ashworth has addressed his considerable acumen over the course of his career thus far. And it is surely telling that 20 leading academics tackle only some of the topics that a single individual has written upon with such easy authority and accomplishment.

The essays in the first section of the book broadly address the role of principles in criminal law—in respect of which Ashworth has, of course, led the field with the several editions of *Principles of Criminal Law* and many pioneering articles. The first essay by John Gardner asks the logically prior question of what we mean by principles. Gardner's essay examines Ashworth's insistence that the law should be principled by exploring his deployment of and commitments to principle;[11] the relationship between principles, rules and reasons, and policies; and by questioning whether principles are any more than arguments that 'cannot be easily overridden'. Nicola Lacey picks up on the relationship between principles and policies. She celebrates Ashworth's contribution to the identification and elaboration of core principles immanent to criminal law and criminal justice and his insistence on the need for their defence.[12] Her essay goes on to examine how those principles have been put under pressure by trends towards over-criminalization and punitiveness. Lacey asks whether a principled approach can really prevail when political pragmatism dominates criminal policy, and she questions the role that policy considerations play in the light of the criminal law's regulatory objectives.

The next three essays each address the articulation and application of principles in criminal law doctrine. Jeremy Horder considers the challenges posed by applying core principles in the Ashworthian subjectivist tradition to inchoate liability. He examines, in particular, the significance of the principles of legality and maximum

[10] M Taggart, 'Gardens or Graveyards of Scholarship? Festschriften in the Literature of the Common Law' (2002) 22 OJLS 227, 246.

[11] See eg A Ashworth, 'Towards a Theory of Criminal Legislation' (1989) 1 Criminal Law Forum 41; A Ashworth, *Principles of Criminal Law* (6th edn, Oxford: Oxford University Press, 2009).

[12] A Ashworth, 'Is the Criminal Law a Lost Cause?' (2000) 116 LQR 225.

certainty for the criminalization of attempts.[13] Horder explores Ashworth's concerns about the compatibility of criminal attempt with the rule of law, considers problems of vagueness in the definition of attempts, and how potential problems of accountability might be met by the use of guidelines. A core principle on which Ashworth has made important contributions, the presumption of innocence,[14] is the subject of Antony Duff's essay, which explores its meaning and normative foundations. Duff examines the nature of the burden imposed by the presumption of innocence, explores the meanings of innocence, and the implications for, and plight of, the presumption in recent legislation. Another of Ashworth's major contributions is his analysis of 'fair labelling' in criminal law, and this is the focus of Tadros' essay.[15] Tadros builds upon Ashworth's exposition of fair labelling to explore variant forms of unfairness in the labelling of crimes and the holding of perpetrators to account. He examines the principles which should guide the definition of offences and why fair labelling is important: both in fulfilling the condemnatory function of the criminal law and in securing public solidarity and confidence in law.

The remaining three essays in this section each address issues arising at the very limits of criminal liability. Douglas Husak's essay examines Ashworth's reservations about punishing persons for harms caused negligently and contrasts this with the general acceptance of liability for recklessness.[16] Husak examines how the boundaries between recklessness and negligence should be drawn, paying particular attention to the concepts of awareness, knowledge, belief, and distraction. Intriguingly, Husak raises the question of whether persons are aware of the risk they disregard in cases in which they have forgotten about a risk they have created. Andrew Simester likewise considers an area in which Ashworth has made an important contribution, the bases for justifications and excuses in criminal law.[17] He suggests a new typology of exculpatory defences: namely, irresponsibility defences, justifications, rationale-based excuses, and defensive mistakes. Simester goes on to differentiate justifications from excuses, to consider the operational implications in law of distinguishing between them, and, in so doing, to advance Ashworth's own attempt to understand the moral structure of blame in criminal law. Barry Mitchell's essay also tackles a controversial basis for criminal defence, namely provocation—a defence that was the subject of some of Ashworth's earliest

[13] A Ashworth, *Principles of Criminal Law* (6th edn, Oxford: Oxford University Press, 2009), Chs 2 and 3.

[14] A Ashworth, 'Four Threats to the Presumption of Innocence' (2006) 123 South African Law Journal 62; A Ashworth and M Blake, 'The Presumption of Innocence in English Criminal Law' [1996] Crim LR 306.

[15] See eg A Ashworth, 'The Elasticity of *Mens Rea*' in CFH Tapper (ed), *Crime, Proof and Punishment* (London: Butterworths, 1981).

[16] A Ashworth, *Principles of Criminal Law* (6th edn, Oxford: Oxford University Press, 2009), 187–8.

[17] eg A Ashworth, 'Testing Fidelity to Legal Values: Official Involvement and Criminal Justice' in S Shute and AP Simester (eds), *Criminal Law Theory: Doctrines of the General Part* (Oxford: Oxford University Press, 2002), 299.

critical contributions,[18] which has only recently been abolished and replaced by 'loss of control'. Mitchell's essay revisits the difficulties in the old provocation defence and offers a critical evaluation of the new law, which suggests that its failure to satisfy Ashworth's insistence on the principle of maximum certainty raises questions about its likely success.

The essays in the second section address different aspects of the criminal process, due process protections, and adherence to human rights. All these are areas in which Ashworth has played a leading role, not least in his successive editions of *The Criminal Process* and *Human Rights and Criminal Justice,* as well as his important Hamlyn Lectures, *Human Rights, Serious Crime and Criminal Procedure.*[19] Liora Lazarus's essay engages with Ashworth's more recent, important work in the field of human rights[20] to address fundamental questions about how positive rights claims have shaped the criminal law and criminal justice process. She examines the framing of positive duties, and the relationship between protective duties and the right to security. Lazarus concludes by warning of the consequential danger that these developments license unduly coercive activity by the state—or, as she aptly phrases it, the risk of 'the coercive sting in the tail of positive duties'.

Mike Redmayne's contribution on entrapment addresses a difficult area at the heart of policing and the criminal process and, again, one on which Ashworth made an early contribution and about which he has gone on to write seminal articles.[21] Redmayne's essay draws upon Ashworth's analysis to show that it provides a coherent account of the bases for entrapment but to suggest that a number of difficulties remain in drawing the distinction between illegitimate and legitimate entrapment. In his essay, Redmayne offers refinements to Ashworth's account that, nonetheless, follow and defend his principled approach. Paul Roberts' essay is prompted by another of Ashworth's early and important essays: on the exclusion of improperly obtained evidence.[22] Roberts' essay, like Ashworth's earlier contribution, explores the ramifications of the 'protective principle'—a principle that has passed into the standard terminology of criminal procedure scholarship. This essay revisits Ashworth's protective principle in the light of developments in criminal procedure law and scholarship over 30 years. Roberts finds Ashworth's work

18 A Ashworth, 'The Doctrine of Provocation' (1976) 35 CLJ 292; A Ashworth, 'Sentencing in Provocation Cases' [1975] Crim LR 553.

19 A Ashworth and M Redmayne, *The Criminal Process* (Oxford: Oxford University Press 2010); B Emmerson, A Ashworth, and A Macdonald, *Human Rights and Criminal Justice* (London: Sweet & Maxwell, 2011); A Ashworth, *Human Rights, Serious Crime and Criminal Procedure* (London: Sweet & Maxwell, 2002).

20 eg, A Ashworth, *Human Rights, Serious Crime and Criminal Procedure* (London: Sweet & Maxwell, 2002); A Ashworth, 'Criminal Law, Human Rights and Preventative Justice' in B Mcsherry, A Norrie, and S Bronitt (eds), *Regulating Deviance: The Redirection of Criminalisation and the Futures of Criminal Law* (Oxford: Hart Publishing, 2009), 87; B Emmerson, A Ashworth, and A Macdonald, *Human Rights and Criminal Justice* (London: Sweet & Maxwell, 2011).

21 Including A Ashworth, 'Defences of General Application: The Law Commission Report No 83: (3) Entrapment' [1978] Crim LR 137; A Ashworth, 'What is Wrong with Entrapment?' [1999] Singapore Journal of Legal Studies 293, 305; A Ashworth, 'Re-Drawing the Boundaries of Entrapment' [2002] Crim LR 161.

22 A Ashworth, 'Excluding Evidence as Protecting Rights' [1977] Crim LR 723.

remarkably prescient in anticipating current controversies bearing on the status of constitutional principles and human rights and their implications for the admissibility of evidence in criminal trials. He further elaborates the protective principle for a post-Human Rights Act era and opens up new the lines of enquiry suggested by Ashworth's original conception. The essay by Andrew von Hirsch and Vivian Schorscher draws directly upon von Hirsch's longstanding collaborations with Ashworth that articulate a proportionate theory of sentencing.[23] Their essay considers the possibility of establishing a system of criminal justice with international jurisdiction to proscribe serious human rights violations as crimes and an international court with authority to prosecute and punish those convicted. They explore whether such a system would be justified and why. In so doing, they draw directly on the von Hirsch and Ashworth account of criminal punishment as justified by both deontological and consequentialist reasons that embrace censure and crime prevention simultaneously.

The essay by Dirk van Zyl Smit is prompted by Ashworth's contributions on the relationship between non-custodial sanctions and human rights and on the place of human rights principles in the development of European criminal justice.[24] His essay explores the idea that there is a distinctively European approach to non-custodial penalties generally and to community sanctions and measures in particular. It compares the human rights-based approaches to European policies on custody with approaches to non-custodial penalties and considers whether these developments have served to strengthen or weaken the original human rights impetus that underlay their introduction. Finally, van Zyl Smit considers how the human rights of those subject to non-custodial sanctions can be protected better in Europe in the future. All the essays in this section make clear that by placing due process protections and human rights at the centre of his scholarship, Ashworth provides the basis for trenchant critique of criminal justice practices and shows the way for the more effective advancement of basic rights.

The third and final section addresses questions arising in respect of sentencing, an area in which Ashworth's work has had unparalleled influence in academic, policy, and judicial domains. In addition to his many articles and chapters exploring all aspects of sentencing, Ashworth is the author of one of the leading sentencing texts in England and Wales, now in its fifth edition.[25]

The first essay in Part III by Kate Warner examines the tensions between two competing principles, namely 'equality before the law' and 'equal impact'.[26] Her essay examines

[23] eg A Ashworth, 'Social Control and Anti-Social Behaviour: the Subversion of Human Rights' (2004) 120 LQR 263; B Emmerson, A Ashworth, and A Macdonald, *Human Rights and Criminal Justice* (London: Sweet & Maxwell, 2011).

[24] A Ashworth, *Sentencing and Criminal Justice* (5th edn, Cambridge: Cambridge University Press, 2010).

[25] Of which the most extended is A von Hirsch and A Ashworth, *Proportionate Sentencing: Exploring the Principles* (Oxford: Oxford University Press, 2005).

[26] A Ashworth, *Sentencing and Criminal Justice* (5th edn, Cambridge: Cambridge University Press, 2010); also A Ashworth and E Player, 'Sentencing, Equal Treatment and the Impact of Sanctions' in A Ashworth and M Wasik (eds), *Fundamentals of Sentencing Theory* (Oxford: Clarendon Press, 1998), 252.

the applications of these principles in respect of financial penalties and issues of employment status. In particular, Warner focuses on the ways in which the unit fine has been deployed in the attempt to tackle issues of economic and social inequality and to reconcile principles of equality with principles such as proportionality and parsimony in sentencing. Elaine Player's essay tackles a related but distinct set of questions about equality in sentencing by examining the implications of the Gender Equality Duty introduced under the Equality Act 2006. Her essay explores the 'radical implications' for sentencing policy and practice posed by this duty and it considers how concepts of justice and equality can shape the sentencing of women. Like Warner, Player draws upon Ashworth's recognition of individual difference, his advocacy of equal impact in sentencing, and the limits placed upon both by an overarching principle of proportionality. The proportionality principle is also a central theme of Malcolm Thorburn's essay. In it he expands upon the 'strong proportionality principle' and the 'state monopoly principle' as furnishing a jurisdictional conception of sentencing that asks who has the jurisdiction to punish and what punishers have the jurisdiction to do. Building upon this conception,[27] Thorburn explores difficult questions about the authority to punish, the place of punishers within a legitimate constitutional order, and the implications of Ashworth's jurisdictional approach for political theory and the rule of law.

The final two essays address more substantive issues that pose conundrums for sentencing practice, both of which have been curiously overlooked by sentencing scholars. The essay by Martin Wasik examines what he rightly describes as an 'issue of great practical importance but one which has been neglected in theory', namely the challenges posed by the sentencing of multiple offences. The difficulties thrown up by concurrent and consecutive sentences for multiple offences, Ashworth has argued, 'should not be allowed to stifle the search for some general principles'.[28] In this essay Wasik explores the development of the 'totality principle' for the sentencing of multiple offences and the difficulty of rendering this consistent with proportionality, such that the resultant sentence does not normally exceed the category range. The complex accounting problems posed are admirably disentangled by Wasik who shares, with Ashworth, extensive first-hand experience of developing sentencing guidelines that are not only principled but also workable in practice.

Michael Tonry also addresses an oddly neglected but equally important question in sentencing theory, namely why the wealth of attention rightly given to wrongful convictions has not also been awarded to wrongful acquittals and unduly lenient sentences. Building upon Ashworth's own contributions,[29] Tonry offers a perceptive

[27] Set out in A von Hirsch and A Ashworth, *Proportionate Sentencing: Exploring the Principles* (Oxford: Oxford University Press, 2005), but also in many of Ashworth's sole authored works on sentencing.

[28] A Ashworth, *Sentencing and Criminal Justice* (5th edn, Cambridge: Cambridge University Press, 2010), 264.

[29] A Ashworth, 'Criminal Attempts and the Role of Resulting Harm under the Code, and in the Common Law' (1988) 19 Rutgers Law Review 725; A Ashworth, 'Taking the Consequences' in S Shute, J Gardner, and J Horder (eds), *Action and Value in Criminal Law* (New York: Oxford University Press, 1993).

account of why these everyday occurrences do not attract the same level of concern. He considers whether moral luck provides any plausible insights into why we treat some offenders less severely than their culpability warrants and he concludes by warning against possible remedies to the twin problems of wrongful convictions and unduly lenient sentences. In particular, Tonry warns against abrogating the double jeopardy rule and argues against allowing prosecutorial appeals against sentence. These, says Tonry, are 'bad ideas' that should not be enacted or, where enacted, should be repealed.

In 2013 Andrew Ashworth retires as Vinerian Professor of English Law at the University of Oxford. This collection of essays is a testament to the extraordinary range, volume, and quality of the scholarship that he has produced during the course of his career so far. We anticipate, and for the sake of criminal law and criminal justice also sincerely hope, that he will continue to publish in the many areas to which he has made such a signal contribution. We have been immensely fortunate to have Andrew as a colleague and as a friend. We dedicate this collection to him as a small token of our admiration and respect.

Acknowledgements

This important volume could not have been produced without the assistance of a number of people—most obviously the authors whom we thank warmly for their excellent contributions. We would like to express our gratitude to Alex Flach, Natasha Flemming, Zoë Organ, and Fiona Stables at Oxford University Press for their continued support in bringing the volume to fruition. We thank Ailbhe O'Loughlin for providing invaluable research assistance in the final editing of this volume. We would also like to acknowledge the financial support of the Faculty of Law at the University of Oxford.

Lucia Zedner
Julian V Roberts

Oxford
February 2012

Contents

Table of Cases

Table of Legislation

UNITED STATES

List of Contributors

R.A. Duff is Professor Emeritus in the Department of Philosophy at the University of Stirling and is also a Professor at the University of Minnesota Law School.

John Gardner is Professor of Jurisprudence at the University of Oxford and a Fellow of University College.

Roger Hood is Emeritus Professor of Criminology at the University of Oxford and an Emeritus Fellow of All Souls College, Oxford.

Jeremy Horder is the Edmund-Davies Professor of Criminal Law at King's College London.

Douglas Husak is Professor of Philosophy and of Law at Rutgers University.

Nicola Lacey is Senior Research Fellow, All Souls College, Oxford, and Professor of Criminal Law and Legal Theory.

Liora Lazarus is Senior Fellow and Tutor in Law at St Anne's College, Oxford and Lecturer in Human Rights Law at the Law Faculty, University of Oxford. She is also a member of Oxford's Centre for Criminological Research, and a Research Associate at the Centre for Legal and Applied Research, Faculty of Law, University of Cape Town.

Barry Mitchell is Professor of Criminal Law and Criminal Justice at Coventry University Law School.

Elaine Player is Professor of Criminology and Criminal Justice at King's College London.

Mike Redmayne is a Professor of Law at the London School of Economics.

Julian V Roberts is Professor of Criminology at the University of Oxford and a Supernumerary Fellow of Worcester College.

Paul Roberts is Professor of Criminal Jurisprudence at the University of Nottingham and Adjunct Professor, University of New South Wales, Faculty of Law.

Vivian Schorscher is completing her doctorate in Law at the University of São Paulo, Brazil.

Andrew Simester is Professor of Law at the National University of Singapore and a Fellow of Wolfson College, University of Cambridge.

Victor Tadros is Professor of Criminal Law and Legal Theory at the University of Warwick.

Malcolm Thorburn is Canada Research Chair in Crime, Security and Constitutionalism at the Faculty of Law, Queen's University, Canada.

Michael Tonry is Professor of Law and Public Policy at the University of Minnesota.

Dirk van Zyl Smit is Professor of Comparative and International Penal Law at the University of Nottingham.

Andreas von Hirsch is Honorary Professor of Law at the Goethe University, Frankfurt am Main, and Emeritus Honorary Professor of Penal Theory and Penal Law at the University of Cambridge.

Kate Warner is a Professor of Law at the Faculty of Law, University of Tasmania, Australia.

Martin Wasik is Professor of Criminal Justice at Keele University.

Lucia Zedner is Professor of Criminal Justice at the Faculty of Law and Corpus Christi College, University of Oxford, and a Conjoint Professor at the Faculty of Law, University of New South Wales, Sydney.

List of Abbreviations

CLJ	Cambridge Law Journal
CLP	Current Legal Problems
Crim LR	Criminal Law Review
ECHR	European Convention on Human Rights
ECtHR	European Court of Human Rights
EEPR	Excluding Evidence as Protecting Rights
GED	Gender Equality Duty
HRA	Human Rights Act
IACtHR	Inter-American Court of Human Rights
ICCPR	International Covenant on Civil and Political Rights
IPP	Indeterminate Sentence for Public Protection
LQR	Law Quarterly Review
MLR	Modern Law Review
OJLS	Oxford Journal of Legal Studies
PACE	Police and Criminal Evidence Act
PoI	Presumption of Innocence

PART I

CRIMINAL LAW

1

Ashworth on Principles

*John Gardner**

Does Andrew Ashworth's peerless body of work[1] on criminal law and the criminal justice system have a unifying theme? The most striking is his emphasis, at almost every turn, on the importance of *principles*. Ashworth sees principles in the law and advocates fidelity to them. He also stands up for principles that, in his view, ought to guide and constrain the law's development and official use, even if they are not to be found in the law. In what he acknowledges to be a triumph of hope over experience, Ashworth yearns for a principled criminal law as well as a principled approach, among politicians and officials, to decisions about whether and how to resort to it. Here are two typical passages—two among many—expressing that yearning:

> Legislatures frequently create or re-enact offenses without proper consideration of the extent of their conformity with general principles or of the justification for departures. The argument here is for a more structured and more principled approach.... In an ideal system, the legislature would make a principled inquiry into the need for a criminal sanction, the form of the offense, the relative seriousness of the crime, and the case (if any) for derogation from first principles, before enacting any offense.[2]

* Professor of Jurisprudence, University of Oxford.

[1] I will be drawing on the following sample: A Ashworth, 'Towards a Theory of Criminal Legislation' (1989) 1 Crim LR 41 (hereafter 'Towards a Theory'); A Ashworth, *Principles of Criminal Law* (3rd edn, Oxford: Oxford University Press, 1999) (hereafter *Principles 3e*); A Ashworth, 'Testing Fidelity to Legal Values: Official Involvement and Criminal Justice' (2000) 63 MLR 633 (hereafter 'Testing Fidelity'); A Ashworth, 'Is the Criminal Law a Lost Cause?' (2000) 116 LQR 225 (hereafter 'Lost Cause'); A Ashworth, 'Is Restorative Justice the Way Forward for Criminal Justice' (2001) 54 Current Legal Problems 347 (hereafter 'Restorative Justice'); A Ashworth, 'Criminal Justice Reform: Principles, Human Rights and Public Protection' [2004] Crim LR 516 (hereafter 'Criminal Justice Reform'); A Ashworth, 'A Change of Normative Position: Determining the Contours of Culpability in Criminal Law' (2008) 11 New Criminal Law Review 232 (hereafter 'Normative Position'); A Ashworth, 'Defending the Criminal Law: Reflections on the Changing Character of Crime, Procedure, and Sanctions' (2008) 2 Criminal Law and Philosophy 21 (with Lucia Zedner) (hereafter 'Defending the Criminal Law'); A Ashworth, *Principles of Criminal Law* (6th edn, Oxford: Oxford University Press, 2009) (hereafter *Principles 6e*). By referring to two editions of *Principles of Criminal Law* published ten years apart I am enlarging the stock of material on which we may draw to establish and confirm Ashworth's views. The book has been substantially rewritten over that period. Nevertheless, where I quote passages from *Principles 3e* that do not appear in *Principles 6e*, it is, I believe, only the formulations that have been abandoned and not the views that they represent.

[2] 'Towards a Theory', 41 and 54.

> [My] main purpose has been to develop two lines of argument. The first is that the criminal law is indeed a lost cause, from the point of view of principle . . . The second line of argument is more constructive, in seeking to identify a principled core of criminal law. The core consists, it is submitted, of four interlinked principles . . . It is not claimed that they should be regarded as absolute rules, and indeed at various points above some possible qualifications to them have been discussed. Derogations from them should be argued as derogations, and should be principled in themselves.[3]

These passages, and many others like them, give us various clues as to what Ashworth thinks a principle is. He typically provides conceptual orientation by connecting principles (more or less contrastively) with rules,[4] values,[5] policies,[6] doctrines,[7] interests,[8] and various other things. But so far as I am aware he never spells out the criteria for something to qualify as a principle, or for someone to qualify as principled. Nor is it incumbent upon him to do so. He is not writing primarily for philosophers. Yet there is sufficient philosophical depth in Ashworth's writings to make the question 'What exactly does he mean by a principle?' a live one, and one to which we might reasonably expect to find an answer by working back from the many scattered remarks he makes in which principles are mentioned or endorsed.

That answer is important to anyone who wants to think critically about Ashworth's views on the criminal law and the criminal justice system. Until we know what a principle is, it is hard to know whether Ashworth's warmth towards principles and their use is warranted. Not all moral and political philosophers share the warmth. Some, indeed, are antagonistic towards principled thinking in practical matters. But could that simply be because they have a different view from Ashworth of what a principle is, or of what it means for something or someone to be principled? Quite possibly. In what follows I will attempt to work out Ashworth's views on these matters, adding some critical commentary, and some comparisons with other possible views, as I go along. Section 1 clears up a couple of preliminary issues about the scope of our discussion. Sections 2 to 5 explore, by turns, four properties which Ashworth seems to ascribe to principles: generality, special force in argument, non-instrumentality, and categoricality. Section 6 reflects on links that may be thought to hold between these four properties, and arrives at a somewhat sceptical conclusion.

1. Some Preliminaries

On any plausible view, including Ashworth's,[9] principles, policies, and rules have this much in common. All are taken to provide reasons (or in other words to

[3] 'Lost Cause', 253 and 255.
[4] eg 'Testing Fidelity', 635; 'Lost Cause', 245; *Principles 6e*, 45.
[5] eg 'Towards a Theory', 41; 'Defending the Criminal Law', 39.
[6] eg 'Lost Cause', 225; *Principles 6e*, 45.
[7] eg 'Testing Fidelity', 642; 'Normative Position', 236.
[8] eg *Principles 3e*, 49.
[9] *Principles 3e*, 59.

militate in favour of or against something) by any person who endorses them. But do they provide the reasons they are taken to provide? Only—one might assume—if they are good principles, policies, and rules. If one endorses them, necessarily one takes them to be good. But one may be mistaken. In which case one takes a principle, policy, or rule to provide a reason that it doesn't actually provide. In truth it does nothing to support the thing that it is supposed by its endorsers to support. At any rate, so one might assume.

Yet there is a rival view, very much alive in British politics and public culture. According to this view, the mere fact of endorsement makes a principle, policy, or rule reason-giving for the endorser, even if the principle, policy, or rule is (otherwise) worthless and does not deserve the endorsement. For example, politicians are criticized by some for departing from their own policies, however dire. They are also admired by some for sticking to their own principles, however bizarre or fanatical. Indeed, one common way of understanding what makes a person 'principled'—where this is treated as an honourable thing to be—is that he or she sticks to his or her principles doggedly, never mind which principles they are.

Occasionally Ashworth speaks as if this is his understanding. He would apparently prefer politicians that have and stick to 'their own principles'.[10] He also seems to set some store by the fact that certain principles are already endorsed by the law, as if the law should be assessed according to its conformity with the principles that it already endorses, because it endorses them.[11] However, most of the time Ashworth's interest in principles (and for that matter in policies and rules) appears to be more critical. He is interested in which principles and policies and rules they are, and he wants them to be the right ones. We all know that he would not enthuse about a system of criminal justice that stuck to its principle of presuming guilt, or its policy of remanding suspects in custody indefinitely, or its rule that no crimes can ever be excused. Would he nevertheless regard it as a slight redeeming feature of such a system that at least it has its principles and sticks to them? Or would he think, as I do, that having and following its dreadful principles might make the system even worse than it would be if it did the very same dreadful things without any principles at all?[12] Ashworth's position in this debate is less clear. Even if he does not think that principles mitigate evildoing, he may think, with Lon Fuller,[13] that they militate against evildoing.[14] The question need not, however, detain us for long. For the purpose of understanding what exactly a principle might be, we will concern ourselves (and assume that Ashworth concerns himself) with sound principles only, and likewise, for parity, with sound policies and rules.

We will also avoid landing Ashworth with any commitment to the desirability of having principles, or of being principled, outside the roles of law-maker and

[10] 'Lost Cause', 256.

[11] *Principles 3e*, 59; 'Criminal Justice Reform', 528.

[12] A recurrent theme of Hannah Arendt's work, especially *The Origins of Totalitarianism* (New York: Harcourt Brace Jovanovich, 1973).

[13] L Fuller, *The Morality of Law* (revised edn, New Haven, CN: Yale University Press 1969), 154.

[14] See 'Testing Fidelity', 634–5, for remarks of Ashworth's that might be read as supporting either the 'mitigate' or the 'militate against' view.

law-applier (and some allied roles). Many who harbour doubts about principles and principled reasoning are thinking of the ways in which such things might figure in non-institutionalized aspects of everyday life.[15] They are thinking about ordinary people who do what they do (refusing to pay their bank charges, boycotting an airline, declining to eat meat, advocating capital punishment, buying fair-trade chocolate, wearing eyeliner to school, not talking to their neighbours, speaking French, demanding compensation, etc) 'on principle' or 'as a matter of principle'. George Bernard Shaw lampooned such people as quintessentially English moral obfuscators, concealing their reasons for action behind a veil of righteousness with a view to forestalling any call (even from themselves) for a proper justification.[16] André Gide expressed the same charge less affectionately: 'One shouldn't expect any kind of sincerity from [people of principle].'[17] I have sympathy for these negative reactions. But I do not think that they—or the various more measured and focused philosophical critiques that echo their themes[18]—typically have the same force in relation to the use of principles by law-makers and law-appliers as they have in relation to the use of principles by non-institutional agents. In fact one possible worry about the prestige that some people attach to principled thinking outside the law is that it may betray too legalistic a view of life, placing too much faith in certainty, clarity, prospectivity, generality, consistency, finality, and other desiderata of legality, and sacrificing thereby some attention to the particularity of each situation.[19] The law needs to live up to the desiderata of legality—one might well think—precisely because most of what life throws at us, including its everyday moral demands, does not live up to them at all. By this backdoor route one could arrive at a critique of the place of principles in practical thought, and in the art of life, which makes a unique exception for, and even gives principles pride of place in, the special business of legal thought and legal practice.

This might be Ashworth's own position. He says nothing to suggest that his hallmark enthusiasm for principles extends beyond the making and applying of law (and allied activities). And he often juxtaposes his advocacy of a principled criminal

[15] This is true of all the authors cited in nn 16, 17, 19, 26, and 27 below.

[16] 'There is nothing so bad or so good that you will not find Englishmen doing it; but you will never find an Englishman in the wrong', says Napoleon in Shaw's *The Man of Destiny*. 'He does everything on principle. He fights you on patriotic principles; he robs you on business principles; he enslaves you on imperial principles; he bullies you on manly principles; he supports his king on loyal principles, and cuts off his king's head on republican principles.' GB Shaw, *Plays Pleasant* (Harmondsworth: Penguin, 1946), 205–6.

[17] '*[Les gens à principes] sont, reprit Ménalque en riant, ce qu'il y a de plus détestable en ce monde. On ne saurait attendre d'eux aucune espèce de sincérité; car ils ne font jamais que ce que leurs principes on décrété qu'ils devaient faire, ou, sinon, ils regardent ce qu'ils font comme mal fait.*' A Gide, *L'Immoraliste* (Paris: Mercure de France, 1972), 116.

[18] Shaw and Gide do not make clear whether they are casting aspersions on all uses of principles, or whether there are some honest uses that survive the critique. A philosophical critic could echo the theme by explaining what it is about principles that makes them so open to dishonest use, even if they are also capable of having honest uses. I take some first steps in section 5 below.

[19] See Bernard Williams' critique of principled moral thinking in 'Persons, Character and Morality' in A Rorty (ed), *The Identities of Persons* (Berkeley: University of California Press, 1976), and his critique of the 'peculiar institution' view of morality in his *Ethics and the Limits of Philosophy* (London: Fontana, 1985), Ch 10.

law with remarks on the importance, especially in the criminal law, of the desiderata of legality. His case for a 'more principled approach' to criminal legislation relies on principles that are 'strongly related' to those of 'certainty, consistency, comprehensibility, and accessibility'.[20] Elsewhere he writes:

> The... disadvantages [of vaguely defined criminal defences] are that the broader issues of principle raised by certain arguments for exculpation are unlikely to be considered thoroughly, and that the law cannot function properly as a source of guidance for conduct if the boundaries of permissible conduct are undefined... [C]oherence is an important value in the criminal justice system—coherence not merely as the absence of contradiction, but more positively as a network of mutually supporting rules and principles.[21]

Is there an implicit 'therefore' after the conjunction in the first sentence? Does Ashworth think that the law's failing to confront 'broader issues of principle' is bad at least partly because it detracts from the ability of the law to guide people (ie because it detracts from the law's compliance with the rule of law)? That is a credible view, at least in the common law systems, where there is often nothing to rely upon for guidance except a line of cases.[22] If it is Ashworth's view, as I will assume it is, then it already puts some distance between him and those who are enthusiasts for principled thinking across the whole arc of human life. I think the existence of that distance is much to Ashworth's advantage, but I will not be arguing the point any further here.

2. Principles as General

In some cases the courts, according to Ashworth,

> ... make high statements of principle, which may raise hopes that a consistent framework is to be established... In the past, any hopes of a consistent judicial approach have usually been dashed, as the supposed principle is progressively whittled away or, more damningly, simply ignored.[23]

Here we have another passage connecting a principled criminal law with one of the desiderata of legality—this time, consistency. But what is meant by 'consistency'? Does it mean absence of conflict, which is what it is usually taken to mean in discussions of the desiderata of legality? Apparently not. It is true that, when a principle is 'simply ignored', that makes for a new conflict in the law. When a principle is 'whittled away', however, the reverse is true. Whittling away leaves less law than we had before, and so tends to reduce legal conflict.[24] What is sacrificed by

[20] 'Towards a Theory', 41.

[21] 'Testing Fidelity', 634.

[22] For a measured defence, avoiding common-law romanticism, see J Raz, 'The Politics of the Rule of Law' (1990) 3 Ratio Juris 331.

[23] *Principles 6e*, 166.

[24] Unless what is whittled away is a closure rule for resolving a legal conflict, eg a rule giving priority to statute over common law.

the whittling away is not consistency in the sense of conflict-avoidance, but consistency in the sense of generality, quite a different desideratum of legality. As the principle is whittled away it applies to fewer cases. This, for Ashworth, is already a loss to the law. More importantly for our purposes, it turns a principle, according to Ashworth, into a 'supposed' principle.

This tells us one thing that Ashworth believes about principles. He believes that principles provide not just reasons but general reasons, reasons of general application. Or does he? Quite often, as in the first passage quoted at the start of this essay, he speaks of the importance of 'general principles'.[25] That may be taken to imply that there can also be non-general principles. But there are other possible readings. Perhaps all principles are general but some principles are more general than others, so that 'general principles' means 'more general principles'. Or perhaps—more likely—'general principles' is a pleonasm used by Ashworth to remind us of the built-in generality of all principles.

That principles provide reasons of general application, or have a built-in generality, seems to me undeniable. But as it stands the point does not help to differentiate principles from anything else in the neighbourhood. All reasons are of general application. If the fact that it is raining is a reason to put up an umbrella, then the fact that it is raining on Monday is a reason to put up an umbrella on Monday, the fact that it is raining on Tuesday is a reason to put up an umbrella on Tuesday, the fact that it is raining on Wednesday is a reason to put up an umbrella on Wednesday, and so on. A complication arises, to be sure, if Wednesday's rain, unlike Monday's or Tuesday's, is combined with high wind. Not only is the fact of the high wind a distinct reason not to put up an umbrella (the umbrella will be wrecked and then will need to be replaced in time for Thursday's windless downpour). It also has the consequence that the fact of the rain on Wednesday is not after all a reason for putting the umbrella up (the umbrella, wrecked as soon as I put it up, won't keep me dry for even a moment). Yet that does not go to show that the reason we are considering, the advertised reason to put up an umbrella, is of less than perfectly general application. It only goes to show that we have not yet stated the reason in full.

The advertised reason to put up an umbrella, more fully stated, is the fact that it is raining coupled with the fact that putting up the umbrella will help to keep me dry in the rain. Since *ex hypothesi* the second fact does not hold on windy Wednesday, the reason to put up the umbrella does not extend to that day. Fine tuning of the reason, revealing that it is incompletely stated even after this emendation, can go on for many further steps. There is the fact that I will be cycling to work on Friday, the fact that on Saturday I will be in training for a damp Scottish fell-run, the fact that I deserve a good soaking after my grumpy remarks last Sunday about people with umbrellas, and so on. In fact it is possible to distinguish different rainy days and different potential umbrella users along a potentially infinite number of lines in respect of the umbrella-favouringness of

[25] 'Towards a Theory', 41; 'Lost Cause', 255; *Principles 6e*, 154; 'Testing Fidelity', 644.

the rain. At each step, however, what we may call the *generality thesis* holds: nothing counts as a rationally salient difference between any two situations unless it is a difference between two generic types of situations, unless there are facts that hold in one of the situations that do not hold in the other, facts that add up to explain why the situations are different in respect of the reasons for action that each affords to whom.[26] If one is to preserve rational intelligibility, one cannot say 'that reason won't apply next Sunday' without identifying the imaginably repeatable feature or features of next Sunday in virtue of which the reason supposedly won't apply then.

Is there some stronger sense of 'general', going beyond this requirement of rational intelligibility, in which principles are supposed by Ashworth to be general? Probably there is. But it is not at all clear what it is. His remark about 'whittling' principles away such that they turn into merely 'supposed' principles suggests that he might want to deny that reasons are principled as soon as any proviso is entered—as soon as the high wind breaks the constant umbrella-favouringness of the rain, or (to generalize) as soon as the constant rational salience and valence of any given fact is interrupted or complicated by the introduction of another fact. Among moral philosophers, the word 'principles' is sometimes reserved for reasons of such pristine constancy.[27] It is armed with this understanding of what principles are; indeed, that some have come to doubt whether morality (or practical life as a whole) has much or any space for principles.[28]

But Ashworth does not help himself to this 'purist'[29] account of principles. Recall what he says about derogations:

> Derogations from [principles] should be argued as derogations, and should be principled in themselves.[30]

Doesn't 'derogation', when done a bit at a time, come to the same thing as whittling? If so, why is the process presented here as consistent with the whittled-away principle remaining a principle, when elsewhere it demotes it to the status of a 'supposed' principle? Is it perhaps a matter of degree, such that an apparently principled reason becomes less principled with each successive whittling, even when the whittling itself conforms to the generality thesis? That is a possible interpretation of what Ashworth says. But notice that, in arriving at or defending this interpretation, it does not help much to know that for a principle to remain a principle, any whittlings must be 'principled in themselves'. To know what that means we would already need to know how 'principled' derogations differ from

[26] For more on this thesis see J Raz, *Engaging Reason* (Oxford: Oxford University Press, 1999), 219–25.

[27] See eg M Singer, 'Moral Rules and Principles' in A I Melden (ed), *Essays in Moral Philosophy* (Seattle: University of Washington Press, 1958), 169: 'Moral principles hold in all circumstances and allow of no exceptions; they are invariant with respect to every moral judgment and every moral situation.'

[28] See notably J Dancy, *Ethics Without Principles* (Oxford: Oxford University Press, 2004), and many of the essays, largely inspired by Dancy's work, in B Hooker and M Little (eds), *Moral Particularism* (Oxford: Clarendon Press, 2000).

[29] 'Towards a Theory', 45.

[30] 'Lost Cause', 255.

those that simply meet the requirements of the generality thesis, ie those that are rationally intelligible. And that is the very thing that we are trying to find out.

3. Principles as Powerful

Maybe the answer lies in Ashworth's remarks about the *force* of principles, by which I mean their ability to defeat countervailing considerations in cases of conflict. He believes that '[a]rguments of principle cannot be easily overridden'.[31] Maybe he thinks that whatever makes principles resistant to override also makes them resistant to derogation. In fact, he does not always cleanly distinguish override from derogation, and he may not attach much importance to the distinction. For example, he writes:

> In certain spheres there may be other values and interests that are regarded as so strong as to displace the general principle of equal treatment.[32]

What does 'displace' mean? Does it mean 'render inapplicable'? Or does it mean 'defeat', which, on the contrary, presupposes continued applicability? In a similar vein Ashworth writes:

> These are put forward as core principles. It is not claimed that they should be regarded as absolute rules, and indeed at various points above some possible qualifications to them have been discussed.[33]

The word 'qualification' brings to mind what above I called a 'proviso', a limit built into the scope of the principle. But in that case, why is a 'qualified' principle being contrasted with an 'absolute' rule, which is presumably a rule of such force that, whatever the limits of its application, it defeats all opposition wherever it applies? Maybe what Ashworth sometimes presents as the generality of principles is not so much a distinctive scope as a distinctive force that allows them to prevail over other reasons so that they are more often (hence: more generally) decisive?[34]

The suggested contrast with 'absolute rules' is intriguing in a second way. It suggests that for Ashworth all principles, or at least some of them, are rules, even if not absolute ones. That sounds right to me. It was Ronald Dworkin who encouraged us to think otherwise. He famously proposed that no principles are rules, because rules 'are applicable in an all or nothing fashion' whereas '[p]rinciples… have a dimension of weight or importance'.[35] This contrast is doubly misleading. First, it confuses the scope question with the force question. The weight of a principle is part of its force, and tells us nothing about when it applies. The supposed 'all or nothing' application of a rule, conversely, tells us nothing about its force. Secondly, and more importantly, rules necessarily do have a dimension of

[31] 'Restorative Justice', 369.
[32] 'Lost Cause', 245.
[33] 'Lost Cause', 255.
[34] cf *Principles 3e*, 59: principles are 'strong arguments… rather than absolute precepts'.
[35] R Dworkin, *Taking Rights Seriously* (London: Duckworth, 1977), 24 and 26.

'weight or importance'. They can conflict with other rules and then it has to be decided which rule is the more important. It is true that when two *legal* rules conflict, and one is found to be more important, it is tempting for lawyers to tidy up by declaring the more important rule to be (henceforth) the only rule, or by attempting to accommodate such force as the less important rule has by way of exception or proviso to the more important. But this points to nothing special about the rational force of rules. It only draws attention to the pressure on the law to conform to the desiderata of legality, including the consistency desideratum, in its *dealings* with rules (whatever their rational force may be before and after those dealings).[36]

Yet there is certainly something special about the force of rules. Rules are what Dworkin calls 'trumps'.[37] They defeat at least some countervailing considerations by kind and not (only) by weight. It follows that on some occasions they do not need to rely on their weight (or their weight alone) in order to prevail. What Ashworth calls an 'absolute' rule is presumably one that never needs to rely on its weight in competition with other considerations, except for other considerations of the same kind, because it defeats them all by kind alone. They are all trumped, or (as it is sometimes more technically put) 'excluded from consideration' by the rule.[38] That Ashworth regards at least some principles as having at least some of the same exclusionary force is readily apparent. True, this is not entailed by his claim that '[a]rguments of principle cannot be easily overridden', which is consistent with the view that principles are just relatively weighty reasons. But consider:

> [T]he principle of *mens rea* ought to operate as the primary restraint upon the pursuit of other aims such as social defense. This, indeed, is the significance of the doctrine of fair opportunity... True, public safety is one of the reasons for having criminal laws, but it does not follow that, where the element of social danger arising from certain conduct is high, this supplies a strong justification for dispensing with the doctrine of fair opportunity.[39]

So the principle of *mens rea* is not defeated by mere increases in the weight of the considerations of 'social defence' that conflict with it. Why not? Why does victory not turn simply on how weighty the conflicting considerations of 'social defence' become, and how slight is the departure from the principle of *mens rea* that they call for? For Ashworth things are plainly not so simple. The countervailing considerations of 'social defence' are defeated by kind rather than by weight. Or at any rate they are downgraded by kind in such a way that they count for less than their

[36] In the early work that we are drawing on here, Dworkin seems to be committed to another thesis which would make it impossible for him to grant this. He seems to be committed to the thesis that, when a case is rightly decided, it does not change the law. Hence, in the (rightly decided) cases in which I would say that the court is resolving the conflict between two rules, Dworkin would say that there was no conflict to resolve. See R Dworkin, 'No Right Answer?' in PMS Hacker and J Raz (eds), *Law, Morality, and Society* (Oxford: Clarendon Press, 1977). I assume that Ashworth has no truck with this thesis.

[37] Dworkin, n 35 above, xv and 85.

[38] The language of exclusion, and the associated apparatus, is owed to J Raz. See his *Practical Reason and Norms* (London: Hutchinson, 1975), 35 ff.

[39] 'Towards a Theory', 53.

weight in competition with the principle of *mens rea*.[40] And the point may apparently be generalized to a range of other principles, if not to all. Once the law is 'objectionable in principle' there is often, in Ashworth's work, a relatively quick move to the law's being 'absolutely indefensible'.[41] The move is quick, I take it, because principled objections have a built-in advantage in their conflict with other considerations. They do not need to rely on their weight alone to prevail.[42]

4. Principles as Non-instrumental

The passage just quoted introduced us, in passing, to another recurrent theme in Ashworth's treatment of principles. Here it comes into the foreground, and with it comes a puzzle:

> In considering the interaction between the principles [of criminal legislation] and other arguments, usually based on social defense, we have noticed various criteria for derogation from the principles.[43]

The puzzle: why should the contrast class of 'other arguments' be differentiated, even 'usually', by a value that figures in them ('social defence'), unless principles are also differentiated by some value that figures in *them*? Another iteration of the puzzle:

> Greater use of fixed penalties, of plea bargaining, and summary trials in England and Wales might all be seen as examples of managerialist techniques that sacrifice principle... for effectiveness.[44]

Why is 'principle' contrasted with 'effectiveness' here? That does not seem to be a contrast of like with like. A principle (we have already gleaned) is a rule or something like it. So it is something in which values could be embodied, reflected, or encapsulated, whereas 'effectiveness' is surely just one of the values that might be so embodied, reflected, or encapsulated. One might think that there has been some kind of category mistake when a device for engaging with value, a principle, is contrasted with one or more of the values that it might be used to engage with.

Or maybe not. One might instead be reminded of another contrast once drawn by Ronald Dworkin, namely the contrast between principles and policies. A policy, for Dworkin, 'sets out a goal to be reached' (or a 'present feature to be protected from adverse change'), whereas a principle is 'a requirement of justice or fairness or some other dimension of morality', where morality is understood not to require the

[40] On the ability to downgrade the weight of competing reasons as a type of exclusionary force, see S Perry, 'Judicial Obligation, Precedent and the Common Law' (1987) 7 OJLS 215, 222–3.

[41] 'Defending the Criminal Law', 46–7. See similarly 'Lost Cause', 11–12.

[42] Which leaves open the possibility that they can still 'on occasion' be outweighed even by ordinary reasons: *Principles 3e*, 59.

[43] 'Towards a Theory', 57.

[44] 'Defending the Criminal Law', 39–40.

reaching or maintaining of some goal.[45] Ashworth too draws a principle–policy contrast, and he may well mean to draw it along Dworkinian lines:[46]

[Principles] amount to strong arguments based on moral or political foundations rather than absolute precepts . . . Reference is also made below to certain policies founded on arguments about what is expedient rather than what is right in principle.[47]

English criminal law both is shaped and ought to be shaped by a number of principles, policies and other standards and doctrines. One of the purposes of this chapter is to draw together and to discuss critically some of the foremost principles that ought to exert an influence on the substance of English criminal law . . . The justifications for upholding each principle are discussed, and each principle is followed by a policy or other instrumental goal that may often run counter to the principle in practice.[48]

So a policy is a kind of 'instrumental goal'. What does that mean? The expression may be elliptical. To judge by Ashworth's main examples of policies, it is not the goal that is supposed to be instrumental, but rather the policy that is supposed to be instrumental towards the goal. The goal is the thing that is served instrumentally; it is a state of affairs to the realization of which actions conforming to the policy contribute, to the extent that they do, in a causal as opposed to a constitutive way. That is why—to return to the puzzling contrast between 'principle' and 'effectiveness'—the question of effectiveness arises in connection with a policy. But it does not arise, we may glean, in connection with a principle. For a principle is not there to serve a goal, or perhaps even to contribute to a state of affairs, unless you count the state of affairs in which the principle has been conformed to, a state of affairs to the realization of which the conforming action made a constitutive, as opposed to a causal, contribution.[49]

This way of distinguishing principles from policies has odd implications. It entails that Bentham's 'principle of utility'[50] is not an unsound principle, for it is not a principle at all; likewise the 'precautionary principle' favoured by some policy-makers,[51] the 'harm principle' set out by John Stuart Mill,[52] and the Roman Catholic 'principle of subsidiarity'.[53] None are principles. Nor, for that

[45] Dworkin, n 35 above, 22.

[46] Ashworth sometimes refers to Dworkin's work on nearby questions (eg 'Towards a Theory', 44 and 45; *Principles 6e*, 24 and 35), but I have not found an instance where Ashworth names Dworkin as the source of the principle–policy contrast that he has in mind. Hence my note of hesitation here.

[47] *Principles 3e*, 58–9.

[48] *Principles 6e*, 45.

[49] cf Dworkin, n 35 above, 22–3, where it is noted that any action can be presented as contributing to the state of affairs in which that action has been performed. Dworkin's suggestion that this is a way of disguising a principle as a policy suggests that the distinction between the two drawn in the text above is the same one that he is advancing.

[50] JH Burns and HLA Hart (eds), *An Introduction to the Principles of Morals and Legislation* (London: Athlone Press, 1970), 11 (Ch 1: Of the Principle of Utility).

[51] See eg J Cameron and J Abouchar, 'The Precautionary Principle: A Fundamental Principle of Law and Policy for the Protection of the Global Environment', (1991) 14 Boston College International and Comparative Law Review 1.

[52] JS Mill, 'On Liberty' in JS Mill, *Utilitarianism; On Liberty; Essay on Bentham* (Warnock: Glasgow, 1962) 126, 136.

[53] Pope John Paul II, *Centesimus Annus* (Rome, 1991), [15] and [48].

matter, are the desiderata of legality the principles that Ashworth himself proclaims them to be. As he says:

> [A] legal system . . . should adhere to rule-of-law principles in its criminal law, by ensuring fair warning, maximum certainty of definition, subjective requirements for criminal liability, and so on. . . . By these means, as H.L.A. Hart put it: 'First, we maximize the individual's power at any time to predict the likelihood that the sanctions of the criminal law will be applied to him; Secondly, we introduce the individual's choice as one of the operative factors determining whether or not these sanctions shall be applied to him.'[54]

Maximal or optimal freedom under the law is a goal, which is served only instrumentally by the desiderata of legality.[55] There is a live question of their effectiveness in securing it.[56] So if those desiderata must be classified as either principles or policies, then according to the criterion under scrutiny here, which is supposedly Ashworth's own criterion, they should surely be classified as policies, not—*pace* Ashworth—as principles. This pushes us towards the conclusion that the criterion under scrutiny here is not, after all, Ashworth's criterion, or at any rate not the criterion he is looking for.

5. Principles as Categorical

Something went astray in Ashworth's characterization of a policy as an 'instrumental goal'. My suggested explanation is this. Talk of a 'goal' sends out two different signals. On the one hand it suggests something that can be pursued instrumentally. On the other hand it suggests something to which one need not, but might, become rationally committed. In the latter sense, I have my goals and you have yours. Some of my reasons for action are given to me by my goals. Given my goal of running the Glasgow half-marathon, for example, I have an extra reason to go running this morning that many people lack. Notice that this is an example of a goal in the second sense which is not a goal in the first. At the end of my training, I can run the Glasgow half-marathon only by running it, and then what I do will contribute constitutively, not causally, towards my fulfilment of the goal.[57] Governments and public authorities can have goals in this sense too, qualifying as goals not by virtue of the instrumentality of the actions taken in their pursuit, but rather by virtue of the rational optionality, as we might call it, of the pursuit itself. The institution has some rational latitude in respect of which goals it adopts, and when it adopts a goal as its own it acquires new reasons that it would not otherwise have had.

[54] 'Normative Position', 237.

[55] See J Gardner, 'Introduction' in HLA Hart, *Punishment and Responsibility* (Oxford: Oxford University Press, 2008).

[56] Ibid, xxxvii–xxxviii.

[57] Maybe even my training contributes constitutively to my fulfillment of the goal, depending on how you interpret the goal.

In the sense that Ashworth often has in mind, it seems to me, the reasons given by policies belong to this class of goal-dependent reasons. Possibly policies are themselves goals in the relevant sense (so Ashworth was right to speak of a 'policy or other . . . goal') and that is why the reasons to which policies give rise are goal-dependent.[58] Principles are different. One has reason to conform to sound principles irrespective of one's goals. They supply what are sometimes called 'categorical' reasons, reasons which one cannot lose merely by changing one's goals.

This is the contrast between principle and policy that is suggested by the link that Ashworth sometimes forges between policy questions on the one hand and 'collective goals' or 'social goals' on the other, where such goals, and the priority among them, 'should be a matter for democratic (participatory) decision-making'.[59] Here 'social goals' are not goals *for* a society (as Dworkin's use of the same expression sometimes suggests)[60] but goals *of* a society. Their adoption gives the government, and the authorities more generally, reasons different from those they would have had, had different goals (or different priorities among goals) been adopted. Policy depends on such adoptions, thinks Ashworth. But principle prevails irrespective of the adoption of any goals by anybody, whether democratically or otherwise.

You may think that this way of distinguishing principle from policy (or this aspect of the distinction) flies in the face of the fact, already noted, that people often have their *own* principles. Clearly they may adopt principles in the course of adopting or shaping their goals; they may even end up with highly principled goals (to save the planet, to uphold justice, etc). Yet once they have their principles, people hold those principles to give them categorical reasons for action. They do not regard their principles as binding on them only for as long as they continue to have the same goals. It is often thought to be part of being a 'principled' person; indeed, that one resists a change of personal goals that would allow one to escape from the tyranny of what one now regards as principles, by allowing one to stop regarding them as principles and to start regarding them as something more like policies. Such resistance requires a certain capacity for obstinate self-deception that may provide the beginnings of an explanation for the ribald and scathing views that Shaw and Gide respectively took of principled people. But that is not yet an indictment of principles themselves. It is an indictment of the natural tendency to elevate what are really goal-dependent reasons to the status of categorical ones. Having had some categorical reason to ϕ, and having responded to it by making

[58] I tend to think that A's policies are A's goals concerning how (constitutively or causally) A is to ϕ, which give A goal-dependent reasons to ϕ in that way, where the reasons to ϕ which militated in favour of adopting such policies may or may not themselves have been goal-dependent. If I am right about this, then one may have a policy for conforming to a principle. That seems to me to be an advantage of the account. I am not so sure, however, that Ashworth would find it an advantage. Sometimes he seems to expect policy to be founded on principle: eg 'Lost Cause', 242 (policy-making must be on principled grounds) and 255 (only principled derogation from principle is acceptable). On other occasions, however, it seems that he envisages a more exclusive contrast according to which policies are '*founded on* arguments about what is expedient rather than what is right in principle': *Principles 3e*, 60.

[59] *Principles 6e*, 26.

[60] Dworkin, n 35 above, eg 22–3.

ϕing one's goal, it is a short step to self-righteously thinking of *all* one's reasons to ϕ as categorical ones, forgetting that some of them come of the fact that one adopted ϕing as one's goal. The designation 'principled' is sometimes reserved for the tiresome people who do this.

There is nothing in this that need worry Ashworth, to whom (you will recall) we are attributing no views about the role of principles in personal life. Yet there is much in it to support what I take to be part of his view about what principles are, viz. that the reasons they give us, when they are sound enough to give us reasons, are categorical ones. If that were not so then the foregoing remarks about the psychology (or the pathology?) of 'principled' people would not hang together as they do.

6. Combining the Criteria

There is a view according to which morality is a body of principles, where all principles are understood to give reasons for action that are (a) distinctively general, not only satisfying the generality thesis to which all reasons are subject, but also being (as I put it above) pristine in their constancy; (b) of absolute force, defeating all competing reasons by kind; (c) non-instrumental, in the sense that the value in conforming to them is constituted rather than caused by that conformity; and (d) categorical, in the sense that their rational hold over us does not depend on what personal goals we have at the time. In Kant's work all of these features of morality were said to follow from morality's unconditionality or universality, a vague idea that was interpreted in numerous different and often inconsistent ways by Kant. Each of the proposed criteria (a) to (d) reflects a different interpretation of that vague idea. As has often been said, Kant's urge progressively to strip away all kinds of conditionality from morality left less and less rational space for morality to inhabit.[61] Probably, if moral considerations must meet all of the criteria that Kant set for them (which (a) to (d) do not exhaust) then there are no valid moral considerations. Even criteria (a) to (d), without more, are capable of eliminating the whole of moral life, depending on their further interpretation. And if (a) to (d) are understood as criteria for something to qualify as a principle, moral or otherwise, then quite possibly there are no sound principles of anything anywhere in the world.

There is no reason to think that Ashworth is wedded to the Kantian illusion of an unconditional morality. And as we have seen, he is certainly not wedded to conditions (a) to (d) as conditions for something to count as a principle. Yet, as we have also seen, he echoes all of them in his work. He embraces diluted versions of (a) and (b). He expects constancy from his principles, but he is no 'purist' about it (section 2 above). He regards principles as having a special force, an ability to prevail by kind and not only by weight, but he does not expect it to be absolute

[61] This is the main lesson of T Nagel, 'Moral Luck' (1976) 50 Proceedings of the Aristotelian Society Supplementary Volume 137.

(section 3). In the spirit of (c), he contrasts arguments of principle with instrumental arguments, but does not uphold the contrast in all his examples (section 4). Only (d), towards which he only gestures, seems to square with everything he says (section 5).

Nevertheless, in the role he gives to principles throughout his work, Ashworth does seem to court, or give succour to, the loosely Kantian idea that criteria (a) to (d) fit naturally together. He gives the repeated impression, including in many of the passages quoted above, that considerations with the force of principles should be expected to apply with the generality of principles, that considerations with the force of principles should also be expected to be categorical, that categorical considerations should be expected to be non-instrumental considerations, that non-instrumental considerations should be expected to be general and categorical, and so forth. In this essay, I have tried to show how these false expectations arise.

By and large, I have suggested, they come of small and understandable conceptual slips. As we saw in sections 2 and 3, it is all too easy to run together the question of scope raised by (a) with the question of force raised by (b), thanks to the equivocality of words like 'derogate' and 'displace'. As we saw in sections 4 and 5, it is all too easy to confuse the criterion of non-instrumentality in (c) with the criterion of categoricality in (d), thanks to the different signals sent out by the word 'goal'. We did not stop to add, but it would not take too long to show, that the status of being categorical is easily and commonly taken to entail having a special force in conflict, thereby linking (d) to (b), and compounding the other small slips with another.

These small slips add up to give a misleading picture of practical rationality as a whole, even as it bears on the law. Although at some times and in some places there may be a case, a rule-of-law case, to build up a body of law that works at a high level of generality, that is treated as forceful in argument, and that is presented as non-instrumental and not contingent on political goals, there is nothing otherwise—*nothing apart from this body of law*—to suggest that categorical considerations tend to have more rational force than goal-dependent ones, that non-instrumental considerations tend to have more rational force than instrumental ones, that more general considerations tend to have more rational force than less general ones, that less general considerations are more likely to be instrumental and goal-dependent than non-instrumental and categorical, that goal-dependent considerations are more likely to be instrumental than non-instrumental, and so on. In the ordinary logic of reasons, all these properties vary independently of each other. In particular, there is no shortcut to showing that a certain consideration has the force necessary to defeat another consideration in a particular conflict; all one can do is show that that is the force it has in the context of that particular conflict. Its generality, its non-instrumentality, and its goal-independence tell us nothing about how it is going to fare in competition with other considerations.

All of this is consistent with holding, with Ashworth, that '[a]rguments of principle cannot be easily overridden' and that principles provide 'strong arguments', even for the purposes of debate outside the courts (eg in forming or legislating criminal justice policy). But the points I have just made tend to suggest a reversal of Ashworth's inference. Ashworth gives the impression, in various remarks we have quoted, that an argument of principle cannot easily be overridden because it is an argument of principle, ie because it already satisfies his other criteria for being a principle, such as (d) and his diluted version of (a). I tend to think, by contrast, that an argument counts as an argument of principle because it cannot easily be overridden. In other words, we use the language of principle, as I think Ashworth himself does in practice, to assert that something is important (that it carries a lot of weight, or wholly or partly excludes some other considerations). It may be that, within the relevant class of important considerations, we restrict the title 'principle' to those that also happen to satisfy some other criteria, such as (a) or (d) or both. But there is no reason to think that satisfaction of those other criteria is what *gives* a consideration its importance. Its importance always calls for some independent defence.

2

Principles, Policies, and Politics of Criminal Law

*Nicola Lacey**

The contributor to Andrew Ashworth's Festschrift is confronted by an embarrassment of riches. Ashworth's work encompasses doctrinal, institutional, and theoretical analysis; and it has ranged across every aspect of criminal justice scholarship: from the substantive law, through evidence and procedure to sentencing. Moreover, his work has left a defining mark on scholarship, teaching, and practice in each of these areas. In this essay, I shall address one of Ashworth's key methodological and substantive contributions to criminal law scholarship. This is the argument that, notwithstanding diversity and a measure of conflict, a number of principles are immanent to criminal law. These may be identified, elaborated, and enriched with broader values as yet unrecognized or incompletely recognized in criminal law, and put to normative work. This methodology implies a strong degree of responsiveness between theory and practice. Given the developments in criminal law during the two decades since the first edition of *Principles of Criminal Law*, it is therefore worth asking how the various principles have fared in an era of punitiveness and 'over-criminalization', and whether the 'principles' methodology has been put under pressure in a world where political pragmatism shapes so many decisions about criminal policy.

In what follows, I set Ashworth's book within the context of a longer tradition of positing 'general principles' of criminal law, drawing out various distinctive features of his approach. I then argue that it is those distinctive features—and notably the way in which Ashworth's principles are derived not merely from the substantive criminal law but also from an understanding of the criminal process as a complex social and political institution—which underpin their intellectual strength and practical utility.

This part of the argument presents both an assessment of the range of principles and a more detailed analysis of some key examples. In conclusion, I trace connections between Ashworth's book and the recent revival of criminalization scholarship in the United Kingdom and the United States, and make some suggestions about how best his approach can be interpreted so as to allow us to make sense of criminal

* I am very grateful to Lindsay Farmer, Celia Wells, and Lucia Zedner for their astute comments on an earlier draft of this essay; and to Zelia Gallo for excellent research assistance.

law in an era of pragmatically driven criminalization in which it is sometimes tempting to regard the criminal law as 'a lost cause'.[1]

1. The Quest for 'General Principles': The Place of Ashworth's Book in the Tradition of the Criminal Law Treatise

When Ashworth published the first edition of *Principles of Criminal Law* in 1991, he was joining—and, one assumes, to some degree aligning himself with—a distinguished tradition in criminal law scholarship. Throughout the post-war era, the idea that doctrinal analyses of criminal law might productively be organized around a set of principles widely if not universally applicable across the whole range of offences had gripped the imagination of many commentators. The two most obvious examples, one on either side of the Atlantic, are Glanville Williams, whose massive *Criminal Law: The General Part*[2] set the standard for principles-based criminal law scholarship in England and Wales, and Jerome Hall, whose *General Principles of Criminal Law*[3] had done the same, somewhat earlier, in the United States.[4] We might see such texts, with their focus on immanent, judicially articulated principles, as modern iterations of a common law tradition stretching back to Coke, Hale, and Blackstone.

These texts stand, however, in an interesting relation to the doctrinal literature on criminal law of the 19th and earlier 20th centuries. As Lindsay Farmer has shown, notwithstanding the failure of the codification projects of the early 19th century, a gradual rationalization of criminal law during the century is powerfully reflected in a flourishing of treatises, primarily written for practitioners. This tradition was supplemented and even superseded in the late 19th and 20th centuries by the student-oriented textbook, a product of the development of university education in law from the late 19th century.[5] While, as Brian Simpson argued, these treatises all presented criminal law as a unity—and hence as a discrete object of professional interpretation and deployment—they were not concerned to present criminal law as a principled, coherent body of doctrine; nor did they look very deeply into the rationale for or distinctiveness of criminal law as a form of legal

[1] A Ashworth, 'Is the Criminal Law a Lost Cause?' (2000) 116 LQR 225.

[2] 1st edn, 1953; 2nd edn, 1961.

[3] 1st edn, 1947; 2nd edn, 1960.

[4] On the parallel—but independent—development of such a tradition in Scotland, see L Farmer, 'The Idea of Principle in Scots Criminal Law' in J Chalmers, F Leverick, and L Farmer (eds), *Essays in Honour of Sir Gerald Gordon* (Edinburgh: Edinburgh University Press, 2010), 86–102. Farmer charts the varying fortunes of two rather different conceptions of 'principle' in Scottish treatises: principle as accumulated practice and principle as general rule or standard on the basis of which practice should be structured or assessed. As we shall see, Ashworth's approach is an interesting combination of these two different conceptions.

[5] L Farmer, 'Of Treatises and Textbooks: The Literature of the Criminal Law in Nineteenth Century Britain' in M Dubber and A Fernandez, *The Idea of the Legal Treatise* (Oxford: Hart Publishing, forthcoming); see also M Lobban, 'The English Legal Treatise and English Law in the Eighteenth Century' (1997) 13 Iuris Scripta Historica 69.

regulation.[6] Both Smith and Farmer suggest that the turning point, and the analysis which both foreshadowed Williams' post-war text and provided some of its foundations, was the work of JWC Turner—an academic at Cambridge, where Williams later took up a chair[7]—who, from the 1930s on, 'began to promote the idea of subjective fault drawing on sources such as the Criminal Law Commissioners of 1833–45'.[8] As editor of the classic treatises of Russell and Kenny,[9] Turner was able to reconstruct the analytic framework within which the texts presented criminal law, notably including significantly longer sections on subjective fault principles and criticizing aspects of the law which failed to accord with these principles.[10] Thus began what amounted to a revolution in the way in which treatises and student texts present criminal law.

The first edition of CS Kenny's *Outlines of Criminal Law*, published in 1902 (and also deriving from the Cambridge Law Faculty), followed a pattern already familiar in the 19th century.[11] The pattern consisted of a preliminary and relatively cursory treatment of the nature of crime and punishment; a treatment of what we would now call 'general part' issues occupying a little over 10 per cent of the book; a substantial treatment of a range of offences, organized loosely in terms of the interests which they seek to protect, and occupying about half of the book; and a treatment of evidence and procedure occupying about a quarter of the book—substantially more than that occupied by the general part. Only 50 years later, building on the work done by Turner, Glanville Williams produced a text of over 700 pages dealing exclusively with the 'general part'[12]—an analysis which was regarded as so decisive that Williams abandoned his original intention of producing an accompanying volume on the 'special part'.

Two things are striking about the post-Turner, Hall/Williams genre of 'general principles' texts, as compared with 19th- or early 20th-century treatises. The first is that these texts are trained predominantly—indeed, leaving aside a brief treatment of punishment, almost exclusively—on the substantive criminal law.[13] Apart from their treatment of a few key issues, such as the principle of legality and the burden of

[6] AWB Simpson, 'The Rise and Fall of the Legal Treatise: Legal Principles and the Forms of Legal Literature' (1981) 48 University of Chicago Law Review 632–79.

[7] Williams wrote the first edition of *The General Part* while holding the Quain Chair of Jurisprudence at University College London.

[8] Farmer, n 5 above.

[9] JWC Turner, 'The Mental Element in Crimes at Common Law' (1936) 6 CLJ 31, republished in L Radzinowicz and JWC Turner, *The Modern Approach to Criminal Law* (London: Macmillan, 1945). See KJM Smith, *Lawyers, Legislators and Theorists* (Oxford: Clarendon Press, 1998), 297–304.

[10] Farmer, n 5 above: Smith, n 9 above, 301–4, comments on Turner's 'conceptual colonisation' of Russell and Kenny.

[11] See N Lacey, 'In Search of the Responsible Subject: History, Philosophy and Criminal Law Theory' (2001) 64 MLR 350–71; 'Contingency, Coherence and Conceptualism' in A Duff (ed), *Philosophy and the Criminal Law* (Cambridge: Cambridge University Press, 1998), 9.

[12] See n 2 above: the second edition in 1961 had swollen to over 900 pages. Its structure virtually unchanged from that of the first edition, just two chapters, 72 pages in all, dealt with the principle of legality and the burden of proof, with the other 21 chapters treating in elaborate detail non-procedural issues pertaining to the general part.

[13] Lindsay Farmer has suggested to me that this shift of focus may have had to do with the changing audience for criminal law treatises, with students gradually replacing practitioners. This change would

proof, they provide little by way of reflection on the content or importance of criminal evidence or procedure, and no systematic analysis of the judicial dimension of punishment, namely sentencing decisions. Secondly, within their treatment of the substantive criminal law, and among the many issues of principle which might have commanded attention, the focus is on principles to be derived from 'the general part': in other words, general doctrines pertaining to *mens rea*; *actus reus*, including causation; secondary liability for complicity; inchoate liability; criminal capacity (including that of corporations); and the defences. The offences themselves, encompassing the interests which criminal law seeks to protect, and the values and social goals which it seeks to further through the articulation of particular offences, are virtually absent from the picture provided by Hall's and Williams' (in other respects rather different) texts. This is particularly striking in light of the fact that it is those interests, goals, and values which provided the implicit rationalizing frame for texts and treatises throughout the modern history of criminal law in the English-speaking world up to the Second World War. Partly as a result of this, and partly as a result of their schematic or non-existent treatment of the procedural and institutional dimensions of criminal law, these texts give the reader only an attenuated sense of the way in which criminal law doctrines operate within and form part of a broader institutional practice.

A brief analysis of the structure of Ashworth's *Principles of Criminal Law* reveals that he has been writing as much against as within the tradition to which his title draws attention. Taking the sixth edition of 2009 as an example, we see a rather different structure from that of Hall and Williams. The book opens with a brief but serious treatment of the institutional framework of criminal justice and of its main aims and functions. Just under half of the rest of the book deals with the 'general part' as understood by Hall and Williams (*actus reus* and *mens rea*, criminal capacity, defences, inchoate and secondary liability), while a little over a third of the book deals with substantive offences: homicide, non-fatal violations of the person, and offences of dishonesty. This is a highly selective group of offences as compared with that analysed in, say, the first edition of Kenny's *Outlines of Criminal Law* a century earlier.[14] But it is the object of a very substantial analysis as compared with that offered by Hall and Williams. Nor is this the only difference. The remaining portion of the book—about one eighth of the text as a whole—presents an entirely new object of analysis: a group of principles—ranging from the highly abstract to the relatively concrete; from the general to the criminal justice-specific—themselves interspersed with policy considerations which sometimes compete with the principles in the three areas to which they pertain: the determination of the range of criminal law; the specification of fair criminal procedures

have been more or less complete by Turner's time: the fact that Kenny chose to place his 1902 text with a University Press rather than a law publisher is also significant.

[14] As well as the offences covered by Ashworth, Kenny dealt with arson and other malicious injuries to property; forgery; 'offences against the safety of the state' including treason and offences such as riot and unlawful assembly; perjury; bigamy; libel; offences against international law; and offences of vagrancy: CS Kenny, *Outlines of Criminal Law* (Cambridge: Cambridge University Press 1902), xx–xxi.

trained on respect for the rule of law; and the specification of the conditions of liability. It is this distinctive balance in Ashworth's text, and in particular the content of the principles and policies which he presents in Chapters 2 and 3 of the latest edition, which underpin the quality of his book as not only a radical departure from the Hall/Williams 'principles' tradition but also a major and innovative contribution to both criminal law scholarship and criminal justice scholarship more generally. It is accordingly these two chapters of the book, understood in the context of the project as a whole, on which I shall concentrate in the rest of this essay.

2. Ashworth's Distinctive 'Principles of Criminal Law'

The principles and policies as a whole

Ashworth's treatment of the principles of criminal law undoubtedly owes something not merely to the Hall/Williams tradition, but also to more philosophical treatments of criminal law such as that of HLA Hart.[15] As he himself puts it in the preface to the latest edition, 'the aim of the book is to focus on issues of principle, some of which are immanent in existing legal rules and practices, some of which are not recognized (or not fully recognized) and which are commended here on normative grounds'.[16] In the genre of criminal law theorists who aspire to develop 'middle order' rationalizations of criminal law which encompass non-ideal as well as ideal theory, Ashworth's analysis moves back and forth between criminal law rules, doctrines, procedural tenets, and (unlike many other theorists) institutional arrangements and social context, and more abstract moral, social, and political values. In doing so, it seeks to tease out principles implicit or immanent in particular doctrines or associated features of criminal law, and to subject them to further normative analysis and refinement in the light of more abstract principles to which a liberal society purports to be committed. At the core of these abstract principles, introduced in Chapter 2, lies the principle of individual autonomy, which underpins a number of the more concrete principles apposite to shaping and constraining criminal law: the principle of respect for human rights and the principle that criminalization be used as a last resort, to name but two.[17] Twinned with the principle of autonomy, however, and not infrequently in tension with it, lies the principle of welfare, which at a more concrete level implies the harm

[15] *Punishment and Responsibility* (1968; 2nd edn, Oxford: Oxford University Press, 2008); Hart's book, of course, helped to inspire a flourishing genre of philosophical criminal law theory, distinguished recent contributions to which include RA Duff, *Answering for Crime* (Oxford: Hart, 2007); J Gardner, *Offences and Defences* (Oxford: Oxford University Press, 2007); and V Tadros, *Criminal Responsibility* (Oxford: Oxford University Press, 2005).

[16] A Ashworth, *Principles of Criminal Law* (6th edn, Oxford: Oxford University Press, 2009), v–vi.

[17] Ashworth, n 16 above, 23–6, 31–3.

principle and a focus on public wrongs.[18] While the principle of autonomy should generally prevail in the design of fair processes and the specification of conditions of liability, the principle of welfare has a substantial role to play in the determination of the range of criminal law.

The explicit recognition that two potentially competing principles lie at the heart of criminal law already marks Ashworth's approach out from most philosophical analyses, which tend to struggle for a neat accommodation of relevant values and principles by means of a division of conceptual labour (as in Hart's case) or a clear ranking of values. The sense of criminal law as a complex dialectic intensifies in Chapter 3, where Ashworth begins to introduce the policy considerations which compete with and sometimes threaten or undermine the realization of the more concrete principles which can be derived from the principles of autonomy and welfare. It also demonstrates how the concrete specification of principles relevant specifically to criminal law itself introduces inevitable moral complexity into the legislative and judicial roles. Again, this hallmark of his approach is signalled in the preface, where he states that:

> The contention is not that English criminal law is grounded in a stable set of established doctrines: on the contrary, there is ample evidence that the arguments and assumptions that influence the development of the law form a disparate group, sometimes conflicting and sometimes invoked selectively. Often there are political factors influencing shape of legislation or the activities of law enforcement officers, and reference is made to these below.[19]

Even leaving policy issues aside, difficult judgments between competing values have to be made. Accordingly, in determining the proper scope of criminal law, the principle of minimum criminalization, for example, must be interpreted in the light of the principle of social responsibility, which must itself be aligned and negotiated with the principle of liability for acts and not omissions.[20] And in relation to the procedures through which the range, scope and application of criminal laws are to be determined, the non-retroactivity principle must be brought into accommodation with the 'thin ice' principle,[21] which itself has a ticklish relationship with the principle of maximum certainty, the principle of strict construction, and the presumption of innocence.[22] Some of these tensions are resolved by clear prioritization within the structure of the European Convention on Human Rights: Ashworth argues, for example, that the thin ice principle should give way to the principle of legality under Article 7, which Article 15 defines as a non-derogable right.[23] But,

[18] Ashworth, n 16 above, 26–31. On the relationship between autonomy and welfare in the liberal and communitarian theories of punishment, see N Lacey, *State Punishment: Political Principles and Community Values* (London: Routledge, 1988), Ch 8.

[19] Ibid, v.

[20] Ibid, 53–6.

[21] Ibid, 63: this principle implies that those who 'sail close to the wind' by knowingly acting on the borderlines of illegality may fairly be taken to have accepted the risk of criminalization. This is a good example of a principle which might easily have been cast as a policy.

[22] Ibid, 57–73.

[23] Ibid, 63.

much in the style of the common law tradition, Ashworth resists any temptation to reduce the diversity of principles to any general hierarchy.

Yet more troubling, the principles and doctrines which make up the criminal law's conception of fair procedures adequate to guaranteeing the rule of law—the non-retroactivity principle, the 'thin ice' principle, the principles of maximum certainty and strict construction and the presumption of innocence—must confront insistent policy considerations such as social defence and a concern with ease of proof.[24] Constructive liability and a concern with efficient administration may threaten the *mens rea* principle, while the latter is sometimes difficult to interpret consistently with other principles such as correspondence and contemporaneity of *actus reus* and *mens rea* or considerations such as the relevance of prior fault.[25] This dialectical approach lacks, of course, the pleasing conceptual neatness which is such a striking feature, indeed aesthetic, of ideal theories of criminal law. But the complexities to which Ashworth draws attention must be confronted by anyone who, like him, recognizes that an understanding of institutional realities as well as of values is a necessary component of the effort to make the criminal law better than it currently is.

Two further features of Ashworth's 'principles of criminal law' distinguish them markedly from both the principles emerging from either ideal theories or the Hall/Williams tradition. First, both Williams' 'general part' and Hall's 'general principles' bore primarily on what Ashworth calls the conditions of liability—the doctrines of *mens rea, actus reus*, and defence—supplemented by a less fully realized concern with procedural values such as legality. This growing dominance in criminal law scholarship of 'the general part', which reached its height with the publication of Williams' text in 1953, and which dominated criminal law scholarship for the next 30 years, is decisively subverted in Ashworth's analysis, which gives equal emphasis not only to a range of values relevant to due process, but also to principles relevant to the proper range and boundaries of criminalization which pertain to the so-called 'special part' of criminal law. He generally works within a tripartite structure distinguishing principles and policy issues pertaining to the range of criminal law, to fair procedures, and to conditions of liability (or, sometimes, range, scope, and conditions of liability—it is not absolutely clear whether this is precisely the same grouping). Yet many of the principles and policy considerations which Ashworth identifies and defends or analyses cut across that structure in the sense of having implications for, or being substantively related to, values primarily relevant to one of the other sections within the tripartite structure. Take, for example, the principle of fair labelling, which dictates that 'widely felt distinctions between kinds of offences and degrees of wrongdoing are respected and signalled by the law, and that offences are subdivided and labelled so as to represent the nature and magnitude of the law-breaking'.[26] Though it speaks primarily to the conditions

[24] Ibid, 57–73. In Ashworth's scheme, the costs associated with proof and the practical advantages of broadly worded statutes which allow interpretive leeway to the courts in the interest of effective social defence count as policy considerations; but note that their cognate relationship with the principle of thin ice, acknowledged by Ashworth on p 66, suggests some relationship with the abstract principle of welfare.

[25] Ibid, 75–82.

[26] Ibid, 78.

of liability, this label has obvious implications for the range of criminal liability: in dictating that the contours of criminal liability must track social understandings, it interacts with our understandings of minimum criminalization, and of what is required by social responsibility.

Secondly, and related to his innovative way of carving up the conceptual issues, Ashworth's vision of the principles of criminal law, across all three subsections of concern, is consistently informed by his deep understanding of human rights, of the criminal process, of the law of evidence and issues of proof, and of the sentencing process. With the publication of the first edition of his criminal process text in 1994, Ashworth committed himself to the regular updating of no fewer than three major criminal law/criminal justice texts, a task which he has sustained over nearly 20 years. *Principles of Criminal Law* is testimony to the rich intellectual benefits of this Stakhanovite endeavour. It is no exaggeration to say that *The Criminal Process: An Evaluative Study*,[27] *Sentencing and Criminal Justice*,[28] and his Hamlyn Lectures, *Human Rights, Serious Crime and Criminal Procedure*[29] echo through every page of the book. For example, the principle of liability for acts rather than omissions,[30] which bears primarily on the range of criminal law, has implications for both the principle of contemporaneity and the doctrine of prior fault,[31] which bear on the conditions of liability. Furthermore, Ashworth's principles of criminal law are implicitly (and sometimes explicitly) embedded within a vision of criminal justice as a complex social process which is realized through interlocking practices framed within a range of institutions which are subject to distinctive pressures and preoccupations. For example, the principle of fair labelling,[32] which has relevance primarily to the conditions of liability, assumes that criminal justice is a social practice which aims to co-ordinate behaviour through the delivery of evaluative judgments which—in order to fulfil that very role—must command legitimacy; it has implications in turn for fair process, since laws which violate the principle of fair labelling may give rise to intractable problems of enforcement.[33] In short, Ashworth's is not a vision of criminal law as an autonomous body of doctrine; rather, it is of criminal law's doctrines and practices as procedurally, institutionally, and indeed socially embedded.

[27] (Oxford: Clarendon Press, 1994). First published in 1994; Mike Redmayne joined as Ashworth's co-author from the third edition, entitled simply *The Criminal Process* (Oxford: Oxford University Press) in 2005; the fourth edition appeared in 2010.

[28] First published as *Sentencing and Penal Policy* (London: Weidenfeld and Nicolson, 1983) and now in its fifth edition (Cambridge: Cambridge University Press, 2010).

[29] (London: Sweet and Maxwell, 2002).

[30] Ashworth, n 16 above, 54–5.

[31] Ibid, 81–2.

[32] Ibid, 78–80.

[33] On the complex relationship between perceptions of fairness and the enforcement of criminal law, see eg R Kinsey, J Lea, and J Young, *Losing the Fight Against Crime* (Oxford: Basil Blackwell, 1986).

Case studies: the principles of social responsibility and of fair labelling

In this section, I take two examples of principles sketched and defended by Ashworth, in order to subject them to a closer examination. My object will be to reveal more precisely than was possible in the previous section the strong interrelationships between abstract and general principles; between principles pertaining primarily to range, process, or conditions of liability and principles bearing on another of the three areas; between substantive law and evidence; and between principles of criminal law and the imperatives of criminal justice as a practical social activity with both institutional and normative conditions of existence.

Social responsibility

Let us take first the principle of social responsibility, which bears primarily on the proper range of criminal law, and justifies society's using criminal law to make mandatory a 'certain level of co-operation and mutual assistance between citizens'.[34] Since Ashworth's initial discussion of this principle occupies just one page,[35] it might be thought fanciful to suggest that he establishes all the connections mentioned in the previous paragraph. And yet I shall suggest that he indeed does so.

Abstract and general principles

The principle of social responsibility derives from the abstract principle of welfare, but also establishes a link between welfare and autonomy: '[t]he recognition of some social duties is . . . essential if individuals are to have a proper capacity for autonomy'.[36]

Interaction with principles pertaining to process and conditions of liability

The realization of the principle of social responsibility demands that it be brought into accommodation with a number of other principles also bearing primarily on the range of criminal law: principles such as the principle of minimum criminalization and the principle of liability for acts not omissions. But the principle of social responsibility also raises core questions relating to procedure and the realization of principles necessary to the rule of law: it may be argued that with '"extensions" of the criminal law . . . [based on a concern with social responsibility] . . . it will inevitably be unclear what is expected of the citizen',[37] hence potentially violating the principles of maximum certainty and fair warning. And though Ashworth does not mention this in his initial discussion, the principle of social responsibility's capacity to justify exceptional 'omissions' liability raises tricky questions about how the principle of contemporaneity as a condition for liability is to be met, as well as being potentially complicated by issues of prior fault in relation to the defendant's capacity to meet her social responsibility.

[34] Ashworth, n 16 above, 55. [35] Ibid, 55–6. [36] Ibid, 56. [37] Ibid, 55.

Process and sanction

A further challenge confronted by the legislator in interpreting the principle of social responsibility is how to design laws enforcing the principle without undermining accountability of power within the criminal process or compromising the fairness of punishment. The difficulty of defining positive social duties in an adequately clear and circumscribed way gives rise, in real systems, to the danger of broad prosecutorial discretion which, unless held accountable to an adequate degree, threatens to accord prosecutors a quasi-legislative role, which in turn violates tenets of non-retroactivity and legality.

The social role of criminal justice

Underlying Ashworth's brief discussion of the principle of social responsibility is a normative vision of the relations between citizens as entailing a duty of mutual assistance. An implicit political theory—liberalism with a strong social-democratic, even mildly communitarian tinge—motivates the argument here. But equally central to this part of his analysis is a practical vision of criminal law as underwriting only the most egregious breaches of that duty of mutuality. This is not only because of the procedural values and commitment to autonomy which equally underwrite its legitimacy, but also because of the practical limits on criminal law's capacity to shape behaviour.

Fair labelling: criminal law in the perspective of criminology

I have already described the relationships between the principle of fair labelling and the abstract principles of welfare and autonomy, as well as its upshot for principles bearing on fair procedures and the conditions of liability.[38] Here I shall therefore concentrate on what it discloses about Ashworth's overall view about the role of criminal law, and on the way in which that vision is fundamentally informed by his familiarity with criminology. To anyone other than an academic criminal lawyer, the proposition that the concerns of criminal law are deeply connected with those of criminology would appear unremarkable. Yet, as any academic lawyer knows only too well, particularly in British scholarship, legal and criminological concerns all too often float in separate intellectual universes.[39] As his elaboration and deployment of the principle of fair labelling shows, this is very far from being the case in Ashworth's scholarship. The idea of labelling itself derives from a sociological tradition which sees the definition of crime and the criminalization of offenders in terms of a social process of recognition, evaluation, and ultimately self-fulfilling 'othering'.[40] Labelling theory is one of the foundational traditions in 20th-century

[38] See above, text at nn 26 and 32.

[39] See N Lacey and L Zedner, 'Legal Constructions of Crime' in M Maguire, R Morgan, and R Reiner, *The Oxford Handbook of Criminology* (5th edn, Oxford: Oxford University Press, 2012), pp 159–81.

[40] See eg H Becker, *Outsiders* (New York: Free Press, 1966); D Matza, *Becoming Deviant* (Englewood Cliffs: Prentice-Hall, 1969).

criminology. It lies at the core of a vision of how social orders sustain and reproduce themselves around normative commitments, and identifies the influence of a variety of vectors of power in shaping both the definition and the application of criminal labels. Yet until the first edition of Ashworth's text, it was little recognized in criminal law scholarship. This was hardly surprising, for the criminological take on labelling theory is largely dystopian: indeed, it might be summed up in the phrase, 'give a dog a bad name and hang him'. In a brilliant synthesis of criminological and normative considerations, however, Ashworth distances himself from this dystopian aspect of labelling, while taking on board the insight that at some level criminal law judgments are all about how people label and evaluate one another. He goes on to team this up with two further insights. First, for this evaluative process to command any level of stability, it must connect with widely diffused social judgments. Secondly, this process, which—as the criminological literature is concerned to demonstrate—is liable to degenerate into a stigmatizing and divisive practice which may in the long run be inimical to social order, can usefully be subjected to scrutiny in terms of norms of fairness which also find a foothold in widely diffused social attitudes. Fair labelling, then, has its roots both in a sociological conception of criminal law as a social practice and in a view of the normative component of that practice. To put this insight in the terms in which I prefer to think about criminal law, Ashworth's point here is that normative principles of criminal law connect not only with a fundamental concern with criminal law's legitimacy, but also that a baseline of legitimacy is key to criminal law's efficacy as a system co-ordinating evaluation of behaviour and contributing to reasonably peaceable social relations.

3. Challenges for Ashworth's *Principles of Criminal Law* in a World of Pragmatic Criminalization

Like any significant account of the shape and rationale of criminal law, Ashworth's *Principles of Criminal Law* is open to various criticisms. Of these, the most obvious have to do with just how the many principles encompassed in Ashworth's vision are to be weighed up against one another where they come into conflict; how far any clear answer can be given to this sort of question; whether a multi-principle conception of criminal law which features no ordering of those principles really counts as 'principled' in the sense generally understood by philosophers and criminal law theorists; and how far it is either appropriate or realistic to suggest that policy considerations should not, as a matter of principle, be weighed in the same balance as issues of principle. With the exception of the last of these, I shall not address myself to these issues, beyond noting that some of them are oblique to Ashworth's project. For that project is rather to analyse the actual shape of criminal law, while pointing to implicit values which may be related to broader social values and deployed in the service of critique and reform, than to give a complete, principled 'theory of criminal law' in the fully normative sense. Indeed his prefatory remarks on the shape of the project, quoted earlier in this essay, suggest precisely this riposte.[41] But in this section, I do want to explore one potential difficulty for Ashworth's account, and to make some suggestions about how his account might be supplemented so as to enable him to respond most effectively to it. This is the difficulty posed, for any view of the criminal law as—even partially—principled, by the governmental tendency to reach for the criminal statute book to 'fix' a wide array of 'problems', with the goal of political gain.

This, as recent work by Ashworth himself[42] and by Ashworth and Lucia Zedner[43] has been important in demonstrating, is a particular problem in England and Wales today. But, notwithstanding the widely cited claim that, during its first decade in office, the Blair administration presided over the creation of upwards of 3,000 new criminal offences,[44] it is important not to exaggerate the novelty of this feature—or perhaps more accurately, this vulnerability or liability—of English criminal law. After all, Ashworth's work with Meredith Blake in the early 1990s, well before the Blair government succumbed to the political temptations of criminalization as an electoral strategy, showed that a staggering proportion of notifiable offences exhibited reverse burdens of proof or incomplete fault requirements.[45] These features not only violate the principles of criminal law which Ashworth defends in his book but, more important for our purposes, imply that pragmatic criminalization in the pursuit of political gain or regulatory impact was already a well-established feature of the English system before 1997.

The historical roots of this liability of English criminal law are not difficult to unearth. In the systems of the continent of Europe, the modern constitutional settlements which prefigured the growth of an ambitious nation state with a variety of regulatory tasks on its hands went alongside the creation of a new genre of administrative infractions which removed the bulk of administrative offences—

[41] See above, quoted at nn 16 and 19.

[42] Ashworth, 'Is the Criminal Law a Lost Cause?', n 1 above. It is not, of course, a problem confined to this country: see DN Husak, *Overcriminalization: The Limits of the Criminal Law* (Oxford: Oxford University Press, 2008); WJ Stuntz, *The Collapse of American Criminal Justice* (London: Belknap Press of Harvard University Press, 2011).

[43] A Ashworth and L Zedner, 'Just Prevention: Preventive Rationales and the Limits of the Criminal Law' in RA Duff and S Green (eds), *Philosophical Foundations of Criminal Law* (Oxford: Oxford University Press, 2011); see also A Ashworth and L Zedner, 'Preventive Orders: A Case of Under-Criminalization?' in RA Duff, L Farmer, SE Marshall, M Renzo, and V Tadros (eds), *The Boundaries of the Criminal Law* (Oxford: Oxford University Press, 2010), 59–87; A Ashworth and L Zedner, 'Defending the Criminal Law: Reflections on the Changing Character of Crime, Procedure and Sanctions' (2008) 2 Criminal Law and Philosophy 21.

[44] N Morris, 'Blair's "Frenzied Law-Making"', The Independent, 16 August 2006; see also Law Commission, *Criminal Liability in Regulatory Contexts* (Law Com CP No 195, 2010. For critical discussion, see N Lacey, 'Historicising Criminalization: Conceptual and Empirical Issues' (2009) 72 MLR 936.

[45] A Ashworth and M Blake, 'The Presumption of Innocence in English Criminal Law' [1996] Crim LR 306; see also Ashworth and Zedner, 'Defending the Criminal Law...', n 43 above, quoting an unpublished paper by Ashworth, 'Criminalization: What do 2005's New Crimes Tell Us about the Law?'.

so-called *mala prohibita*—from the ambit of the criminal law proper.[46] In England, where modernization of criminal law and criminal justice—though decisive—was piecemeal and took place incrementally over the course of more than a century, no such separation ever occurred. The upshot is that, from at least the middle of the 19th century, when the summary jurisdiction was expanded so as to accommodate a raft of new administrative offences functional to an industrial economy and an urbanizing society, it became increasingly difficult to rationalize the content, let alone the distinctive social functions, of criminal law.[47] The confidence about rationalizing and understanding criminal law in terms of a distinctive set of social values and interests, reflected in William Blackstone's enunciation of a group of 'public wrongs',[48] began to evaporate. (Indeed, as Blackstone's passionate defence of the common law against legislative encroachment implies, criticism of legislation as sullying the doctrinal coherence of criminal law is far from being a new phenomenon: it already exercised 18th-century commentators, and is a recurring theme in the common law tradition.[49]) A conception of certain wrongs or evils as the distinctive concern of criminal law is echoed, certainly, in the more ecumenical 'special part' frameworks of 19th- and early 20th-century treatises; but in its gradual decline, I would argue, lay the origins of the rise and rise of the 'general part'. For, unlike the 'special part' of criminal law, which can only be theorized by confronting the whole range of questions about the social functions and meaning of criminal law—issues which have become ever more diverse and liable to be caught up in political dynamics—the general part allows the theorist or doctrinalist to focus on relatively abstract or procedural values without having to address the substantive questions of what the criminal law should be criminalizing and why.[50] The dominance of 'the general part' in the Hall/Williams tradition had the effect—with a few honourable exceptions, notably Joel Feinberg[51] and Jonathan Schonsheck[52]—of more or less evacuating serious and systematic study of the rationale

[46] See eg JQ Whitman, *Harsh Justice* (Oxford: Oxford University Press, 2003); discussed in N Lacey, *The Prisoners' Dilemma: Political Economy and Punishment in Contemporary Democracies* (Cambridge: Cambridge University Press, 2008), Chs 1 and 2.

[47] For further discussion, see N Lacey, 'What Constitutes Criminal Law' in A Duff, L Farmer, S Marshall, M Renzo, and V Tadros (eds), *The Constitution of Criminal Law* (Oxford: Oxford University Press, forthcoming 2012).

[48] W Blackstone, *Commentaries on the Laws of England, Volume IV* (Chicago: University of Chicago Press, 1979).

[49] The tension between the integrity of a judge-articulated common law and the increasing dominance of legislation is most powerfully reflected in—and rejected by—Jeremy Bentham's swingeing critique of Blackstone: see GJ Postema, *Bentham and the Common Law Tradition* (Oxford: Clarendon Press, 1986), Chs 1 and 5–9; on contemporary complaints about the unprincipled legislative expansion of criminal law in the 18th century, see P King, *Crime and Law in England, 1750–1840* (Cambridge: Cambridge University Press, 2006), 22 ff; D Lieberman, *The Province of Legislation Determined: Legal Theory in Eighteenth Century Britain* (Cambridge: Cambridge University Press, 1989).

[50] This argument has been made most forcefully by Alan Norrie, whose work has consistently drawn attention to the way in which the legitimation of modern criminal law has been projected onto its distinctive form: see A Norrie, *Crime, Reason and History* (2nd edn, London: Butterworths, 2001).

[51] J Feinberg, *The Moral Limits of Criminal Law: Harm to Others; Offense to Others; Harm to Self; Harmless Wrongdoing* (Oxford: Oxford University Press, 1984–8).

[52] J Schonsheck, *On Criminalization* (London: Kluwer Academic, 1994).

for the substance and boundaries of criminalization from criminal law theory for several decades. Criminal law textbooks, meanwhile, contented themselves with variously analytically sophisticated black letter expositions of the doctrinal requirements for serious offences, prefaced by a dutiful if typically schematic rehearsal of the main theories of *mens rea*, *actus reus*, and defence and of the principle of legality.

This imbalance in the normative framework of the criminal law treatise was, as we saw earlier, one the main things which Ashworth's *Principles of Criminal Law* set right. As such, Ashworth's book must count as one of the earliest and most influential works in underpinning the revival of scholarly interest in criminalization.[53] Among texts widely read by students, it still stands alongside only one other book—Lacey, Wells, and Quick's *Reconstructing Criminal Law*[54]—in according equal importance to the rationale of the range of criminal law as to procedure and conditions of liability in assembling its normative framework. But precisely in making that significant advance in scholarship, Ashworth confronted himself with the intractable questions from which Williams had found an escape route half a century earlier: how can we rationalize the substance of criminal offences as an even partially principled matter in a system in which not only 'black letter' lawyers but also the government believe that the criminal law is simply what the legislature decides it to be? As Ashworth himself admits:

> The main determinants of criminalization continue to be political opportunism and power, both linked to the prevailing political culture of the country. Though an attempt has been made in this chapter to identify some general principles, it remains true that key concepts such as harm, wrongdoing and offensiveness may tend to be submerged by the political ideologies of the time.[55]

In a theory specifically oriented to the shape and role of criminal law in a 'broadly liberal democratic society',[56] some use can be made of institutionalized norms such as those enshrined in the Human Rights Act 1998 in tracing limits to, if not rationales for, criminalization. Ashworth makes excellent and imaginative use of this particular resource. But as he himself admits, the teeth of the Act are relatively blunt when it comes to any attempt to counter the sort of rampant criminalization which we have witnessed in recent years. Another strategy is to push the case for changes to the substance of criminal offences or defences which are arguably necessitated by expanded criminalization if principles such as maximum certainty,

[53] A field which is now flourishing: see Husak, *Overcriminalization*, n 42 above; G Lamond, 'What is a Crime?' (2007) 27 OJLS 609; Duff et al, *The Constitution of Criminal Law*, n 47 above, as well as *The Boundaries of Criminal Law*, n 43 above; see also RA Duff and SP Green (eds), *Defining Crimes: Essays on the Special Part of the Criminal Law* (Oxford: Oxford University Press, 2005).

[54] C Wells and O Quick (eds), *Lacey, Wells and Quick's Reconstructing Criminal Law* (4th edn, Cambridge: Cambridge University Press, 2010). In this text, our aspiration was to reverse the usual order of the criminal law treatise by reading criminal law through the prism of, first, social constructions of crime and, secondly, the criminal process. Even though we did not aspire to elicit coherent principles à la Ashworth, it is relevant to note that the task of drawing out clear overall themes driving the social construction of crime became increasingly challenging in successive editions from 1990 onwards.

[55] Ashworth, n 16 above, 39.

[56] Ibid, 39.

which have strong support within existing criminal law, are not to be compromised. This strategy Ashworth has also exploited to good effect, notably in his recent argument for a radical change in the treatment of ignorance of law.[57] But is there more which could be done, within a theoretically sophisticated account of criminal law, to illuminate and explain the nature of the challenge here?

Clearly, a normative account of criminal law cannot in itself counter the political and social forces which have led to the expansion of pragmatic criminalization in recent years: nor can such an account do anything to change the underlying dynamics of the political and social system which has produced those forces. But I would tentatively suggest that some modest progress can be made towards the goals which Ashworth and I share with other liberal criminal law scholars through two related strategies. First, one can locate criminal law more firmly in an analysis of what we might call the political economy of criminal justice—in other words, an analysis of the upshot of recent legislative changes in criminal law for its meaning, functions, and significance as a social institution; and secondly, one can work to develop a more explicit account of two fundamental dynamics which are at work within systems of criminal law. These are the dynamics of what I have called co-ordination and legitimation.[58] Any system of criminal law, whether conceived primarily as a censuring system or as a system of regulation, confronts two structural challenges. The first is to achieve minimum levels of co-ordination: in terms of defining criminal law norms; in terms of motivating compliance with them; and in terms of providing the institutional arrangements which allow for the effective enforcement of criminal law—notably, in modern societies, policing, the trial and sentencing process, arrangements for prosecution and defence, the provision and testing of evidence, and the execution of the sentence of the court. The second is to achieve an effective level of legitimation of the criminal law and criminal process across the populace to which the law is addressed. Note, crucially, that these two structural imperatives are internally related: without adequate co-ordinating institutions, legitimation is beside the point; without adequate levels of perceived legitimacy, co-ordinating institutions are unable to achieve their ends. Just as in the criminal process—'[a]convincing normative theory of the criminal process needs to be properly connected to facts about actual criminal processes'[59]—so in criminal law.

The internal relationship between legitimation and co-ordination is, I take it, precisely what motivates Ashworth's elaboration of the footing which his principles of criminal law already have within legal doctrine, legal practice, and broader social norms. Whatever the aims and functions of criminal law are taken to be, their realization depends not only on a range of effective institutions but also on the foothold which those institutions have in the normative attitudes of the populace to whom they are addressed. This insight can help us to put more flesh on the bones of

[57] A Ashworth, 'Ignorance of the Criminal Law, and Duties to Avoid it' (2011) 74 MLR 1.

[58] Lacey, n 11 above; see also N Lacey, *Women, Crime and Character: From Moll Flanders to Tess of the d'Urbervilles* (Oxford: Oxford University Press, 2008), Ch 1.

[59] Ashworth and Redmayne (4th edn), n 27 above, 23.

a variety of Ashworth's principles, notably the principle of minimum criminalization, of criminalization as last resort, and of not criminalizing where this would be counter-productive. Key areas in which these insights might be yielded—many of them issues on which Ashworth himself has worked in recent years—include the criminalization of drug use, where the evidence of unequal and counter-productive effects is beginning to have a significant impact on popular perceptions of legitimacy; terrorism offences, where the courts have already begun to register concerns; and the anti-social behaviour order, whose practical implementation can be shown to have contributed little to the ostensibly popular goals which it purported to pursue. But a further question is whether, in light of these developments, Ashworth might provide more systematic reflection on the recent changes in the actual boundaries of criminal law—for example, of the intensification of preventive justice which forms the object of his and Lucia Zedner's current work[60]—for the overall shape of criminal law as a social institution: how far do these changes reflect a real shift in the underlying legitimation needs and co-ordinating mechanisms of criminal law? I also wonder whether Ashworth might usefully revisit the division of labour which he ascribes to principles and policies, giving further consideration to whether it is truly feasible to rule out all balancing of policy considerations as normatively unacceptable. If we are prepared to accept that modern English criminal law has regulatory objectives[61]—however inadequately it may fulfil them—does this not imply that it is important to confront how the hard choices between values such as administrative efficiency and, say, maximum certainty should be made, rather than interpreting such choices as inevitably 'unprincipled'?

4. Conclusion

Ashworth's *Principles of Criminal Law* exemplifies all that is best in liberal criminal scholarship of the highest intellectual order. In this essay, I have demonstrated the place which it occupies in a common law tradition reaching back to Ashworth's predecessor in the Vinerian Chair at All Souls College, Oxford, William Blackstone. I have also argued that, in aligning itself with the tradition of theorizing criminal law's 'general principles', Ashworth's book reflects the significant development towards a theorization of criminal law under distinctively English conditions. Most importantly, these conditions feature a criminal law split, since at least the mid 19th century, between quasi-moral and regulatory concerns, implying a scholarly abandonment of efforts to rationalize the substance of criminal offences in favour of a focus on process values and the so-called 'general part'. Ashworth's vision in this book combines the best of both 19th-century and late 20th-century traditions in criminal law treatises. While exhibiting the strengths of the Hall/Williams elaboration of the 'general part'—in Ashworth's terms, the conception of

[60] See references at n 43 above.

[61] See N Lacey, 'Criminalization as Regulation: The Role of Criminal Law' in C Parker et al (eds), *Regulating Law* (Oxford: Oxford University Press, 2004), 144–67.

fair procedures and proper conditions of liability—it equally confronts the increasingly difficult challenge of developing normative insights pertaining to the proper range of the 'special part' of criminal law—the aspect sadly neglected in the Hall/Williams tradition. More tentatively, I have suggested that an extra push on a further dimension of *Principles of Criminal Law*—the implicit vision which it sketches of the role of criminal law as a social institution in a modern liberal polity, accompanied by a more specific acknowledgment of the distinctive dynamics affecting the English system—might yield further benefits within the four corners of the project which Ashworth has set for himself. A Festschrift is, of course, a celebration of work already completed. But my conclusion raises the hope that it may also be an anticipation of work still to come.

3

Criminal Attempt, the Rule of Law, and Accountability in Criminal Law

Jeremy Horder

1. The Rule of Law and the Definition of Inchoate Offences: Ashworth's Account

To an extent far greater than any other British scholar, Andrew Ashworth has sought to bring sophistication, coherence, and breadth of vision to what, during the 20th century, came to be known as 'subjectivism' in criminal law scholarship.[1] Briefly, earlier pioneers of this perspective on the nature and legitimate scope of the criminal law—such as JWC Turner,[2] Glanville Williams,[3] Smith and Hogan[4]—argued that, with limited exceptions, criminal liability should not be imposed unless the subjective state of mind of the accused when doing the act in question was (bearing in mind D's capacities) culpable with respect to all the elements of the offence, or with respect to a defence pleaded. One of Ashworth's most important contributions to the subjectivist tradition has been to enhance and then go beyond it through the development of certain master principles of criminal law, such as the principle of minimalism, the principle of individual autonomy, the principle of fair labelling, and the principle of correspondence.[5] It is with Ashworth's treatment of one of those principles in particular, the demand that the rule of law be respected in the design of criminal law, that I shall be concerned in this essay. Of the significance of this rule-of-law principle to criminal law in general, Ashworth says:

> [It] is a fundamental principle, with both procedural and substantive implications. It expresses an incontrovertible minimum of respect for the principle of autonomy: citizens must be informed of the law before it can be fair to convict them of an offence... and both legislatures and courts must apply the rule of law by not criminalizing conduct that was lawful when done.[6]

[1] See generally R Tur, 'Subjectivism and Objectivism: Towards Synthesis' in S Shute, J Gardner, and J Horder (eds), *Action and Value in Criminal Law* (Oxford: Oxford University Press, 2003).

[2] In his classic essay, 'The Mental Element in Crimes at Common Law' (1936) 6 CLJ 31.

[3] See his *Textbook of Criminal Law* (London: Stevens, 1978).

[4] See the first edition of JC Smith and B Hogan, *Criminal Law* (London: Butterworths, 1965).

[5] A Ashworth, *Principles of Criminal Law* (6th edn, Oxford: Clarendon Press, 2009), Chs 2 and 3.

[6] Ibid, 57–8.

I shall consider the application of this argument to the English law of criminal attempts.

In common with other inchoate offences, criminal attempt may involve only harmless wrongdoing, rather than harm done. Further (and partly in consequence), such offences together cast the net of criminal liability very widely across the field of human conduct. A nod or a wink in private, caught on a mobile telephone camera, may be sufficient evidence to convict someone of conspiracy or of encouraging crime, just as the mere putting of one's hand on another's car door may amount to the conduct element of a criminal attempt to steal. The sheer reach of inchoate liability might therefore seem to make it especially important to secure clarity concerning the kinds of conduct that will amount to an inchoate offence. Certainly, Ashworth links these two issues together:

> [C]onditions in a particular jurisdiction may be such that a properly developed law of inchoate offences places too much power in the hands of the police and puts innocent citizens at risk... [C]onnected to this, is the uncertainty of key definitional terms: the conduct element in attempts has been drawn so vaguely in English law that it sacrifices values of legality...[7]

The principle of legality alluded to here is the principle that, to use the language of Article 7 of the European Convention on Human Rights, '[n]o one shall be held guilty of any criminal offence on account of any act or omission which did not constitute a criminal offence under national or international law at the time when it was committed'. In what way and to what extent does the law of criminal attempt compromise this principle? An initial point to note (one I shall come back to) is that in Ashworth's account the principle is treated as interchangeable with what he calls the 'principle of maximum certainty':

> A connected reason in favour of the principle of maximum certainty is that, if rules are vaguely drafted, they bestow considerable power on the agents of law enforcement: the police or other agencies might use a widely framed offence to criminalise behavior not envisaged by the legislature, creating the very kind of arbitrariness that rule-of-law values should guard against.[8]

A critique of the law governing criminal attempts founded on the principle of maximum certainty works in this way. In English law, it is an offence of criminal attempt to engage in an act that is 'more than merely preparatory' to the commission of an indictable offence, with intent to commit that offence.[9] The phrase, 'more than merely preparatory' gives little other than generic guidance on what kinds of conduct will, and what kinds will not, count as criminal attempts.[10] The issue is effectively left to the judgment of the fact-finder at the trial itself. There is thus a significant risk, so the argument runs, that someone will be found guilty of

[7] A Ashworth, *Principles of Criminal Law* (6th edn, Oxford: Clarendon Press, 2009) Chs 2 and 3, 468.

[8] Ibid, 65–6.

[9] Criminal Attempts Act 1981, s 1(1).

[10] See eg W Wilson, *Criminal Law: Doctrine and Theory* (3rd edn, London: Lexis Nexis, 2008), 499–506.

criminal attempt having engaged in preparatory conduct that it could not confidently have been predicted beforehand would be found to amount in law to a criminal attempt. For Ashworth, the connection with Article 7 is that:

> [M]aximum certainty in defining offences—what are termed the 'fair warning' and 'void for vagueness' principles in United States law . . . may be seen as [a constituent] of the principle of legality . . . [and] . . . a vague law may in practice operate retroactively, since no one is quite sure whether given conduct is within or outside the rule.[11]

This is the so-called 'quality of law' test,[12] a basis for challenge claimed to be part of the prohibition on retroactivity at the heart of Article 7. If Ashworth is right, then his argument is a serious threat to the law of attempt, given the non-derogable status of rights under Article 7.

I will express doubts about the strength of the concerns raised here about the compatibility of criminal attempt with respect for the rule of law. However, whatever one makes of my doubts, they leave undiminished the importance of Ashworth's fresh perspective on the limits of the criminal law. That is because his work opens the way for a critique of criminal law doctrines in the light of the morality of institutional conduct (sound principles of public law), rather than in terms solely of the morality of individual conduct, the critique employed by an earlier generation of 'counter-authoritarian' criminal law scholars in the subjectivist tradition.[13]

2. Criminal Attempts and the Rule of Law: How Important is Article 7?

First, it is hard to see how an Article 7 objection to criminal attempts really strikes with much force at the way in which the conduct element is defined, in terms of a 'more than merely preparatory' act. So far as vague legislative wording is concerned, the European Court of Human Rights has taken an approach that is generous to legislatures. For example, the Court has upheld the validity of the offence in Greek law of 'insulting' the army, even in the absence of legislative or judicial elaboration of the concept of insult.[14] So far as judicial interpretation of the written law is concerned, the European Court has said that Article 7 prohibits instances in which 'existing offences [are] extended to cover facts which did not *clearly* constitute a criminal offence'.[15] On that interpretation, the vagueness that seems to some inherent in the notion of conduct that is 'more than merely preparatory' might

[11] Ashworth, n 5 above, 63–4, citing *Kokkinakis v Greece* (1994) 17 EHRR 397 at [52].

[12] See B Emmerson, A Ashworth, and A Macdonald (eds), *Human Rights and Criminal Justice* (London: Sweet & Maxwell, 2007), Ch 10.

[13] See nn 2–4 above. By 'counter-authoritarian' scholars I mean those who seek to shape substantive criminal law rules such that they form a bulwark against supposed over-criminalization.

[14] *Grigoriades v Greece* [1998] 9 HRCD 103. See the discussion below, nn 44 ff. A breach of Art 10 was found in this case, but (unanimously) no breach of Art 7.

[15] *SW and CR v UK* (1995) 21 EHRR 363, 390 (my emphasis).

be said to open the law of criminal attempts to extension of just that prohibited kind.[16] Having said that, the European Court's approach must be put in context. Even judicial extension of the criminal law can in the Court's eyes be perfectly legitimate if it takes the form of foreseeable 'progressive development', or 'gradual clarification' of the scope of liability, meaning that the offence in question retains its essential character.[17] By contrast, for example, a sudden extension of the common law offence of outraging public decency to encompass the glorification of terrorist acts would clearly fall foul of Article 7. It would fall foul because, to re-formulate the European Court's language in a small but significant way, the glorification of terrorist acts clearly *did not* fall within the scope of the existing offence. The courts' interpretation of the 'more than merely preparatory' test does not offend against Article 7 in this way. If the test is flawed the flaw is one in point of maximum certainty *as opposed to*—not as an example of—a flaw in point of legality. This is because whilst the test certainly requires 'gradual clarification', it is not a test apt to catch conduct that *clearly* (as opposed to arguably) did not constitute an attempt at the relevant time.

Article 7 takes aim at, inter alia, retroactive laws that change the legal status of an act or of a person from some significant point of time in the past, such as when the act was performed or when the person entered or still remained in a jurisdiction.[18] So long as the courts' law-making activity is confined to the gradual clarification or foreseeable progressive development of existing crimes, other than in wholly exceptional situations it is highly unlikely that crimes with open-textured definitional elements will violate the principle of legality, thus understood. Indeed, it is not going too far to suggest that impugning the legitimacy of the open-textured definition of the conduct element of criminal attempts by invoking Article 7 devalues the currency of that fundamental provision. To be sure, open-textured definitions of crimes leave the police and prosecutors with a good deal of discretion in deciding what conduct to pursue as an instance covered by them. However, a court will have the final say, in law, over the success of such an approach, and in liberal democracies agents of the state can be held accountable for prosecutorial actions. Even when existing criminal laws are blatantly misused to enhance state power, the moral integrity of Article 7 can only be properly preserved if it is confined in its application to the issue of whether or not there was a legal norm applicable to D's conduct at the time when it was engaged in (when the principle of legality will be in issue). Article 7 should not itself be extended such that it outlaws legal norms having an application at the relevant time—where the 'applicable law'

[16] There is an irony about such a worry in the present context. If anything, much criticism of the English courts' interpretation of the 'more than merely preparatory' act criterion has focused on the courts' failure to extend it to include anything like enough conduct highly proximate to the commission of the substantive offence: Law Commission, *Conspiracy and Attempts* (Law Com CP No 183, 2007), 171–3.

[17] *SW and CR v UK* (1995) 21 EHRR 363, 399.

[18] See E Edinger, 'Retrospectivity in Law' [1995] 29 University of British Columbia Law Review 5, 10. See also the discussion of *Tot v United States* 319 US 463 (1942) in L Fuller, *The Morality of Law* (revised edn, New Haven: Yale University Press, 1969), 62.

includes instances covered by its foreseeable progressive development or clarification[19]—but that give what some regard as an unacceptably wide scope for the exercise of discretion in interpretation and enforcement (when the principle of maximum certainty is in issue). The latter is not the same evil as the evil involved when the state employs the power of law retroactively. For example, through foreseeable progressive development over many years, a legal rule or concept—such as 'unlawful sexual intercourse' in rape—could ultimately come to mean something quite different from what (if anything) was anticipated at the outset.[20] Even so, the very fact that this significant change occurred through progressive development, and not through a single policy-driven 'lurch' (however, from a cynical viewpoint, predictable that might have been) means that the change can have a legitimacy it would not otherwise possess.[21] As Ronald Dworkin puts it:

> Interpretation folds back into the practice, altering its shape, and the new shape encourages further reinterpretation, so the practice changes dramatically, *though each step in the progress is interpretive of what the last achieved.*[22]

The certainty or the vagueness of a criminal prohibition, and hence its capacity to provide fair warning, are matters of degree. It is hard to be much more categorical about the requirements of the rule of law in that respect than to say, with Professor Gardner, that 'D should be able to know, *more or less*, when her actions will have which types of adverse consequences, such as a criminal conviction'.[23] A jurisdiction respectful of autonomy and dignity will, as Lon Fuller argued long ago, 'put a high value on legislative clarity';[24] but as Joseph Raz has argued, in that respect, 'a lesser degree of conformity [to the rule of law] is often to be preferred precisely because it helps realization of other goals'.[25] In this context, a very significant 'other goal' is the attainment of brevity and simplicity in the definition of criminal offences, virtues that section 1(1) of the Criminal Attempts Act 1981, whatever other faults it may have, exemplifies admirably. Quite rightly, Article 7 is uncompromising in its terms and in its effects, and it should not be modified in its application to take account of such subtleties. To seek to make it do so is to miss its narrow but fundamental point. A more promising human rights-based critique of vagueness in offence-definition might concentrate on the fairness, for Article 6 purposes, of a trial based on official exploitation of such vagueness to ambush

[19] See n 18 above. As Hart rightly remarks, it can be a legitimate part of the relationship between the legislature and the courts that the courts can make law, at least interstitially: see HLA Hart, *The Concept of Law* (2nd edn, Oxford: Clarendon Press, 1994), 275. On interstitial development of the law, see J Raz, 'On the Autonomy of Legal Reasoning' (1993) 6 Ratio Juris 1.

[20] On the issue of 'unlawful' sexual intercourse, see *R v R* [1992] 1 AC 599 (HL).

[21] See *SW and CR v UK* (1995) 21 EHRR 363, and Hart, n 19 above.

[22] R Dworkin, *Law's Empire* (London: Fontana, 1986), 48 (my emphasis). On the legitimacy of judicial creativity in developing the criminal law, see J Horder, 'Criminal Law and Legal Positivism' (2002) 8 Legal Theory 221.

[23] J Gardner, 'Justification Under Authority', University of Oxford Legal Research Paper Series, Paper No 5/2009, 29 (my emphasis).

[24] Fuller, n 18 above, 64.

[25] J Raz, 'The Rule of Law and its Virtue' in J Raz, *The Authority of Law* (Oxford: Clarendon Press, 1979), 228. This point is acknowledged by Ashworth: see n 5 above, 66.

'offenders'. In that respect, there may be an analogy between such exploitation, and the wrongdoing involved in entrapment. Both may, in Ashworth's words when discussing entrapment, in their different ways involve 'an abuse of executive power', and hence threaten 'the integrity of the criminal justice system', undermining the fairness of the trial.[26]

3. Criminal Attempts and the Rule of Law: Professor Dan-Cohen's Argument

That final point brings me to Meir Dan-Cohen's analysis of the American 'void-for-vagueness' doctrine on which Ashworth relies in his critique.[27] As we have seen,[28] Ashworth links his Article 7 objections to the conduct element of criminal attempt in English law to American 'void-for-vagueness' and 'fair warning' requirements. These requirements are in his view an integral part of the prohibition on retroactive laws passed by Congress in section 9 of Article 1 of the US Constitution, which stipulates that 'no Bill of attainder or *ex post facto* law shall be passed'. Dan-Cohen considers the 'void-for-vagueness' doctrine in the light of the decision of the Supreme Court in *Rose v Locke*,[29] in which the constitutionality of a Tennessee statute outlawing 'crimes against nature' was upheld, and its application to cunnilingus affirmed. In Dan-Cohen's view, the wrong approach to such cases is to apply a test that treats detailed legal interpretation (judicial gloss) of the scope of crimes 'against nature' as aimed at the direct guidance of citizens themselves, forming part of the state's 'conduct' rules. On such an approach, sometimes adopted in English cases dealing with analogous problems,[30] the test applied is whether, had D consulted a lawyer, it would have been possible for the lawyer to provide D with a reliable opinion on what the court would rule. Even if one ignores its impracticability in many instances, from Dan-Cohen's perspective this approach runs together the test for the adequacy of 'conduct' rules, for citizens, with the adequacy of 'decision' rules, for officials.[31] In Dan-Cohen's theory, decision rules are rules that govern the decision-making powers of the courts, and (I might add) more broadly the relationship between the legislature, the courts, and other criminal justice agencies or officials. Some decision rules will be set out by the legislature for the benefit of the courts, criminal justice agencies, and the broader legal community, perhaps in the form of guidelines,[32] but decision rules may also

[26] Ashworth, n 5 above, 237. However, Ashworth now appears to reject such an analogy: A Ashworth, 'Ignorance of the Criminal Law, and Duties to Avoid It' (2011) 74 MLR 1, 6.

[27] M Dan-Cohen, 'Decision Rules and Conduct Rules: On Acoustic Separation in Criminal Law' (1984) 97 Harvard Law Review 625.

[28] Text at n 11 above.

[29] 423 US 48 (1975).

[30] *R v Goldstein; R v Rimmington* [2005] UKHL 63, [2006] 1 AC 459.

[31] See further P Alldridge, 'Rules for Courts and Rules for Citizens' (1990) 10 OJLS 487; P Robinson, 'Rules of Conduct and Principles of Adjudication' (1990) 57 University of Chicago Law Review 729.

[32] This is a suggestion of long-standing: see Fuller, n 18 above, 64.

include the case-by-case 'filling out' of open-textured legal concepts by the higher courts. Such cases should be counted under the heading of decision rules, because their main normative function is to add to predictability and certainty within the legal system by creating a high degree of shared understanding between judges, lawyers, and officials, as to the meaning and scope of the legal concepts in question. Decision rules of this kind can contribute to the rule of law by making it clearer to defence lawyers, judges, and juries what case D will have to meet, when charged with an offence (enhancing compliance with Article 6(3)(a) of the European Convention on Human Rights). In Dan-Cohen's view, this virtue of decision rules should not be equated or confused with the nature or quality of guidance they are capable of giving to private individuals subject to the law. However, before taking this argument forward, some refinement of it is needed, as Dan-Cohen somewhat exaggerates the significance of the distinction.

One should not draw too stark a contrast between conduct rules and decision rules.[33] Conduct rules 'for citizens' in (criminal) law are commonly drawn up by the legislature with half an eye on the interpretation that courts, and other officials, are likely to put on them: part of what Gardner calls the 'feedback loop' connecting the legislature and the courts when it comes to the interpretation of legislature wording.[34] Contrariwise, decision rules can in practice be more or less reliably consulted by citizens for conduct guidance purposes;[35] and even though it may not be the main normative function of a decision rule to provide citizens with conduct guidance, a failure by officials to stick to decision rules may be reviewable in the courts.[36] Rather than making classification of a rule as a conduct or as a decision rule the key issue, we would perhaps do better to ask the following question in relation to the governance of a particular area of law such as criminal attempt. If neither kind is sufficient by itself, does the combination of rules aimed more at legal experts than at lay people, and rules aimed more at lay people than at experts, do enough to secure compliance with the rule of law, bearing in mind the other goals that the legislation must achieve or support? With this refinement in place, can Dan-Cohen's argument be applied to resist the view that the conduct element of attempt is, as Ashworth suggests, unacceptably vague?

One way of applying the argument would be to say that cases, or declaratory legislative guidelines, covering commonly encountered situations involving actions preparatory to the commission of offences, should not be regarded primarily as belated attempts to improve what is said to be a defectively vague conduct rule ('more than merely preparatory' conduct), for the purposes of section 1(1) of the 1981 Act. In that respect, as Dan-Cohen puts it, making a more general point:

[33] J Gardner, *Offences and Defences* (Oxford: Oxford University Press, 2007), 116.

[34] J Gardner, 'Legal Positivism: 5½ Myths' (2001) 46 American Journal of Jurisprudence 199.

[35] Think of a company consulting Sch 1 to the Interpretation Act 1978 to discover whether a statute making it criminal for a 'person' to do something includes corporate persons within its scope.

[36] On this point, see the discussion in the concluding section.

> . . . judicial gloss often remedies indeterminacy only by increasing inaccessibility. Consequently, judicial gloss may cripple a statute's ability to communicate to the public a 'fair warning' no less than did the statute's earlier indeterminacy.[37]

Cases (or guidelines) are often better regarded as either facilitating or constituting the development of supplemental decision rules, aimed primarily at improving the understanding between the police, prosecution, defence lawyers, and the judiciary concerning conduct that is fit for arrest and prosecution, and hence concerning the case D will have to meet if arrested or prosecuted. Where, then, lies the conduct-guiding element in the law of criminal attempt?

It is arguable that even the basic requirement for a 'more than merely preparatory' act can itself be regarded as primarily a decision rule added to the true conduct rule. The latter—'Attempts to commit offences must not be committed'—is simply implicit in the generic character of section 1(1) of the 1981 Act. What is more, this implicit conduct rule is sufficient by itself to satisfy the demands of the rule of law, not least because of the special nature of an 'attempt' to commit a crime as a species of wrong. Consider John Gardner's argument that the demands of the rule of law can be met in certain cases, other than simply by bolting subjective fault elements on to conduct elements, by what he calls the 'action-specificity' of the conduct element:[38]

> [A]ction-specificity adds a second and different protection against ambush [by the law]. It enables one to organise one's life so as to avoid even having to worry about committing certain criminal offences . . . [T]he argument only applies where the action in question is one that cannot be performed without noticing that one is performing it. But so long as that condition is met, the specific action's inclusion in the definition of the offence makes a distinct contribution to one's freedom.[39]

'Attempts' have a special normative mixture of fault and conduct elements: we cannot make sufficient sense of the idea of an 'attempt', or indeed of a 'more than merely preparatory' act, as conduct elements, without reference to the fault element, to the requirement that someone's aim be the commission of the substantive offence. For that reason, I suggest that becoming engaged in an 'attempt' to commit a criminal offence has the kind of action-specificity that provides significant protection from ambush, being something that one cannot help but be fully aware that one is doing. The same can be argued to be true of entering into a conspiracy.[40] It may be that, for decision-rule purposes, the law seeks to narrow the class of actions to be regarded as criminal attempts by confining them to 'more than merely preparatory' acts; but that laudable aim should not be confused with what is

[37] Dan-Cohen, n 27 above, 559–60.

[38] Gardner, n 33 above, 241. It should be noted that Gardner does not apply this argument specifically to the conduct element of the 1981 Act.

[39] Ibid.

[40] However, the same point cannot be made of 'assisting' or 'encouraging' an offence, contrary to ss 44 and 45 of the Serious Crime Act 2007, because it is possible to assist or encourage an act unintentionally. So, there is nothing about engaging in the action itself (assisting, encouraging) that will necessarily alert one to its nature.

required by the rule of law in this context, for conduct-rule purposes. This being so, Ashworth's critique of the vagueness, for conduct-guidance purposes, of the term 'more than merely preparatory' may not be as potent as it appears. That term need not be regarded as included in the 1981 Act primarily to guide the public. Its primary function is to guide lawyers and officials (including, for this purpose, juries) on matters such as the case each side has to meet at trial. Accordingly, even if left unsupplemented by case law or guidelines, that term does not stand to be judged by void-for-vagueness provisions in the same way as, for example, an unvarnished prohibition on crimes 'against nature'. No doubt, lawyers and officials welcome the greater clarity for decision-rule purposes that supplemental case law or guidelines may bring; but whilst such supplemental law may enhance the rule-of-law credentials of the 1981 Act when it comes to compliance, it is not essential to them.

Suppose, then, that section 1(1) of the 1981 Act had begun with nothing more than words along the following lines: 'If, with intent to commit an offence to which this section applies, *D attempts to commit* that offence, he is guilty of criminal attempt.' Would anything of real value have been lost, in terms of meeting fair warning and (for want of a better term) specificity requirements, by the omission of words purporting to give greater specificity to 'attempts to commit'? In seeking to answer this question, it would be helpful to go further into Dan-Cohen's arguments. One way in which the US Supreme Court has said that criminal laws can satisfy fair warning and void-for-vagueness requirements is if they incorporate '*scienter*' (knowledge) as a definitional element, namely a requirement for proof that D knew the external elements of the offence would take place.[41] However, on one view, the *scienter* requirement does little to cure vagueness, because its focus is not on whether D was aware that his or her conduct was *in law* criminal. Instead, the focus is simply on whether D knew that, as a matter of fact, his or her conduct would bring about certain results in certain circumstances. As LaFave and Scott put it:

> Because it [*scienter*] is knowledge of the consequences of one's actions and not knowledge of the existence or meaning of the criminal law which is relevant, it seems clear that uncertain language in a statute is not clarified by the addition of a *scienter* element.[42]

However, for Dan-Cohen, such a criticism draws too sharp a distinction between knowledge of the law and knowledge of the facts. Knowledge of the law and knowledge of the facts may overlap when both draw on ordinary language concepts. Accordingly, as Dan-Cohen argues:

> [T]he defendant's state of mind satisfies the mens rea requirement in a criminal statute if the defendant perceives the facts and the nature of his conduct in terms of the statute's ordinary-language description of them . . . So interpreted, the requirement of mens rea can in fact

[41] *United States v National Dairy Products Corporation* 372 US 29 (1963); *Boyce Motor Lines v United States* 342 US 337 (1952), cited by Dan-Cohen, n 27 above, 659.

[42] W LaFave and A Scott, *Handbook on Criminal Law* (St Paul: West Publishing Company, 1972), 11, 86, cited by Dan-Cohen, n 27 above, 660.

serve the interest in fair warning by securing a correspondence between the defendant's own cognitions and the description of the proscribed conduct in the relevant conduct rule.[43]

There are two points to make about this passage, in applying it to the present context. First, in spite of the emphasis on *mens rea* rather than on *actus reus*, it must be kept in mind that in the case of criminal attempt, the fault element is bound up normatively with the conduct element.[44] Secondly, Dan-Cohen errs in supposing that what must be shown in each case is that the individual defendant actually saw his or her conduct 'in terms of the statute's ordinary-language description': that is too generous to defendants.

Subject to what will be said in the concluding section, it may be perfectly legitimate, albeit controversial, for a legislature to criminalize, say, 'threatening', 'abusive', or 'insulting' behaviour likely to cause harassment, alarm, or distress,[45] even when D did not realize that his or her conduct might be regarded as threatening, abusive, or insulting.[46] What matters, first, is whether there is sufficient overlap between the ordinary language and the legal understandings of 'threatening', 'abusive', or 'insulting' to ensure that the conduct rule is one that gives fair warning, and (to a lesser extent) secondly, whether there are sufficiently comprehensive decision rules or guidelines filling out the legal meaning of these terms to ensure compliance with Article 6.[47] Dan-Cohen confuses the normative conditions under which a criminal law employing an ordinary language concept may fairly be regarded as sufficiently 'rule-like' (putting conduct and decision-rule components together), with the ascriptive—blame attributive—conditions under which a line of distinguished scholars and judges have come to regard criminal laws as fair, namely when they require subjective fault elements in some form. For the purposes of fair criminalization of attempts, it is sufficient (in conduct-rule terms) that the legal understanding of an 'attempt' does not move far from the ordinary language understanding. It will be more than sufficient if case law or other decision rules such as guidelines also provide a stable and well-understood basis on which the police, prosecutors, defence lawyers, judges, and juries can respectively enforce, advise on, explain, and apply the law.[48] For some, it might constitute an important improvement, in point of fairness, if the law required that D be aware that ordinary people would regard his or her conduct as 'more than merely preparatory' respecting the commission of an offence; but that improvement, if such it really would be, does not bear on the normative conditions in which the law of criminal attempt operates in accordance with the requirements of the rule of law. Moreover, such a 'subjectivist' development would arguably achieve less, in point of fairness and

[43] Dan-Cohen, n 27 above, 662–3.

[44] Text at n 39 above.

[45] Public Order Act 1986, s 5.

[46] See the judgment of the European Court in *Grigoriades v Greece* [1998] 9 HRCD 103.

[47] See *Grigoriades v Greece*, n 46 above, where no decision rules shedding further light on the meaning of 'insulting' were required, for rule of law purposes. It will, of course, be important that any law constructed on such a basis is well publicized, avoiding widespread ignorance of it: see Ashworth, n 26 above.

[48] For further discussion, see the concluding section.

adequate warning, than the law already achieves through an important point of criminal procedure. It confines the scope of criminal attempt to attempts to commit indictable (more serious) offences.[49] These are offences respecting which no one could reasonably say they had been caught by surprise when they discover that it is an offence to try to bring about, as well as to succeed in bringing about, the wrongful harm in question.

In that regard, though, critics of the *scienter* requirement are on firmer ground when what are in issue are crimes that employ ordinary language that has no prospect of acquiring a relatively settled meaning, because the concepts involved are archaic or essentially contested. For example, in relation to the decision in *Locke*,[50] Dan-Cohen rightly argues that the idea of 'crimes against nature' does not (unlike the idea of, say 'threatening' behaviour) convey a sufficiently meaningful message:

> The Supreme Court completely overlooked the possibility that changes in moral outlook and their reflection in linguistic usage were relevant to the issue of fair warning... [E]xpressions whose linguistic vitality has expired and whose moral connotations are no longer valid, give no fair warning to the ordinary person.[51]

Notoriously, in English law, the inchoate offence of conspiracy 'to corrupt public morals'[52] ought for this reason to be regarded as failing a void-for-vagueness or fair warning test. There has been far too little by way of decision rule-making, whether by case-law development or through the issuing of guidelines, for it to be possible to say that the development of decision rules has sufficiently compensated for the essentially contested or archaic character of the conduct rule. In that respect it is interesting to note that, satisfied that sufficient certainty *had* been created by the accumulation of decision rules over many years relating to the offences of outraging public decency and public nuisance,[53] the Law Commission has recommended the introduction of what would be, in effect, a watered-down requirement of *scienter* for these offences:

> A 'public nuisance' or an instance of 'outraging public decency' is involved when the conduct in question is what ordinary people would regard as a public nuisance or as an outrage to public decency. The fault element will be proven only if D is shown to have intended to cause such a nuisance or outrage, or to have realised that such a nuisance or outrage—one regarded by ordinary people as such—might be caused by his or her conduct.[54]

As this recommendation implies, a *scienter* requirement can only make a meaningful contribution to the rule of law credentials of an offence if there is adequate

[49] Criminal Attempts Act 1981, s 1(4).
[50] See n 29 above.
[51] Dan-Cohen, n 27 above, 664.
[52] *Shaw* [1962] AC 220.
[53] See *R v Rimmington; R v Goldstein* [2005] UKHL 63, [2006] 1 AC 459.
[54] Law Commission, *Simplification of Criminal Law: Public Nuisance and Outraging Public Decency* (Law Com CP No 193, 2010), para 5.28.

certainty concerning its scope created, if not by the original definition itself, then by decision rules or other guidelines (to which I now turn).

4. Attempts and Accountability through Decision Rule-making

No one should conclude from the discussion so far that, just because the relevant conduct and decision rules created by the legislature and the courts can together ensure that the wording employed to define a crime meets the requirements of the rule of law, that is sufficient to justify the existence of that crime. Consider the offence of engaging in abusive behaviour likely to cause harassment, alarm, or distress.[55] Even if it passes muster, in terms of certainty of definition, the way in which it is enforced by officials—too frequently, as an offence committed against police officers themselves—may cast serious doubt on its justifiability.[56] This raises a more general point about Ashworth's distinctive contribution to what I called (broadening out the older 'subjectivist' agenda) the 'counter-authoritarian' perspective on fairness.[57] In relation to the substantive law, earlier subjectivists[58] who adopted that perspective tended to see the ground that needed defending in terms of the way in which offences and defences are defined by the legislature and the courts. They advocated the use of advertent states of mind to define fault, taking account of individual capacities when setting limits to defences, and so on. They saw things in this way, because their primary concern was with what they regarded as the proper (subjective) moral basis on which individuals should be held culpable, in criminal law. Although Ashworth himself also sees things in these terms, he has a broader agenda. As we have seen, his concern with the definition of offences is that, as he puts it, 'if rules are vaguely drafted, they bestow considerable power on the agents of law enforcement'.[59] A problem with offence definition may be, thus, not so much that it is vague but that there is too little accountability in respect of the way in which its vagueness may be exploited by officials. Thus understood, *nemo iudex in sua causa* may be as important a maxim, and *quis custodies ipsos custodiet?* as important an issue, as *actus non facit reum nisi mens sit rea*,[60] in relation to the development and use of the substantive law. So far as criminal attempts are concerned, Ashworth himself sees this point being addressed through the development of legislative (or possibly judge-made) guidelines on the scope of the conduct element.[61] However, such developments need not be confined to bodies with normative powers to change and develop the criminal law itself, bodies which

[55] See n 45 above.
[56] See the discussion in Ashworth, n 5 above, 40–1.
[57] See n 13 above.
[58] See nn 2–4 above.
[59] Text at n 8 above.
[60] Respectively, 'No one is to be a judge is his or her own cause', 'Who will guard the guards themselves?', and 'The act cannot be treated as guilty unless the mind was also guilty.'
[61] Ashworth, n 5 above, 63–4.

cannot themselves be held to account in law for their law-making activities by those affected. Here are two examples.

First, in the criminal law's regulatory sphere, a different approach has been taken to securing the rule-of-law credentials of inchoate (or, more broadly, 'preliminary') offences. This involves government departments or quasi-autonomous agencies creating their own guidelines on what open-ended offences require of citizens or businesses, and thus on what conduct is likely to be targeted by enforcement officials. A well-known example is the set of guidelines provided by the Health and Safety Executive for a whole variety of industries, on what steps employers should take to ensure that they have done what is reasonably practicable to ensure employees' health and safety.[62] Similar guidelines are now provided, to give a less well-known example, for pet owners respecting their obligations under section 9 of the Animal Welfare Act 2006 to take reasonable steps to provide a suitable environment and diet for their pets, as well as to allow pets to exhibit normal behaviour patterns (obligations above and beyond those in section 4 of the 2006 Act concerned with causing unnecessary suffering).[63] Such developments in practice, if not in strict legal theory, make far less significant in securing fairness the normative role of courts (of which much was always expected by traditional counter-authoritarians[64]) through, for example, their application of the presumption of fault to statutory provisions. In the modern world of the criminal law, the burgeoning of secondary norms (rules and standards governing other rules and standards) created by Parliament to determine procedures to be adopted by enforcement agencies[65] threaten to confine that traditional normative role to even more marginal a bit-part than it had before. From self-appointed guardians not only of public safety and order but also of the 'moral welfare of the state',[66] the courts are in many areas being reduced to passive night watchmen, operating at the fringes of a specialist criminal law 'construction industry' concerned more than efficient outcomes and stakeholder management than with criminal prosecution and appeal.

Secondly, returning to the non-regulatory sphere, the House of Lords has shown itself willing to require the Director of Public Prosecutions, in the interests of certainty, to issue guidance on when an offence is more or less likely to be prosecuted. In *R (on the application of Purdy) v Director of Public Prosecutions*,[67] the Law Lords required the DPP 'to clarify what his position is as to the factors that he regards as relevant for and against prosecution',[68] respecting the offence of

[62] See <http://www.hse.gov.uk/guidance/industries.htm> accessed 6 March 2012.

[63] See <http://www.defra.gov.uk/publications/2011/03/29/pb12460-animal-welfare-act/> accessed 19 April 2012.

[64] Accordingly, the sense of betrayal amongst counter-authoritarians, when the courts are deemed to have failed to meet those expectations, is all too evident: see eg G Williams, 'The Lords and Impossible Attempts' (1986) 45 CLJ 33.

[65] See eg the Regulatory Enforcement and Sanctions Act 2008, s 43(2).

[66] See *Shaw v DPP* [1962] AC 220 (HL).

[67] [2009] UKHL 45, [2010] 1 AC 345.

[68] Ibid, at [55].

encouraging and assisting suicide. Following the publication of that guidance,[69] the Association of Chief Police Officers will itself also issue decision-rule guidance to police forces on dealing with such cases, including guidance on seeking prosecutors' advice at an early stage on appropriate lines of investigation.[70] Such guidance does not, of course, concern an offence with an especially open-textured definition of the conduct element. However, the need to issue the guidance (and to stick by it in future) shows the importance of decision rules in enhancing the rule-of-law credentials of an offence. Lest it be thought that this is an exceptional case, it is becoming more common for the Ministry of Justice itself to issue decision-rule guidance on the scope of inchoate offences generally. For example, following the coming into force of Part 2 of the Serious Crime Act 2007, the Ministry issued (non-binding) advice, including examples, on the scope of the offences of assisting and encouraging crime to judges, court officials, prosecutors, police organizations, the Law Society, the Bar Council, and the Criminal Bar Association.[71] Such guidance, coupled with (for example) the Crown Prosecution Service's own guidance on the issue,[72] may considerably improve the rule-of-law credentials of any given offence. Furthermore, the issuing of such guidance opens up the operation of offences to greater public scrutiny (and to scrutiny by other official agencies, including the courts), and in some instances to challenge to official decisions departing from the guidance.[73] It is one of the great virtues of Ashworth's work that it has the potential to provide a broader basis for such a 'counter-authoritarian' analysis and critique of criminal law. This critique moves well beyond the narrow concern of an earlier generation of subjectivists, who were largely taken up with what they took to be law-makers' (including courts') neglect of advertent and capacity-focused culpability elements in offences and defence definitions. Ashworth's critique takes the argument against an expansive criminal law into the realms of public law, of accountability in decision-making, and of human rights in a way that will set the terms of debate for years to come.

[69] See <http://www.cps.gov.uk/publications/prosecution/assisted_suicide_policy.html> accessed 6 March 2012. The guidance is primarily in decision-rule form, but can obviously be used by lay people to guide their conduct.

[70] Ibid, paras 9–10.

[71] See Circular No 2008/04, 29 September 2008, <http://tna.europarchive.org/20081013095030/http://www.justice.gov.uk/docs/serious-crime-act-2007-implementation-part2.pdf> accessed 19 April 2012.

[72] See <http://www.cps.gov.uk/legal/h_to_k/inchoate_offences/index.html#a01> accessed 6 March 2012.

[73] For further discussion on this point, see *R (on the application of Corner House Research) v Director of the Serious Fraud Office* [2008] UKHL 60, [2009] 1 AC 756 at [30]–[44] (especially [44], per Lord Bingham, dealing with cases in which there is a clear legal basis by which to judge an official decision).

4

Presuming Innocence

RA Duff *

1. Introduction

Andrew Ashworth's remarkable intellectual career to date (and there is, of course, much more to come) makes the task of choosing a topic on which to write for this Festschrift both easy and difficult: easy because, given the range of his contributions to criminal law, it would be hard to find an important topic on which one could not engage with his work; but difficult because the authoritative clarity of his writings, their command of both abstract theory and concrete practice, and the humanely liberal good sense that they manifest, set a high standard. With appropriate trepidation, therefore, but with great pleasure in being able thus to honour someone who has done so much to enliven and to deepen principled discussion of the proper workings of systems of criminal justice, I will discuss some aspects of the Presumption of Innocence (PoI)—a topic to which Ashworth has returned several times in recent years.[1]

To ask about the meaning of the PoI and its proper role in the criminal law is to ask what must be presumed, by whom, about whom, to what effect; what can defeat that presumption; and when (if ever) the presumption need not be made. One set of issues that I cannot pursue here concerns the role that the, or a, PoI might play outside the criminal trial. As declared in its classical formulation in English common law and by the European Convention on Human Rights (ECHR), the PoI applies, if not only within the trial, at least only within the criminal process that begins with a criminal charge.[2] As thus understood, it might have implications for such matters as the refusal of bail,[3] the legitimacy of such

* Thanks to the editors, to Victor Tadros, and to Patrick Tomlin for helpful comments.

[1] See especially 'Article 6 and the Fairness of Trials' [1999] Crim LR 261; 'Four Threats to the Presumption of Innocence' (2006) 10 International Journal of Evidence and Proof 241 (hereafter, 'Four Threats'); and (with M Blake), 'The Presumption of Innocence in English Criminal Law' [1996] Crim LR 306.

[2] *Woolmington v DPP* [1935] AC 462, 481 (HL)—'it is the duty of the prosecution to prove the prisoner's guilt' (Viscount Sankey); Art 6(2) ECHR: anyone 'charged with a criminal offence shall be presumed innocent until proved guilty according to the law'.

[3] See eg U Ni Raifeartaigh, 'Reconciling Bail Law with the Presumption of Innocence' (1997) 17 OJLS 1; Ashworth, 'Four Threats', 244.

post-verdict procedures as the making of confiscation orders,[4] and the award of compensation to defendants who are acquitted or have their convictions overturned on appeal;[5] but it has no bearing outside the criminal process. More expansive versions of a PoI are possible, bearing on the way in which the state should treat citizens who are not (yet) within the criminal process, or on how we should treat each other as citizens: in what ways, to what effect, is it legitimate for the state and its officials, or for other citizens, to treat people as if they were guilty of past wrongdoing or likely to engage in future wrongdoing, if they have not been convicted of a criminal offence?[6]

The values underpinning the PoI in the criminal process are certainly connected to those expressed in these more expansive presumptions: all concern the practical attitudes that the state should take towards its citizens and that citizens should take towards each other, the kind of trust that should structure those attitudes, and the conditions under which such trust may be qualified or suspended. There are also, however, significant differences between the PoI in the criminal trial, and such broader presumptions. Within a trial, the issue concerns the conditions under which someone can be convicted and punished for past wrongdoing; outside that context, it more usually concerns the conditions under which someone can be treated as a suspect—as one who might have committed or might in future commit an offence. There are important questions about the normative status of 'suspect'—about how it can be acquired or imposed, about the obligations and liabilities that it can bring—but they are not the questions raised by the role of the PoI in the criminal trial,[7] and we cannot pursue them here.

Instead, I focus on two questions about the meaning and implications of the PoI in the criminal trial: one (section 2) concerns its implications for the allocation of persuasive or evidential burdens; the other (section 3) concerns the meaning of 'innocence'.

2. Whose Burden?

Classical formulations of the PoI leave the question of standard of proof open, but it is natural to add that the proof must be (something like) 'beyond reasonable doubt'.[8] This is suggested by the ordinary meaning of 'proof': if I claim to have

[4] See Ashworth's case comments on *Phillips v UK* (with C Ovey) [2001] Crim LR 817; *Grayson v UK* [2009] Crim LR 200; *Briggs-Price* [2010] Crim LR 139.

[5] See eg R Nobles and D Schiff, 'Guilt and Innocence in the Criminal Justice System' (2006) 69 MLR 80; *Hussain v UK* (2006) 43 EHRR 22.

[6] See eg L Campbell, 'A Rights-based Analysis of DNA Retention: '"Non-conviction" Databases and the Liberal State' [2010] Crim LR 889; cf J Floud and W Young, *Dangerousness and Criminal Justice* (London: Heinemann, 1981), 44, on a citizen's 'right to be presumed free of harmful intentions'.

[7] See L Laudan, 'The Presumption of Innocence: Material or Probatory?' (2005) 11 Legal Theory 333.

[8] *Woolmington v DPP* [1935] AC 462, 481 (HL); *Barberà, Messegué and Jabardo v Spain* (1989) 11 EHRR 360.

proved that Cain assaulted Abel, but the evidence I offer shows only that it is more likely than not that Cain assaulted Abel, you should reject my claim; I have proved only that it is probable that Cain assaulted Abel.[9] But it also rests on more substantive grounds. If we are to justify condemning a person as a wrongdoer (as a criminal conviction condemns the defendant), we must be able to say more than that he is probably guilty: we must claim to know that he is guilty; but knowledge that D is guilty requires more than a proved probability that he is guilty.

Persuasive and evidential burdens

It is therefore inconsistent with the PoI to lay any persuasive burden on the defence, even if the 'proof' need only be 'on the balance of probabilities'. If the prosecution is to prove D's guilt beyond reasonable doubt, it must prove not merely that D committed the crime charged, but that he had no legally recognized defence for doing so.[10] For suppose that *p* is a necessary condition of D's guilt, either as an offence element (eg that D knew or suspected the goods he was handling to be stolen), or as the absence of a defence (eg that D did not act under exculpatory duress); that the law lays on the defence the burden of proving that not-*p* on the balance of probabilities; and that although the defence leads evidence that not-*p* (that D did not even suspect the goods to be stolen; or that D was acting under duress), that evidence does not show not-*p* to be more probable than not. The most we can infer is that it is as probable that *p* as that not-*p*. But even if we could infer that it was probable that *p*, this would not amount to proof beyond reasonable doubt that *p*: for the probability that *p* leaves room for reasonable doubt about whether *p* or not-*p* is the case.[11] This is not to say that we could never justify reverse burdens of proof; only that they would need to be justified as exceptions to the PoI, not as being consistent with it.[12]

What is less clear is whether it is consistent with the PoI to lay on the defence the formal evidential burden of adducing evidence either of the absence of an element of the offence, or of the existence of a defence: evidence that need not prove the matter in question, but that must suffice (if not rebutted by the prosecution) to create a reasonable doubt about D's guilt. Such burdens are sometimes imposed in relation to what is formally categorized as a defence: a shopkeeper who sells 'food

[9] cf G Williams, 'The Logic of Exceptions' (1988) 47 CLJ 261, 265.

[10] We cannot discuss here the burden of proof in relation to matters that bear on the legitimacy of the trial rather than on D's guilt—matters such as D's fitness to plead, or the court's jurisdiction, or whether the trial would amount to an abuse of process.

[11] On this issue in the English and European courts, see Ashworth, 'Four Threats', 257–70; see also P Roberts, 'The Presumption of Innocence Brought Home? Kebilene Deconstructed' (2002) 118 LQR 41; V Tadros and S Tierney, 'The Presumption of Innocence and the Human Rights Act' (2004) 67 MLR 402.

[12] It might be argued that if the traditional verdict of 'guilty but insane' (changed in England to 'not guilty by reason of insanity' by s 1 of the Criminal Procedure (Insanity) Act 1964, but still popular in the USA) was an appropriate way of expressing the implications of a successful insanity defence, the defence could be legitimately required to 'prove', at least on the balance of probabilities, that D was relevantly insane. We cannot discuss the problematic protasis of the previous sentence here.

which fails to comply with food safety requirements' commits an offence, but has a defence if she can prove that she 'took all reasonable precautions and exercised all due diligence' to avoid committing the offence,[13] ie that she was not negligent. Sometimes they are imposed in relation to what is formally categorized as an element of the offence, via a 'presumption' that the court is allowed or required to make: if a civil servant receives a gift from a government contractor, the gift 'shall be deemed to have been . . . given and received corruptly . . . unless the contrary is proved'.[14] In such cases, the burden laid on the defendant might be formally described as a persuasive burden: D must 'prove' the absence of the relevant offence element, or the existence of the defence. In the light of the argument of the previous paragraph, however, and of the courts' willingness to 'read down' apparently persuasive burdens to evidential burdens to reconcile statutes with the European Convention on Human Rights,[15] we can treat such burdens as evidential.

Whether the 'not-*p*' in relation to which the defence bears an evidential burden involves the absence of an element of the offence, or the presence of a defence, the logic of such cases is that if the prosecution proves that *q* (that D sold unsafe food; that D received a gift from a government contractor), D is guilty of the offence unless he adduces evidence that not-*p* (that D did not fail to exercise due diligence; that the gift was not received corruptly)—evidence sufficient to create a reasonable doubt whether *p*, and thus to warrant D's acquittal unless the prosecution proves that *p*. If such provisions are to do any real work, proof that *q* (that D sold unsafe food; that D received a gift) cannot by itself constitute conclusive proof that *p* (that D did not exercise due diligence; that the gift was received corruptly): for if it did constitute such proof, there would be no room for the defence to offer evidence that not-*p*, if it had been proved that *q*. The combination '*q* & not-*p*' must be a possible one, which proof that *q* does not conclusively rule out: it must be possible that a duly diligent shopkeeper sells unsafe food, or that a civil servant receives a contractor's gift non-corruptly.

In that case, however, it looks as if such provisions, as well as those that lay a persuasive burden on the defence, violate the PoI: if *p* (the shopkeeper's lack of due diligence, or the recipient's corruption) is a necessary condition of conviction for the offence, and if proof that *q* (that unsafe food was sold; that a gift was received) does not constitute conclusive proof that *p*, then a prosecutor who proves only that *q* has not proved D's guilt beyond reasonable doubt, and a conviction would violate the PoI even if the defendant offered no evidence that not-*p*. Proof of D's guilt must involve proof that *p*, as well as that *q*; if the PoI is to be respected, it must therefore be for the prosecution to prove that *p*, not for the defence either to prove or to adduce evidence that not-*p*. So have courts been too quick to see the 'reading down' of persuasive burdens into evidential burdens as a simple way to reconcile English

[13] Food Safety Act 1990, ss 8(1), 21(1).

[14] Prevention of Corruption Act 1916, s 2.

[15] See *Lambert* [2001] UKHL 37, [2002] 2 AC 545; *Attorney General's Reference (No 4 of 2002)* [2004] UKHL 43, [2005] 1 AC 264; Ashworth, 'Four Threats', 241; A Stumer, *The Presumption of Innocence: Evidential and Human Rights Perspectives* (Oxford: Hart, 2010), 22–6; also the explanation of 'prove' given in s 118(2) of the Terrorism Act 2000.

law with the ECHR? Have theorists been too quick to accept such evidential burdens as consistent with the PoI? 'Imposing an evidential burden on the defendant', Ashworth says, 'is a common and logical way of dealing with defences, exceptions and provisos to offences': it is not one of the threats to the PoI against which he warns us.[16] But how is it consistent with the PoI?

Justifying evidential burdens: what makes doubt 'reasonable'?

We can render some impositions of evidential burdens consistent with the PoI by reading them as partial stipulations of what makes doubt 'reasonable'. A reasonable doubt is a doubt for which there is good reason. To determine whether it would be reasonable to doubt that *p*, given proof that *q*, we must therefore ask what could give us good reason to doubt whether *p*. The answer given by such provisions as these is that in these contexts, as a matter of law, it is up to the defendant to give the court good reason to doubt whether *p*.

Suppose it is proved that a shopkeeper sold food that failed to comply with the prescribed safety requirements, but she says nothing either before or during her trial to explain how this happened or to describe the precautions that she took: would it be 'reasonable' to harbour any serious doubt about whether she had been negligent as to the safety of the food she sold; or could we be rationally convinced ('beyond reasonable doubt'), in the face of such proof and such silence, of her negligence? The question concerns not just the empirical strength of the evidence provided by whatever the prosecution has proved, but the normative expectations that we should have of each other as citizens, and that the criminal law should formalize. The Food Safety Act gives legal force to an expectation that shopkeepers who sell food should not only take appropriate precautions to make sure that the food they sell is safe; but should also, if they do sell food that is unsafe, be ready to explain what happened, and to offer evidence that they had taken appropriate precautions. Given such expectations, proof that a shopkeeper sold unsafe food creates a presumption that she was negligent, and defeats the PoI; the burden then lies on to her to rebut that presumption of guilt by offering evidence that suffices, if not rebutted, at least to create a reasonable doubt about whether she was negligent. Similarly, the Prevention of Corruption Act formalizes an expectation of civil servants that, if they accept gifts from contractors, they must be ready to explain (to offer evidence) that the gift was not corrupt:[17] given that expectation, proof of the receipt of such a gift creates a presumption of corruption, which it is up to the civil servant to defeat, by offering evidence that suffices to create a reasonable doubt as to whether it was corrupt.

16 'Four Threats', 269. See also Stumer, n 15 above, 18.

17 An expectation made more reasonable by the fact that they could refuse such gifts; food safety laws should not have the chilling effect of deterring people from selling food, but it would not be obviously undesirable if government employees refused gifts from those who seek to do business with the government.

If the imposition of this kind of burden is to be consistent with the PoI, we must at least be confident that an innocent defendant (a non-negligent shopkeeper, or a non-corrupt civil servant) would be able to offer the appropriate evidence;[18] but we can be thus confident, for two reasons. First, when the unavailability of any evidence independent of the defendant's own testimony is consistent with the defendant's innocence, as could well be true in cases of alleged corruption, the defendant's evidential burden could be discharged by an explanation of why or how the gift was given and received: what matters is that the defendant be ready to offer such an explanation, which is then available for testing by the prosecution and appraisal by the court. Secondly, in other cases, including that of food sellers, the law can also partly specify, through a regime of health and safety regulations, what counts as taking reasonable care; what is specified might include the keeping of records that would then be available as evidence.[19]

It is important to be clear about the logic of the argument here. What the shopkeeper is to be convicted for, if the prosecution discharges its persuasive burden and she fails to discharge her evidential burden, is not a strict liability offence of selling unfit food, but selling unfit food through a negligent failure to take precautions. What the civil servant is to be convicted for is not simply accepting a gift from a contractor, but corruptly accepting such a gift. Thus what must be shown is that proof of the sale of unsafe food suffices to create a presumption of negligence, which it is legitimate to require the shopkeeper to rebut; or that proof of the receipt of a gift creates a presumption of corruption, which the recipient can legitimately be expected to rebut. We can show this if we can argue that it is reasonable to expect people in such situations to be ready to offer such exculpatory evidence, and to presume them guilty if they do not.

It might seem that the argument sketched here involves a sleight of hand: the PoI may be formally preserved, but only by a stipulative redefinition of 'reasonable doubt' which negates the values that inform the PoI. For the PoI is often associated with the right of silence, and the idea that the prosecution must prove the defendant's guilt without the defendant's help;[20] but the argument sketched here surely undermines that right. However, first, what belongs with the PoI as a fundamental right is not an unqualified right of silence, but only a right not to be required (on pain of sanctions or of adverse inferences) to respond to accusations, until they are supported by evidence that creates a reasonable suspicion of guilt:[21] it would be consistent with the PoI for the law to hold that whilst a defendant need not respond to mere accusations, he must respond once the

[18] I do not mean that the ease with which D can provide the evidence is what justifies the imposition of such a burden (see below); the point is simply that if the burden is to be justified, it must not be too onerous.

[19] See further RA Duff, *Answering for Crime* (Oxford: Hart, 2007), 243–5.

[20] See eg AJ Ashworth and M Redmayne, *The Criminal Process* (4th edn, Oxford: Oxford University Press, 2010), 312; also 'Four Threats', 246–51; P Duff, 'The Agreement of Uncontroversial Evidence and the Presumption of Innocence: an Insoluble Dilemma?' (2002) 6 Edinburgh Law Review 25.

[21] See K Greenawalt, 'Silence as a Moral and Constitutional Right' (1981) 23 William and Mary Law Review 15; Ashworth, 'Four Threats', 249.

prosecution offers evidence that generates a reasonable suspicion of guilt. Any defence of a more extensive right of silence must appeal not merely to the PoI, but to the need to protect suspected citizens against the oppressive power of the state. What gives the PoI its normative power is that we owe it to our fellow citizens to see each other, not as suspicious strangers and potential enemies who must prove their bona fides before we grant them the most minimal civic trust, but as citizens living under the law. But such mutual civic respect is consistent with the belief that we should be willing to respond to accusations of wrongdoing that are supported by adequate evidence; to show why a civic responsibility to respond should not generate a legal obligation to respond, and thus to defend a legal right of silence, we must appeal to the dangers that state power creates.[22] Indeed, even a sanction-backed legal obligation to respond, once the prosecution had put up a case to answer, would be consistent with the PoI.

This might (and should) still seem a bit too quick: surely the value of the PoI is impaired if defendants are required (on pain of conviction) to offer evidence of their innocence as soon as the prosecution offers evidence that creates a reasonable suspicion of guilt. The answer to this worry, however, is not to hold that evidential burdens are always inconsistent with the PoI, but to set strict limits on the kinds of case in which they are allowed.

One kind of case in which such a burden seems legitimate is that in which it relates to a defence. Offence definitions should specify presumptive wrongs, kinds of action from which we normally, in the criminal law's eyes, have conclusive reason to refrain. If the prosecution proves that D committed a presumptive wrong, it is then reasonable to lay on D the onus of offering an exculpatory explanation for his conduct—to offer a justification or excuse for its commission.[23] We should not have to answer in the criminal court for our conduct unless it is shown to have been a presumptive wrong; but once that is shown, our presumed innocence is put into question, and we must offer some evidence to rebut the inference to guilt that proof of the presumptive wrong would otherwise justify.

Even if this justification for laying evidential burdens on the defence can succeed, further questions arise about when it is properly used. Consider first the shopkeeper who sells unsafe food, and whose evidential burden relates to what is specified, formally, as a 'defence'.[24] This shifts the traditional boundary between offences and defences: what the defendant must now 'prove' is the absence of what would normally count as an aspect of *mens rea* (as an element of the offence); while proof merely of an *actus reus* does not normally warrant a presumption that the act was done with the requisite *mens rea*,[25] proof of the sale of unsafe food legally entitles the court to presume negligence, if the defendant offers no evidence to the

[22] See RA Duff, L Farmer, SE Marshall, and V Tadros, *The Trial on Trial (3): Towards and Normative Theory of the Criminal Trial* (Oxford: Hart, 2007), 203–11.

[23] See further Duff, n 19 above, 220–4, 242–50.

[24] Food Safety Act 1990, s 21(1).

[25] This was the essence of the ringing declaration of the PoI in *Woolmington v DPP* [1935] AC 462, 481 (HL).

contrary.[26] This shift is justified if it is proper to hold food sellers prospectively responsible for taking precautions that would enable them to offer evidence of non-negligence and to require them to answer for any sales of unsafe food; but given the dangers posed by unsafe food, it does not seem unreasonable to expect this of them.

What of the gift-receiving civil servant, however? We could simply forbid civil servants to accept gifts from anyone holding or seeking a government contract, and make breaches of that prohibition a criminal offence; or make it an offence to accept a gift under circumstances that give rise to a reasonable suspicion of corruption:[27] such provisions *might* be justifiable by appealing to the need to guard against both corruption and the trust-undermining suspicion of corruption. But the offence of which the civil servant is to be convicted is an offence of actual corruption,[28] and we must ask whether courts should presume the acceptance of a gift to have been corrupt, given proof only of the acceptance of the gift, and the absence of evidence from the defendant that it was not corrupt. Here we should be more uneasy. It might be argued that, given the corrosive effects of both actual and perceived corruption, we can reasonably expect civil servants not only to avoid both the actuality and the appearance of corruption, but also to be ready, if they accept a gift, to explain why it was not corrupt; and that given proof of a gift, courts may therefore presume corruption, unless the defendant offers evidence to the contrary. But it is still not clear that the offence for which a defendant who cannot offer such evidence should be one of corruption, rather than of creating a suspicion of corruption.

However, my aim here has not been to determine when we can properly impose such an evidential burden on the defence, though I suspect that many such existing impositions are not justifiable;[29] it has only been to show how it can in principle be consistent with the PoI to lay some such burdens on defendants. It is time now to turn to a second question about the implications of the PoI for criminal trials: what kind of 'innocence' is to be presumed?

3. What is Innocence?

The natural answer to the question with which the previous section ended is that what is to be presumed is legal innocence: that 'one is not guilty of whatever may be the elements of a criminal offence'.[30] But is this answer adequate? To answer this question, we can consider some different possible versions of the notorious section 57 of the Terrorism Act 2000.

[26] And negligence must be proved, if the defendant is to deserve the condemnation that a conviction for selling unsafe food involves; see further at n 53 below.

[27] Compare Terrorism Act 2000, s 57, to be discussed in section 3.

[28] The title of s 2 of the Prevention of Corruption Act 1916 is 'Presumption of corruption in certain cases'.

[29] For two obvious examples, see Terrorism Act 2000, s 57(2)–(3) and s 58(3).

[30] *R v G* [2006] EWCA Crim 821, [2006] 1 WLR 2052 at [36] (Lord Phillips CJ); see Stumer, n 15 above, 55.

Possession for terrorist purposes

The section's heading, 'Possession for terrorist purposes', makes explicit the mischief at which it is aimed. Let us accept, for now, both that the primary purpose of this section was to provide for the conviction and punishment of those who possess items for terrorist purposes, and that it is legitimate to criminalize such 'possession with intent'. We need not debate here the conditions under which it can be legitimate to criminalize possession,[31] save to note that 'possession with intent' offences are more likely to be justifiable than are offences of bare possession. The section would then be unobjectionable if it simply read:

A person commits an offence if he possesses an article for a purpose connected with the commission, preparation, or instigation of an act of terrorism.

Suppose, however, that the drafters, concerned about difficulties of proof, added a subsection:

If it is proved that the accused possessed an article in circumstances which gave rise to a reasonable suspicion that his possession was for a purpose connected with the commission, preparation, or instigation of an act of terrorism, the court shall assume that his possession was for such a purpose, unless he proves that his possession of the article was not for such a purpose.[32]

If this laid a persuasive burden on the defendant, it would violate the PoI: the offence requires a terrorist purpose; the onus must therefore lie on the prosecution to prove that purpose; but proof of a reasonable suspicion that *p* cannot constitute proof beyond reasonable doubt that *p*. If, instead, it imposed a merely evidentiary burden,[33] we would need to ask whether we can reasonably expect citizens to be prepared to answer for their suspicion-arousing possession, and reasonably presume them to have terrorist purposes if they cannot offer an exculpatory answer. In the light of the discussion above, it would be hard to justify such an expectation; this subsection would therefore violate the PoI, even if it imposed only an evidentiary burden.

The objection to this version of the offence is that it requires courts to assume a condition that is necessary for conviction (a terrorist purpose) in the absence of conclusive proof of that condition: proof that D's possession of the article aroused a reasonable suspicion of terrorist purposes does not warrant the firm conclusion that, absent an exculpatory explanation from D, he had such purposes. The legislature could avoid that objection by revising the offence definition: instead of defining the suspicion-arousing possession as evidence from which the court is to infer terrorist purpose as an essential constituent of the offence, it could define the offence itself as consisting in the suspicion-arousing possession:

[31] See A Ashworth, 'The Unfairness of Risk-Based Possession Offences' (2011) 5 Criminal Law and Philosophy 237; MD Dubber, 'Policing Possession: The War on Crime and the End of Criminal Law' (2001) 91 Journal of Criminal Law and Criminology 829.

[32] Compare the wording of s 57(2)–(3) of the Act.

[33] Which is how s 118 defines it.

A person commits an offence if he possesses an article in circumstances which give rise to a reasonable suspicion that his possession is for a purpose connected with the commission, preparation or instigation of an act of terrorism.[34]

It might now be objected that such a provision is unduly harsh on those who have suspicious articles for innocent purposes. A legislature has three possible responses to this objection. It could argue, first, that given the serious threat posed by terrorism, and the consequent need to allow early police intervention in planned terrorist activity, to reassure an anxious public, and to avoid diverting investigative resources away from real terrorists, mere suspicion-arousing possession is a mischief that it is reasonable to require citizens to avoid—and to convict and punish them for causing. This response should not persuade the critics, but not because of the PoI. The relevant objection is that the section, as thus understood, violates the negative legal moralist principle that culpable wrongdoing is a necessary condition of just punishment, and therefore of justified criminalization:[35] suspicion-arousing possession is simply not a wrong that merits criminal condemnation and punishment. We can express this objection by saying that this section would punish 'the innocent': it would render liable to criminal punishment people who are innocent of any punishment-worthy wrongdoing. But it does not implicate the PoI: the legislature enacts a misguided view of what constitutes a punishable wrong, but if the prosecution bears the burden of proof, citizens are presumed innocent of that supposed wrong until they are proved beyond reasonable doubt to have committed it.[36] We can therefore leave this response aside, and focus on the two responses that do bring the PoI into the picture.

Secondly, the legislature might agree that suspicion-arousing possession without any actual terrorist purpose is not part of the mischief at which this provision is aimed, but argue that it would be too hard for prosecutors to obtain convictions of the 'truly' guilty, those acting with a terrorist purpose, if they had to prove such purpose; and that we can count on appropriately guided police and prosecutorial discretion to spare innocently suspicion-arousing possessors from prosecution.[37] This response, however, creates an uncomfortable dilemma. On the one hand,

[34] This is the actual wording of s 57(1) of the Act. Compare s 57 of the Civic Government (Scotland) Act, which makes it an offence to be 'found' in a building under circumstances such that 'it may reasonably be inferred that he intended to commit theft', without providing a defence for one who can 'prove' that he had no such intention: see *Fulton v Normand* 1995 SCCR 629; for discussion, see V Tadros, 'Rethinking the Presumption of Innocence' (2007) 1 Criminal Law and Philosophy 193, 198–9.

[35] See eg A Ashworth, *Principles of Criminal Law* (6th edn, Oxford: Oxford University Press, 2009), 27–30, 34–7; DN Husak, *Overcriminalization: The Limits of the Criminal Law* (Oxford: Oxford University Press, 2008), Ch 2 (on the 'wrongfulness' and 'desert' constraints on the scope of the criminal law).

[36] See Ashworth, 'Four Threats', 252–6; Tadros, n 34 above, 203; Stumer, n 15 above, 53–68. On what might follow from such a reading of the PoI, see P Tomlin, 'Extending the Golden Thread? Criminalization and the Presumption of Innocence', Journal of Political Philosophy (forthcoming).

[37] Compare the government's response to parliamentary concern that ss 9 and 14 of the Sexual Offences Bill 2003 would criminalize two young people aged 15 who engaged in sexual activity with each other. 'That is not the intention of the Bill; nor will it be its effect in practice… [I]f we find no other way to deal with this question… we shall be able to trust the Crown Prosecution Service to

suppose that there was a declared prosecutorial policy of prosecuting only in cases in which the prosecutor was convinced that the possession was actually for terrorist purposes;[38] a policy so authoritative that we could say that what is in effect criminalized is possession for terrorist purposes. Such a law would violate the PoI: people convicted under it would be in substance, and would be publicly understood as being, convicted and punished for possession for terrorist purposes; but the prosecution would not have proved them guilty of that, since it would have had to prove only suspicion-arousing possession. On the other hand, suppose that any such prosecutorial policy remained informal and non-public (and thus less reliable). But such a law would again provoke the objection that it defines as criminal, and threatens with punishment, conduct that does not constitute a punishment-worthy wrong—and that, in this case, the legislature does not even believe to be punishment-worthily wrong.

The question that concerns me here, however, is whether this law would be objectionable because it would violate the PoI. But before tackling that question, we must note a third possible response. Moved by such objections, but still wanting to ease the prosecutorial burden, the legislature might preserve the 'arousing suspicion' offence definition, but add that:

> It is a defence for a person charged with an offence under this section to prove that his possession of the article was not for a purpose connected with . . . terrorism.

Mindful of the European Court's rulings about the PoI, it might also stipulate that, when it is a 'defence' for a defendant to 'prove' a particular matter:

> [If] the person adduces evidence which is sufficient to raise an issue with respect to the matter the court shall assume that the defence is satisfied unless the prosecution proves beyond reasonable doubt that it is not.

This brings us very close to the actual provisions of section 57(1)–(2) of the Terrorism Act 2000, read in the light of section 118—with one significant difference. The title of section 57 is 'Possession for terrorist purposes': that is the offence for which someone convicted under section 57 is convicted; the section is thus substantially identical to the version considered above,[39] which defined the offence in terms of actual terrorist purpose, but required that purpose to be presumed, given proof only of suspicion-arousing possession and the defendant's failure to offer evidence of innocent possession. This version therefore also violates the PoI: the court is to assume the existence of a terrorist purpose when this has not been proved beyond reasonable doubt.

Suppose, however, that the legislature changed the section's title to 'Possession arousing suspicion of terrorist purposes'? The offence definition would then match

ensure that that intention is followed.' Paul Goggins, a Home Office minister, in Hansard, HC vol 409, col 248 (15 July 2003).

[38] Compare <http://www.cps.gov.uk/publications/prosecution/assisted_suicide_policy.html> accessed 6 March 2012: the guidelines for cases of assisting suicide published by the DPP.

[39] See nn 32–3 above.

its title; proof of suspicion-arousing possession would be proof of commission of the offence; the 'defence' would be formally a defence—an exculpatory explanation of the commission of the offence as thus labelled and defined. We might still find the section objectionable: but would it now be part of our objection that it violates the PoI?[40]

We thus have two possible versions of a revised section 57: both define the offence in terms of possession arousing suspicion of terrorist purposes; the unadorned version allows no defence to someone proved to have committed the offence; the adorned version provides a defence for someone who adduces evidence of lack of terrorist purpose. Our question now is: does either of these versions violate the PoI?[41]

For a formal reading of 'innocence'

On a formal reading of the PoI, the unadorned version of section 57 respects it. For what must be presumed is that:

> . . . one is not guilty of whatever may be the elements of a criminal offence. One must not confuse innocence of a criminal offence with innocence of blameworthy conduct.[42]

One whose possession arouses reasonable suspicion of terrorist purposes might be innocent of blameworthy wrongdoing, but is legally guilty of what the law defines as an offence; so long as the prosecution must prove the suspicion-arousing possession, the PoI is respected.

Matters are more complicated with the adorned version, whether the burden it lays on the defendant is persuasive or evidential. I suggested earlier that it would be hard to justify laying even an evidential burden on the defendant in relation to his lack of terrorist purpose:[43] is the adorned version therefore inconsistent with the PoI? I think it is, but we must be clear about the reason. What is inconsistent with the PoI is to require defendants to answer for suspicion-arousing possession, *on pain of being presumed to have (and convicted for having) terrorist purposes* if they could offer no exculpatory answer. Now conviction under the unadorned version would be a conviction not for terrorist purposes, but simply for suspicion-arousing possession. If the same would be true of the adorned version, it would also be consistent with the PoI on a formal reading: a defendant who offered no evidence of lack of terrorist purpose would still not be presumed to have, or be convicted of having, terrorist purposes; he would be convicted merely of suspicion-arousing possession. But this is not a plausible reading of the adorned version: to allow a defence of lack of terrorist purpose implies that those convicted under the section

[40] I ignore here the objectionable provisions concerning proof of possession in s 57(3) of the actual Act.

[41] Compare the debate over *Kebilene* [2000] 2 AC 326 (HL) between Roberts, n 11 above, and Tadros and Tierney, n 11 above.

[42] *R v G* [2006] EWCA Crim 821, [2006] 1 WLR 2052 at [36] (Lord Phillips CJ); see Ashworth, 'Four Threats', 252–6.

[43] See n 33 above, and the argument of s 2.

are really being convicted not for merely suspicion-arousing possession, but for possession for terrorist purposes; one whose possession is proved to have aroused suspicion, and who offers no evidence of lack of terrorist purpose, is thus once again being presumed to have a terrorist purpose—which is again inconsistent with the PoI.

It might now be argued that this shows the inadequacy of a formal reading of the PoI. On that reading, section 57 could be rendered consistent with the PoI merely by changing its title, and by removing the defence that section 57(2) offers; but this undermines the PoI's protective power, and makes it too easy for legislatures 'to evade the protections provided by article 6(2)' of the ECHR.[44] We should rather understand innocence as innocence of the kind of 'conduct which the creation of the offence was intended to deter or control' or of the *supposed* 'public wrong' at which the statute is aimed.[45] With or without its actual title, with or without the defence, section 57 is obviously aimed not against non-terrorist possession that arouses even a reasonable suspicion of terrorist purposes, but against possession that *is* for terrorist purposes. It is that kind of conduct, that supposed public wrong, of which citizens should be presumed innocent until proved guilty; but the section does not respect that presumption. On this reading, the PoI not only requires trial procedures to be such that prosecutors must prove all the elements of the offence as defined by the law; it requires legislatures so to formulate statutes that they define as criminal only the kinds of conduct that the legislation is intended to deter or control, only the kinds of conduct that the legislature takes to constitute public, punishment-worthy wrongs. The PoI, as thus understood, 'provides citizens with real protections against state power':[46] a kind of protection that, on a formal reading, it cannot provide. It would surely, we might add, be very odd to condemn the adorned version of the section, which gives innocently purposed possessors the chance to avoid conviction, as inconsistent with the PoI, whilst holding that an unadorned version which gives them no such chance is consistent with the PoI.

Ashworth is, I now think, right to argue against any such substantial reading, and for a formal reading of the PoI.[47] If a statute criminalizing the intentional or reckless causing of injury required a defendant who was proved to have caused injury to disprove intention or recklessness, it would violate the PoI;[48] if instead the statute created a strict-liability offence of causing injury, it would be 'a shining example of compliance' with the PoI. Such a strict-liability offence would be objectionable, but not as violating the PoI: it would rather violate a different principle, of 'no criminal liability without fault'.[49] It might be tempting, given the rhetorical power of the PoI as the 'golden thread' running 'throughout the web of the English criminal law',[50] and its legal force as enshrined in the ECHR, to try

[44] Tadros and Tierney, n 11 above, 413.
[45] Ibid, 413; Tadros, n 34 above, 200.
[46] Tadros and Tierney, n 11 above, 413–14.
[47] And I was therefore, along with Tadros and Tierney, wrong: see Duff, n 19 above, 195–201.
[48] Even, I would add, if the defendant's burden was only evidential: see s 2 above.
[49] Ashworth, 'Four Threats', 254.
[50] *Woolmington v DPP* [1935] AC 462, 481 (HL) (Viscount Sankey): it had to be quoted.

to expand it to cover an ever wider range of defects in the criminal law: but we would do better to recognize that it is just one of a number of principles that should govern the criminal law in a liberal polity.

In some of those principles, 'innocence' will have a substantial, extra-legal meaning: we can say, for instance, that innocent conduct must not be criminalized, meaning by 'innocent' conduct that is not culpably, punishment-worthily wrongful.[51] This principle, of 'no criminal liability without culpable wrongdoing', bears most directly on what may be criminalized: it is violated if the legislature defines as criminal conduct that cannot legitimately be classed, and condemned, as a public wrong; it is flouted if the legislature defines as criminal conduct that it does not even believe to constitute a public wrong. In other principles, however, including particularly the PoI, 'innocence' should carry a more formal, legal meaning: the principle that citizens must be 'presumed' innocent until 'proved' guilty bears particularly on the criminal process, and concerns the conditions under which, and the ease with which, citizens should be liable to conviction and punishment for the commission of whatever it is that the criminal law defines as an offence.

Someone convicted of suspicion-arousing possession under the unadorned version of section 57, and whose purposes had nothing to do with terrorism, has grounds for complaint: that she is convicted and punished for conduct that is not only not wrongful, but is not even believed by the legislature to be punishment-worthily wrongful. All citizens can complain that they are required to refrain, on pain of conviction and punishment, from conduct (suspicion-arousing possession) that is not even believed by the legislature to be punishment-worthily wrongful. The legislature is not even trying or claiming to respect the principle of 'no criminal liability without culpable wrongdoing'. If the legislation also allowed people to be convicted of this offence in the absence of proof, beyond reasonable doubt, of suspicion-arousing possession,[52] defendants would have an additional complaint: that the legislature is violating the PoI. That violation might be less serious than it would be if conviction was for possession for terrorist purposes, since being unjustly convicted of suspicion-arousing possession is a less grievous injustice than being unjustly convicted of possession for terrorist purposes; but it is a distinct violation.

The thought that there is something odd about accepting that the unadorned version of the offence, which allows no defence, satisfies the PoI, whilst holding that the adorned, defence-allowing version violates the PoI, is also misguided. The adorned version does indeed offer defendants more protection against conviction than does the unadorned version, but it offers them protection against a different fate: for introducing the defence also changes the offence.

What the unadorned version criminalizes is suspicion-arousing possession: one convicted under that section is not convicted of, or condemned or punished for, possession for terrorist purposes; no such purpose is supposed or presumed. Once the defence is added, however, it becomes clear that the purported wrong that is to

[51] See at n 35 above.

[52] If, for instance, it required 'possession' to be presumed on the tenuous basis specified in s 57(3) of the Act.

be condemned and punished is possession for terrorist purposes: for that is why it can constitute a defence to offer evidence of the lack of any such purpose.[53] Someone convicted under the adorned section is thus convicted of and condemned for *that* purported wrong, not merely for suspicion-arousing possession; which is why the adorned section violates the PoI. The unadorned section respects the PoI, because what is to be presumed there is innocence of suspicion-arousing possession, and defendants are presumed innocent of that until the prosecution proves such possession. The adorned section violates the PoI because what must now be presumed is innocence of possession for terrorist purposes; but the prosecution does not bear the burden of proving such a purpose.

A Pyrrhic victory?

It might now be argued that this shows the inadequacy of formalism. For surely it would be obvious to all that the mischief at which the unadorned section was aimed was still that of possession for terrorist purposes, not that of mere suspicion-arousing possession; someone convicted under the unadorned section would thus be understood to be being convicted and punished as someone with terrorist purposes—and the statute, as it would actually be applied and understood, would thus still be aimed at the wrong of possession for terrorist purposes, and would still violate the PoI by not requiring the prosecution to prove such purposes.

What this objection shows is not that the formal reading of the PoI is inadequate (though it reminds us that the PoI does not protect citizens against every kind of legislative injustice), but rather that whilst it does in one way make it easy for legislatures 'to evade the protections provided by Article 6(2)' of the ECHR,[54] such evasion is likely to constitute a rather Pyrrhic victory. A legislature that is to avoid the charge of paying mere lip service to the PoI, whilst violating it in substance, will need to make clear that what is being criminalized is precisely suspicion-arousing possession; prosecutors will need to avoid giving any impression that they pursue only cases in which there is really a terrorist purpose; courts will need to make clear what the defendant is being convicted of—perhaps by making it explicit that the defendant's purposes might have been entirely innocent; and sentences for those convicted of the offence will need to be modest, given the minor nature of the offence as it is now defined. But if all that is done, and if the real target of the legislation was possession for terrorist purposes, the achievement of that aim is also likely to be frustrated: for it is plausible that the legislation could be effective in the pursuit of that aim only if citizens believed that, and courts acted and sentenced as if, those convicted of the offence were really guilty of possession for terrorist purposes. In making clear that the statute respects the formal PoI, by making clear what those convicted under it are convicted of the legislature would undermine the statute's intended effect.

[53] Just as to allow self-defence as a defence on a charge of murder is to make clear that the wrong which the law of murder defines is not killing, but killing that is not defensively necessary.

[54] Tadros and Tierney, n 11 above, 413; see at n 44 above.

A formal reading of the PoI, as urged by Ashworth, does make it easier for legislatures to evade the demands of the ECHR. But, first, that evasion comes at a high cost. Secondly, though the protections provided by the ECHR are limited in their scope, the proper solution is not to try to extend them by stretching the meaning of the principles that underlie them. It is, as Ashworth argues, to insist on the importance of other principles, such as 'no criminal liability without fault',[55] that should also constrain legislatures.

[55] Or without culpable wrongdoing: see at nn 35, 51 above.

5

Fair Labelling and Social Solidarity

*Victor Tadros**

One kind of unfairness in the criminal law, the most familiar kind, involves defendants who are convicted of a criminal offence despite demonstrably not having breached the criminal law. A second kind of unfairness involves defendants who have breached the criminal law, but where it has not adequately been demonstrated that they have done so. Justice, in this case, is not done in virtue of its not being seen to be done. A third kind of unfairness involves cases where the defendant has demonstrably breached the criminal law, but where the state lacks standing to hold the defendant responsible for what she has done, for example if the state is complicit in the offence that the defendant has committed. A fourth unfairness occurs when the defendant breaches the criminal law, but his conduct ought not to have been criminal at all. This occurs when the state over-criminalizes.

In this essay, we are concerned with a fifth kind of unfairness. In the cases we are concerned with, the defendant has demonstrably breached the criminal law and the state has standing to call the defendant to account. Furthermore, it is appropriate that her conduct is criminalized. But the law describes the defendant's conduct unfairly. The idea is that justice imposes restrictions not only on the scope of the criminal law, but also on the way that content is divided up and described. This is one way to understand the issue of fair labelling.

We can see the problem clearly by thinking about the extreme case—it would be unfair to convict a person who has taken the property of another without consent as a rapist, or to convict a person who has not caused death as a murderer. But the principle of fair labelling also seems to have force when we think about the criminal law as it is. For example, we might doubt that it is fair to convict both those who are grossly negligent in killing another person, or who kill as a result of a single punch, along with those who intentionally kill but are (only just) entitled to the defence of diminished responsibility of the same offence. This is so not merely because these offenders deserve different sentences, but also because we ought to mark out the

* School of Law, University of Warwick. Email: v.tadros@warwick.ac.uk. I have benefited from discussion of the ideas in this essay with members of the AHRC funded Criminalization project—Andrew Cornford, Antony Duff, Lindsay Farmer, Christine Kelly, Sandra Marshall, and Massimo Renzo. I have also benefited from Lucia Zedner's comments. Thanks to them, and to the AHRC, for supporting this work. Most of all, thanks to Andrew Ashworth, who has tirelessly supported and stimulated good scholarship, and mine as well.

differences in the moral gravity of their conduct by convicting them of different offences.[1]

Fair labelling is an important principle that helps us to evaluate the legitimacy of the criminal law, and Andrew Ashworth's work has done a great deal to develop it and to promote recognition of its importance. The principle was first marshalled by Ashworth to criticize the relationship between *actus reus* and *mens rea* in the criminal law of England and Wales in a range of contexts.[2] He has also argued that the principle could motivate a more finely grained criminal law: one that distinguishes more precisely between different kinds of wrongful conduct.[3] And fair labelling is identified as a general principle of criminal law in his influential *Principles of Criminal Law*.[4] One reason why the principle of fair labelling is important is simply the fact that we should seek to discover unfairness and seek to promote greater fairness where we can. Labelling can be unfair to defendants, describing them in ways that overestimate or otherwise mislead others about the gravity or the kind of conduct in which they have engaged. It may be unfair to victims, failing to reflect adequately the wrong that they have suffered. Unfair labelling is a distinct kind of unfairness and it is important to identify inadequacies in the criminal law of this kind and to encourage governments and courts to correct them.

But fair labelling is also important because reflecting on it encourages us to think not only about the boundaries of the criminal law, but on the way in which it structures and distinguishes between crimes.[5] Traditionally, philosophical reflection on criminalization has mostly been concerned with its boundaries.[6] What principles can be adopted to restrain the criminal law from intruding too greatly into the lives of its citizens? This question is undoubtedly important. But there is a distinct question that philosophical reflection has done less to answer. How should the content of the criminal law be structured? How should we distinguish wrongs from each other, and how should their content be articulated? The principle of fair labelling has led us to consider these questions carefully in a range of offence contexts.

Focusing on the structures of, and distinctions between, crimes may also help us to develop a more careful and plausible account of the boundaries of the criminal law that has traditionally occupied legal and political theorists.[7] One reason why

1 See, for further discussion, the essays in CMV Clarkson and S Cunningham, *Criminal Liability for Non-Aggressive Death* (Aldershot: Ashgate, 2008).

2 A Ashworth, 'The Elasticity of *Mens Rea*' in CFH Tapper (ed), *Crime, Proof and Punishment: Essays in Memory of Sir Rupert Cross* (London: Butterworths, 1981).

3 See A Ashworth, 'Towards a Theory of Criminal Legislation' (1989) 1 Criminal Law Forum 41, 42.

4 For his latest account, see A Ashworth, *Principles of Criminal Law* (6th edn, Oxford: Oxford University Press, 2009), 78–80.

5 The focus of scholars on this issue was also sharpened by the collection of essays in RA Duff and SP Green (eds), *Defining Crimes: Essays on the Special Part of the Criminal Law* (Oxford: Oxford University Press, 2005).

6 The best developed account is D Husak, *Overcriminalization: The Limits of the Criminal Law* (Oxford: Oxford University Press, 2007).

7 See also RA Duff, *Answering for Crime* (Oxford: Hart, 2007).

this might be so is that any set of general principles that determine the scope of the criminal law is likely to be indeterminate. Focusing on the content of particular offences and families of offence is necessary to make more determinate recommendations about how the criminal law should be shaped, and the principle of fair labelling has a role to play in this project.

For example, once we have a better grasp of the different ways in which sexual autonomy may be undermined, we will also have a better grasp of the best way in which the criminal law can protect sexual autonomy both by criminalizing some sexual behaviour and decriminalizing other sexual behaviour. By focusing on the fact that there are different kinds of wrongful sex, we are also likely to develop a more nuanced view about the proper boundaries of the criminal law. We will see that there are important moral differences between offenders who force others to have intercourse with them and those who exploit the fact that the victim was unconscious. This will help us focus on the circumstances in which force on the one hand and lack of capacity on the other should result in a criminal conviction and for which offence.[8]

My aim in this essay is not to advance particular recommendations of this kind, but rather to consider in greater depth one important motivation behind fair labelling. I do this in an attempt to deepen our understanding of the importance of the principle, and not to advance understanding of what it is that makes a label fair. Fair labelling, I will argue, has an important role to play in the conception of social justice to which I think we should be committed. And I will attempt to show how pursuing it may be possible within divided societies such as ours.

1. Two Justifications of Fair Labelling

As with other kinds of fairness, the fairness of a label depends not only on the idea that unfair labelling might be unfair *to the defendant*. The fairness of a label might be established for other reasons. For example, it might be fair to distinguish between defendants who have caused harm and those who have not, even if the degree of culpability of these defendants is identical. It might be fair not because it would be unfair to the defendant who has not caused harm to label her in the same way as the defendant who has caused harm, but rather because victims have a right that the suffering that a defendant's wrongdoing has caused them is recognized by the law. I don't say that this is true, though I suspect that it is, but only that there is nothing wrong in principle with justifying a label to the defendant on the grounds that the label is important in securing the rights of others.

Of course, it would typically be wrong to imply something false about the defendant for this reason. If referring to the outcomes of the defendant's conduct wrongly implies a degree of control over the outcome that he lacked, it would be wrong to refer to it even if recognizing the suffering of the victim is an important

[8] See further V Tadros, 'Rape Without Consent' (2006) 26 OJLS 515.

goal of the criminal law. But assuming that this is not so, that we can perfectly well understand that outcomes are not within the complete control of defendants, and that bad outcomes need not reflect a high degree of culpability, there is nothing wrong in principle in referring to outcomes in offence definitions.

Furthermore, defendant-centred considerations are unlikely to provide a full account of the *importance* of fair labelling. The idea that criminal responsibility is not affected by the outcome of the offender actions is a challenge to the orthodox view about what counts as a fair label.[9] But before considering what counts as a fair label, we need an account of the importance of fair labelling. We might rather think about the range of ends that fair labelling should hope to secure. Fair treatment of the defendant is undoubtedly one of these aims. But it may not be the most important end. The idea of fair labelling may be motivated by a range of considerations beyond attempting to ensure that the defendant is treated fairly.

There may be other ways of ensuring fair treatment of the defendant, even if he is not really labelled at all. On some accounts of the criminal law, the traditional idea of fair labelling—the idea that the criminal law should be composed of discrete criminal offences which reflect the adequate distinctions in degree and kind to reflect the moral significance of criminally wrongful conduct—is more or less abandoned. Larry Alexander and Kim Ferzan advocate abolishing the 'special part' of the criminal law, understood in this way, in favour of a list of a range of legally protected interests that might be threatened intentionally or recklessly by defendants.[10]

Their account of fairness to defendants shares some significant commitments with Ashworth—they too believe that the criminal law should aim at giving defendants what they deserve, and they too believe that desert is determined by culpability and not by outcomes. But even if we thought that their revisionist proposals were good at satisfying the aims of fairness to defendants, we might disagree that they serve all of the aims that might properly be pursued through the criminal law in an adequate way. Again, I don't say that this is true, only that it may be true, and that until we have a proper account of the deeper-lying justification of the principle of fair labelling, we will not be able to evaluate its truth.

Ashworth provides two main justifications for the principle of fair labelling that he thinks guides criminal law. The first focuses on the range of practical effects of labelling. The bad effects of unfair labelling help to vindicate its importance. For example, if the offence that a defendant is convicted of conveys the impression that his conduct was graver than it was, judges may tend to pass sentences that are more severe than they ought to be, the public may tend to shun the defendant on inadequate grounds, he may find it more difficult to find employment as a result,

[9] For Ashworth's scepticism about the significance of outcomes to the criminal law, see 'Taking the Consequences' in S Shute, J Gardner, and J Horder (eds), *Action and Value in Criminal Law* (Oxford: Oxford University Press, 1993). I discuss the idea further in 'Obligations and Outcomes' in R Cruft, M Kramer, and M Reiff (eds), *Crime, Punishment, and Responsibility: The Jurisprudence of Antony Duff* (Oxford: Oxford University Press, 2011).

[10] L Alexander and K Ferzan, *Crime and Culpability: A Theory of Criminal Law* (Cambridge: Cambridge University Press, 2009).

and so on. These practical effects of labelling are, of course, significant, and they cannot be ignored in a complete account of fair labelling. They have also provided a central focus in the important account of fair labelling developed by James Chalmers and Fiona Leverick.[11] My aim is not to make any progress with this aspect of the theory of fair labelling. The most important practical considerations that might motivate fair labelling have been nicely identified and evaluated by Chalmers and Leverick.

My aim is rather to develop an account of fair labelling that will help to underpin Ashworth's second idea, an account which, I hope, helps to clarify and deepen our understanding of it. This second idea is less clearly articulated in Ashworth's work. Ashworth claims that the criminal law should reflect the moral judgements that the public makes about the relevant conduct. This yields more particular ideas. For example, 'where people generally regard two types of conduct as different, the law should try to reflect that difference'.[12] The motivation for this idea, and its significance, are not entirely clear from Ashworth's account. Nevertheless, there is something intuitive about the criminal law being unfair if its distinctions are too far detached from those used in ordinary morality.

This idea should not be pursued uncritically. The public may also have mistaken ideas about moral conduct, and the criminal law should not reflect *those* judgements. Indeed, it may have a role in helping to correct them.[13] The criminal law may sometimes be guilty of reflecting a kind of popular morality that is grounded in prejudice or ignorance. This may lead to the underestimation or overestimation of the significance of some conduct. Or it may distinguish between conduct that is morally indistinct, or alternatively fail to distinguish between conduct that is importantly distinct. It may be difficult for criminal law to play a leading role in shaping moral responses to conduct.[14] Nevertheless, this is undoubtedly a valid role for it to play, and one that it has sometimes played with some success, for example in the criminalization of marital rape and the incitement of racial hatred.

Despite this caveat, it does seem important that *valid* distinctions that the public makes between different kinds of wrongdoing are reflected in the criminal law. The criminal law may be criticized if it replaces the kinds of ideals and judgements that are familiar from ordinary moral discourse with abstract or technical rules or rules whose content in no way reflects familiar moral discourse. In this way, the law may fail to speak adequately to its citizens. This is important not only in the role that the law has in guiding citizens' conduct, but also during trials and in condemning offenders for what they have done.

[11] J Chalmers and F Leverick, 'Fair Labelling in Criminal Law' (2008) 71 MLR 217.

[12] Ashworth, n 4 above, 79.

[13] See further V Tadros, 'The Distinctiveness of Domestic Abuse' in RA Duff and SP Green (eds), *Defining Crimes: Essays on the Special Part of the Criminal Law* (Oxford: Oxford University Press, 2005).

[14] See P Robinson, 'Criminalization Tensions: Doing Justice, Empirical Desert and Changing Norms' in RA Duff, L Farmer, SE Marshall, M Renzo, and V Tadros (eds), *The Structures of the Criminal Law* (Oxford: Oxford University Press, 2011).

Ashworth is not entirely clear why the second of these ideas is important. Why should the criminal law reflect the moral views of the community about wrong-doing insofar as those views are valid? What aims does ensuring this advance? In the absence of an account, it is tempting to believe that this idea is not of profound importance, and to focus primarily on the kinds of practical considerations with which Chalmers and Leverick are mainly concerned.

My aim is to show that Ashworth's second idea plays an important role in advancing a particular conception of social justice that we have reason to value. Furthermore, there is good reason to think that Ashworth is sympathetic to this general project. He also sees the principle of fair labelling as part of a more general project of ensuring that the criminal law treats citizens with the respect that they are due in a liberal democracy.[15]

The version of social justice that I will outline has two dimensions. The first is that the set of rules that the state enforces are guided by respect for autonomous agents, and the protection and promotion of their interests (as well as the interests of those who lack autonomy). But this ambition is coupled with another—to ensure that each citizen of the state has confidence both that this is the case and that all are abiding by that public set of rules. This conception of social justice is one that is secured not simply by ensuring that the state has the right moral content in its rules, but also by providing each citizen with the confidence that she is to be treated as fundamentally important both by the state as a whole, in laying down the law, and by other citizens, in adhering to it. Adhering to the principle that the criminal law should reflect the valid moral ideas of the citizens that it governs helps to foster this ideal.

2. Public Commitment

The criminal justice system has a range of social functions. Three of the most important are that it guides conduct, it prevents and deters crime, and it condemns wrongdoers for what they have done. Fair labelling has some role to play in all three of these functions. The labels that we use in the criminal law help it to provide a guide to conduct. And they contribute to its deterrence function. But at their heart is the condemnatory function of the law. Perhaps the central concern when a person is labelled unfairly is that her conduct is condemned by the state in inappropriate terms. This has a range of bad practical effects, but the unfairness involved is not reducible to those practical effects.

The condemnatory function of the criminal law is important for a range of reasons. Ashworth believes that it is more important in the justification of punishment than I do.[16] In my view, censure occurs at the moment of conviction, and punishment does not play an important role in censuring offenders. My aim is not

[15] See Ashworth, n 3 above.

[16] See eg A Ashworth and A von Hirsch, *Proportionate Sentencing: Exploring the Principles* (Oxford: Oxford University Press, 2005), especially Ch 2.

to defend any particular position on that issue, though. I am interested, rather, in the value of condemnation itself. I will focus here mainly on one value that it has, but one of the most significant. Condemnation has the function of reaffirming a public commitment to ensure trust and confidence that a public scheme of justice is adhered to.

The idea is this. When a person violates the criminal law she will often attack a particular victim or set of victims, and it is important to recognize this fact. But beyond that, the offender sets back an ideal that we strive towards through a public system of laws. The ideal is that we, as members of a political community, live by a fair scheme of shared public laws that provide each with confidence that her moral significance is protected and her interests are advanced on equal terms with all other members of the political community. Breaching a just criminal law not only attacks the particular victim whose interest the law is there to protect. It also erodes our ability to advance towards this ideal.

The condemnatory function of the law thus not only affirms the significance of any particular rights that have been violated. This is, of course, an important role for condemnation to play. But it is not its *only* important role. It also affirms the importance of an ideal to which we must all aspire, but which is threatened by criminal offending. Breaching a just rule of the criminal law is wrong not only because of the particular interests that are set back through the breach. It may also be wrong because it further erodes our collective project of living together peacefully under a just set of rules—something that is a central ideal of social justice.

This also indicates why it may be wrong to breach a just criminal law, even if the interest that the criminal law is designed to protect is not set back. For example, if a person carries a knife, she may not intend to harm anyone. And her conduct may, independently of the law, not be wrong. But a rule prohibiting possession of knives may be justified on the grounds that such a rule does not significantly erode liberty and is required to advance security. Breach of this rule, and rules like it, erodes the possibility of us living together under a public scheme of rules with confidence. And, regardless of any actual threat imposed on others, breach of the rule may therefore be wrong and may be condemned. It is condemned in part to affirm the public project of living together under a just scheme of rules, something that has great value.[17]

This provides part of the *public* aspect of the criminal law. One idea of the criminal law as public is that the criminal law is concerned with wrongs that require a public response—wrongs that it is appropriate to condemn publicly. And one way to understand what is involved here is that public wrongs are wrongs of the gravity

[17] I emphasize this partly to correct a deficiency in V Tadros, 'Crimes and Security' (2008) 71 MLR 940. There I indicated that breach of a just rule of the criminal law is wrong regardless of whether the interest that the law is designed to protect is advanced. But I did not indicate clearly why. Thanks to Andrew Cornford for alerting me to the deficiency. For contrasting further discussion of the permissibility of the criminalization of possession of offensive weapons, see V Tadros, 'Wrongdoing and Criminalization' in A Marmor (ed), *The Routledge Companion to Philosophy of Law* (London: Routledge, forthcoming) and A Ashworth, 'The Unfairness of Risk-Based Possession Offences' (2011) 5 Criminal Law and Philosophy 237.

and kind that demand condemnation in virtue of the effects that they have on particular victims. I am not sure how significant this idea is in marking out the criminal law in particular over other aspects of law, and hence in governing the proper boundaries of the criminal law, but publicly affirming particular rights of victims is undoubtedly an important element of the condemnatory function of the criminal law.

Here I emphasize something else that is public about the criminal law. The criminal law contributes to a particular form of social justice: one in which the confidence of citizens that everyone abides by the full set of rules of justice is central. This is a uniquely public project, and one that the criminal law helps to advance. It is set back when confidence that others will abide by the rules is eroded, as it is through criminal offending. And that requires a public response in order to affirm collective commitment to the project of advancing this kind of social justice.

3. The Role of Content

It might seem that this project does not require that the criminal law have any particular content. What is required is only that the defendant is condemned for breaching the rules of the criminal law. It is not required that the defendant is condemned in any particular way. What is required for public confidence is adherence to a just set of laws. What is required when this is breached is condemnation for undermining the project of ensuring that we comply with a just set of laws.

This appearance is illusory. The idea of a political community governed by a set of rules that are outlined in public, and that we each have confidence in, is not best understood in this formalistic way. The rules that we adopt in social justice can bind us together in the proper way only if we grasp their point. For the idea of social justice is not advanced simply by a scheme of laws that in fact treat each citizen with respect. Public solidarity in a political community can be developed only if each person is confident that her moral significance and her interests are adequately reflected in the scheme of laws. Beyond her confidence that each person will obey the law, each person must recognize that the scheme of laws is one whose content demonstrates that the community is properly committed to respecting her as an autonomous agent, and to ensuring that her interests are protected and advanced through common adherence to the law.[18]

For this reason, when the law communicates to citizens the importance of complying with it, it is essential to ensure that citizens have confidence in the general project of ensuring compliance with a scheme of just laws, but also confidence that the content of the law has appropriate moral foundations. This ideal will be advanced if the content of the criminal law not only has an appropriate

[18] I say more about why respect for autonomy and interests guide the content of the law in V Tadros, 'Independence Without Interests?' (2011) 31 OJLS 193 and V Tadros, 'Harm, Sovereignty, and Prohibition' (2011) 17 Legal Theory 35.

scope, but also if the law is articulated in terms that can foster an appreciation of their value and significance. It will help to facilitate this ideal if the moral foundations of the criminal law as a whole are easy to grasp.

Furthermore, this ideal will be advanced if particular interests and moral judgements that it is appropriate for the law to reflect are well captured by the definitions of offences such that their significance is publicly affirmed. This affirmation of these interests and judgements can then be expected to command adherence by the population, as well as playing a role in shaping the attitudes of citizens who have failed, or failed fully, to grasp those interests and judgements.

There are different ways of advancing the project of ensuring that each person has confidence that the content of the law reflects their moral significance and interests in the appropriate way. One of the most important ways in which we can help to ensure that people are confident that the law is shaped by appropriate respect for each citizen is to shape it through democratic processes. In this way, objections to the law by those affected by it can be raised and responded to. If the content of the law is difficult to grasp, and some criminal law will inevitably be difficult to grasp, the role of the democratic process is especially important.

The rapidity with which criminal offences are developed and passed, and the impoverished level of consultation and debate that often accompanies them, not only undermines the quality of legislation, but also the confidence that citizens can have that the content of the criminal law is shaped in a way that is sensitive to values and interests that citizens can be expected to endorse as part of a liberal polity.[19] This failure to consult fosters a sense of separation between the polity and the law that governs it, eroding the sense that the criminal law imposes proper limits on our conduct as part of a shared project of advancing our interests and ensuring respect for our independence.

But confidence in the content of the law is also more easily secured if the law itself has a content that is clearly articulated in terms such that the public can understand the moral ideals that it is attempting to secure. Ultimately, a law that is passed through the right process, but which has a content that citizens find difficult to grasp when it is communicated to them, will do less to secure and foster the kind of public solidarity that I have argued we should aim at. This provides a significant motivation to ensure that the criminal law is reasonably simple and precise in its content, but also that it contains the kinds of moral distinction between offences that citizens should expect to find if their judgements and attitudes properly reflect the rights that we ought to protect in liberal society.

4. Conflict and Content

Now let us face an objection. The idea that the content of the criminal law should directly reflect the moral ideas of the citizenry might also seem naively to suppose

[19] Ashworth played a significant role in orienting scholarship to this concern in 'Is the Criminal Law a Lost Cause?' (2000) 116 LQR 225.

that the citizenry has a uniform idea of the values that ought to lie behind the criminal law. In reality, moral and political conflicts will inevitably leave some members of the community alienated from the criminal law, whilst others endorse its content.

This might be thought unproblematic insofar as some members of the community make *unreasonable* mistakes about wrongdoing. As I noted at the outset, we ought not to approach the idea that the criminal law must reflect the moral distinctions that the community recognizes as important in an uncritical way. It is legitimate for the criminal law to help to shape community attitudes about wrongdoing as well as reflecting them. Furthermore, any set of laws, however just, will alienate the unreasonable. Just as equal opportunities policies may alienate sexists and racists, so may stricter laws on domestic abuse, rape, and inciting racial hatred. But this is hardly an argument against stricter laws on domestic abuse, rape, and inciting racial hatred.

More troubling is the idea that those with different reasonable conceptions of the good will disagree about the content of offences. Let me explore a single but important example. Different people have different conceptions of the idea of rape. Some people think that rape constitutes an attack on sexual autonomy. These people typically see intercourse without consent as an instance of rape even if consent is not undermined by violence. Other people think that force or violence is essential to the idea of rape. They may think that intercourse without consent is wrong, even criminally wrong, when unaccompanied by violence, but they don't think that it is rape.

Some jurisdictions, including the law of England and Wales, define rape around the absence of consent. Others, including some US states, treat violence as essential to conviction of rape. They may decriminalize other instances of non-consensual sex. That may be unreasonable. But it is not obviously *unreasonable* to create a lesser offence of intercourse without consent that is distinguished from rape on the grounds that violence is not used to undermine consent in these cases. We may doubt that this is the *best* view, but it is not an unreasonable view.

These different views may reflect different underlying ideas about what makes sex wrong, when it is wrong. These may depend on different views about well-being. One possibility is that the goods of life—goods that may either be set back or promoted—determine the moral significance of a life. And the goods of life are determined by the quality of the experiences that the person living the life has. Typically at least, on this view, a good life is a life of positive experiences and a bad life is a life of negative experiences. Wrongdoing, on this view, involves acting in a way that either does, or tends to, result in negative experiences, or that frustrates a person's ability to have positive experiences.

Those who believe this may tend to conclude that violence has a special role to play in rape. For violence will typically make a great deal of difference to the experiences of the victim. Those victims of non-consensual sex whose autonomy is undermined, say by involuntary intoxication, may typically not feel the degree of terror and trauma felt by victims of violent non-consensual sex. Non-consensual sex, even on this view, is wrong. For non-consensual sex also tends to result in negative experiences, or to frustrate a person's ability to have positive experiences. But the direct and powerful negative experiences of violent non-consensual sex may be sufficiently greater to warrant reserving the label rape to cases involving violence. This idea may well have provided part of the motivation for law reform in Canada, where the gravity of a sexual offence is determined by the degree of violence that accompanies it.[20]

I doubt that this is the best view of rape.[21] I suspect that whilst experiences of victims are important in determining the significance of wrongdoing, this view of rape tends to fail to recognize sufficiently the moral significance of a person's authority over her own sexual life. Interference with a person's ability to shape her sex-life has, I believe, the appropriate degree of gravity to constitute rape regardless of the quality of the experiences of the victim. That is not to say that the law should ignore experiences in the way in which it defines rape, but only that it should be possible to convict a person of rape where the victim lacks the negative experiences typically found in cases of violent rape.[22]

This alternative account of rape draws on a different conception of wrongdoing: one that regards autonomous agency as a more fundamental idea in determining the quality of wrongdoing. Autonomous agency is important not only for the reason that protecting it will typically lead people to have better experiences. Underpinning this view is the idea that we must show respect for each other's independence. Failing to do this may constitute a profound form of wrongdoing regardless of the experiences of the person who is affected in this way. We need not believe that this is the *sole* idea behind wrongdoing to recognize its importance.[23]

My aim here is not to defend this account of rape. It is rather to point to the fact that the account of rape that we endorse may depend on deep and difficult questions about the nature of moral wrongdoing. And these questions about moral wrongdoing themselves rest on deeper ideas about what features of a person ground her moral significance. The first conception of rape depends on a moral view that I believe to be false, but one which has many intelligent and thoughtful defenders. Consensus on the best view of wrongdoing is unlikely to be achieved in the near future. Indeed, it may be inevitable that such consensus will not emerge at least insofar as we are governed by liberal institutions. As John Rawls memorably puts it: 'The diversity of reasonable comprehensive religious, philosophical, and moral doctrines found in modern democratic societies is not a mere historical condition that may soon pass away: it is a permanent feature of the public culture of democracy.'[24]

What this suggests is that particular choices about the content of the criminal law are likely to reflect one side better than another in the kinds of deep debates that are

[20] Another controversial feature of the Canadian position is that it abandoned the label 'rape' altogether. See Criminal Code of Canada, ss 271–3.

[21] See Tadros, n 8 above.

[22] For a suggestion how both violence and sexual autonomy might be reflected in a definition of rape, see ibid.

[23] See further the articles cited in n 18 above.

[24] J Rawls, *Political Liberalism* (New York: Columbia University Press, 1993), 36.

unlikely to be resolved soon. And I believe that this will *inevitably* be the case, for I very much doubt that there is a basis on which we can decide how to define the law of rape that is not motivated by one moral conception or the other. There is no way to define rape in a way that is neutral between the different moral conceptions that I have outlined.

This is not least because the gravity of the law's condemnatory message depends on reflecting the moral quality of wrongdoing in its offence definitions. Those who disagree with the moral conception of a wrong articulated in the law will, according to their own reasonable view, believe that the law is too severe or too lenient in the condemnatory message that it sends out, depending on how the offence is designed. If rape includes all cases of non-consensual intercourse, those who have the first conception of moral wrongdoing that I identified will be dissatisfied with the communicative operation of the law. If it does not, those who have the second conception of moral wrongdoing will be equally dissatisfied. And, I suspect, there is no policy choice that is neutral between these views.

This fact about the way in which particular and deep moral views are inevitably reflected in particular policy choices in the criminal law need not undermine any project of political liberalism of the kind that Rawls hoped to defend, though it does threaten some accounts of that liberal view. For example, Rawls believed that, in the course of establishing the constitutional essentials and matters of basic justice, it would be wrong to appeal to particular comprehensive doctrines that others could reasonably reject.[25] But that may not mean that those defending particular policy choices, such as the proper definition of rape, may not appeal to comprehensive doctrines in the course of public discourse, though Rawls does sometimes seem to imply this.[26] The latter idea—that we must refrain from referring to comprehensive moral doctrines in public debate about particular policy choices—seems much more demanding than the idea that the institutional and constitutional essentials of a political community should be acceptable to those with a range of comprehensive views.[27]

I suspect that we ought not to expect debates about particular policy choices, such as the proper definition of rape, to be pursued without appealing to more basic and fundamental comprehensive moral views, and that indeed it may be damaging to attempt to constrain public reason in this way.[28] But this does also result in a certain kind of loss, though that loss is, I believe, unavoidable. The loss is a reduction in the degree of solidarity that we can expect to find around particular public policies, including the criminal law, in liberal communities. We may expect to be able to find a consensus on the basic features of our institutions and

[25] J Rawls, *Political Liberalism* (New York: Columbia University Press, 1993), 224.

[26] Ibid, 242–3.

[27] For a recent defence of the view that we may not appeal to comprehensive moral views even in shaping particular policy choices, see J Quong, *Liberalism Without Perfection* (Oxford: Oxford University Press, 2011), Ch 9.

[28] See also R Dworkin, *Is Democracy Possible Here? Principles for a New Political Debate* (Princeton: Princeton University Press, 2006), Ch 3.

constitutional principles. We cannot expect to find consensus on the content of even our most basic criminal laws such as the law of rape.

Nevertheless, I do not believe that this loss of solidarity need inevitably be profound. There are two reasons why. First, if the law is shaped through the right process, and is formulated with the appropriate degree of clarity, whilst not all reasonable individuals will *agree* with the judgements that the criminal law reflects in condemning offenders, all can nevertheless *see the point* of these judgements. They can come to see that those who take a different moral view from them may conclude that the law is justified, and this may help to bolster acceptance of, if not agreement with, the law.

Secondly, by passing laws through the right kind of process, citizens can see that the state, constituted by the public reasoning of its members, takes each agent of moral concern seriously. They can see pursuit of the aspiration that each person is treated as having the right kind of importance, even if they think that the basis on which it is pursued in particular cases is misguided.

This can help to build a certain kind of solidarity even with those with whom we disagree, a solidarity that cannot be shared in hierarchical societies, for example, that do not even aim, in determining the content of the criminal law, to take seriously the fundamental moral conceptions and values that people endorse. In this way, although the set of judgements that are reflected in the criminal law cannot command universal agreement, they can command a measure of universal respect, the kind of respect that we can have towards another person whose judgement on a difficult issue is well thought out and well motivated, but which differs from our own.

Again, this is not to underplay the frustration that a person can feel when his moral convictions are not well reflected in the law. It is only to say that there is a different kind of solidarity, that can be shaped through political processes, which is nevertheless important in developing a valuable kind of political and social solidarity, the only kind of political and social solidarity that is possible in the face of the substantial disagreement about basic moral judgements that we must expect to find in liberal societies.

The criminal law, through its communicative function, has a role to play in fostering and sustaining this kind of social solidarity. We allow it to play this role by ensuring that decisions to criminalize are taken with the proper degree of care, taking into consideration the proper range of views about what constitutes the kind of wrongful conduct that the state is permitted to condemn and punish. But we also enhance its potential to contribute to this aim by ensuring that the criminal law has a content which, insofar as possible, tracks the reasonable moral convictions of the community, and if this goal is unattainable, to ensure that its point is at least easy to grasp so that those who disagree can have a kind of respect for the content of the law even in the face of their disagreement with it.

5. Conclusion

The principle of fair labelling has seemed less important to many people than other principles that guide the criminal law. This is perhaps because the principle of fair labelling does not, in itself, determine who is punished and who is not. Nor does it have a direct influence over the magnitude of the sentence which offenders will serve (though it may indirectly play a role in this regard[29]). For these reasons, whilst the kind of unfairness involved in unfair labelling is seen as important, it is often seen as less important than the kinds of unfairness involved when the trial is defective, or when the criminal law is too expansive.

I agree that the unfairness to defendants involved in fair labelling may be less important than other kinds of unfairness in the criminal process. There are undoubtedly problematic cases where defendants are stigmatized, for example as sex offenders or as terrorists, where this is entirely unwarranted.[30] But this kind of unfairness is perhaps less serious than the unfairness of convicting a person of an offence where his conduct ought not to have been criminal at all, or failing to provide adequate protections against conviction through trials and punishments.

But even if it is true that these defendant-centred reasons are less profound in the case of fair labelling than they are in other contexts, we should not be led to relegate the importance of fair labelling. For fair labelling plays an important function in securing public solidarity and confidence in the law. This connects the idea of fair labelling with another of Ashworth's most important ambitions: to reveal the extent to which the criminal law as a whole is one that we can have confidence in.[31] With Ashworth, I believe that this valuable goal is increasingly being set back by the range of trivial offences, obscurely defined and chaotically distinguished, which ensure that the criminal law as a whole is properly treated with suspicion, rather than with pride by the community that it is supposed to serve. We might doubt that we can expect citizens to obey a fragmented and obscure criminal law like this given the difficulties of knowing exactly what is prohibited.[32] We might also doubt that we can expect citizens, including defendants, offenders, and victims, to have confidence that the content of the law shows adequate respect for them as individuals. With Ashworth I can only hope, rather than expect, that one of the most important causes that the criminal law could serve—that is, securing public solidarity—is not lost.

[29] See Chalmers and Leverick, n 11 above, 224–5.

[30] See, for further discussion, J Hodgson and V Tadros, 'How to Make a Terrorist out of Nothing' (2009) 72 MLR 984.

[31] Ashworth, n 19 above.

[32] See further, Ashworth's excellent discussion of ignorance of the law: A Ashworth, 'Ignorance of the Criminal Law and Duties to Avoid it' (2011) 74 MLR 1.

6

Distraction and Negligence

*Douglas Husak**

1. Recklessness, Negligence, and Belief

The determination of whether a given defendant is reckless or negligent is often crucial in assessing his liability. Suppose, for example, that a defendant commits homicide by causing the death of another. If he is reckless, he is probably liable for manslaughter. But if he is negligent, he may not be liable at all. Some jurisdictions do not punish negligent homicide, and those that *do* impose a sentence far less severe than in cases of manslaughter. Of course, homicide statutes provide only a single illustration of the practical significance of contrasting recklessness with negligence. Even though all Anglo-American jurisdictions punish *some* acts of negligence, they do so infrequently. The Model Penal Code, for example, imposes liability for negligence in only a handful of cases. Thus negligent defendants are far more likely than reckless defendants to evade penal liability altogether.

Andrew Ashworth shares the reluctance of positive law to punish negligent conduct. Although he describes several reasons to reject it altogether, Ashworth eventually allows liability for negligence when '(i) the potential harm is great; (ii) the risk of it occurring is obvious; (iii) D has a duty to try to avoid the risk; and (iv) D has the capacity to take the required precautions'.[1] In the absence of further explanation, it is hard not to construe his position as a compromise between unpalatable extremes: liability for negligence should not be ubiquitous, but should not be rejected categorically. At the end of the day, Ashworth readily concedes that 'views may differ' about whether defendants who satisfy these conditions are sufficiently culpable to merit blame and penal liability.[2] Needless to say, no one exhibits comparable ambivalence about punishing recklessness.

But how should the contrast between criminal recklessness and negligence be drawn? In a previous essay, I described as 'scandalous' the failure of theorists to

* Professor of Philosophy and Law, Rutgers University. Thanks to Lucia Zedner and members of the criminal law theory workshop at Brooklyn and NYU schools of law. Generous support for this project was provided by The Straus Institute for the Advanced Study of Law and Justice, NYU.

[1] A Ashworth, *Principles of Criminal Law* (6th edn, Oxford: Oxford University Press, 2009), 187–8.

[2] Ibid, 188.

defend criteria to decide whether defendants in given scenarios are reckless or merely negligent.[3] The examples on which I focused involve *forgetting*. When a defendant creates a condition that becomes risky because he forgets he has created it, under what circumstances, if any, should we categorize his behaviour as reckless or as negligent?[4] Unless this question can be answered, we have little basis to identify what crime, if any, he has committed. A somewhat similar question confronts us in cases of *distraction*. When a defendant is engaged in an activity that becomes risky because he is distracted, under what circumstances, if any, should we categorize his behaviour as reckless or as negligent? I propose to examine the latter question largely by comparing and contrasting the culpability of defendants who forget with that of defendants who are distracted. As we will see, some theorists regard these kinds of case as raising identical issues. After all, it is plausible to suppose that distraction causes us to forget the propositions of which we were aware before we became inattentive. Despite their similarities, however, I will contend that these kinds of case are importantly different. A finding of recklessness in cases of distraction is generally stronger than in cases of forgetting. In neither kind of situation, however, is the argument in favour of recklessness conclusive. Moreover, not all cases of distraction or forgetfulness are amenable to the same analysis; distinctions must be drawn *within* these categories. In order to classify given examples correctly, I contend that penal theorists need to make more progress to identify the propositions defendants *believe*.

I conclude Ashworth is correct about his major point. No *general* position about negligence is defensible. Cases of forgetting are similar to but different from cases of distraction, which in turn are similar to but different from cases of true negligence. By *true negligence*, I mean situations in which it never occurs to a defendant (until after the harm occurs) that he has created a risky condition.[5] Casebooks often include examples of true negligence, but we should not employ them as a basis for generalizing about all cases. Commentators should stop trying to determine whether individuals are blameworthy in every situation in which they deviate from a standard of reasonable care and instead should proceed by separately evaluating different kinds of case.

The practical importance of the distinction between recklessness and negligence requires us to contrast these two culpable states carefully. As a matter of definition, the contested issue is easily described. In many jurisdictions in the United States, recklessness—which nearly everyone concedes to be a mode of culpability—is distinguished from negligence—which is highly controversial—by a single factor: the presence or absence of *conscious awareness* of a substantial and unjustifiable risk

[3] D Husak, 'Negligence, Belief, and Criminal Liability: The Special Case of Forgetting' (2011) 5 Criminal Law and Philosophy 199.

[4] Henceforth I assume that other necessary conditions in statutory definitions of culpable states are satisfied. Liability for both recklessness and negligence requires the risk to be substantial and unjustifiable, and involves a gross deviation from the standard of care taken by the reasonable person in the actor's situation.

[5] Perhaps the most well-known case to appear in casebooks is (probably) an instance of true negligence. See *State v Williams*, 484 P.2d 1167 (1971).

the defendant disregards. If the defendant *is* aware of the risk, he is reckless. If he is *not* aware, he is negligent as long as he *should* have been aware; that is, if a reasonable person in his situation *would* have been aware of the risk. As commentators such as Ashworth have insisted, the normative basis for holding persons to the standard of the reasonable person presupposes that they possess the mental and physical capacities to have taken the necessary precautions.[6] Thus the blameworthiness in negligence, according to Ashworth, consists in 'the culpability of unexercised capacity'.[7] Both the specification of these capacities as well as the reliability of the evidence that given defendants possess or lack them can be problematic, but I will not pursue these familiar difficulties here. Instead, I seek to clarify the concept of *awareness* that is central in contrasting uncontested from highly disputable impositions of blame and penal liability.

When *is* a person *aware* of something? In particular, when is a person aware of a risk? My answer is speculative and tentative. The Model Penal Code provides some guidance in its definition of knowledge, which it equates with awareness.[8] Thus I will tentatively suppose as a matter of positive law in the United States that the contrast between recklessness and negligence depends on whether or not the defendant *knows* he is creating a risk. Pursuant to this supposition, the negligent defendant, unlike the reckless defendant, does not know he is creating a risk, even though a reasonable person in his situation would have known. One might suspect that this definition would not succeed in advancing the inquiry, since we are just as likely to be uncertain about whether or not a given defendant knows he is imposing a risk. Unlike the concept of awareness, however, the concept of knowledge has been analysed extensively by epistemologists. Perhaps their efforts can shed light on our topic.

Nearly all philosophers agree that S knows that p only if S *believes* p and p is *true*. Moreover, they largely concur that a third condition—roughly described as *justification*—is needed to complete the analysis. In what follows, I make two simplifying assumptions. First, it is *true* that the defendant is subjecting another to a risk. Secondly, he is *justified* in believing that he is subjecting another to a risk. If these two simplifying assumptions are granted, the difference between the reckless and the negligent defendant is simply a function of their beliefs: the reckless defendant, unlike the negligent defendant, *believes* that he is creating a risk.[9]

[6] Ashworth, n 1 above, 186, in discussion of HLA Hart, *Punishment and Responsibility* (Oxford: Oxford University Press, 1968), Chs 2 and 5.

[7] Ibid, 186, citing A Simester, 'Can Negligence Be Culpable?' in J Horder (ed), *Oxford Essays in Jurisprudence* (4th series, Oxford: Oxford University Press, 2000), 106.

[8] Model Penal Code, s 2.02(2)(b)(i).

[9] We must also be clear about exactly *what* a reckless defendant must believe. At least two problems arise. First, must the defendant by aware of the risk of the exact harm the statute requires, or is an amorphous sense that his conduct is risky sufficient? See KK Ferzan, 'Opaque Recklessness' (2001) 91 Journal of Criminal Law and Criminology 597. Secondly, must the defendant simply believe that he has created a risk, with the question of whether that risk is substantial and/or unjustifiable determined by the judge or jury? Or must he also believe that the risk he has created is substantial and unjustifiable? See KW Simons, 'The Distinction between Negligence and Recklessness is Unstable' in PH Robinson, SP Garvey, and KK Ferzan (eds), *Criminal Law Conversations* (New York: Oxford University Press, 2009), 290.

Ashworth appears to endorse this position. In the course of voicing his reservations about the fairness of imposing penal liability for negligence, he indicates that 'the principle of *mens rea* also encompasses the belief principle, which holds that criminal liability should be based on what defendants believed they were doing or risking, not on actual facts which were not known to them at the time'.[10] If Ashworth is correct to link the 'belief principle' to the normative case for imposing liability for negligence—as I think he is—we need to inquire whether given defendants often treated as negligent might actually possess the relevant beliefs that would establish them to be reckless and thus place their penal liability beyond serious controversy.

In particular, we must decide whether persons believe they have created a risk when they are distracted—the topic of my inquiry. Throughout this essay I will refer to the following case (which I regard as something of a paradigm): Claire is a motorist who hears the familiar chime indicating that someone has sent her a text message while she is driving. She takes her eyes off the highway for several moments to type an unimportant greeting to her friend. When she finally glances back at the road, she is horrified to see a child running from the kerb to retrieve a ball. She slams on her brakes but cannot stop in time, hitting and killing the victim. Had she been looking at the road the whole time, she would have been able to avoid the collision. Did Claire believe she was creating a risk when she struck the child, even though the accident was the furthest thing from her mind while she concentrated on her message? If so, we have a ground to find her to be reckless (and presumably guilty of vehicular manslaughter). If not, her act of killing is at most negligent.

If the determination of whether drivers such as Claire are reckless or negligent has so much practical significance, why has it not been resolved? Frankly, the question is puzzling, but one partial answer is as follows. Many jurisdictions enact special statutes to address the problems posed by distracted drivers. Although the laws governing driving vary widely, all but a handful of states in the United States expressly prohibit texting while driving.[11] Many of these statutes do not mention a culpable state and appear to impose strict liability. When a death occurs because a driver is texting, the breach of a statutory duty may involve all of the evidence of culpability the law requires. Even so, the problem of categorization remains important and continues to vex those philosophers of criminal law who struggle to understand the elusive boundary between recklessness and negligence.

[10] Ashworth, n 1 above, 159.

[11] See National Institute of Highway Safety, 45:10 *Status Report* (28 September 2010) 1, <http://www.iihs.org/externaldata/srdata/docs/sr4510.pdf> accessed 9 March 2012. Paradoxically, these bans appear to have slightly increased the rate of crashes per mile driven. Theorists disagree about why these laws have failed to reduce accidents. Perhaps drivers who are not deterred text more furtively, thus creating even greater hazards.

2. Do Distracted Persons *Believe* They Have Created a Risk?

In order to sort cases correctly, we must be able to determine when it is true that S [the defendant] believes p [that she is creating a substantial and unjustifiable risk]. Before moving to the enormous perplexities that surround this question, I begin with a crucial observation with which I hope all commentators agree: awareness (or belief) need not be *occurrent.* The exact nature of occurrent belief is mysterious. But it is clear that defendants need not have an explicit thought about the risk before their conscious minds in order to be reckless. In other words, reckless persons need not be saying to themselves 'This is risky' when they inflict injury. To be sure, defendants who entertain occurrent thoughts about risk provide the least controversial examples of recklessness. Still, few of us would ever be reckless if we needed to rehearse such thoughts at the moment we cause harm. Phenomenologically, we rarely articulate propositions to ourselves in order to qualify as believing them. And for good reason. Persons who are keenly aware of a risk and seek to minimize it learn *not* to lose focus from their task by mentally entertaining such propositions. For example, the experienced marksman who fires his weapon at a distant target does not think to himself 'I might miss'. Such thoughts would sap his attention from the job at hand. Yet I assume that no one would infer that this marksman is unaware of and does not believe he is at risk of missing. *Of course* he is aware of this risk. But even though this observation is tremendously important in clarifying what belief need *not* involve, it does not go very far in helping us understand what it *does* involve.

With this point of agreement in place, I return to an analysis of the conditions under which S believes p. Contemporary epistemologists have said disappointingly little about this matter. They have generated countless theories about what is required to elevate belief to knowledge, but almost nothing about what is involved in having a belief in the first place. An adequate analysis, I assume, would support the conclusion that our marksman is well aware of the risk of missing his target—even though his belief is not occurrent. Beliefs that are not occurrent might be called *tacit,*[12] and the standard analyses of tacit belief are *dispositional.*[13] The details of these analyses vary widely. Roughly, S is said to believe p tacitly when he has the disposition to behave in given ways, most notably when he has the disposition to assent to utterances of p in the right sorts of circumstance (eg, when he comprehends the language, has no stake in deception, and the like). If the reckless defendant need only believe p dispositionally, it should be possible to describe tests that provide strong (but not conclusive) evidence of his tacit belief ('I have

[12] See WG Lycan, 'Tacit Belief' in RJ Bogdan (ed), *Belief* (Oxford: Oxford University Press, 1986), 61.

[13] Dispositional analyses need not be ontological theses about what beliefs *are*, but rather epistemological accounts of why belief ascriptions are warranted.

created a risk').[14] These tests may be applied to decide whether persons believe they have created a risk when they are distracted.

What criteria should we invoke to decide *what* Claire believes at the moment she is creating a risk by texting? I attempt to make progress on this matter by drawing from my earlier thoughts about cases of forgetting. I use the example of Joe, an otherwise loving parent who is busy giving a bath to his one-year-old son. The phone rings; he quickly leaves the bathroom to travel a few short steps down the hall to answer it, and becomes completely engrossed in the ensuing unimportant conversation. He forgets about the bath, and his son has drowned by the time he finally remembers. How are the arguments for or against the judgment that Claire believes she has created a risk similar to and different from the same arguments about Joe? In other words, to what extent are cases of forgetting amenable to the same analysis as cases of distraction?

Matters are complicated because I reached no straightforward conclusion in my examination of cases of forgetting. Neither ordinary language nor philosophical analysis yields an unequivocal answer to the question whether S (eg, Joe) tacitly believes p (eg, my baby is at risk) when S has temporarily forgotten about the condition (eg, my baby is in the bathtub) that creates the risk. I assume that Joe believes (by any respectable dispositional analysis) that babies left alone in bathtubs for more than a few moments are at risk of drowning. If at t2 (while he talks on the phone) he tacitly believes that his baby is in the bath for more than a few moments, we have a strong basis to find him to be reckless rather than negligent for creating the risk that led to the death. What tests should we use to decide whether Joe believes p at t2? Are these criteria equally applicable in cases of distraction?

The most general such tests that are potentially applicable to both contexts cite effects that are best explained as having been caused by beliefs.[15] Some of these effects are purely physiological. We have evidence that Claire knows she is creating a risk by texting if her skin temperature rises slightly or if her heart beats a bit faster than when she texts in a safer environment. Other effects are wholly behavioural. Thus we have evidence that Claire knows she is creating a risk if she makes more mistakes in typing her message than when she is able to give the keyboard her undivided attention. Our marksman knows he is at risk of missing his target because he aims his gun carefully. Unless some plausible explanation of these effects can be offered that is consistent with a *lack* of belief, we have reason to infer that they know they have created a risk. Of course, we may not be in a position *ex post* to gather this kind of data, but the outcome of these dispositional tests *would* provide powerful evidence that Claire has the relevant belief, even in the absence of an occurrent mental state. But I doubt that these tests should be applied to show that

[14] Unfortunately, these tests are not conclusive. Some of the difficulties in inferring the existence of beliefs from behaviour are described by TS Gendler, 'Alief and Belief' (2008) 105 Journal of Philosophy 634.

[15] The behavioural effects best explained by beliefs (or unconscious mental states) are surprising and diverse. See DM Wegner, *The Illusion of Conscious Will* (Cambridge, MA: MIT Press, 2002). Among the most spectacular examples is *blindsight.* See L Weiskrantz, *Blindsight: A Case Study and Implications* (Oxford: Oxford University Press, 1990).

Claire is reckless rather than negligent. A wealth of empirical research demonstrates that *unconscious* mental states—those of which persons are unaware—frequently influence judgement and conduct.[16] As we have seen, however, recklessness requires *conscious* belief. I assume that the rationale for this requirement is that the beliefs a person is unable to access through introspection cannot be employed in practical reasoning. As a result, they should not be cited to show that a defendant is sufficiently culpable to be liable for an offence involving recklessness.

How might we proceed if these physiological or behavioural tests are unavailable or inapplicable? Notice first that some of the very same considerations that allegedly show Joe not to be reckless can be borrowed to defend the same outcome for Claire. According to this train of thought, distraction and forgetting are amenable to a similar analysis. I stipulate (because the issue may be in doubt) that Joe is not at fault for leaving his baby unattended in the bath for a few moments. Similarly, Claire is not at fault for taking her eyes off the road for a brief instant. Their fault, if any, comes later. At this later time, however, they are not attending to the hazards they have created. Thus some legal philosophers who oppose liability for negligence tend to assimilate forgetting with distraction. Larry Alexander and Kim Ferzan are among these theorists. They write: 'An injunction to notice [or] remember . . . is an injunction no human being can comply with, so violating this injunction reflects no moral defect.'[17] Their point is that Claire may not believe she is creating a danger at the time she is distracted for the same reason that pertains to Joe.

I contend that a finding of recklessness in cases of distraction is generally stronger than in cases of forgetting. Typically, we *can* comply with the injunction 'Pay Attention!' even though the command 'Remember!' is more problematic. The former but not the latter injunction can play a significant role in our practical reasoning. Here, then, is a very important dissimilarity between the two kinds of case. In any event, I propose to contrast forgetting from distraction by distinguishing the practical syllogisms that might apply to each. When Joe forgets his baby, he might have reasoned:

(1) I believe that leaving babies unattended in a bath for more than a few moments creates a substantial and unjustifiable risk;
(2) I believe I have left my baby unattended in a bath for more than a few moments; therefore
(3) I believe that I have created a substantial and unjustifiable risk to my baby.

The foremost obstacle to finding Joe to be reckless, of course, is that (arguably) he does *not* believe (2). Since he has forgotten about his baby, we may doubt that he believes he has left him unattended in the bath for more than a few moments. Matters are otherwise, however, for Claire. The comparable syllogism is:

[16] See EL Uhlmann, DA Pizarro, and P Bloom, 'Varieties of Social Cognition' (2008) 38 Journal for the Theory of Social Behaviour 293.

[17] L Alexander and KK Ferzan with S Morse, *Crime and Culpability* (Cambridge: Cambridge University Press, 2009), 71.

(1*) I believe that texting while driving creates a substantial and unjustifiable risk to others on the road;
(2*) I believe that I am texting while driving; therefore
(3*) I believe that I have created a substantial and unjustifiable risk to others on the road.

It is much harder to defend the claim that Claire does not believe (2*) than that Joe does not believe (2). Except in the most bizarre circumstances, no one should dispute that Claire is aware she is texting while she is driving. As we have seen, however, there is ample room to doubt that Joe believes the parallel proposition—that he has left his baby unattended for more than a few moments. If I am correct so far, it is simply false that cases of forgetting are amenable to the same analysis as those involving distraction.

Moreover, if the second of the above syllogisms is sound, Claire is reckless, rather than negligent. For two reasons, however, this argument is inconclusive. First, it is much harder to defend the claim that Claire believes (1*) than that Joe believes (1). How do we determine whether Claire believes that texting while driving is risky? All of the difficulties of belief ascription about the conclusion resurface about the premise. Notice that the case in favour of recklessness is not established simply because Claire believed (1*) at *some* point in her life. Perhaps she has gained ample experience at texting while driving, and is convinced she has become proficient at multi-tasking.[18] Propositions cannot play a role in practical reasoning if they are no longer held. Secondly, even if Claire *does* believe (1*) and (2*), she still may not believe (3*). This possibility arises because Claire (or Joe) might fail to draw the relevant inference. Clearly, persons may believe both premises in a sound syllogism, even though they do not believe the conclusion. Claire may fail, as it were, to 'put two and two together'. What criteria should we apply to determine whether Claire has a current dispositional belief that she is creating a risk to others on the road?

No criterion is obviously correct. Still, I propose the following test(s) as the most apt. Suppose persons are prompted without being led to the correct answer. Joe should *not* be asked: 'Don't you know that your baby is unattended in the bathtub for several moments?' Similarly, Claire should not be asked: 'Don't you know that you are creating a risk by texting while driving?' These questions, I submit, are analogous to impermissibly leading a witness at trial or to contaminating a suspect during an interrogation. Instead, Claire should be asked a more neutral question such as 'Do you create a risk if you text while driving?' This latter question does not lead Claire in any particular direction.[19] If she (sincerely) answers the neutral question affirmatively, she satisfies my dispositional test for belief. Thus *she* (and not merely a reasonable person in her circumstances) actually believed she was

[18] A good many motorists probably do *not* believe texting while driving is dangerous. See n 23 below. I stipulate, however, that Claire has no illusions about her ability to drive safely while texting.

[19] Of course, in many circumstances even this supposedly neutral question may give persons grounds for suspicion that something is amiss. In some situations, a purely neutral question may be impossible to formulate.

creating a risk at the time of the accident, and we have reason to conclude that she is reckless rather than negligent.

Again, the case for finding Claire to be reckless is stronger than the parallel case for Joe.[20] The disparity arises because a different but seemingly equally appropriate dispositional test yields the opposite result for our forgetful parent. We may have ample evidence that Joe is a loving and caring father. But loving parents who believe their babies are unattended in bathtubs do not behave like Joe. Instead, they rush to the bathroom to see if their babies are safe. The fact that Joe behaves as he does is evidence that he does not believe his baby is at risk. The parallel argument in Claire's case, however, is less compelling. The fact that Claire texts while driving is less evidence of her belief in the absence of risk than in her deviation from a standard of care. Hence the argument that gives us pause in the case of Joe is less worrisome in the case of Claire. In her case, the appropriate dispositional tests I have proposed do not pull us in contrary directions.

Theorists have additional reason to differentiate typical cases of forgetting from those involving distraction. Except in highly unusual circumstances, people do not choose to forget. The same cannot be said for distraction. We tend to distinguish situations in which the distracting event is initiated by the defendant from those in which it has an external source. A driver can become distracted from the road by a billboard depicting her favourite movie star, for example. In this latter case, the distraction seems less voluntary and merely negligent, rather than reckless.[21] Of course, the difference between voluntary and non-voluntary distraction is probably a continuum allowing for borderline cases that elude simple categorization. Still, sympathy for distracted drivers erodes when we learn that the source of their distraction is internal and governed by choice. If distraction *happens* to someone, rather than being the result of something that someone actively *does,* we cannot impose liability through what might be called a 'culpability in causing' or 'tracing' rationale: when someone is culpable for causing the conditions in which he alleges his culpability is reduced, we tend to hold him culpable for those latter conditions.[22] I intend the case of neither Joe nor Claire to be amenable to such an approach; in neither example is the agent culpable for the event that causes the subsequent state of forgetting or distraction.

These considerations reveal an important point about judgments about recklessness and negligence: examples of distraction or forgetfulness should not be treated

[20] Additional reasons to differentiate between Joe and Claire might be given. We might be more lenient towards Joe because he has suffered a great loss. By the same token, we might be less punitive towards Claire if she herself is seriously injured in the fatal accident. For a general discussion, see D Husak, 'Already Punished Enough' in D Husak, *The Philosophy of Criminal Law: Selected Essays* (Oxford: Oxford University Press, 2010), 433.

[21] If sufficiently severe, an external distraction might defeat voluntariness altogether. See the hypothetical swarm of bees discussed in *Hill v Baxter* [1958] 1 QB 277.

[22] Culpability-in-causing rationales should not be endorsed without qualification. See PH Robinson, 'Causing the Conditions of One's Own Defense: A Study of the Limits of Theory in Criminal Law Doctrine' (1985) 71 Virginia Law Review 1. Culpability-in-causing arguments involve what some moral philosophers call *tracing.* See M King: 'The Problem with Negligence' (2009) 35 Social Theory and Practice 577.

alike. Not all cases of distraction are reckless and not all cases of forgetfulness are merely negligent. Instead, the relevance of further details about particular examples indicates that our judgments about blame and liability are highly fact-sensitive and do not admit of a general resolution. Commentators should stop pretending that we can sort all cases of distraction and/or forgetting into simple categories. Sweeping generalizations about the blame or liability of forgetful or distracted persons should be avoided.

3. Reservations about My Position

I have argued that the case for finding Claire to be reckless rather than negligent is fairly strong—and certainly stronger than the comparable case for Joe, our forgetful parent. How might those commentators respond who regard forgetfulness and distraction to be analogous and hold Claire to be merely negligent? They might reject dispositional tests of tacit belief altogether. More plausibly, they might reject any of the particular dispositional tests I have proposed. In either event, the challenge for them is to offer an alternative criterion to decide whether S believes p. As far as I can see, neither friends nor foes of liability for negligence have met this challenge. In fact, they do not seem to appreciate that this challenge must be met—the situation I earlier described as scandalous. Once we recognize that occurrent beliefs are not needed for awareness, the unfinished task is to formulate one or more tests to allow us to decide whether given defendants tacitly believe that they have created a risk.

At this juncture, however, it might be protested that my strategy has gone seriously awry. I have construed the inquiry about whether a defendant is consciously aware of a risk to depend on whether he tacitly believes he is creating that risk at the moment harm is caused. But conscious awareness, the protest continues, requires *something more* than tacit belief. Perhaps it even requires something more than a belief that can be accessed through introspection. My proposal to equate awareness with belief, especially when belief is tacit and non-occurrent, is to *alter*, not to *interpret*, the concepts of recklessness and negligence. Like the forgetful defendant, the distracted defendant lacks this missing element. Even if Joe and/or Claire *believe* they have created a risk, the argument concludes, they are not *aware* that they have done so. For all I know, this protest might be sound. But what *is* this mysterious 'something more'? And why should we suppose that whatever allegedly elevates tacit belief to awareness should be required for culpability and thus will serve the normative purpose of distinguishing recklessness from negligence? Perhaps a satisfactory answer can be supplied. My basic worry is that the concept of awareness is poorly understood and requires much more elaboration than penal theorists have offered. In particular, clarification is needed before we should be confident that defendants who are inattentive are negligent rather than reckless and thus are dubious candidates for criminal liability. In the absence of an account of the supposed missing element lacked by Claire that shows her to be merely negligent, I doubt that this protest is persuasive. I persist in claiming that the controversy about defendants such as Claire and Joe depends on an analysis of what they tacitly believe and can access through introspection.

Still, most of us remain uncertain about whether Claire is reckless. One source of uncertainty might be as follows. Recklessness requires that persons disregard substantial risks by grossly deviating from the standard of care taken by the reasonable person in the actor's situation. But do drivers actually cause a *substantial* risk by texting? Admittedly, distraction is the most common cause of automobile accidents. And automobile accidents, in turn, are the most common cause of death among persons from age 15 to 40 in the United States today.[23] Still, distraction is ubiquitous, and a miniscule percentage of persons who text while driving cause a crash. This activity is tremendously risky in the aggregate, but creates only a tiny risk each particular time we engage in it. Moreover, the fact that no one is perfectly attentive at all times makes it difficult to support the judgment that inattentive persons are reckless. If distraction is so pervasive, can it really be true that it involves a gross deviation from the standard of care taken by the reasonable person?[24]

Although troublesome, this reservation threatens to prove too much. If we doubt that texting causes a *substantial* risk, or that texting while driving is not genuinely *unreasonable,* we are no more able to convict Claire of negligence than of recklessness. As I have said, the sole difference between these two (alleged) culpable states consists in whether a person is *aware* of the risks she disregards. If these risks are minor, or if it is reasonable to disregard them, it is hard to see how Claire has *any* degree of culpability. This implication, I think, amounts to a *reductio* of the foregoing argument. Despite our intuitive ambivalence about Claire's degree of culpability, it is hard to see that she is ineligible for *any* amount of blame for her inattentive behaviour.

In any event, respondents should not be uncertain about several important intuitive judgments. Surely Claire's culpability is higher than that of a defendant in a case that involves *true* negligence. Suppose Cheryl is texting while driving but (somehow) has no idea that it is dangerous. Imagine that she satisfies *none* of the dispositional tests that would allow us to conclude that she believes she has created a risk. In other words, she does not believe (1*). Although Cheryl may be more stupid than Claire, I concede that Claire is more culpable. It is equally apparent, however, that Claire's culpability is lower than that of Jane, a driver who texts while entertaining the occurrent belief that she is creating a risk. Although she is thinking to herself that her activity is dangerous, she engages in

[23] If texting is a major source of distraction, and distraction causes large numbers of accidents and fatalities, why do so many drivers do it? The best answer is that crashes are so infrequent that we come to believe we are capable of driving competently even though we are distracted. Surprising numbers of persons think they are better than others at multi-tasking and do not suppose they are imposing substantial risks while texting and driving. '[P]eople are confident that they can drive and [text] simultaneously precisely because they almost never encounter evidence that they cannot.' See C Chabris and D Simons, *The Invisible Gorilla* (New York: Random House, 2010), 37.

[24] In general, distraction does not operate by significantly impairing skills to do familiar and simple tasks like steering. Instead, it reduces the probability that we will recognize and react to unfamiliar and unexpected hazards. Psychological evidence shows that we are surprisingly inept at noticing rare and surprising events, but are even worse at noticing them when we are distracted. See ibid, especially 25.

it anyway, consciously disregarding the risk she knows she is posing to other users of the highway,

Claire's culpability is between a case of true negligence exemplified by Cheryl and a case of undisputed recklessness exemplified by Jane. Perhaps we can offer a tentative explanation of why her culpability lies on this boundary. To do so, begin by asking why a person who knowingly causes harm is more culpable than a person who knowingly creates a mere risk of the same type of harm. Although no general theory of culpability has attracted a consensus among criminal law theorists, one plausible perspective on this matter appeals to counterfactuals: the person who knowingly causes only a risk of harm might well have changed his behaviour had he realized the risk would materialize.[25] By contrast, the defendant who knowingly causes harm already demonstrates through his behaviour what he would do in the very circumstances in which the reckless defendant might have done otherwise. If we are tempted by this line of argument, we might be able to show why Claire's case should be contrasted from those of Cheryl and Jane. Claire's culpability should be distinguished from that of defendants like Cheryl, who satisfy none of the criteria of belief because the conduct of the latter might have changed had she held the same beliefs as Claire. By contrast, defendants like Jane who hold an occurent belief that their conduct is risky have already demonstrated by their behaviour what they would do in the very circumstances in which Cheryl and Claire might have done otherwise.

The following tentative hypothesis emerges from recognizing that Claire's degree of blame is less than Jane's but greater than Cheryl's: a defendant deserves less blame to the extent that her belief becomes more and more distant from an occurrent belief.[26] As beliefs recede from actual consciousness, persons have greater difficulty bringing them to bear on their practical reasoning, and eventually are unable to do so at all. This hypothesis places the relative culpability of the foregoing drivers in the correct order: Jane, Claire, and Cheryl, from highest to lowest. Of course, the law must draw relatively sharp boundaries. As long as we work with only two culpable states from which to choose, we are stuck with the problem of whether to conceptualize the culpable state of Claire as closer to undisputed recklessness (eg, Jane) or to true negligence (eg, Cheryl).

We might hazard different responses to this difficulty. First, we might add a third culpable state between that of Jane and Cheryl. This culpable state would be less than undisputed recklessness but greater than true negligence (which might well involve no culpability whatever).[27] This solution has the obvious advantage of not forcing us to pigeonhole Claire's culpability into one of two existing categories. Unfortunately, it adds

[25] See KW Simons, 'Rethinking Mental States' (1992) 72 Boston University Law Review 463, especially 497–8.

[26] This hypothesis makes the controversial assumption that beliefs are distant from actual consciousness along a single dimension.

[27] Nothing I have written bears on the fundamental question of whether and under what circumstances persons are liable for true negligence. For thoughts on this basic issue, see H Smith, 'Non-Tracing Cases of Culpable Ignorance' (2011) 5 Criminal Law and Philosophy 115.

complexity to the law that would further strain the capacities of jurors.[28] Moreover, if we concede that culpability belongs on a continuum as beliefs deviate further and further from occurrent mental states, why should we stop at three? Soon we would face pressure to expand the number of culpable states still more.

An even more radical possibility is that the means by which positive law distinguishes manslaughter from negligent homicide—which depends on whether or not defendants believe they have created a risk—is defective and should be replaced by some other device to mark the contrast. In other words, the presence or absence of belief may not be the most salient factor in assessing relative culpability. If it is so difficult to decide whether given defendants do or do not believe they have created a risk, we have ample incentive to rethink whether the problem is worth trying to solve. I have some sympathy for this position. The task, of course, is to defend a preferable device to contrast recklessness from negligence—a device that does not depend on whether the defendant has or lacks a particular tacit belief. I cannot pursue this formidable task here—even if I were confident about how to do so.[29]

My reservations notwithstanding, I claim to have described a criterion that supports a finding of recklessness and thus of criminal liability in (some) cases of distraction. We have reason to believe that Claire, who satisfies at least some of the appropriate dispositional criteria for tacitly believing she has created a risk, is reckless rather than negligent. We certainly have more reason to hold Claire to be reckless when she causes a risk through distraction than to hold Joe to be reckless when he causes a risk through forgetfulness. Forgetfulness and distraction pose distinct issues. But I have not insisted that my arguments for holding Claire to be reckless are demonstrably sound. I have described some of the challenges that must be met to sustain my conclusion. Finally and perhaps most importantly, I agree that Ashworth is correct to conclude that not all examples of distracted behaviour can be resolved by a simple, single analysis.

[28] See FX Shen et al, 'Sorting Guilty Minds' (2011) 86 New York University Law Review 1306.

[29] An even more extreme alternative is to deny that moral or criminal responsibility requires the sort of control involved in practical reasoning. For a rival to voluntary control theories of responsibility, see A Smith, 'Control, Responsibility, and Moral Assessment' (2008) 138 Philosophical Studies 367.

7

On Justifications and Excuses

*Andrew Simester**

Substantively and evidentially, the criminal law draws a distinction between offences and defences. If a person satisfies the specified *actus reus* and *mens rea* elements of an offence, prima facie she commits the offence. But a prima facie offence will not be a crime if the defendant has a supervening defence, ie a defence that denies neither *actus reus* nor *mens rea* but, rather, seeks to avoid liability by reference to accompanying considerations not contemplated in those elements of the offence definition. A person commits no assault, for example, when she uses reasonable force to protect herself when attacked. She may commit the prima facie offence, but criminal liability does not follow.[1]

That legal distinction, between offence and defence, often tracks a corresponding moral distinction. Suppose that D has a duty not to ϕ. If D ϕs, she commits a *pro tanto* wrong. Yet, even if she ϕs intentionally, it may not follow that D is culpable for ϕing. Additional factors can preclude that conclusion.

Not always. Within the criminal law, certain supervening defences have no implications for an agent's culpability. Claims of statutory limitation or diplomatic immunity, for example, oust the defendant from the realm of the pertinent court, without further moral evaluation. Even so, many such 'defences' operate better as procedural bars to trial than as defences in their own right. And it comes as no surprise to find that Andrew Ashworth has made a leading contribution to untangling all these defences.[2] As so often, his characteristically principled approach

* Grateful thanks are due to Bob Sullivan and Andreas von Hirsch for comments on an earlier draft of this essay.

[1] Admittedly, there is a line of authority in the common law to the effect that she does not even commit a prima facie offence, purportedly on the grounds that the *actus reus* of assault requires 'unlawful' force. For criticism of that approach, see AP Simester, 'Mistakes in Defence' (1992) 12 OJLS 295.

[2] A Ashworth, 'Testing Fidelity to Legal Values: Official Involvement and Criminal Justice' in S Shute and AP Simester (eds), *Criminal Law Theory: Doctrines of the General Part* (Oxford: Oxford University Press, 2002), 299. On 'non-exculpatory' defences generally, see eg PH Robinson, *Structure and Function in Criminal Law* (Oxford: Oxford University Press, 1997), 71 ff. Certain kinds of privileges can only operate as substantive defences: one controversial example is consent (where it operates as a defence, rather than an element of the *actus reus*), eg to bodily injury under the Singaporean Penal Code, s 87.

unlocks the philosophical underpinnings of our legal doctrines, illuminating how those foundations can, and should, inform the criminal law.

The mainstream criminal defences are therefore a subset of the supervening. They speak distinctively to the grounds for withholding blame from a defendant who ϕs. This essay concerns how they do so.

In particular, the essay addresses the differences between justifications and excuses, their respective characters and basic structures. I will argue in what follows that justifications and 'rationale-based' excuses such as duress are fundamentally similar, and that their differences have relatively few implications for the criminal law. It is often claimed that justifications are 'about the act' and excuses 'about the actor': but they are about both—and equally so. Both rationale-based excuses and justifications are personal, and impersonal, alike to the actor. While their differences track a categorical moral distinction about the normative status of an agent's conduct—and in that much I will side with those who contend that justification has priority over excuse—the main driver of that difference is whether the agent's rationale for acting was, or was not, what Raz calls an 'excluded' reason. If not excluded, a justification may well lie. Even if excluded, it may ground an excuse. So there are key differences in how, morally speaking, the defendant's rationale is relevant to her exculpation. But that same rationale leads in either case to blameless acquittal. The starting point is the same. The end point is the same. There are some idiosyncratic stop signs, as we shall see. But basically, the difference is the routes. So, I will claim, there is no fundamental difference of output in the criminal law, at least for individual defendants. Rather, from the perspective of the law, the main differential consequence regards actions by the state. State action may be justifiable, but it is inexcusable.

1. Four Kinds of Exculpatory Defences

First, however, it is helpful to begin by separating out the four main kinds of exculpatory defences. Traditionally, theorists have subdivided them just once, into 'justifications' and 'excuses', although that pattern is starting to change. In what follows, I propose to separate the excuses into three distinct classes.

The first class of defences is often called 'excuses', but for clarity I will term it *irresponsibility* defences.[3] These defences are predicated on a denial of the defendant's moral responsibility for ϕing. They recognize her inadequacy as an agent capable of moral deliberation, one able to process and apply moral reasoning to her ϕing. Rather than seeking to give any exculpatory explanation of the defendant's choice to ϕ, defences such as insanity and infancy take the defendant out of the realm of moral agents.[4] These kinds of defences are *context-insensitive*, in as much as

[3] The leading articulation of this distinction is J Gardner, 'The Gist of Excuses' in *Offenses and Defences* (Oxford: Oxford University Press, 2007), Ch 6.

[4] Admittedly, the criminal-law version of these defences does not always capture well the underlying moral phenomenon. Notoriously, under the M'Naghten Rules, D may be quite mad yet fail to qualify

their availability is independent of the nature of the action, its appropriateness, and proportionality to the occasion. Irresponsibility defences are capacity-based. As such, they contain no requirement of reasonableness, no evaluation of the defendant with respect to her action. They do not speak to culpability assessments. They simply don't get that far.

Like all the exculpatory defences, irresponsibility defences are act-specific. A condition of insanity is exculpating only in so far as the defendant's condition affects his moral responsibility for the relevant action. Even a radically psychotic killer may be perfectly competent to buy groceries or obey the traffic laws. Irresponsibility can also come in degrees, something implicitly acknowledged by the modern defence of diminished responsibility. More general defences, such as infancy, draw only very rough lines, marking a boundary where, typically, actors are thought to have sufficient capacities for moral reasoning to be counted as morally responsible agents, so that formal assessments of culpability are appropriate.

It is important, though not always done, to keep irresponsibility defences apart from the next two main classes of defences, which are *rationale-based*. Irresponsibility defences may help to explain how it was that something came to be done, but there is an important sense in which they do not address *why* it was done. By contrast, a rationale-based defence affirms D's responsibility for her action and articulates the reasons why she did it. The rationale-based defences are choice-based explanations of *pro tanto* wrongdoing. They are predicated upon the reasons for which D deliberately acted as she did.

In turn, for D's explanation to exculpate, her reasons must either *justify* or *excuse* her ϕing. It is the narrower class of rationale-based excuses that is, in many ways, like justifications rather than like irresponsibility defences. This point is obscured when irresponsibility defences are also called 'excuses'. John Austin, for example, characterized justification as an acceptance of responsibility alongside a denial that the action was bad; whereas, he said, excuses 'admit that it was bad but don't accept full, or even any, responsibility'.[5] Similarly, George Fletcher states that claims of justification 'challenge whether the act is wrongful; claims of excuse concede that the act was wrongful, but seek to avoid the attribution of the act to the actor'.[6] Not so. Irresponsibility defences speak to whether the actor is morally 'accountable', or fully morally responsible, for her act. Rationale-based excuses don't. They speak to culpability. Thus the *basic* distinction is between irresponsibility and rationale-based defences, rather than between justifications and excuses. In *Principles of Criminal Law*, Ashworth rightly treats the former in a separate chapter.[7] Unlike irresponsibility defences, both justifications and rationale-based excuses are context-dependent, in that their exculpatory power depends on the nature and

as legally insane, and vice versa. For critical discussion, see AP Simester, JR Spencer, GR Sullivan, and GJ Virgo, *Simester and Sullivan's Criminal Law: Theory and Doctrine* (4th edn, Oxford: Hart Publishing, 2010) §§ 19.1, 22.2(i) and references there cited.

[5] JL Austin, 'A Plea for Excuses' (1956) 57 Proceedings of the Aristotelian Society 1, 3.

[6] GP Fletcher, *Rethinking Criminal Law* (Boston: Little, Brown and Co, 1978), 759.

[7] A Ashworth, *Principles of Criminal Law* (6th edn, Oxford: Oxford University Press, 2009), § 5.2 (insanity) and Ch 6 (excuses); contrast earlier editions, where both were handled in Ch 6.

seriousness of D's action, as well as upon the circumstances in which it was committed. This is why all true justifications and excuses contain some form of proportionality or reasonableness condition, some element that imposes an objective constraint upon D's claim to exculpation. (For convenience of expression, in what follows I will generally use 'excuses' as shorthand for rationale-based excuses.)

The fourth class of defences is mistake-based. I use 'mistake' here loosely, to include other forms of inadvertence or ignorance. However, I do not mean to suggest that mistakes are necessarily a matter of supervening defences at all. Where a mistake concerns an element of the *actus reus*, it is very likely to result in an absence of *mens rea*. Suppose that I am in a jungle, where I see what I think is a dangerous animal about to attack.[8] I shoot and injure the creature. Unfortunately, the 'creature' turns out to be a human being, stumbling about lost. In such a case, there is no 'defence' of mistake. I am not guilty of any kind of assault or malicious wounding, simply because I lack *mens rea*.[9]

As with law, so with morality. Before we get to the realm of exculpatory moral explanations, a positive case of (*pro tanto*) culpability for one's ϕing must be established. Mistaken ϕing rules out choice-based culpability, and falls to be considered under negligence.[10] It may or may not be culpable. But whether it is culpable is not a question for the exculpatory defences. By contrast, mistake-based *defences* are parasitic. They involve mistakes that concern elements of a rationale-based defence: where, if the mistaken belief were true, the defendant's choice to ϕ would have been justified or excused.

Mistakes can themselves be justified or excused.[11] Either way, they are not like primary mistakes that lead a defendant to ϕ inadvertently, and the law should treat them differently. Or so I have argued elsewhere.[12] In this essay, however, my main concern is with the second and third classes of defence. Given their basic similarity, obvious questions arise. In particular, what is the difference between a justification and an excuse, and why does it matter?

[8] See eg *State Government of Madhya Pradesh v Rangaswami* AIR 1952 Nag 268, 1951 Cri LJ 1191 (tiger); *Waryam Singh v Emperor* AIR 1926 Lah 554 (ghost).

[9] cf the analysis in the controversial case of *Morgan* [1976] AC 182, 214 (HL), on a charge of rape which then required awareness of the risk of non-consent: 'Once one has accepted, what seems to me abundantly clear, that the prohibited act in rape is non-consensual sexual intercourse, and that the guilty state of mind is an intention to commit it, it seems to me to follow as a matter of inexorable logic that there is no room either for a "defence" of honest belief or mistake . . . Either the prosecution proves that the accused had the requisite intent, or it does not.'

[10] On these two distinct, positive grounds of culpability, see AP Simester, 'A Disintegrated Theory of Culpability' in DJ Baker and J Horder (eds), *The Legacy of Glanville Williams: The Sanctity of Life and the Criminal Law* (Cambridge: Cambridge University Press, 2012).

[11] eg, a mistake may be made for good reasons (a justified mistake; *not* justified ϕing) or, say, because D was understandably distracted by news of his mother's death (excused). This is to disagree with John Gardner's claim that 'the structure of excuse [including mistake-based defences] derives from the structure of justification. To excuse an action is not, of course, to justify that action. Rather, one justifies one's belief that the action was justified.' Gardner, n 3 above, 110. But I cannot pursue the point here.

[12] Simester, n 1 above.

2. Distinguishing Justification from Excuse

A justified action is a morally appropriate response to the circumstances and is, for that reason, permissible. D has a justification when his reasons for ϕing are sufficient to defeat those that militate against ϕing, so that ϕing is morally permitted. Permitted, not tolerated. Douglas Husak suggests that 'an act is permissible when it is tolerated'.[13] That may be true—legally speaking. Not morally. Something that is morally permissible does not call for toleration, because there is nothing wrong with it. One can only tolerate something that one considers to be wrongful.[14] Justified ϕing is not like that. It may be harmful in some way. It may generate reasons for regret. But where it is morally justified, ϕing is not, all things considered, wrongful.

Notice that the foregoing definition takes account of D's own reasons. In putting it this way, I am embracing a thesis that, for reasons of space, cannot be defended here:[15] that justification depends upon D's actual or 'subjective' reasons for ϕing, and not solely[16] upon any guiding—'objective'—reasons that are in fact available to justify ϕing.[17] Hence it is not sufficient that ϕing be justifi*able* in the circumstances. D's own reasons must themselves be valid,[18] and sufficient, for D's act of ϕing to be justi*fied*.

For convenience, let me call this the motivational thesis. While controversial,[19] its validity will be assumed here. In any case, that debate concerns the scope of reasons eligible to justify D's ϕing. The important point to start with is that, whatever reasons are treated as eligible, justification requires those reasons to be sufficient. They must pass an evaluative, objective,[20] test of whether, taken as a whole, they supply D with good reasons to ϕ. Overall, they must defeat, or at least

[13] 'On the Supposed Priority of Justification to Excuse' in D Husak (ed), *The Philosophy of Criminal Law: Selected Essays* (Oxford: Oxford University Press, 2010), 287, 296–7.

[14] See eg P King, *Toleration* (New York: St Martin's Press, 1976), 44–54; J Raz, 'Autonomy, Toleration, and the Harm Principle' in R Gavison (ed), *Issues in Contemporary Legal Philosophy* (Oxford: Oxford University Press, 1987), 313.

[15] Elsewhere, see AP Simester, 'Why Distinguish Intention from Foresight' in AP Simester and ATH Smith (eds), *Harm and Culpability* (Oxford: Clarendon Press, 1996), 71, 87 ff; AP Simester, 'Wrongs and Reasons' (2009) 72 MLR 648, 659–63.

[16] Or even primarily (contra Gardner): Simester (2009), ibid.

[17] The terminology of 'guiding' reasons invokes the distinction drawn by Raz between guiding (objective, applicable-in-fact) and explanatory (subjective, motivating) reasons: J Raz, *Practical Reasons and Norms* (2nd edn, Princeton: Princeton University Press, 1990), 16–20.

[18] Conversely, it is not, therefore, a purely subjective test.

[19] The so-called *Dadson* debate: (1850) 2 Den 35. For a contrary view, see PH Robinson, 'Competing Theories of Justification: Deeds versus Reasons' in AP Simester and ATH Smith (eds), *Harm and Culpability* (Oxford: Oxford University Press, 1996), 45.

[20] This should not be read to mean that the validity and weight of reasons—and thus the range of what is morally permissible—is universal rather than society-independent; or even that it is independent of law. The point here is simply that the evaluation of D's reasons is not up to D. In criminal law, it is a matter for the court: contra *Scarlett* [1993] 4 All ER 629 (CA).

match, the reasons D has not to ϕ. They must make it morally okay—or as Greenawalt puts it, warranted—to ϕ.[21]

No such requirement exists for excuses. That said, there is a tendency to relegate excuses to a catch-all dustbin. Expressed most generally, D can be said to have an excuse if the reasons why he ϕs are such that he is not culpable for doing so. Unfortunately, while that definition is appealingly simple, it can be applied more-or-less to all four kinds of the exculpatory defences we identified earlier, and certainly to justifications. No surprise, then, that writers tend to add a proviso that excused conduct is unjustified, or that they sometimes conflate irresponsibility defences with rationale-based excuses.

Excuses differ from irresponsibility defences in that they address D's own reasons for action, not his capacity for reasoning. D's ϕing is excusable if, in choosing to ϕ, he exhibits no shortcoming of a kind that grounds blame—no shortfall of the character or moral judgement that we should expect of an ordinary, decent person. D need not be perfect. We all have limitations, even decent folk. Exoneration requires only that the limitations explaining why D ϕed be normal ones, ones that do not reflect badly on D. Perhaps supererogation was possible. Perhaps D could have exhibited abnormal levels of altruism, etc, and refrained from ϕing. But blame does not turn on D's failure to merit praise. It requires that he fall short, not of standards of perfection, but of standards of reasonableness. And excuses require only that his failings be, so to speak, understandable or reasonable ones.

Like justifications, and unlike the irresponsibility defences, all rationale-based excuses therefore require that D's reasons for ϕing be subjected to evaluative assessment. Moreover, the assessment is not relativized to any personal limitations of virtue that the defendant might have. The difference lies in the conclusion of that assessment. When justified, there is no moral error—it is morally okay for D to ϕ. In the case of excuse, D is not culpable for ϕing even though ϕing may not be okay. Any moral error by D is understandable, the kind of error that a decent person might well make.

The priority thesis

Put this way, justifications and excuses can overlap. Legally speaking, that presents no problem. Redundancy is possible in the law's schema of rationale-based defences. Suppose that Frances shoots and injures George, her attacker. Frances may qualify for overlapping defences of self-defence, necessity, and duress. Under the legal heading of duress, we may acquit her because she acted in response to a threat of death. At the same time, Frances may avail herself of a lesser-evils necessity

[21] K Greenawalt, 'The Perplexing Borders of Justification and Excuse' (1984) 84 Columbia Law Review 1897, 1903. I hesitate to adopt Greenawalt's terminology, mainly because his account does not distinguish between warranted and entitled (see especially the discussion at 1904–5). Sometimes, it is permissible to act wrongfully—a matter of rights and liberties, not justification. I am not concerned with such cases here.

defence: it is better that injury be suffered than that death result. Even more aptly, her act qualifies as a legitimate use of proportional force in self-defence.

This kind of doctrinal overlap shows only that the legal categories are somewhat rough-and-ready, and there is nothing wrong with that. Allowing multiple defences in a particular situation is an instance of complementariness rather than contradiction, partly because the verdict is the same either way: acquittal, provided at least one defence is made out. In practice, if the same facts are relied on to establish a justification and an excuse, the former is normally treated in court as supervening over the latter. We should ask, however, whether that practice tracks the underlying moral categories. Duress is paradigmatically (though not necessarily) excusatory,[22] self-defence justificatory. Can one really be simultaneously justified and excused? Or is there supervenience in morality too? Should we accept the widely held *priority thesis* (or more properly, *theses*): that justifications and excuses are mutually exclusive, with the former taking priority over the latter?[23]

In principle, one's being attacked can generate both justificatory and excusatory grounds for exculpation. The fear of death may make D's response understandable, whether or not permissible. Normally, where his response is also justified, there will be a convergence, so that the very reasons that tend to excuse will simultaneously support D's justification. But consider Doug Husak's example, where the two remain separate:[24]

> [Case I] Suppose, for example, that a defendant is threatened with serious bodily harm unless he inflicts a somewhat greater harm on the next person to walk into his office. By chance, this next person happens to be a personal enemy who begins to attack the defendant. In this example, the defendant has two independent, sufficient[25] reasons to inflict personal injury, each of which constitutes a defense from liability. His first reason, duress, is generally categorized as an excuse; his second reason, self-defense, is almost always categorized as a justification.

Assuming that D acts for both reasons, he is at once justified and excused.

Husak intends this as a counterexample to the priority thesis. Specifically, his example undermines the claim of mutual exclusivity. Notice, however, that in Husak's scenario the excuse and the justification are predicated on concurrent but independent reasons. It is, in that sense, a special case. It shows that justifications and excuses are not just act-specific but rationale-dependent. If D acts for multiple rationales, some of those rationales may (individually or collectively) be sufficient to justify the action, while others may excuse without justifying. By contrast, those who claim that justifications and excuses are mutually exclusive are usually

[22] As is implicit in the case of Frances and George, the legal criteria of duress can include scenarios where D's response is justified. My concern here is not with the legal defences as such.

[23] See D Husak, 'On the Supposed Priority of Justification to Excuse' in *The Philosophy of Criminal Law: Selected Essays* (Oxford: Oxford University Press, 2010), 287, 287–90 for a large collection of priority thesis supporters.

[24] Ibid, 298–9 (footnotes omitted).

[25] I take it here that Husak means sufficient in a motivational sense.

concerned with defences that arise out of the very same rationale. Let us vary the hypothetical:

[Case II] E is threatened with serious bodily harm by F, a personal enemy, and realises that the only way to save himself will be by inflicting a somewhat greater harm on F. When F walks into E's office and begins to attack E, E has one sufficient reason to inflict personal injury, which constitutes a defence from liability.

The excusatory force of case II seems no less than in case A. Yet most theorists would straightforwardly regard E as being justified *rather than* excused. The very reason why E acts is sufficient to make her conduct permissible, and not (merely) non-culpable.

Perhaps there is no harm in saying, with Husak, that E is both justified and excused in this case. But to the extent that 'excused' means something distinct from 'not culpable', it is misleading to describe E's defence as an excuse. Excuses do meaningful moral work only when they do not render the agent's conduct permissible; when they relate to an unjustified wrongful act. Suppose, this time:

[Case III] T credibly threatens to kill G's family unless G inflicts a substantial harm on the next person to walk into his office. G attacks and seriously injures that person, V.

This case *is* one of excuse. Despite his rationale, G's conduct remains wrongful—it is not permissible. Yet we should be reluctant to fault him. Notwithstanding that G's reason for acting was (objectively speaking) inadequate, it is understandable that G should have acted for that reason. Even a decent person might, like G, have attacked V out of fear for his family's lives. As such, we cannot make the inference of culpability that would normally entitle us to blame G for her actions. Hence, an excuse.

All this suggests that we need to refine the definition of rationale-based excuses with which we began. An agent's rationale for ϕing is—distinctively—excusatory when it establishes that he is not culpable for ϕing, without sufficing (either alone or in tandem with any other reasons why the agent ϕed) to make ϕing permissible. In the same vein, a partial excuse ameliorates his culpability for ϕing while falling short of full exculpation.[26]

This reformulation is compatible with the mutual exclusivity thesis. Moreover, it survives Husak's counterexample in case I.

The reformulation also maintains the priority of justification over excuse. Intuitively, within the realm of rationale-based defences, most of us would rather be justified than (merely) excused in our actions. Better not to make the moral error at all than to do so understandably, and blamelessly. Yet this second aspect of the priority thesis is also denied by Husak, who sees 'no general reason why a defendant should prefer to be acquitted on the ground that his behaviour is [permissible] than because he is excused'.[27] He offers two intuitive counterexamples. Here is the first:[28]

[26] Thus the law's distinction between substantive partial excuses and post-conviction culpability-related mitigation is primarily operational. It does not reflect a fundamental moral distinction.

[27] Husak, n 23 above, 297. [28] Ibid.

> Smith and Jones deliberately inflict a fairly serious but not life-threatening injury on White. Imagine that the story is embellished in either of two ways. In the first scenario, Smith's behaviour is barely tolerable, although no one would regard it as commendable. Suppose White is a deranged thief who is escaping with Smith's television set. Smith's act, I assume, is permissible and thereby justified. In the second scenario, Jones is well below the age of criminal responsibility, and injures White in a schoolyard brawl. Even if Jones has not acted in self-defense, I assume he is excused. From a moral point of view, why should we conclude that Smith's defense is superior to that of Jones?

Quite. But notice that Jones's defence is one of irresponsibility, not rationale-based. Irresponsibility defences are logically prior to rationale-based defences, to *both* justifications and excuses. Whether or not a defendant might prefer them, they come first. Only responsible actors can claim rationale- or mistake-based defences. By the same token, however, Husak's first example cannot establish that justifications lack priority over rationale-based excuses. Neither can his second hypothetical:[29]

> Perhaps I am permitted to push someone from a plank to save myself.[30] Suppose further that mistakes about justifications, even when reasonable, give rise to an excuse rather than a justification. Perhaps I am excused when I falsely but reasonably believe that I must push a single individual from a lifeboat to save two others. Again, why think that the justification casts the agent in a better moral light than the excuse?

Again, the comparison is with a different category of supervening defence. It is telling, I think, that Husak does *not* offer an intuitive example comparing a justification with a genuine rationale-based excuse. And it remains hard to see, within the realm of rationale-based defences, why one wouldn't prefer to be justified than excused: to not be in the wrong at all.

3. Operational Implications

Why else would it matter whether one is justified or excused? Partly, because justifications and excuses operate internally in different ways. Hence, even as an agent may be excused without being justified, she may be justified without being excused (or in rare cases such as Husak's, both). Their border-lines are not merely fuzzy. They are not even contiguous. To see all this, however, we need to expose two common myths.

The difference is one of degree?

It is sometimes envisaged that justifications and excuses lie on an exculpatory spectrum, or continuum, of explanation, where the difference is one of degree. According to Clarkson, for example:[31]

[29] Ibid. [30] For simplicity, I assume that Husak envisages repulsion rather than expulsion.
[31] C Clarkson, 'Necessary Action: A New Defence' [2004] Crim LR 81, 85.

> ... in reality there is a continuum of pressurised conduct with it being impossible to distinguish clearly ... It becomes a question of judgment as to when understandable reasons become sufficient ones.

On this view, justification is essentially *more* exculpatory: where the reasons D has to ϕ are stronger than they are when D is excused, so much so that their conduct crosses not merely a first threshold of being non-culpable but a second, higher one of being genuinely okay. Conversely, one might say, of a person who offers a very bad reason for ϕing, that the person is 'not excused let alone justified'.

This way of thinking about the difference is misleading because the exculpatory force of reasons works differently for justifications than it does for excuses; and the difference is one of kind rather than degree. What counts for justification is whether D's reasons were good ones, ones that defeated those militating against her ϕing. Determining that is an evaluative matter, involving the logic of practical reasons. It is also an all-or-nothing matter: the justification either succeeds, defeating the counter-reasons not to ϕ, or it doesn't. Either ϕing is permitted, or it is not. Justification does not come in degrees.[32]

By contrast, when considering whether D is excused, we do not assess *whether* D acted wrongfully, but why. Our concern lies not with the objective, practical quality of D's reasons, but with why D came to act upon them and what vices, if any, he displayed in doing so. Sometimes there may be a connection. Wrongful acts can be more excusable when they came very close to being justified.[33] Indeed, this is one reason why the law should not test the proportionality of a self-defensive act 'on jeweller's scales';[34] because some misjudgement, especially in emergencies, is likely anyway to be excusable. So the objective force of a guiding reason to ϕ will sometimes be relevant to the question whether D fell short in acting on it.

Typically, however, excuses admit of grounds for exculpation quite apart from the guiding reasons for action themselves. In the case of provocation, D has no valid reason to kill his victim. Yet he is understandably—even rightly—angry. We recognize how it was that he came to attack the victim, overreacting in a manner that even a reasonable person might have done. D's response remains impermissible, and indeed culpable, but the explanation diminishes his culpability.

Notice that there is no element of justification about the killing here *at all*. When Ashworth states that provocation rests on a 'partial justification',[35] I do not take him to be denying this. Perhaps some other aggressive but less serious response by D would have been justified; and the reasons why so are relevant to the excusatory power of the case. But to accept that is not to admit that D has any kind of 'partial reason' to kill.

[32] Contra Husak, n 23 above, 302–3. But Husak does not show how an action can be partially permissible.

[33] Not always: especially when the counter-considerations are authoritatively excluded (itself, perhaps, a finely balanced matter). One familiar example is the legal status of euthanasia.

[34] cf *Reed v Wastie* [1972] Crim LR 221 (DC).

[35] A Ashworth, 'The Doctrine of Provocation' (1976) 35 CLJ 292, 307.

The same can hold even for full excuses, such as duress—which is one reason why it is a mistake to think that there is an underlying relationship between excusing duress and justifying necessity.[36] Suppose that a terrorist organization bursts into a house and threatens to shoot E's family unless he assists to murder V, a policeman.[37] In terms of justification, it is irrelevant here that V is elderly and, say, in the early stages of a terminal illness. It is irrelevant because the terrorist threat supplies E with *no valid reason at all* to kill V. This is implicit in V's having a right to life. That right invalidates certain kinds of reasons. It excludes from consideration many factors that might otherwise seem to favour killing V,[38] such as the benefit to E's family. The existence of those benefits adds no weight to any objective, justificatory case for killing V. They cannot be weighed up against V's life when deciding what is permissible.

E has no claim to justification, not even the beginnings of one. Morally speaking,[39] however, he has an excuse. Even though E has no sufficient grounds for preferring the lives of his family to those of policemen, it is quite understandable that he should act as if he does. It is quite understandable that the 'reason' was good enough for him. That same rationale, irrelevant to his justification, is central to his excuse. In being motivated to comply with the terrorists' threat, E does not fall short of the qualities we expect in a decent person. Indeed, in caring about his family's welfare so much, he demonstrates a virtue rather than vice.[40]

It can readily be seen from this that excuses involve a quite separate kind of inquiry. Excuse is no mere shadow of justification. Moreover, as the provocation example shows, excuses can come in degrees. They may diminish culpability even when they do not cancel it. And one's degree of excuse may be independent of the force of one's claim to justification. Unjustified actions, by contrast, are unjustified *tout court.*

Still more tellingly, it is possible for actions to be justified without being excusable. That occurred in *Re A (Children)*,[41] in which the Court of Appeal ruled that it would be lawful for surgeons to separate conjoined twins, even though the known consequence was that one twin would die within minutes.[42] Here, the

[36] cf the so-called 'duress of circumstances' cases in English law: AP Simester et al, n 4 above, § 20.1(ii).

[37] A variant on *DPP for Northern Ireland v Lynch* [1975] AC 653 (HL).

[38] Though not all: it may be a valid and unexcluded reason to shoot V that doing so will protect D's family from attack *by V*. Implicit in this analysis is the crucial importance of 'excluded' reasons for understanding the difference between justifying and excusatory rationales. See Raz, n 17 above, § 1.2. For elaboration of this point in the context of necessity and duress, see AP Simester, 'Necessity, Torture and the Rule of Law' in V Ramraj (ed), *Emergencies and the Limits of Legality* (Cambridge: Cambridge University Press, 2008), 289, § II.

[39] Not legally, as the common law stands: *Howe* [1987] AC 417 (HL).

[40] The example shows that excuses, as well as justifications, can be role-related. Cf *Hasan* [2005] UKHL 22, [2005] 2 AC 467 at [21(3)], restricting the scope of duress to threats directed at those close to the defendant.

[41] [2001] Fam 147 (CA).

[42] The 'weaker' twin's own heart and lungs were inadequate to sustain her life, and would fail within minutes upon separation. She was incapable of independent existence. Unfortunately, the heart of the other twin was not strong enough to sustain both lives: inevitably, both would die within a few months if left conjoined.

question for the Court turned on whether such an operation by the surgeon would be justified: does the case for protecting one life warrant an intervention that kills the other? Otherwise, however, the surgeon has no possibility of an excuse. There is no factor here, apart from the very claim to justification, available to exculpate the deliberate killing of one twin. This is not a scenario where morally erroneous action occurs in an emergency, under pressure of circumstances, threats, or other motivating factors which might make wrongdoing understandable. To operate in such a case is to take morality into one's own hands, as it were. Like the rule of law, the rule of morality requires that doing so be justified, not excused. The reasons supporting a justification, therefore, have no necessary implication for the question whether one is excused. The two overlap but do not dovetail.

Justifications are repeatable, and about the act; excuses are ad hoc, and personal to the actor?

Let us turn now to the second myth. It is often said that justifications are about the act, and excuses about the actor.[43] Justifications apply to actions that others in like circumstances could legitimately perform, whereas we would hope or even expect other actors to refrain from repeating a person's excused act.[44]

That distinction works well when applied to irresponsibility defences, which are paradigmatically personal. Insanity, infancy, and the like accommodate incapacities that are particular to the defendant. They do not purport to say anything more generally about the defendant's conduct. But the same distinction does not hold for the rationale-based defences.

Even so, there is a grain of truth in it. Not a bushel. The truth resides in the fact that, to justify her ϕing, D's reasons for acting must be sufficient objectively, qua valid guiding reasons. But it does not follow that D's objective reasons for action are independent of D or of D's circumstances. It is *D's act of ϕing* that must be justified, not ϕing in general. For those who embrace the motivational thesis of justification, this requires that D herself act for the reasons that make her ϕing permissible.[45] Moreover, there are other ways in which the applicability of justifying reasons can depend in part on the actor. A mother may have reasons to discipline her child that others do not. Alternatively, suppose that P launches a violent attack on E, in circumstances where E can easily fend P off. E may not be entitled to use pre-emptive force that F, who is less mobile or strong, would have been permitted to use. Justifications are personal too.

[43] cf J Dressler, *Understanding Criminal Law* (3rd edn, Newark, NJ: Lexis Publishing, 2001), 202–3; Fletcher, n 6 above, 761–2; D Husak, 'Justifications and the Criminal Liability of Accessories' (1989) 80 Journal of Criminal Law and Criminology 494, 496–7; PH Robinson, *Criminal Law Defenses* (St Paul, MN: West Publishing Co, 1984), vol 1, 100–1.

[44] eg Greenawalt, n 21 above, 1915: 'Justifications typically arise out of the nature of the actor's situation, excuses out of the actor's personal characteristics.' Greenawalt himself recognizes difficulties with this 'basic distinction', although his analysis is affected by a failure to segregate irresponsibility defences from rationale-based excuses.

[45] See above.

To accommodate these points, one might clarify the claim that justification is about acts by allowing that it is ϕing in the same circumstances (including D's role, physical capacities,[46] and the like) that is repeatable.

Yet, once the claim is clarified, we can see that it applies to excuses too. Excuses are themselves subject to restrictions that are external to the agent; and to that extent, they are susceptible to generalization. In other words, excuses are impersonal too. To say that D is excused is to say that *anyone* in the same circumstances (including D's role, physical capacities, and the like) would be excused—because they have not fallen short of the standards of decency in action that undergird blame. It is *not* to say anything distinctive about D. The 'concession', if it be one, is to human beings as a whole, not to any frailty of the agent.[47] So it goes too far to say, as does Mitchell Berman, that 'a justified action is not criminal, whereas an excused defendant has committed a crime but is not punishable'.[48] Much too far. The excused defendant's action is wrongful. Indeed, it is unlawful (more on which below). But it is not criminal. Neither is the defendant a criminal.[49] What the law criminalizes, what it condemns, is not unjustified wrongdoing per se; but culpable unjustified wrongdoing.

Of course, this analysis of the exculpatory nature of excuses depends on D's motivation: but, according to the motivational thesis, that is equally true of justifications. Both justification and excuse start by asking why D ϕed, and subject D's reasons and circumstances to critical evaluation. If made out, both exculpate D. The difference lies only in what they are being evaluated for; what is the basis of exculpation.

Much the same goes for third-party interventions. Famously, one key distinction is said to be that, when D's ϕing is justified, bystanders may help her and should not interfere with her doing so. By contrast, if her ϕing is merely excused, others should not assist. Indeed, they may intervene to resist.[50]

That approach makes the mistake of over-abstraction, of objectifying justifications and excuses. *Both* are, in part, personal. Suppose that T is a bystander when P attacks Q. Whether T is justified in interfering to protect Q must be assessed with respect to T; is not determined by whether Q is permitted to shoot back at P. Here, it is *T's act of shooting P* (say) that must be justified. To be sure, the required analysis for each party overlaps, and the considerations that warrant Q's self-defensive response will also support T's intervention. But suppose that T does not know that P is attacking Q; he is an old enemy of P's and has sworn to shoot P on sight.

[46] I leave to one side the difficult question whether justification accommodates certain other types of limitation, such as intellectual capacities. I think it does, but cannot pursue that issue here.

[47] cf *Howe* [1987] AC 417, 432–5 (HL).

[48] M Berman, 'Justification and Excuse, Law and Morality' (2003) 53 Duke Law Journal 1, 4 (emphases omitted).

[49] Ibid, 18 ff, especially n 20.

[50] See eg PH Robinson, 'Competing Theories of Justification: Deeds versus Reasons' in AP Simester and ATH Smith (eds), *Harm and Culpability* (Oxford: Oxford University Press, 1996), 45, 59: 'Whether the deed is or is not actually justified is central to whether the law should allow it to be resisted.' Cf GP Fletcher, 'The Right and the Reasonable' (1985) 98 Harvard Law Review 949, 971 ff.

At least if one subscribes to the motivational thesis, T is not justified in shooting P, even though Q may be.[51]

Bootstrapping, authority, and lawfulness

Still, at least one practical consequence does attend the justification–excuse distinction. Because excuses address the culpability of an agent's reasons for acting wrongfully, they generally exclude reliance on the fact that ϕing can itself be excusable. D had better not choose to ϕ *because* she thinks she has an excuse. Agents who act under duress are exculpated because they act directly out of fear; not because they think it is blameless, let alone lawful, to do so. Within the criminal law, therefore, a defendant cannot rely on the legal status of her excuse as a motivation for her action. Excuses supply rules of adjudication, not rules of guidance for conduct.[52] They constitute grounds of exculpation; in the criminal law, of acquittal. They do not constitute reasons to ϕ. Justificatory reasons do. Hence, by contrast with exceptions, the lawfulness of a justification may be something the defendant is morally, and legally, permitted to consider.

This distinction affects other parts of the legal system: especially public law, where the divide between justification and excuse also matters to the lawfulness of one's action. In general, official action constituting a prima facie crime can only be lawful because justified, not because excused. Where ϕing is justified, it is permissible—ie, lawful. There is good (sufficient) reason to do it. Otherwise, the action is unlawful. There is no middle ground. Thus, from the point of view of public law, official torture remains inexcusable, even if we were to concede that it might (*possibly*) be justifiable.[53]

The generalization offered here applies to rationale-based defences, not to mistake-based defences. Actions by officials can be lawful, even law-creating, notwithstanding that they are predicated on mistakes. A policeman who arrests the wrong person can still effect a valid arrest. To a large extent this is a pragmatic matter, predicated on the need for officials to have decision-making powers that are authoritative. If we allow the validity of those decisions to be second-guessed whenever the official is mistaken, we undermine their very authority. So we cannot always require officials to be right. Yet that does not mean that decisions are, or should be, unimpeachable. Perhaps we can require their mistakes to be reasonable. Either way, however, we should deny that officials may choose to act wrongfully.

So far, this is a point about the lawfulness of ϕing. A stronger claim is that the state cannot be *exculpated* by excuses. If this stronger claim is right, it follows that

[51] The point that justifications are actor-specific also helps to create logical space for the possibility of conflicting justifications (contra Fletcher, ibid). I cannot explore that issue here.

[52] See eg PH Robinson, *Structure and Function in Criminal Law* (Oxford: Oxford University Press, 1997).

[53] See Simester, n 38 above, 300–3. I have sought here to clarify some aspects of that earlier discussion in the light of a very thoughtful essay by F Tanguay-Renaud, 'Puzzling about State Excuses as an Instance of Group Excuses' in RA Duff, L Farmer, S Marshall, and V Tadros (eds), *The Constitution of Criminal Law* (Oxford: Oxford University Press, 2012).

public wrongs such as official torture are conceptually inexcusable even in a criminal proceeding;[54] by contrast with a private act of torture, which might in principle—though surely rarely—be excusable.

We need to be careful about what the stronger claim entails. Ashworth has argued that, under the right-to-life provisions in Article 2 of the European Convention on Human Rights, state agents such as police officers should not be entitled to rely on unreasonable factual mistakes to found a successful claim of mistaken self-defence.[55] His argument is not that unreasonable mistakes should be disallowed for *all* agents when they generate perceived scenarios of self-defence.[56] It is that they should be disallowed specifically for police officers, soldiers, and the like. However, my stronger claim does not support that distinction. When a policeman, like anyone else, is tried for a crime, she is tried as an individual, qua subject-citizen, not qua state official. The conviction is personal, not official. There are, to be sure, some crimes that can only be committed by a state official (eg some forms of corruption), just as there are some crimes that can only be committed by factory owners, but in such cases the role is partly constitutive of the wrong. Self-defence contexts are not ones where the agent's official role is constitutive of the wrong. As such, officials are entitled to personal excuses and mistake-based defences too.

Still, the state itself can be a defendant. When it is, the stronger claim would allow justifications and deny it any excuses.

Two lines of thought support the stronger claim. The first is metaphysical. Suppose that we accept a theory of group agency whereby corporate organizations, including the state, are moral agents in their own right, whose choices and intentions are not reducible to those of individual, constituent human members.[57] The intentions, beliefs, and decisions of the organization are the upshot of an internal constitutional framework that co-ordinates the inputs of its various members in such a manner that the results distinctively belong to the organization, rather than to the individual members. On that account, the organization may be a moral agent; but it is not a human being. Indeed, it is not even quasi-human, in as much as the irreducible upshots that mark out the organization are essentially cognitive rather than affective. They do not seem to include the kinds of human 'frailties', such as the ability to experience and be motivated by fear, that underpin excuses. Rationale-based excuses are personal—one cannot experience them vicariously.

Needless to say, that line of objection rests on a controversial theory of corporate agency. It is circumnavigated by abandoning the idea that corporate organizations are autonomous moral agents. Instead, one might analyse corporate agency through some theory of identification with the acts and intentions of their members. In that

[54] As such, the excuse remains available in a criminal trial; where defendants are charged as individuals, not qua officials. Cf s 134(4) of the Criminal Justice Act 1988 (UK).

[55] *Principles of Criminal Law* (6th edn, Oxford: Oxford University Press, 2009), 124–5. See also F Leverick, *Killing in Self-Defence* (Oxford: Oxford University Press, 2006), Ch 10.

[56] *That* argument is made in Simester, n 1 above.

[57] See eg C List and P Pettit, *Group Agency: The Possibility, Design, and Status of Corporate Agents* (Oxford: Oxford University Press, 2011).

case, the attribution of an individual official's excuse might plausibly be thought to run alongside the attribution of her acts and intentions. We allow the official an excuse qua individual: why not pass that on to the state in whose name she acts?

A second line of objection, then, rests on the state's claim to legitimate authority over its citizens.[58] It is widely accepted that the state has moral constraints upon its ends. Mill's formulation of the Harm Principle, for example, rules out enforcing morality for its own sake.[59] Beyond that, however, the state also has constraints upon the means by which it goes about its ends. One key constraint is that it should act within the law. At the heart of the state's relationship with its citizens, and central to its claim of authority, is respect for the complex web of rules by which the legal system is constituted and by which the society is governed. Not only must the state act lawfully, *it must seek to do so*. If that is right, then it is not open for the state to defend its conduct by reference to an excuse. Excuses involve deliberate wrongdoing, deliberately unlawful conduct. If admitted, they would threaten to dissolve the glue that legitimates recognition of the state itself.

Suppose that we accept these lines of thought. It follows that even emergency action by state officials, such as shooting down the hijacked aeroplane flying toward an office building,[60] is inexcusable. In my view, that's a payoff. Cases such as these are profoundly difficult. But the difficulty is not about whether shooting the plane down involves a confession of human frailty, normal or abnormal. References to excuse just obscure the true question here, which is whether shooting down the aeroplane is morally *permissible*; whether it is okay to shoot down the plane. The real issue is one of justification.

4. Revisiting the Boundary between Irresponsibility and Rationale-Based Excuses

Let's return to our basic set of distinctions between irresponsibility defences, justifications, rationale-based excuses, and defensive mistakes. It is worth pausing to raise some final doubts about whether even the rationale-based excuses are unitary in kind. I am thinking, in particular, of the possibility of hybrid defences, defences that might straddle the line between irresponsibility and excuse (or mistake). At least in some cases, this possibility has been embraced by the law of provocation.[61]

[58] As such, its application is restricted to the domestic arena, and not to contexts where the state is a subject.

[59] JS Mill, *On Liberty* (1859), Ch 1.

[60] There is now a lot of writing on this topic. See eg T Hörnle, 'Shooting Down a Hijacked Plane—The German Discussion and Beyond' (2009) 3 Criminal Law and Philosophy 111, together with other papers in that issue.

[61] Now displaced in the UK by a statutory defence of 'loss of control', pursuant to the Coroners and Justice Act 2009, ss 54–56.

In the short-lived decision by the House of Lords in *Smith (Morgan)*,[62] it was held that the key statutory question,[63] whether a given piece of provocation was enough to make 'a reasonable man' act as did the defendant, should be evaluated inter alia by reference to D's own peculiarities, such as depression, which bear on the degree of self-control fairly to be expected of him. The decision was rightly criticized,[64] in as much as such cases really involve a claim of diminished capacity, of partial irresponsibility. As John Gardner put it, the provocation defence 'depends on the reasonableness of the provoked person's reaction to the provocation'.[65] In his classic article on provocation, Ashworth made a similar point: 'Where an individual who is congenitally incapable of exercising reasonable self-control is provoked by a petty affront, his loss of self-control must surely be ascribed to his own personality rather than to the provocation he received.'[66] These characterizations place provocation squarely within the realm of rationale-based defences. Persons who claim such defences do not rely on abnormal incapacities: they live up to the standard of the reasonable human being. By contrast, it is through the irresponsibility defences that we allow for people such as Morgan Smith, who fail in some way to be full moral agents. A rationale-based excuse is compatible with there being no diminution of respect for the defendant. An irresponsibility defence is not, or at least not entirely.[67]

No doubt the decision in *Smith (Morgan)* was misguided. But it is easy to see its attraction. The pull is strongest in cases such as *Ahluwalia*,[68] where the provocation involves a long history of abuse. One feature of 'battered woman syndrome' is the effect of that history on the defendant's ability to make rational decisions. In a sense, it explains why the defendant's moral responsibility was itself diminished. It can do so, I think, without diminishing our respect for the defendant. And as such, it has a genuine excusatory force. Suppose that even a reasonable person, exposed to the defendant's history, may have exhibited diminished powers of self-restraint at the time of her action. If that is the case, then the defendant did not fall short of our expectations. And to that extent, she is morally entitled to an excuse. Certainly this is not a paradigm rationale-based excuse. Neither, however, is it a simple case of partial irresponsibility. It is a hybrid excuse. Irresponsibility defences do not measure D's response against any criteria; they do not ask whether D fell short on any dimension of the reasonable person. Excuses do. Even in *Ahluwalia*.

[62] [2001] 1 AC 146; abandoned in *A-G for Jersey v Holley* [2005] UKPC 23 and not revived by the Coroners and Justice Act 2009.

[63] Homicide Act 1957 (UK), s 3.

[64] eg J Gardner and T Macklem, 'Compassion without Respect? Nine Fallacies in *R v. Smith*' [2001] Crim LR 623.

[65] Gardner, n 3 above, 134.

[66] Ashworth, n 35 above, 312.

[67] Gardner, n 3 above, 181.

[68] [1992] 4 All ER 889 (CA). (After waiting for her abusive husband to fall asleep, D got a can of petrol, poured it over his bed, and set the bed on fire.)

5. In Closing

It is a challenging task to generalize very far about the ingredients of blaming judgements. Moreover, the pay-offs for the legal system are not always substantial. As this essay has suggested, the moral distinctions between justifications and rationale-based excuses have relatively few implications for criminal law verdicts. On the other hand, the distinction in morality between rationale-based and irresponsibility defences has fundamental implications for the structure of their corresponding defences in law. The analogy that Fletcher drew between duress and 'normative' involuntariness, for instance, turns out to be profoundly mistaken.[69] Involuntariness is context-insensitive: duress is not. The rules of the criminal law reflect that distinction. And so they should. Criminal-law verdicts and sentences involve a form of institutional moral censure. As such, a good system of criminal law ought to track the moral foundations of those judgements. So academics are right to seek an understanding of the moral structure of blame. They are right when they look to identify and to implement the basic normative principles that should shape the contours of the criminal law. And that is, of course, precisely the project that Andrew Ashworth has advanced. It is no surprise that his textbook is entitled *Principles of Criminal Law*. Building on the work of the other two great English criminal lawyers of the 20th century, his writings have contributed enormously to the development of a principled account of the criminal law; and, above all, to the perception that such an account is not only possible but worth striving for.

[69] Fletcher, n 6 above, 802–7.

8

Years of Provocation, Followed by a Loss of Control

Barry Mitchell

On 4 October 2010 the old common law plea of provocation which, if successful, reduced murder to voluntary manslaughter, was abolished and replaced by the partial defence of loss of control.[1] This was the culmination of a crescendo of criticism and frustration over three or four decades of case law, especially (but not exclusively) about (1) the requirement of a loss of self-control, and the apparent bias in favour of male reactions to provocation, and the law's inadequate accommodation of female reactions; and (2) the nature of the normative element in the law and the extent to which personal characteristics of the defendant could be taken into account. In 2003 the Law Commission was asked to review the law, and following a consultation process, proposals for reforming the plea were put forward in 2004.[2] The government then invited the Commission to undertake a wider review of the homicide law and their final report, which reiterated their proposals, was published towards the end of 2006.[3] The new law, which is set out in the Coroners and Justice Act 2009, adopts some of the Law Commission's proposals, but there are some important differences between the structure and wording of those proposals and the new plea.

This essay contains a brief review of some of the key elements and concerns about the old common law before turning to explore its statutory replacement. In so doing, it will argue that the decision to base the new law on a loss of control requirement is fundamentally misguided. Whilst the use of ambiguous words and phrases may allow the courts a necessary measure of discretion, it will simultaneously risk injustice to some deserving defendants. The essay will also suggest that the objective requirement in the new plea has not been adequately thought through.

[1] Coroners and Justice Act 2009, s 56, abolishes the old provocation plea, and ss 54 and 55 replace it with loss of control. In Northern Ireland the change in the law took effect from 1 June 2011.

[2] See Law Commission, *Partial Defences to Murder* (Law Com No 290, 2004), especially Part 3.

[3] See Law Commission, *Murder, Manslaughter and Infanticide* (Law Com No 304, 2006), especially paras 5.1–82.

1. The Old Law of Provocation

The old common law on provocation had been recognized, albeit in slightly different forms, since the 17th century.[4] The law which prevailed until its abolition was based on the definition offered by the then Devlin J in *Duffy*, that provocation 'is some act, or series of acts, done by the dead man to the accused, which would cause in any reasonable man, and actually causes in the accused, a sudden and temporary loss of self-control, rendering the accused so subject to passion as to make him or her for the moment no longer master of his mind'.[5] Various adjustments were made to this over the years. For example, as Andrew Ashworth has pointed out,[6] although in practice the provocation commonly did originate from the deceased, following section 3 of the Homicide Act 1957 the law was not restricted in this way,[7] nor did the provocation have to be directed at the accused.[8] Nevertheless, the principal features of the old common law were that the defendant had to show that she had been provoked by some form of human action, that that had caused her to lose her self-control (which she had not regained at the time of inflicting the fatal assault), and that a reasonable person would have killed had she been provoked in the same way. Some commentators doubted the law's restriction of provocation to human conduct:

> Mere circumstances, however provocative, do not constitute a defence to murder. Loss of control by a farmer on his crops being destroyed by a flood, or his flocks by foot-and-mouth, a financier ruined by a crash on the stock market or an author on his manuscript being destroyed by lightning, could not, it seems, excuse a resulting killing. An 'Act of God' could hardly be regarded as 'something done' within s.3. Since, where there is a provocative act, it no longer need be done by the victim, this distinction begins to look a little thin. If D may rely on the defence where the crops or the manuscript were destroyed by an unknown arsonist or the stock exchange crash was engineered by other anonymous financiers, why should it be any different where no human agency was involved? The provocation is no more and no less.[9]

Indeed, the common law's insistence that the defendant's reaction be triggered by some form of human conduct was probably rooted in its origins when only a very limited set of circumstances were regarded as sufficient for a successful plea. It was arguably also the result of a failure fully to get to grips with the underlying rationale

[4] Excellent accounts of the emergence and historical development of the provocation plea can be found in J Kaye, 'The Early History of Murder and Manslaughter' (1967) 83 LQR 365, 569; A Ashworth, 'The Doctrine of Provocation' (1976) 35 CLJ 292; and J Horder, *Provocation and Responsibility* (Oxford: Clarendon Press, 1992).

[5] [1949] 1 All ER 932 (CCA).

[6] A Ashworth, *Principles of Criminal Law* (6th edn, Oxford: Oxford University Press, 2009), 251, 252.

[7] See eg *Davies* [1975] QB 691 (CA).

[8] See eg *Pearson* [1992] Crim LR 193 (CA).

[9] See D Ormerod, *Smith and Hogan Criminal Law* (12th edn, Oxford: Oxford University Press, 2008), 491. See also BJ Mitchell, RD Mackay, and WJ Brookbanks, 'Pleading for Provoked Killers: In Defence of *Morgan Smith*' (2008) 124 LQR 675, 683.

behind the plea and to pinpoint precisely what it is that warrants a reduction of liability.

Nevertheless, the major criticisms of the law arose from the loss of self-control and normative requirements.

Loss of self-control

Over the years the courts adopted various epithets in their attempts to explain what they regarded as an appropriate response by the defendant, one of which was a loss of self-control.[10] Although the Court of Appeal in *Richens*[11] stated that it was wrong to say that the defendant must have completely lost his self-control such that he did not know what he was doing—for that would be more indicative of automatism, which is a complete defence—there was never any clear definition of this subjective requirement. There was a fundamental ambiguity in the law because it was uncertain whether it required an incapacity to control one's reaction to the provocation, or whether a mere failure to do so would suffice.[12] Given the volume of criticism heaped upon the loss of self-control requirement, it is somewhat ironic that, as both Ashworth and the author discovered, the courts did not necessarily go to any great lengths to see that this theoretical condition was actually fulfilled in the individual case.[13] Nevertheless, regardless of what sometimes happened in practice, whilst this stretching of the law as set out in *Duffy* may have enabled the courts to return what were perceived to be more just verdicts (eg, in cases of battered women who killed their abusive partners), Ashworth observed that it also 'weakened the excusatory force that derives from acting in uncontrolled anger'.[14] Clearly, any excusatory force would have to be founded on some other form of mental or emotional disturbance.

The 'suddenness' requirement

As Ashworth commented, the further requirement that the loss of self-control be 'sudden' was only introduced by Devlin J in *Duffy* and was unsupported by any precedent.[15] The intention behind the suddenness requirement was to distinguish genuine deserving cases from revenge killings.[16] Ashworth rightly criticized the

[10] See the references in n 4 above.

[11] [1993] 4 All ER 877 (CA).

[12] Interestingly, the Law Commission referred to a comment made to them by psychiatrists that those who do lose their self-control when provoked can usually afford to do so. 'An angry strong man can afford to lose his self-control with someone who provokes him, if that person is physically smaller and weaker.' See Law Commission, No 290, n 2 above, para 3.28.

[13] Ashworth, n 4 above, 316; B Mitchell and S Cunningham, 'Defences to Murder' in Law Commission, No 304, n 3 above, Appendix C.

[14] Ashworth, n 6 above, 254.

[15] Ibid, 252, 253.

[16] Though it was subsequently argued that this is a false distinction because the usual motive for killing whilst out of control is revenge; see R Holton and S Shute, 'Self-Control in the Modern Provocation Defence' (2007) 27 OJLS 49.

suddenness restriction for its bias—'it favours those with quick tempers over others with a slow-burning temperament (but no less intensity of emotion), and it favours those with the physical strength to act quickly'.[17] This latter form of bias was linked to the perception that the law favoured men over women, although empirical research conducted for the Law Commission did not support such favouritism.[18] Initially at least, the suddenness requirement effectively restricted the scope of the plea to cases where there was little time lapse between the provocation and the defendant's reaction to it; the fact that the defendant had lost self-control at the time of inflicting the fatal assault was not sufficient per se. Regrettably though, the courts appeared to be inconsistent in this respect. As Ashworth pointed out, in cases such as *Fantle*[19] and *Simpson*[20] the courts admitted evidence of the background leading up to the fatal assault, whereas in *Brown*[21] Bridge J thought that the earlier events were irrelevant.[22] Ashworth's view was that Bridge J was wrong: '[o]ne straw may indeed break a camel's back',[23] and 'the significance of the deceased's final act and its effect upon the accused—and indeed the relation of the retaliation to that act—can be neither understood nor evaluated without reference to previous dealings between the parties'.[24] His criticism of Bridge J was subsequently underlined when in cases of 'cumulative provocation' the courts felt that the time lapse between the provocation and retaliation was merely relevant but not a conclusive factor.[25] Indeed, as Ashworth again pointed out, there were occasions on which the 'sudden and temporary' requirement seemed to have been completely overlooked, as in *Pearson*, where the defendant struck his abusive father twice with a sledgehammer even though there had apparently been no final act of provocation to which the defendant's action was a sudden response.[26]

Although the common law provocation plea has been abolished, its replacement is loss of (self-)control, and so the concept is still enormously relevant under the new law.

The normative element

Whilst the loss of self-control requirement in the old common law often proved a stumbling block for battered women and various other deserving defendants,[27] it

17 Ashworth, n 6 above, 253.

18 See RD Mackay, 'The Provocation Plea in Operation: An Empirical Study', in Law Commission, No 290, n 2 above, Appendix A.

19 [1959] Crim LR 585.

20 [1957] Crim LR 815.

21 [1972] 2 All ER 1328, 1332 (CA).

22 A Ashworth, 'Sentencing in Provocation Cases' [1975] Crim LR 553, 557.

23 Ibid.

24 Ibid, 559.

25 See especially Lord Taylor CJ in *Ahluwalia* (1993) 69 Cr App R 133, 139 (CA).

26 The author's own research also indicates there are unreported cases which are similar to *Pearson* in this respect; see B Mitchell, 'Distinguishing between Murder and Manslaughter in Practice' (2007) 71 JCL 318.

27 Some of these were able to avoid a murder conviction and mandatory life sentence by pleading diminished responsibility, though that was not necessarily an entirely satisfactory course to adopt.

was the objective requirement which arguably attracted most criticism. Its basic aim was to ensure that the plea would only be available to those who showed a reasonable level of self-control and it thus sought to provide some justification for the loss or angry reaction. The normative requirement was initially articulated in purely objective terms, but this was revised by the House of Lords in *Camplin.*[28] In a much-quoted speech Lord Diplock stated that when applying the objective test the jury might take some of the defendant's personal characteristics into account. The trial judge 'should.... explain to [the jury] that the reasonable man referred to in the question is a person having the power of self-control to be expected of an ordinary person of the sex and age of the accused, but in other respects sharing such of the accused's characteristics as they think would affect the gravity of the provocation to him'.[29] In other words, the defendant's sex and age might be taken into account even though they are only relevant to the defendant's capacity to exercise self-control, along with other characteristics which were the object of or relevant to the provocation.

In 1976, shortly before the House of Lords' decision in *Camplin*, an article by Ashworth was published in the Cambridge Law Journal[30] in which he essentially put forward the argument which was used by Lord Diplock. In this seminal article, Ashworth argued that, with the possible exception of serious assaults, the gravity of any provocation can only sensibly be judged in relation to people of a particular class. '[T]he sight of two persons indulging in sexual intercourse cannot properly be described as a grave provocation—for it would hardly provoke the unrelated intruder to anything more than embarrassment—without adding that it would be grave for someone who is married, engaged or related to one of the participants.'[31] In advocating a narrower range of personal characteristics to be taken into account than that which had been proposed by the Criminal Law Revision Committee,[32] he submitted that (with the exception of age and gender) those which bore only on the defendant's powers of self-control should be ignored (unless, of course, they were the object of the provocation). Such a distinction necessarily followed from the purpose of the objective requirement, namely to stipulate and apply a general standard of self-control.

To lay down a test of 'a man with reasonable self-control and with an unusually excitable temperament' would indeed be illogical; but a test of 'an impotent man with reasonable self-

Although some women clearly have developed mental abnormalities through the abuse, others have not. Critics of the law argued that not only is a conviction for diminished manslaughter stigmatizing in itself, but the circumstances leading up to the killing should themselves be sufficient to reduce liability without the need to plead a medical or psychiatric excuse.

28 [1978] AC 705 (HL).

29 Ibid, 718.

30 See Ashworth, n 4 above.

31 Ibid, 300.

32 See Criminal Law Revision Committee, *Working Paper on Offences against the Person* (London: HMSO, 1976), para 54, where it was proposed that 'any physical characteristics of the accused' could be taken into account when applying the objective test, but the Committee went on to say that 'any disability, physical or mental, from which he suffered' should also be included.

control' contains no logical contradiction, for these two characteristics can co-exist and the reference to impotence assists in interpreting the gravity of the provocation.[33]

It is fair to say that the use of the reasonable man/person as the benchmark against which the defendant's reaction should be compared probably caused much confusion and misunderstanding. It was surely not intended to be used in the same way as it is in other areas of the law, such as the tort of negligence. In the civil law the reasonable person test is used as setting a minimum standard of acceptable conduct, and the defendant either meets that standard (and incurs no legal liability) or does not. In *Morhall* Lord Goff explained that in provocation the test's function was to induce the court to compare the defendant's reaction with that of an ordinary person with a normal capacity for self-control.[34] In effect, it was a means whereby the courts could distinguish the deserving from the undeserving cases. As a consequence of section 3 of the Homicide Act 1957, once there was evidence that the defendant had been provoked to lose self-control the matter then had to be passed to the jury, who would decide whether a reasonable person would have reacted as the defendant had.

Ashworth also used causal reasoning as a means of understanding the rationale behind provocation, and he linked it to the issue of relevant characteristics. Where there is some significant or grave provocation, the defendant's loss of self-control could be attributed to it, whereas in cases of trivial provocation the loss of self-control is due more to a weakness in the defendant's make-up than the provocation.[35] It is, of course, in cases of trivial provocation that the defence are more likely to want personal characteristics to be taken into account; these are cases where the characteristic, such as some form of mental abnormality or personality deficiency (which are discussed below), provides an explanation or excuse for the loss of self-control.

The case law which emerged after *Camplin* was confusing and inconsistent. It was not simply that the courts sometimes ignored the distinction which Ashworth and Lord Diplock had advocated, nor that the hypothetical reasonable man became increasingly (and impractically) anthropomorphized; ultimately the confusion and disagreement reached its height on whether undesirable or discreditable characteristics, or mental abnormalities could be taken into account. In *Morhall* the House of Lords held that in the light of section 3 of the Homicide Act 1957 juries should be directed to take account of anything they thought was relevant to the assessment of the strength of the provocation. This seemed to include discreditable characteristics such as irascibility or racial prejudice. From a purely pragmatic perspective it might be suggested that it was enough to leave it to the jury's good sense to decide whether a characteristic was so discreditable that it should not be used to enable the defendant to reduce his liability. But in principle there was arguably no good explanation for such an approach. Morhall was an addicted glue-sniffer who was

[33] Ashworth, n 4 above, 301. The reference to the defendant's impotence is clearly a reference to the case of *Bedder v DPP* (1954) 38 Cr App R 133 (HL) which was overruled on this point by *Camplin*.

[34] *Morhall* [1995] 3 All ER 659, 665 (HL).

[35] Ashworth, n 4 above, 308.

taunted about his addiction. How, one might wonder, would a jury take this into account when applying the objective test?[36]

More fundamentally, Ashworth argued that this is unsatisfactory on the ground that the objective test should exclude attitudes and reactions which are inconsistent with the aims and values which the law seeks to uphold.[37] He also demonstrated his desire to be guided by principle when considering the merits of other characteristics such as culture. If the law was trying to ensure that deserving defendants have shown a reasonable level of self-control, then youth should be regarded as relevant because 'there is good reason to maintain that a lower standard may be accepted'. Conversely, cultural background may well be relevant to assessing the seriousness of the provocation, but there is no clear reason why it should justify the reduction of the expected standard of self-control unless greater weight is attached to the desire for 'cultural pluralism'.[38] Two simple observations can be made here. First, the law should not expect a person to exercise a level of self-control that he was incapable of exercising, and secondly, a decision had to be made—and still has to be made under the new law—about whether provocation was the appropriate plea where there was an incapacity or reduced capacity.

The other major controversial issue relating to characteristics that are relevant to the objective test concerned mental disorders and personality disorders, and here the conflict in the case law was ultimately between the Privy Council and the House of Lords. In *Luc Thiet Thuan*[39] the majority of the Privy Council declined to take account of the defendant's brain damage when applying the reasonable man standard. Lord Goff took the same view as that taken by Ashworth,[40] that the provocation plea was designed for ordinary 'normal' people, not for those suffering from some form of mental abnormality. This, of course, follows the distinction advocated by Lord Diplock and Ashworth in that only characteristics relevant to the provocation should be taken into account. However, in *Smith (Morgan)*[41] the majority of the House of Lords decided that in the light of section 3 of the Homicide Act 1957 juries should be able to determine which characteristics to take into account, including mental abnormalities. Two of their lordships (Lords Hobhouse and Millett) took the same view as Ashworth that those who seek to rely on mental abnormality to reduce their liability should base their defence on diminished responsibility. But the majority thought that the distinction between characteristics relevant to the provocation and those relevant to the power of self-control is unrealistic. Moreover, although certain characteristics such as pugnacity, undue excitability, short temper, or morbid jealousy should always be excluded,

[36] Similarly, one might wonder how the jury would take account of the defendant's immaturity and attention-seeking in *Humphreys* [1995] 4 All ER 1008 (CA), and 'obsessive and eccentric' personality in *Dryden* [1995] 4 All ER 987 (CA).

[37] Ashworth, n 6 above, 256.

[38] Ibid. In *Ali* [1989] Crim LR 736 the Court of Appeal explained that age is not always relevant. There the fact that the defendant was 20 years old at the time was immaterial; it mattered not whether he was 20 or, say, 35; one would expect the same general level of self-control in either case.

[39] [1997] AC 131 (PC).

[40] Ashworth, n 4 above, 312.

[41] [2001] 1 AC 146 (HL).

they felt that the primary concern was to do justice in the circumstances of the case, even if that might cause some uncertainty or lack of clarity as to the law. One particular dimension of this was that the law should not expect people to exercise self-control when, though no fault of their own, they were incapable of doing so.[42]

But the Privy Council had the last word on the issue. In *A-G for Jersey v Holley*[43] a majority (six to three) of the court effectively overruled *Smith (Morgan)* and held that unless they are relevant to the provocation, mental abnormalities should be excluded when applying the reasonable person standard. Thus the principle expressed by Ashworth and adopted by Lord Diplock in *Camplin* prevailed; the law of provocation required a reasonable level of self-control from provoked defendants regardless of any mental abnormalities. The Court of Appeal subsequently accepted this interpretation of the law.[44] Those who had been provoked but sought to rely on a mental abnormality as the explanation for loss of self-control should plead diminished responsibility instead.

A further dimension to the objective requirement—proportionality

There was another, perhaps less obvious, objective dimension to the old common law which concerned the relationship between the provocation and the defendant's reaction to it. This was once known as the 'reasonable relationship rule',[45] but it ceased to be a rule of substantive law and became instead one of evidential significance.[46] Section 3 of the Homicide Act 1957 required the court to be satisfied that the provocation 'was enough to make the reasonable man *do as he did*' (emphasis added).[47] The obvious ambiguity here was whether those last four words mean that the reasonable man would have killed in precisely the same way as the defendant did or whether it merely means that the reasonable man would have lost control and killed in some way. In *Phillips*[48] Lord Diplock said that common sense dictated that loss of self-control is a matter of degree and that the nature of a person's reaction to provocation will depend on its gravity. In other words, the nature and gravity of the provocation should be reflected in the nature of the defendant's reaction to it. The implication behind this was that the reasonable person would carry on behaving reasonably even after losing his self-control.

[42] For contrasting views about *Smith (Morgan)* see eg J Gardner and T Macklem, 'Compassion without Respect? Nine Fallacies in *R v Smith*' [2001] Crim LR 623; T Macklem and J Gardner, 'Provocation and Pluralism' (2001) 64 MLR 815; RD Mackay and BJ Mitchell, 'Provoking Diminished Responsibility: Two Pleas Merging into One?' [2003] Crim LR 745; J Chalmers, 'Merging Provocation and Diminished Responsibility: Some Reasons for Scepticism' [2004] Crim LR 198; J Gardner and T Macklem, 'No Provocation without Responsibility: A Reply to Mackay and Mitchell' [2004] Crim LR 213; RD Mackay and BJ Mitchell, 'Replacing Provocation: More on a Combined Plea' [2004] Crim LR 219.

[43] [2005] UKPC 23.

[44] See *Mohammed* [2005] EWCA Crim 1880; *James* [2006] EWCA Crim 14, [2006] QB 588.

[45] Following the decision in *Mancini v DPP* [1942] AC 1 (HL).

[46] After the decision in *Brown* [1972] 2 QB 229 (CA).

[47] In *Camplin* Lord Diplock included a similar condition in his model direction.

[48] [1969] 2 AC 130, 137 (PC).

Ashworth has persuasively argued, however, that the 'reaction' in this context has not always been properly understood. It should refer to the degree of loss of self-control, rather than the extent of the violence in D's reaction, as being in proportion to the gravity of the provocation.[49] Thus, since the defendant must necessarily have been provoked so as to lose his self-control, it makes no sense to stipulate that the reasonable person would have done exactly what the defendant did.[50] Our desire for proportionality is surely satisfied if the provocation was sufficiently grave to justify the angry loss of self-control which resulted in the use of fatal force.

2. The Review of the Old Law

At the end of its review the Law Commission identified three principal problems with the old law—(1) there was a lack of judicial control over pleas, so that even where there was only very trivial provocation the judge had to allow the matter to be determined by the jury; (2) the sudden and temporary loss of self-control requirement was problematic—there was a tension between it and slow-burn cases, and there was also some difficulty applying the law (which was clearly based on anger) to situations where the predominant emotion was fear; and (3) the inconsistencies in the case law regarding the defendant's characteristics, which may be relevant to the reasonable person standard.[51]

The Commission recommended a reformed partial defence of provocation[52] based on two limbs, namely (i) a fear of serious violence; and (ii) gross provocation in the sense of words and/or conduct which caused the defendant to have a justifiable sense of being seriously wronged.[53] The first of these was meant to fill a gap in the law where defendants fear serious violence and overreact by killing the aggressor in order to thwart an attack. The government doubted whether many such cases actually arose, but accepted the Commission's wider point that shoe-horning these cases into a plea based on anger is difficult.[54] As to the second limb of the Commission's proposal, the government felt that as a general rule people should be able to control their reactions when they think they have been wronged but accepted that there is a small number of situations in which the provocation is so strong that some allowance should be given to them.[55] The government therefore

[49] Ashworth, n 4 above, 305.

[50] Ashworth, n 6 above, 259.

[51] Law Com No 304, n 3 above, paras 5.15–46.

[52] The Law Commission recommended a restructuring of the substantive law, so that (if successful) provocation would effectively reduce murder in the first degree to murder in the second degree; n 3 above, para 9.6. The previous New Labour government was not persuaded to implement the proposed restructuring, and the Coalition government concluded 'that the time is not right to take forward such a substantial reform of our criminal law'; see Ministry of Justice, *Report on the Implementation of Law Commission Proposals* (London: TSO, 2011), para 54.

[53] Law Com No 304, n 3 above, para 9.17.

[54] Ministry of Justice, *Murder, Manslaughter and Infanticide: Proposals for Reform of the Law: Consultation Paper CP19/08* (London: Ministry of Justice, 2008), paras 26 and 27.

[55] Ibid, paras 31–4. The government cited an example from the Law Commission's report of a rape victim who kills his attacker after being taunted about what happened.

decided to abolish the old common plea[56] and replace it with words and/or conduct which constituted circumstances of an extremely grave character and which caused the defendant to have a justifiable sense of being seriously wronged.

Whereas the Law Commission considered that the loss of self-control concept had been so troublesome that it should be abandoned, and that undeserving cases would nonetheless be excluded by the safeguards they incorporated elsewhere in their recommendations, the then government took a more pessimistic and cautious approach. The Ministry of Justice remained 'concerned that there is a risk of the partial defence being used inappropriately, for example, in cold-blooded, gang-related or "honour" killings. Even in cases which are less obviously less unsympathetic, there is still a fundamental problem about providing a partial defence in situations where a defendant has killed while basically in full possession of his or her senses, even if he or she is frightened, other than in a situation which is complete self-defence.'[57] At the same time, the government decided to remove the 'suddenness' requirement 'to make plain that situations where the defendant's reaction has been delayed or builds gradually are not excluded'.[58]

As to the third of the principal problems with the old law, both the Law Commission and the government favoured the majority view in *Holley* and that of Ashworth and Lord Diplock, that there should be a general standard of self-control.[59] Concessions to the defendant's capacity to exercise self-control should be made only by taking account of her age and gender. The difficulty here is that there are no clear objective or scientific data about consistency in levels of self-control. We do not know how much consistency there is in people's *views* about when self-control should or should not be exercised, nor do we know the degree of similarity in people's *ability* to exercise self-control in any given set of circumstances. The Law Commission and the government also rightly felt that judges ought not to have to direct juries on provocation (now loss of control) where the evidence is very poor.[60] Otherwise, there is a greater risk of inconsistencies and verdicts which fly in the face of the law.

3. The New Law of Loss of Control

By virtue of ss 54 and 55 of the Coroners and Justice Act 2009 the court must now be satisfied that the defendant's participation in the killing resulted from a loss of self-control which was triggered in one of two ways. Either it must have been

[56] The government took the view that the term 'provocation' had acquired such 'negative connotations' that it should be abandoned (ibid, para 34), though Andrew Ashworth suggests that the term will continue to be used in practice; see n 6 above, 261.

[57] Ibid, para 36. The Ministry confirmed this view after the consultation process was completed (para 62).

[58] *Murder, Manslaughter and Infanticide: Proposals for Reform of the Law: Summary of Responses and Government Position: Response to Consultation CP(R)19/08* (London: Ministry of Justice, 2008), para 66.

[59] Ibid, para 78.

[60] Ibid, para 80.

triggered by the defendant's fear of serious violence from the victim against the defendant or someone else, or it must have been prompted by something done and/or said which was of an extremely grave character and caused the defendant to have a justifiable sense of being seriously wronged. Whichever trigger is appropriate, the court must also be satisfied that (a) the trigger was something other than sexual infidelity;[61] (b) the trigger was not self-induced; (c) the defendant must not have acted 'in a considered desire for revenge'; and (d) 'a person of D's sex and age, with a normal degree of tolerance and self-restraint and in the circumstances of D, might have reacted in the same or a similar way to D'.[62] Thus, the reasonable person test at common law has been replaced by a person of normal tolerance and self-restraint etc, and instead of referring to the defendant's characteristics when applying the objective test, we should henceforth refer to the defendant's circumstances.

At the time of writing this essay there has been just one reported case, *Clinton*,[63] in which the new partial defence has been raised, and it is obviously impossible to know at this stage how far that case reflects the way in which the courts will interpret the new law. That said, the Lord Chief Justice, Lord Judge, warned that some aspects of the new legislation 'are likely to produce surprising results'.[64]

The triggers

The first of the two possible triggers of the defendant's fatal assault is a fear of serious violence from the victim against the defendant or another identified person. In broad terms this is surely a welcome development. The precise boundary between serious and non-serious violence may sometimes not be immediately apparent, but the government required that the fear must be of 'serious' violence in order to exclude unmeritorious cases.[65] The law does not expressly stipulate that the fear must be of *imminent* violence, but the government is relying on the loss of self-control condition, the need to fulfil the person of normal tolerance test, and evidence (for example) whether the defendant had sought other protection as being sufficient safeguards to ensure that only deserving cases benefit from the new plea.[66]

The alternative form of the plea arises where the loss of self-control was triggered by words and/or conduct which constituted circumstances of an extremely grave character and caused the defendant to have a justifiable sense of being seriously wronged. One of the central aims of the new law is to reduce the number of cases in which defendants reduce their liability from murder to manslaughter and to limit the application of the new pleas to 'exceptional circumstances'[67]—hence the 'extremely grave character' requirement. There is also a desire to stipulate general standards of reaction to provocation, and the 'justifiable sense of being seriously

61 Coroners and Justice Act 2009, s 55(6)(c).
62 Ibid, s 54(1)(c).
63 [2012] EWCA Crim 2.
64 Ibid, at [2].
65 *Response to Consultation CP(R)19/08*, n 58 above, para 28.
66 Ibid, paras 29 and 30.
67 Ibid, para 36.

wronged' requirement is one element of this. An obvious concern here is the ambiguity and uncertainty of the language—'extremely grave' and 'seriously wronged'. Some of the wording in section 55(4) is based on the Law Commission's recommendation, and the Commission thought that the word 'justifiable' should be construed objectively.[68] The government took the same view, believing it is unnecessary to 'spell that out',[69] but the statute does not make this clear and, as Simester et al commented, there must surely be a risk that it will be confused with 'excusable' or 'understandable'.[70]

Sexual infidelity by the victim was regarded by the previous New Labour government as an inadequate ground, and if it is one aspect of a wider set of circumstances then it should be disregarded when deciding whether those circumstances should suffice to reduce murder to manslaughter. But it is not easy to appreciate why the previous administration felt it was necessary expressly to exclude sexual infidelity from the words or conduct trigger, and indeed there may well be good reason to suspect that a potential conflict has been created within the new law. On the face of it, it seems that the New Labour government was heavily influenced by the support it received for the exclusion from various organizations. In contrast, it also felt that perpetrators of 'honour killings' should not benefit from the new plea, but instead of expressly excluding this category as well it was content that 'the high threshold for the words and conduct limb of the partial defence will have the effect of excluding "honour killings" because such cases will not satisfy the requirements that the circumstances were of an extremely grave character and caused a justifiable sense of being seriously wronged'[71]—together with the exemption of cases where the killing resulted from a considered desire for revenge. Why should not the same be true of sexual infidelity?[72] Moreover, as Simester et al argue, if having been properly directed by the judge a jury concludes that a person with normal tolerance and self-restraint would also have reacted with fatal violence, it is difficult to see why the plea should be denied.[73]

The prohibition of sexual infidelity as a qualifying trigger is especially problematic.[74] What, for example, does 'sexual infidelity' mean? It is not defined in the 2009 Act. Should it be confined to the words and acts of sexual intercourse, so that the effects of it are not excluded? Must there be some form of relationship between the parties and, if so, what?

[68] Law Com No 290, n 2 above, para 3.70.

[69] *Response to Consultation CP(R)19/08*, n 58 above, para 45.

[70] See AP Simester, JR Spencer, GR Sullivan, and GJ Virgo, *Simester and Sullivan's Criminal Law: Theory and Doctrine* (4th edn, Oxford: Hart, 2010), 399 and 400.

[71] *Response to Consultation CP(R)19/08*, n 58 above, para 56.

[72] The government went out of its way to exclude any trace of sexual infidelity from the new law. 'We believe that where sexual infidelity is one part in a set of circumstances which led to the defendant losing self-control, the partial defence should succeed or fail on the basis of those circumstances *disregarding the element of sexual infidelity*' (emphasis added); ibid, para 55.

[73] Simester et al, n 70 above, 399.

[74] For a fuller discussion of these problems, see Professor David Ormerod's comments in *Smith and Hogan's Criminal Law* (13th edn, Oxford: Oxford University Press, 2011), 520–22.

By a combination of analysis of the structure and wording of sections 54 and 55 of the 2009 Act together with careful scrutiny of comments by government ministers about the purpose and intended effect of the new law, the Court of Appeal in *Clinton*[75] concluded that (i) sexual infidelity could not *by itself* constitute a qualifying trigger; but (ii) evidence of sexual infidelity may be admissible because of its relevance to the circumstances in which the defendant reacted to a (legally acceptable) qualifying trigger.[76] The Court stressed the need to consider the context in which the loss of control occurred. Lord Judge CJ illustrated this by reference to a situation in which the defendant returned home unexpectedly to find her spouse having consensual sexual intercourse with her sister. When the defendant complained about what she discovered, her unfaithful spouse justified what he had done, shouting and taunting the defendant in hurtful language that it is she (the defendant) who was really responsible for the infidelity. The taunts and distressing words, that do not constitute sexual infidelity, may be treated as a qualifying trigger (under section 55(4)). 'The idea that, in the search for a qualifying trigger, the context in which such words are used should be ignored represents an artificiality which the administration of criminal justice should do without.'[77]

The loss of self-control requirement

At the heart of the new law there remains the need for a loss of self-control, and it is difficult to avoid the conclusion that this will necessarily prevent much of the reform and improvement in the law which had been sought. The Law Commission was worried that a loss of self-control requirement would inevitably favour men over women and thought that there was no overriding need to replace it with some other form of subjective requirement;[78] rather, it would be sufficient to stipulate that the provocation had not been triggered by a considered desire for revenge, that the defendant should not have 'engineered' or incited it, and that either judges could exclude undeserving cases or that juries could be trusted to do so.[79] Ashworth, though, criticized the Commission's approach on theoretical rather than practical grounds—it 'seeks to detach the provocation defence from one of its true rationales, which is that a good reason for partially excusing such defendants is that they acted during a distinct emotional disturbance resulting from what was done to

[75] [2012] EWCA Crim 2.

[76] Ibid, at [34]–[44].

[77] Ibid, at [23].

[78] The Law Commission did consider the alternative concept in the American Model Penal Code, 'extreme mental or emotional disturbance', but consultation with academics and judges yielded much criticism of vagueness and indiscrimination; and the Commission also feared it would produce considerable case law; see Law Com No 304, n 3 above, para 5.22. The Commission did, though, acknowledge that EMED 'has formed the basis for a provocation defence in at least some American jurisdictions, and cannot therefore be dismissed as unworkable'. Other commentators have argued that EMED is a more accurate and more defensible concept than loss of self-control; see eg Mitchell et al, n 9 above.

[79] Law Com No 304, n 3 above, paras 5.17–27.

them'.[80] Ashworth's concern is not with the proposal to abolish the loss of self-control requirement but with the suggestion that there should be nothing put in its place. Interestingly, Horder had earlier floated the idea of what he called 'provoked extreme emotional disturbance' as a substitute subjective requirement.[81] Indeed, various alternatives to the loss of self-control requirement have been offered, some of which also seek to put emotional disturbance at the core of the subjective test. Such suggestions have been criticized essentially for their uncertainty. Regrettably though, the government's preferred condition, that there must be a loss of self-control, remains undefined and vague, and there is no apparent reason to assume that the case law on it will be any more consistent than it was under the old common law.

Prima facie, the only apparent difference between the old and the new law is that the loss of self-control need no longer be 'sudden and temporary'. Quite how a loss of self-control could be anything other than temporary is hard to envisage, and the more significant questions surround the suddenness requirement. Its removal under the new law appears to indicate a wish to formally accommodate slow-burn cases. Yet one obvious category of such cases—battered women who kill their abusers—would still have to surmount the loss of self-control hurdle, and previous experience clearly indicates that many of these women would not be able to rely on the new plea.[82] Welcoming the Law Commission's proposal to include the fear of serious violence trigger, the government stated that it should be available even though the violence is not imminent.[83] It is, however, not easy to imagine a situation in which the defendant was fearful of non-imminent serious violence and still lost his or (perhaps more likely) her self-control. Although concern about this was expressed by consultees, the government asserted that a loss of self-control is not always 'inconsistent with situations where a person reacts to an *imminent* fear of serious violence'.[84] Unfortunately, there was no comment on cases where the fear is not imminent.

The paradigmatic provocation case under the old common law was based on the idea that the defendant 'exploded' with anger (and lashed out with fatal violence), and the anger then subsided. But whether the new law will be noticeably different in this respect from the common law is open to doubt. It has already been suggested that this distinction between the old and the new law ought not in fact to make much difference. A loss of self-control can only occur 'as a moment of departure from

[80] Ashworth, n 6 above, 254.

[81] See J Horder, 'Reshaping the Subjective Element in the Provocation Defence' (2005) 25 OJLS 123, 134–9. 'Where, on a charge of murder, the judge considers there to be evidence that D was provoked to play his or her part in the killing in a state of extreme emotional disturbance, he or she should direct the jury that the offence may for that reason be found to be manslaughter. Further, ' "extreme emotional disturbance" is confined to circumstances in which it is produced by a combination of gravely provoked anger and D's fear for his or her own safety (or the safety of another), being no mere pretext for the taking of premeditated revenge.'

[82] See eg *Ahluwalia* (1993) 96 Cr App R 133 (CA); and *Thornton (No 2)* [1996] 2 Cr App R 108 (CA).

[83] *Consultation Paper CP19/08*, n 54 above, paras 26 and 29.

[84] Ibid, para 63, emphasis added.

being in control'.[85] Moreover, the decision to admit evidence of cumulative provocation over a lengthy period, so as to provide the context in which the final incident (which may have been relatively trivial) occurred, effectively undermined the element of suddenness. Conversely, as has already been indicated, the new plea will automatically fail if the defendant acted in a considered desire for revenge, and the longer the time gap between the trigger and the fatal assault, the greater is the risk that the court will infer that the killing was vengeful.[86]

Thus, it has elsewhere been suggested that rather than focus on the physical nature of the defendant's reaction, the law should concentrate on the impact of the trigger (provocation) on his mind[87]—after all, the defendant receives and processes the trigger in his mind; the physical response follows from that and is merely (ambiguous) evidence of the impact of the trigger. Arguably therefore, the law should instead put some form of mental or emotional disturbance at the heart of the plea.[88] One consequence of that would be the avoidance of the problem in both the old and the new law of satisfactorily reconciling the loss of self-control requirement with acceptance of a time lapse before the fatal assault.

The objective requirements

As well as losing self-control through one of the two triggers, the defendant will only succeed under the new law if a 'person of D's age and sex, with a normal degree of tolerance and self-restraint and in the circumstances of D, might have reacted in the same or in a similar way to D'. As under the old law the assumption behind this is that there is a generally recognized and recognizable standard of tolerance and self-restraint that most people could and would exercise when provoked or fearful. But no evidence to support this has ever been produced, so the government's aim of setting a general normative standard is based more on hope and assumption than on reliable data. Moreover, even if the assumption is well-founded, it is almost inevitable that juries will vary in their precise location of the maximum level of self-restraint, and there is thus a real risk that the cases will result in inconsistent decisions in the interpretation of this requirement.

The phrase 'circumstances of D' specifically excludes 'those whose only relevance to D's conduct is that they bear on D's general capacity for tolerance and self-restraint'.[89] In essence, this reproduces the law after the decision in *Holley* so that, apart from age and gender, individual characteristics of the defendant will only be attributable to the 'person with normal tolerance and self-restraint' if they are relevant to the triggering event. As under the old common law, trial judges will

[85] A Norrie, 'The Coroners and Justice Act 2009—Partial Defences to Murder (1) Loss of Control' [2010] Crim LR 275, 288.

[86] Simester et al, n 70 above, 397.

[87] See Mitchell et al, n 9 above.

[88] As indicated above, Ashworth criticized the Law Commission for not recommending something such as an 'element of emotional disturbance' to put in place of the loss of control requirement; n 6 above, 260.

[89] Coroners and Justice Act 2009, s 54 (3).

have to direct juries very carefully about this distinction and which characteristics they can and cannot take into account, in what circumstances and for what purpose. One of the main criticisms of the old law before *Holley* was that those courts which took the same approach as in *Smith* effectively subjectivized (and, in so doing, diluted) the normative elements in a way which was morally repugnant (eg, by taking account of the defendant's discreditable characteristics) and this predictably led to calls for 'purer' objective requirements. At the same time though, Ashworth pointed out that if the principle of autonomy is to be maintained, an objective test should be subject to capacity-based exceptions.[90] The principle of autonomy, that each person should be treated as responsible for his own conduct, implies that each individual has sufficient free will to choose how to behave in any situation and thus should be regarded as an independent agent. If the conduct breaches the law the individual can rightly be held liable and punished. The danger in adopting objective requirements is that any individual may, through no fault of his own, be incapable of acting in a way which would have avoided contravening the law. This, of course, echoes the concern of Lords Hoffmann and Clyde in *Smith* that the law would be unjustified in expecting a person to conform to a standard of which he is, through no fault on his part, incapable of achieving.

Given the New Labour government's desire to 'toughen up' this part of the law it is not surprising to find that the new plea is littered with objective requirements—apart from the obvious 'person with a normal degree of tolerance and self-restraint . . . ' test, those who rely on the fear trigger must fear *serious* violence, which will surely be construed according to what the court treats as serious; those who rely on the words and/or conduct trigger will only succeed if the court thinks they are of an *extremely grave* character and that they caused the defendant to have a *justifiable* sense of being *seriously* wronged. In some cases the facts are likely to be such that it is clear whether these tests are or are not fulfilled, but there will be many where there is no such certainty.[91] Thus, any benefits which may be derived by adopting a stricter normative requirement are, at least in the early years before any line of authority or clarity is established, likely to be at the cost of maximum certainty.

Judicial directions to the jury

At this relatively early stage in the life of the new law it is obviously difficult to predict with confidence how it will work in practice, but it is impossible not to be concerned that juries will find it perplexing. In addition to the ambiguities in some of the words and phrases in ss 54 and 55 of the 2009 Act, the structure and wording of it is complicated, and judges are likely to be hard-pressed to explain it in clear and simple terms. The jury needs to be told that the burden is on the prosecution to

[90] Ashworth, n 6 above, 189.

[91] Moreover, there is the danger that a purely objective interpretation of these words will lead to injustice by denying the plea to deserving defendants such as battered women or very young defendants.

satisfy them that the plea fails.[92] They should be advised to consider evidence of one of the two recognized triggers. For the fear trigger, was it of *serious* violence; did the defendant fear the violence would emanate from the victim; was the feared violence directed at the defendant or another? For the words or conduct trigger, did this constitute something of an *extremely grave character; and did it cause the defendant to justifiably feel she had been seriously wronged?* In relation to either trigger, was it self-induced? If the killing was prompted solely through sexual infidelity or in considered desire for revenge, the plea must fail. Whichever trigger is appropriate, the defendant must have lost her self-control and not regained it at the time of the assault, and the jury must be made aware of what constitutes such a loss. Then they have to consider the objective test, whether a person of the defendant's age and sex, 'with a normal degree of tolerance and self-restraint, and in the defendant's circumstances, might have reacted in the same or in a similar way'. The judge will have to identify which of the defendant's circumstances might be applicable. He will have to tell the jury to ignore any morally repugnant or discreditable characteristics, and only take account of any mental abnormalities if they were relevant to the trigger. The new law thus surely makes very heavy demands both of judges and juries.

The relationship between loss of self-control and diminished responsibility

Evidence of both loss of self-control and diminished responsibility might arise in the course of any individual case, even though following the Privy Council's decision in *Holley*, and certainly under the Coroners and Justice Act 2009, the two pleas should now be regarded as mutually exclusive: if pleaded in the same case they ought to be considered in the alternative.[93] Where a person was suffering from an 'abnormality of mental functioning' (as defined in section 52 of the Coroners and Justice Act 2009) which caused him to lose his self-control and strike out with fatal violence, then he may plead diminished responsibility, regardless of any provocation to which he may have been subjected. Evidence of such abnormality may also be relevant where the defendant pleads loss of self-control (under the words and/or conduct trigger) if it is the object of the provocation. To that extent therefore, the defendant can raise both pleas, but this presents a potential problem. Where diminished responsibility is relied on, the burden of proof lies with the defendant and the burden must be discharged on a balance of probabilities;[94] whereas it is for the prosecution to disprove beyond reasonable doubt a loss of self-control.[95] Clearly, there is a real likelihood that these differences in the burdens and standards of proof will cause considerable difficulties for juries.

[92] Coroners and Justice Act 2009, s 54(5).

[93] The author has begun to monitor the operation of the new law and has already encountered cases in which both pleas are being raised, but the basis on which they are raised is unknown.

[94] Homicide Act 1957, s 2(2), and *Dunbar* [1958] 1 QB 1 (CCA).

[95] Coroners and Justice Act 2009, s 54(5) and (6).

Sentencing

It is worth making some brief comments about sentencing in provocation manslaughter cases as well as on the substantive law. The guidelines drafted by the then Sentencing Guidelines Council in 2005 indicate that, as Ashworth had suggested many years earlier,[96] the dominant consideration when determining the appropriate sentence in provocation manslaughter should be the objective seriousness of the provocation itself.[97] Other factors include the extent and timing of the retaliation, post-offence behaviour, and the use of a weapon. Judges need to have clear lines of direction. For example, where there is a short time between the provocation and the loss of self-control the defendant's culpability is likely to be less, but longer gaps between the two should not necessarily imply greater culpability in cases of cumulative provocation. The use of a weapon prima facie suggests greater culpability, but only if it was carried to the scene by the defendant—if it was used simply because it was conveniently at hand, no real increase in seriousness is implied. In addition, there may be an important difference between a man and a woman—who may be significantly weaker than her victim—using a weapon.

The SGC guidelines state that where there is a high degree of provocation over a short period, the starting point should be three years' custody, up to a maximum of four years. In cases of substantial provocation (over a short period) the starting point should be eight years, within a range of four to nine years; and if the provocation was at a low level over a short time, the starting point should be twelve years, and the range ten years to life imprisonment. Bearing in mind that offenders serving a year or more in prison can expect to be released at the half-way stage,[98] Ashworth indicated that some of these sentences—where the provocation is high—seem very low.[99] Provocation (now loss of control) manslaughter is a form of mitigated murder, and on average murderers can expect to spend at least 15 or 16 years in prison before being able to apply for release on licence.[100] As Ashworth explained, the justification for the low sentences must be based on the offender's reduced culpability arising out of the loss of self-control and partial justification for that loss. But, not surprisingly perhaps, the political tide appears to have turned in favour of tougher sentences where the harm is so serious, and as Ashworth rightly suggests, the current guidelines may have to be revised. It has recently been suggested that one consequence of the enactment of Sch 21 to the Criminal Justice Act 2003 will be a general ratcheting up of sentences for all serious crimes, including manslaughter by provocation/loss of control.[101] Indeed, dealing with

[96] AJ Ashworth, 'Sentencing in Provocation Cases' [1975] Crim LR 553, 560.

[97] Sentencing Guidelines Council, *Manslaughter by Reason of Provocation* (London: SGC, 2005), paras 3.2 and 4.2.

[98] Criminal Justice Act 2003, s 244.

[99] A Ashworth, *Sentencing and Criminal Justice* (5th edn, Cambridge: Cambridge University Press, 2010), 122.

[100] Statistics kindly provided to the author by the National Offender Management Service. The shortest minimum term which a convicted murderer is likely to serve is about 6 years.

[101] D Jeremy, 'Sentencing Policy or Short-term Expediency?' [2010] Crim LR 593.

an appeal against sentence in an unlawful and dangerous act manslaughter case the Lord Chief Justice commented that following the 2003 Act 'crimes which result in death should be treated more seriously and dealt with more severely than before'.[102]

4. Provocation and Principles

It was not surprising to find such a strong desire to be rid of the old provocation plea, though one of the underlying problems was the struggle to identify a clear rationale behind it. Some commentators have categorized it as essentially excusatory, on the basis that the defendant was acting out of control (as a consequence of the provocation) and was thus less culpable.[103] Others, such as Ashworth, acknowledged this but also recognized an element of justification in the loss of self-control.[104] Yet a third school of opinion preferred to regard the rationale as one of partial responsibility because of the disturbed mental or emotional state of mind of the defendant.[105] But much of the criticism of the provocation plea must surely be attributed to a failure to consistently follow or apply legal principles and policies. An obvious concern with both the old and almost certainly the new law is the failure to comply with the principle of maximum certainty.[106] There was uncertainty about how far the courts would look closely at the evidence of a loss of self-control, about which characteristics would be treated as relevant to the objective test (especially whether they would adopt the *Smith* or *Holley* approach), and thus about the relationship between provocation and diminished responsibility.

The latter two issues appear to have been settled under the new law, but it remains to be seen how the courts construe the central concept of loss of self-control. If they regard it in the same light as under the old law, then much of the potential benefit to battered women from the introduction of the fear of serious violence trigger will effectively be frustrated (as under the old law). In addition, much of the terminology of the new law—especially in the words and/or conduct trigger (extremely grave character, justifiable sense of being seriously wronged)—is ambiguous, so that certainty will depend on the emergence of a clear and consistent body of case law. It is perhaps too early to be really critical, and as Ashworth reminds us, the principle is of *maximum* not *absolute* certainty,[107] so that some uncertainty is inescapable in order to avoid undue rigidity.[108]

Concerns have also been raised about the extent to which the old law complied with the principle of proportionality. One of the central criticisms of the old law was

[102] *Appleby* [2009] EWCA Crim 2693, [2010] 2 Cr App R (S) 46.

[103] See eg J Dressler, 'Provocation, Partial Justification or Partial Excuse?' (1998) 51 MLR 467.

[104] Ashworth, n 6 above, 254.

[105] Mitchell et al, n 9 above.

[106] Referring to the obvious potential ambiguity of the wording in s 55(3) and (4), Lord Judge CJ warned in *Clinton* [2012] EWCA Crim 2 at [11]: '[T]here is no point in pretending that the practical application of this provision will not create considerable difficulties.... The statutory language is not bland.'

[107] Ashworth, n 6 above, 66.

[108] Ashworth refers to this as part of a policy of social defence, n 6 above, 66, 67.

that it accommodated undeserving defendants, inter alia because the courts did not always insist on a loss of self-control, and because they sometimes took account of inappropriate characteristics of the defendant instead of adopting a tougher normative approach. In other words, there was a lack of proportion between the real mitigation and the verdict. The courts were encouraged to look at the relationship between the gravity of the provocation and the defendant's retaliation to it, whereas Ashworth argued that it should have been between the provocation and the defendant's loss of self-control (rather than the nature of the violence he used against the victim). Ashworth's worry that some cases resulted in disproportionately short prison sentences being imposed, when compared to the minimum terms imposed in murder cases, is a further obvious example of his concern to maintain a principled approach. It remains to be seen how the principle of proportionality will be addressed under the new law. The government clearly hopes that fewer pleas under the 2009 Act will succeed, and judges can now exclude consideration of loss of control in what are viewed as weak cases. Nevertheless, there must be a real fear that the retention of the loss of self-control requirement will continue to thwart many deserving cases.

PART II

CRIMINAL PROCESS AND HUMAN RIGHTS

9

Positive Obligations and Criminal Justice: Duties to Protect or Coerce?

*Liora Lazarus**

Andrew Ashworth's prodigious body of work on criminal law, criminal law theory, and sentencing theory has more recently been complemented by a relatively newer strand of enquiry on the relationship between criminal law, criminal justice, and human rights.[1] I have been privileged to co-teach two graduate courses with Professor Ashworth on this area. The relationship between human rights, criminal law, and criminal justice is relatively under-explored, as it requires an intimate knowledge of more than one field of law. Few are better placed than Ashworth.

Ashworth's scholarship in this area is wide ranging, and he has produced a body of work which provides a framework within which to balance respect for human rights and the pursuit of safety and security, or 'the reduction of harm and reduction of the risk of harm',[2] through the criminal law. Much of his work has focused on unearthing the human rights safeguards aimed at constraining coercive activity through criminal procedure. He has sought to outline the ways in which habeas corpus and fair trial rights can be used as principles to regulate the criminal process as a whole, and to tame the excesses of political pursuits of security and

* Fellow in Law, St Anne's College, Oxford. My thanks must go to Julia Lowis for her excellent case research work in support of this essay, and to Miles Jackson and the editors of this volume for their feedback. Any errors are my own.

[1] Some examples include: A Ashworth, *Human Rights, Serious Crime and Criminal Procedure* (London: Sweet & Maxwell, 2002); A Ashworth and B Emmerson, *Human Rights and Criminal Justice* (London: Sweet & Maxwell, 2001); A Ashworth, 'Criminal Law, Human Rights and Preventative Justice' in B McSherry, A Norrie, and S Bronitt (eds), *Regulating Deviance: The Redirection of Criminalisation and the Futures of Criminal Law* (Oxford: Hart, 2009); A Ashworth and D van Zyl Smit, 'Disproportionate Sentences as Human Rights Violations' (2004) 67 MLR 541; A Ashworth, 'Criminal Procedure, Human Rights and Balance' in T Elholm et al (eds), *Ikke kun Straf: Festskrift til Vagn Greve* (Copenhagen: Jurist- og Økonomforbundet Forlag, 2008); A Ashworth, 'Security, Terrorism and the Value of Human Rights' in BJ Goold and L Lazarus (eds), *Security and Human Rights* (Oxford: Hart Publishing, 2007); A Ashworth, 'Criminal Justice Reform: Principles, Human Rights and Public Protection' [2004] Crim LR 516; A Ashworth and M Strange, 'Criminal Law and Human Rights' [2004] European Human Rights Law Review 121.

[2] A Ashworth, 'Criminal Law, Human Rights and Preventative Justice' in B McSherry, A Norrie, and S Bronitt (eds), *Regulating Deviance: The Redirection of Criminalisation and the Futures of Criminal Law* (Oxford: Hart Publishing, 2009).

public protection.[3] But in his more recent work, Ashworth acknowledges that while 'the constraints imposed by the European Convention on Human Rights (ECHR) are significant in relation to criminal procedure', they are 'slightly less significant in matters of sentencing and not extensive at all in the criminal law itself'. He is led to conclude that the 'Convention leaves large gaps in the normative coverage, having nothing to say on major issues'.[4]

As a consequence, Ashworth, whose concern is with the unjustified expansion of the criminal law, seeks to develop human rights principles to underpin a 'liberal theory of criminalisation' based on the principle of harm.[5] He, along with Lucia Zedner, is right to be worried about the spread of the preventative justice model of criminal law and the potential for coercive overreach.[6] Ashworth's use of human rights (in particular, rights under the ECHR) is thus directed to the limitation of the preventative measures that have proliferated in recent years. His focus on the limiting powers of rights such as liberty (Article 5 ECHR) and fair trial (Article 6 ECHR) is at the core of this project.

What I propose to do in this essay is to explore the relationship between criminal law, criminal process, and human rights from a slightly different perspective. I will seek to demonstrate that while human rights may well be used to limit the excesses of security and law and order politics, the nature of the relationship between human rights and criminal justice cannot be captured alone by the view of rights as a limit on the coercive reach of the criminal law and criminal justice institutions. Increasingly, human rights, cast as positive rights, have resulted in claims for the extension of the criminal law, the creation of preventative duties or 'protective policing measures',[7] for the intensification of policing and prosecution of sexual and violent crimes in particular, and threats to security or public protection in general.

The story is a complex one which is intimately linked to the growing international acceptance of human rights as including positive rights, and hence a shift from a conception of rights as a limitation on state action to one which now views rights as demands for such action.[8] The result is a process whereby the human rights of those subject to harm—such as the right to life, the right against torture, inhuman and degrading treatment, the right to private life, the right against discrimination, and the right to security—have now combined to create what I argue are most accurately described as *coercive duties* on the state to criminalize, prevent, police, and prosecute harmful acts. In short, I want to suggest that human rights may have more to say on the big questions of normative coverage of the

[3] Ashworth, n 2 above. [4] Ibid, 87, 93. [5] Ibid, 87, 94.

[6] A Ashworth and L Zedner, 'Just Prevention: Preventive Rationales and the Limits of the Criminal Law' in RA Duff and S Green (eds), *Philosophical Foundations of the Criminal Law* (Oxford: Oxford University Press, 2011).

[7] A Mowbray, *The Development of Positive Obligations under the European Convention on Human Rights by the European Court of Human Rights* (Oxford: Hart, 2004), 15.

[8] S Fredman, *Human Rights Transformed: Positive Rights and Positive Duties* (Oxford: Oxford University Press, 2008); Mowbray, n 7 above. See also discussion in L Lazarus et al, *The Evolution of Fundamental Rights Charters and Case Law: A Comparison of the United Nations, Council of Europe and European Union Systems* (Brussels: European Parliament Directorate General for Internal Policies, 2011), Part A.

criminal law than Ashworth accepts, and as a consequence we need to remain vigilant about the direction of positive duties which require coercive action from the state.

This trend is not only located within the jurisprudence of the European Convention on Human Rights, but is found within international law, as well as domestic constitutions and constitutional adjudication around the world.[9] Any account that seeks to capture adequately the relationship between criminal law, justice, and human rights will have to account for the ambiguity that human rights present: both as limiting coercion by the state and as requiring it. Moreover, accounts by human rights lawyers of the benefits of positive rights and duties in general[10] need to take account of the coercive potential which arises out of the logic of positive rights claims and rhetoric in relation to the criminal law.

The essay will start by outlining key areas where positive rights claims have shaped the criminal law and criminal justice process. It will then examine the relationship between positive rights and coercion and critique the language used to frame certain positive duties. Finally, the essay will use the right to security as a case study through which to demonstrate the concerns raised by the development of coercive duties.

1. Right to Life and Positive Duties

In a variety of jurisdictions, the right to life gives rise to positive duties that the state must fulfil in order to protect life. Here we will focus on the jurisprudence of the European Court of Human Rights (ECtHR). In *Osman v United Kingdom*, the Court developed a wide-ranging general duty out of the right to life, which set aside the exclusionary rule in the United Kingdom preventing the police from being held liable in negligence claims for failure to investigate crime.[11] According to the

[9] International human rights treaties have always protected positive rights, in particular socio-economic and cultural rights. The language of 'respect, protect, promote and fulfil' suffuses the various rights instruments, implying that even civil and political rights are not merely negative protections against the state. The political struggle for the equal recognition of economic, social, and cultural rights gained particular impetus at the 1993 Vienna World Conference and has been consistent since then. See Lazarus et al, n 8 above. The European Court of Human Rights (ECtHR) is by no means the pioneer regional court on the development of positive rights. The Inter-American Court of Human Rights laid out the basis for positive duties and due diligence requirement 20 years before this in *Velasquez-Rodriquez v Honduras*, judgment of 29 July 1988, IACtHR (series C) No 4. At the domestic level, the German Federal Constitutional Court developed the notion of positive duties even earlier in the 1970s (E Friesenhahn, 'Der Wandel des Grundrechtsverständnisses' in H Koätz (ed), *Verhandlungen des 50 Deutschen Juristentages* (Munich: Beck, 1974) G1; HH Rupp, 'Vom Wandel der Grundrechte' [1976] AöR 161). This also relates to the concept of protective duties which were used to protect the unborn foetus in 1975 (*BVerfGE* 39, 1).

[10] Mowbray, n 8 above; J McBride, 'Protecting Life: A Positive Obligation to Help' (1999) 24 European Law Review Human Rights Survey HR/43; JG Merrills, *The Development of International Law by the European Court of Human Rights* (Manchester: Manchester University Press, 1993), 102 f; K Starmer, *European Human Rights Law* (London: Legal Action Group, 1999), Ch 5; A Clapham, *Human Rights in the Private Sphere* (Oxford: Clarendon Press, 1993).

[11] *Osman v United Kingdom* (App no 23452/94) (2000) 29 EHRR 245.

ECtHR, a state has a *general* duty to individuals to protect the right to life. It is required to legislate 'effective criminal law provisions to deter the commission of offences against the person backed up by law-enforcement machinery for the prevention, suppression and sanctioning of breaches of such provisions'.[12]

Given that the specific duties of the state in these cases are also related to tortious liability, the ECtHR acknowledges that it cannot place 'an impossible or disproportionate burden on the authorities' as it has to keep 'bearing in mind the difficulties involved in policing modern societies, the unpredictability of human conduct and the operational choices which must be made in terms of priorities and resources'.[13] It also notes that 'another relevant consideration is the need to ensure that the police exercise their powers to control and prevent crime in a manner which fully respects the due process and other guarantees which legitimately place restraints on the scope of their action to investigate crime and bring offenders to justice, including the guarantees contained in Articles 5 [right to liberty] and 8 [right to private life] of the Convention'.[14]

As a consequence, 'not every claimed risk to life can entail for the authorities a Convention requirement to take operational measures to prevent that risk from materialising'.[15] Hence, states are only under a *specific* obligation 'in certain well-defined circumstances' to take proactive 'preventive operational measures to protect an individual whose life is at risk from the criminal acts of another'.[16] This specific obligation only arises where 'the authorities knew or ought to have known of the existence of a real and immediate risk to the life of an identified individual, and that they failed to take measures within their powers which, judged reasonably, might have been expected to avoid that risk'.[17] This delimited specific duty is clearly framed and informed by tortious notions of causation and responsibility.[18]

Since *Osman* was decided, a range of cases have been brought to Strasbourg involving the specific positive duty arising under the right to life,[19] and the question of whether the state has fulfilled the general positive duty.[20] The cases where a

[12] *Osman v United Kingdom* (App no 23452/94) (2000) 29 EHRR at [115].

[13] Ibid at [116].

[14] Ibid at [116].

[15] Ibid at [116].

[16] Ibid at [115].

[17] Ibid at [116].

[18] D Fairgreave, *State Liability in Tort: A Comparative Law Study* (Oxford: Oxford University Press, 2003); L Hoyano, 'Policing Flawed Police Investigations: Unravelling the Blanket' (1999) 62 MLR 912.

[19] Some examples include: *LCB v UK* (App no 2341/94) (1998) 27 EHRR 212; *Keenan v UK* (App no 27229/95) (2001) 33 EHRR 242; *Rantsev v Cyprus and Russia* (App no 25965/04) (2010) 51 EHRR 1; *Kilic v Turkey* (App no 22492/93) (2001) 33 EHRR 1357; *Mahmut Kaya v Turkey* (App no 22535/93) (ECHR 28 March 2000); *Nuray Sen v Turkey* (App no 25354/94) (ECHR 30 March 2004); *Akkoc v Turkey* (App no 22947/93) (2002) 34 EHRR 51; *Kontrova v Slovakia* (App no 7510/04) (ECHR 31 May 2007); *Demiray v Turkey* (App no 27308/95) (ECHR 21 November 2000); *Oneryldiz v Turkey* (App no 48939/99) (2005) 41 EHRR 325.

[20] *Rantsev v Cyprus and Russia* (App no 25965/04) (2010) 51 EHRR 1; *Kilic v Turkey* (App no 22492/93) (2001) 33 EHRR 1357; *Mahmut Kaya v Turkey* (App no 22535/93) (ECHR 28 March 2000); *Nuray Sen v Turkey* (App no 25354/94) (ECHR 30 March 2004); *Akkoc v Turkey* (App no 22947/93) (2002) 34 EHRR 51; *Shanaghan v UK* (App no 37715/97) (ECHR 4 May 2001); *Nachova v Bulgaria* (App no 43577/98) (2004) 39 EHRR 793; *Kontrova v Slovakia* (App no 7510/04) (ECHR

breach of the general duty has been found have mostly centred on the state's failure properly to investigate a death.[21] This constitutes a breach of an ancillary procedural obligation under Article 2 (right to life) to 'conduct an effective investigation into the death and instigate criminal proceedings where necessary'.[22] The duty to investigate supplements the general duty of the state to put in place criminal law and policing measures to prevent and deter violations of the right to life. In the ECtHR jurisprudence, breach of the investigative duty is particularly likely to be found where the state has failed properly to investigate a killing which may have been racially motivated, and which also engages Article 14 (prohibition on discrimination).[23] The procedural obligation to investigate deaths also presupposes the setting-up of an efficient judicial system, and in some circumstances recourse to criminal law.[24]

Despite the potentially expansive scope of the general duty under *Osman*, the ECtHR's jurisprudence regarding the right to life has thus far given rise to clearly identifiable and delimited positive duties, which places the standard of fault very high. Given that murder is very likely to be criminalized, the general positive duties that have arisen out of this case law have dealt with serious deficiencies in the investigation, prosecution, and trial flowing from deaths. There is a number of cases where applicants have argued for the extension of the criminal law to acts resulting in death.[25] In two cases of medical negligence, one dealing with the death of an unborn foetus,[26] the Court held that civil law remedies were sufficient and that the right to life did not automatically require recourse to criminal law sanctions where breaches occur.

But the threshold at which criminal law sanctions are required by Article 2, or at which sanctions should be imposed, is not always set this high. In *Oneryildiz v Turkey* the state was held liable for being too lenient on local mayors whose 'negligent omissions' resulted in the death of a number of Turkish citizens where

31 May 2007); *Demiray v Turkey* (App no 27308/95) (ECHR 21 November 2000); *Mastromatteo v Italy* (App no 37703/97) ECHR 2002-VIII 689; *Calvelli v Ciglio v Italy* (App no 32967/96) (ECHR 17 January 2002); *Vo v France* (App no 53924/00) (2005) 40 EHRR 259; *Oneryldiz v Turkey* (App no 48939/99) (2005) 41 EHRR 325.

[21] *Angelova and Iliev v Bulgaria* (App no 55523/00) (26 July 2007); *Rantsev v Cyprus and Russia* (App no 25965/04) (2010) 51 EHRR 1; *Kilic v Turkey* (App no 22492/93) (2001) 33 EHRR 1357; *Mahmut Kaya v Turkey* (App no 22535/93) (ECHR 28 March 2000); *Nuray Sen v Turkey* (App no 25354/94) (ECHR 30 March 2004); *Akkoc v Turkey* (App no 22947/93) (2002) 34 EHRR 51; *Kontrova v Slovakia* (App no 7510/04) (ECHR 31 May 2007); *Demiray v Turkey* (App no 27308/95) (ECHR 21 November 2000).

[22] See, on standards of the investigation, *Keenan v UK* (App no 27229/95) (2001) 33 EHRR 242; *Jordan v UK* (App no 24746/94) (2003) 37 EHRR 2.

[23] *Menson v UK* (App no 47916/99) (ECHR 6 May 2003); *Nachova v Bulgaria* (App no 43577/98) (2004) 39 EHRR 793; *Angelova and Iliev v Bulgaria* (App no 55523/00) (ECHR 26 July 2007); but see *Shanaghan v UK* (App no 37715/97) (ECHR 4 May 2001), where the obligation to investigate possible racist overtones was not viewed as mandatory unless there was a real and legitimate concern of discriminatory practice.

[24] *Vo v France* (App no 53924/00) (2005) 40 EHRR 259; *Demiray v Turkey* (App no 27308/95) (ECHR 21 November 2000).

[25] *Calvelli v Ciglio v Italy* (App no 32967/96) (ECHR 17 January 2002); *Vo v France* (App no 53924/00) (2005) 40 EHRR 259; *Oneryldiz v Turkey* (App no 48939/99) (2005) 41 EHRR 325.

[26] *Vo v France* (App no 53924/00) (2005) 40 EHRR 25.

a rubbish dump collapsed on their shacks after a methane explosion.[27] The mayors were held guilty of 'negligent omissions in the performance of their duties' (§230 of the Turkish Criminal Code) and given a suspended fine, which was the lowest available penalty. The ECtHR took the view that the criminal provision in question did 'not in any way relate to life-endangering acts or to the protection of the right to life within the meaning of Article 2' and hence there was no 'acknowledgment of any responsibility for failing to protect the right to life'. The Court argued further that there was no 'precise indication that the trial court had sufficient regard to the extremely serious consequences of the accident; the persons held responsible were ultimately sentenced to derisory fines, which were, moreover, suspended'. As a consequence the ECtHR concluded:

> It cannot be said that the manner in which the Turkish criminal justice system operated in response to the tragedy secured the full accountability of state officials or authorities for their role in it and the effective implementation of provisions of domestic law guaranteeing respect for the right to life, in particular the deterrent function of the criminal law. In short, it must be concluded in the instant case that there has also been a violation of Article 2 of the Convention in its procedural aspect, on account of the lack, in connection with a fatal accident provoked by the operation of a dangerous activity, of adequate protection 'by law' safeguarding the right to life and deterring similar life-endangering conduct in future.[28]

Oneryildiz is only one example of how the right to life can have an intensifying effect on the shape and implementation of the criminal law, on the exercise of prosecutorial discretion, the conduct of a criminal trial, and on the type and gravity of sentence. There are other instances where the ECtHR has held that ordinary criminal law protections were not effective enough due to basic defects in the ambit and implementation of the criminal law. Many of these are very extreme cases in the south-east region of Turkey and concern the criminal law regulation of official killings of Kurds suspected of supporting the PKK.[29] But not all successful applications are limited to such politically extreme circumstances. In *Kontrova v Slovakia*,[30] the ECtHR found the state in breach of the right to life where the police had failed to respond adequately to an initial complaint of domestic violence, which was directly related to the deaths of two children. In this case, the ECtHR was particularly critical of the fact that 'one of the officers involved assisted the applicant and her husband in modifying her criminal complaint of 2 November 2002 so that it could be treated as a minor offence calling for no further action'.[31] This action, and other dereliction of police duties in response to the emergency calls of the applicant, were seen as leading directly to the death of the applicant's two children and were key in the success of this application.

[27] *Onerlydiz v Turkey* (App no 48939/99) (2005) 41 EHRR 325 at [118].

[28] Ibid at [116]–[117].

[29] *Mahmut Kaya v Turkey* (App no 22535/93) (ECHR 28 March 2000); *Kilic v Turkey*, (App no 22492/93) (2001) 33 EHRR 1357 and *Akkoc v Turkey* (App no 22947/93) (2002) 34 EHRR 51 held that the transfer of jurisdiction to national security forces for terrorist crimes was incompatible with Art 6.

[30] *Kontrova v Slovakia* (App no 7510/04) (ECHR 31 May 2007).

[31] Ibid at [54].

The case law on the right to life is instructive in respect of how positive rights claims, most frequently arising out of tortious actions against the state, can shape the criminal law and its enforcement in a variety of circumstances. Later in this essay, the broader implications of such duties will be explored. Suffice it to say, at this stage, that the rhetoric of positive duties in relation to the right to life is not confined to the court rooms. Politicians and state actors are all aware of, and quick to deploy, a justification for an increasing range of preventative criminal law measures based on the right to life. This is also mirrored in the language of the right to security in a range of jurisdictions and will be explored in a later part of this essay. In short, case law is one thing, it is another matter how states and governments translate the messages they are hearing from the ECtHR and other constitutional courts, and how they are incorporating these messages into the rhetoric of public protection. The risk of coercive overreach may not lie then in the specific decisions of the courts, but rather in the reception of the messages in question within a broader politics of security.

2. Gender Violence and Positive Duties

Since the Convention on the Elimination of All Forms of Discrimination Against Women (CEDAW) was adopted by the UN General Assembly, gender violence has been the subject of extensive international law activity.[32] This includes the 19th General Recommendation of the CEDAW Committee,[33] which notes that states should 'take appropriate and effective measures to overcome all forms of gender-based violence, whether by public or private act' and 'ensure that laws against family violence and abuse, rape, sexual assault and other gender-based violence give adequate protection to all women, and respect their integrity and dignity'.[34] Similarly, the General Assembly Declaration on the Elimination of Violence Against Women (DEVW) enshrines a 'due diligence' standard and enjoins states to 'pursue by all appropriate means and without delay a policy of eliminating violence against women' including: exercising 'due diligence to prevent, investigate and in accordance with national legislation, punish acts of violence against women, whether those acts are perpetrated by the state or by private persons'.[35] The international duty of due diligence with respect to the treatment of violence against women is also supported by the Committee of Ministers of the Council of Europe in their Recommendation (2002), which obliges states to penalize all non-consensual sexual acts, including where the victim does not show resistance.[36]

Much of this international activity is directed towards systemic reform of the treatment of victims of gender violence and could not be said to establish positive

[32] L Lazarus, 'The Human Rights Framework Relating to the Handling, Investigation and Prosecution of Rape Complaints', Annex A to *The Stern Review* (London: Home Office, 2010).

[33] General Recommendation 19 of 29 January 1992.

[34] Ibid, s 24.

[35] General Assembly Resolution 48/104 of 20 December 1993, Art 4.

[36] Recommendation no R (2002) 5 adopted by the Committee of Ministers on 30 April 2002 and Explanatory Memorandum. H/Inf (2004).

duties directed at the coercion of perpetrators of gender violence. Nevertheless, there is little question that the activities have led to an extension of the criminal law, and a strong intensification of the policing and prosecution of acts of gender violence. This was particularly evident in the case of *MC v Bulgaria*, where the ECtHR declared itself:

> . . . persuaded that any rigid approach to the prosecution of sexual offences, such as requiring proof of physical resistance in all circumstances, risks leaving certain types of rape unpunished and thus jeopardizing the effective protection of the individual's sexual autonomy. In accordance with contemporary standards and trends in that area, the Member States' positive obligations under Articles 3 [prohibition on torture, inhuman and degrading treatment] and 8 of the Convention must be seen as requiring the penalisation and effective prosecution of any non-consensual act, including the absence of physical resistance by the victim.[37]

The international law obligations, soft law, and jurisprudence of the ECtHR have all played into domestic court interpretations of the right to sexual autonomy and rape. This is evident in both the South African and English cases, which we will return to below.[38]

3. Domestic Violence and Violence against Children

A number of decisions by the ECtHR have developed protective duties with respect to domestic violence and violence against children. *Opuz v Turkey* dealt with a pattern of domestic violence culminating in a murder.[39] The authorities repeatedly failed to take special measures to protect the victims, on the grounds that they were limited by the applicable domestic law. Here the ECtHR incorporated a broader view of the discriminatory nature of violence against women. The decision, which was heavily influenced by the CEDAW Committee's work and the Recommendations of the Committee of Ministers of the Council of Europe, declared that the ineffectiveness of domestic remedies and the failure to take pre-emptive protective measures in relation to domestic violence constituted a violation of Article 14, as well as Articles 2 and 3 (prohibition on torture, inhuman, and degrading treatment) in this context. The Court was highly critical of the authorities' failure to consider properly the risks and threats that the offender posed. It rejected the government's arguments that there was no 'tangible evidence' that the life of the victim was in danger.[40] The Court noted that no attempt had been made to balance the risks and consider the proportionality of particular protective measures.[41] Notably, however, it added, citing decisions of the CEDAW Committee, that:

[37] *MC v Bulgaria* (App no 39278/98) (2005) 40 EHRR 20 at [166].

[38] *R v G* [2008] UKHL 37, [2009] 1 AC 92; *S v Chapman* 1997 (3) SA 342 (SCA); *The State v Baloyi* (2000) 1 SACR 81 (CC).

[39] *Opuz v Turkey* (App no 33401/02) (ECHR 9 June 2009).

[40] Ibid at [147].

[41] The ECtHR was equally critical of the Croatian authorities for failure to implement protective measures that had been ordered against an abusive husband in *A v Croatia* (App no 55164/08) (ECHR 14 October 2010). Here the Court found a violation of the victim's personal and psychological

In any event, the Court underlines that in domestic violence cases perpetrators' rights cannot supersede victims' rights to life and to physical and mental integrity.[42]

It is striking that the countervailing rights and interests of those subject to protective measures received so little regard here. This is a theme to which we return at a number of points later in this essay.

In *Opuz*, the ECtHR identified women and children as 'vulnerable groups entitled to State protection'.[43] This is consistent with a range of decisions regarding violence against children. One of these cases, *A v UK*,[44] resulted in a clear extension of the criminal law by redefining the context in which the defence of 'reasonable chastisement' could be invoked. The Court took the view that 'beating of a child aged 9 year old with a garden cane applied with considerable force reached the severity [of treatment] prohibited by Article 3'.[45] It was clear that Article 3 placed positive obligations on the state, and hence 'children and other vulnerable individuals in particular are entitled to State protection, in the form of effective deterrence, against such breaches of personal integrity'.[46] Hence placing the burden of proof on the prosecution to 'establish beyond reasonable doubt that the assault went beyond the limits of law punishment' meant that the 'law did not provide adequate protection to V against treatment contrary to article 3, constituting a violation of article 3'.[47] *A v UK* remains one of the least popular decisions of the ECtHR in the United Kingdom, having clearly extended criminal law protections against parental chastisement.

Three further ground-breaking cases regarding domestic abuse of children gave rise to a significant change in tort law in the United Kingdom.[48] These all involved the failure of local authorities to prevent gross or sexual abuse of children, giving rise to potential breaches of Articles 3 and 8. The Court held that 'the obligation imposed by art. 3 requires that the State take measures to provide effective protection, in particular, of children and other vulnerable persons and take reasonable steps to prevent the ill-treatment of which the authorities had or ought to have had knowledge'.[49] While the threshold of this substantive test was not met in *DP*, all cases rejected the rule in *X v Bedfordshire*, which protected local authorities from liability in negligence in respect of the exercise of their statutory duties to protect children.[50] The *X v Bedfordshire* rule was held to violate Article 13 ECHR (right to

integrity under Art 8 of the Convention (right to private life). The Court did not find sufficient evidence to ground a claim of discrimination against women however, and was not persuaded that the actions were discriminatory.

42 *Opuz v Turkey* (App no 33401/02) (ECHR 9 June 2009) at [147].

43 Ibid at [160].

44 *A v UK* (App no 25599/94) (ECHR 23 September 1998).

45 Ibid at [21].

46 Ibid at [22].

47 Ibid at [23]–[24].

48 *Z v UK* (App no 29392/95) (ECHR 10 May 2001); *E v UK* (App no 33218/96) (ECHR 26 November 2002); *DP v UK* (App no 38719/97) (ECHR 10 October 2002).

49 *E v UK* (App no 33218/96) (ECHR 26 November 2002) at [88].

50 *X (Minors) v Bedfordshire CC* [1995] 2 AC 633 (HL).

an effective remedy), which requires a 'mechanism for establishing any liability of State officials or bodies for acts or omissions involving the breach of their rights under the Convention'.[51] The child protection cases demonstrate clearly how protective duties arising from international and regional human rights law obligations can transform the contours of domestic tort law, even where the implications for criminal law are not as evident.

4. Protective Duties and the Right to Security

A range of protective duties have arisen out of the right to security in South Africa where the right is enshrined in the Constitution.[52] The Constitutional Court and Supreme Court have been faced with a number of applications regarding the failure of police to protect individuals who have been subject to serious violence and sexual violence.[53] As with the ECtHR in *MC v Bulgaria*, these cases often raise the right to security in conjunction with other rights such as the prohibition on gender-based violence in international law. While the South African courts have accepted a broad duty to 'protect the right of everyone to be free from violence',[54] they have (again like the ECtHR) constrained the coercive duties arising from this right by considerations of reasonableness, proximity, and resource constraints.[55]

This legal taming of far-reaching demands for state coercion arising out of the right to security is welcome, but similarly to the ECtHR jurisprudence most of these cases have involved claims against the state in respect of its failure to act. Here it is the Court's decision whether the state is at fault, and responsible for wrongs committed in circumstances where it has failed to arrest individuals (*Carmichele*), granted bail to suspects (*Carmichele*), released individual offenders or allowed offenders to escape (*Van Eeden*), or failed to secure the security of individuals on commuter trains (*Metrorail*), where there was an evident risk of harm occurring. Because these cases are about actionable claims and the clear attribution of responsibility, the construction of the duty here has been intimately connected to the South African equivalent of tort law, the law of delict. Hence, while the founding duty is broadly framed, the obligation on the state is constrained by questions of reasonableness (as is the case in the ECtHR's approach to the right to life). As stated in *Van Eeden*:

[51] *Z v UK* (App no 29392/95) (ECHR 10 May 2001) at [109].

[52] South African Constitution, Art 12(1)(c), obliges the state directly to protect the right of everyone 'to be free from all forms of violence from either public or private sources'.

[53] *S v Baloyi (Minister of Justice Intervening)* 2000 (1) BCLR 86 (CC); *Rail Commuters Action Group v Transnet Ltd t/a Metrorail* 2005 (4) BCLR 301 (CC); *Minister of Safety and Security v Van Duivenboden*, case no 209/2001; *Carmichele v Minister of Safety and Security* 2001 (4) BCLR 938 (CC); *Van Eeden v Minister of Safety and Security* 2003 (1) SA 389 (SCA).

[54] South African Constitution, Art 12(1)(c); *S v Baloyi (Minister of Justice Intervening)* 2000 (1) BCLR 86 (CC).

[55] *Rail Commuters Action Group v Transnet Ltd t/a Metrorail* 2005 (4) BCLR 301 (CC).

A defendant is under a legal duty to act positively to prevent harm to the plaintiff if it is reasonable to expect of the defendant to have taken positive measures to prevent the harm. The court determines whether it is reasonable to have expected of the defendant to have done so by making a value judgment, based *inter alia* upon its perception of the legal convictions of the community and on considerations of policy. The question whether a legal duty exists in a particular case is thus a conclusion of law depending on a consideration of all the circumstances of the case and on the interplay of the many factors which have to be considered.[56]

The delimitation of positive duties in South Africa echoes the approach taken in *Osman* and is also reflected in the ECtHR's restricted approach to local authority liability in the child abuse cases.[57] Clearly these restrictions of the protective duties of the state are welcome. But, as a later part of this essay will demonstrate, this approach does not always travel across to cases where the issue is one of balance between an individual right and the state's protective duty.

5. Positive Rights and the Coercive Sting

Having provided a brief overview of the kind of rights claims that can result in positive duties related to the scope of the criminal law (and tort or delict law) and the way in which criminal justice institutions behave, we might reflect for a moment on how these duties can be properly characterized.

Human rights theorists argue persuasively that a theory of rights conceived only as limits on state action is premised on a set of misplaced conceptions. Fredman argues that a conception of rights as limitations is premised on 'a conception of freedom as absence of interference' and 'a characterization of the State as separate from and opposed to the individual'. In contrast, values of 'substantive equality', 'social solidarity', and participative democracy give rise to a strong claim that rights give rise to a range of duties which involve 'positive action' as well as 'restraint'.[58] Fredman is joined by a range of contemporary rights theorists who are agreed that rights go beyond subjective individual entitlements that place limitations on the state or other duty bearers, and that rights incorporate the notion that states or other actors have duties to respect and protect rights and not merely a duty to desist

56 *Van Eeden v Minister of Safety and Security* 2003 (1) SA 389 (SCA) at [9].

57 The South African and ECtHR approach is also echoed in India, where a series of cases has established that the state could be held liable for negligent acts resulting in the violation of the right to life (what many refer now to as a 'constitutional tort'). See *National Human Rights Commission v State of Arunachal Pradesh* AIR 1996 SC 1234; *M Hongray v Union of India* AIR 1984 SC 1026; *Challa Ramkonda Reddy v State of Andhra Pradesh* (1990) ACJ 668; *R Gandhi v Union of India* AIR 1989 Mad 205; *M/s Inderpuri General Stores v Union of India* AIR 1992 J&K 11; *Manjit Singh Sawhney v Union of India* 2005 Indlaw DEL 379; K Cooper-Stephenson, 'The Emergence of Constitutional Torts Worldwide', presented at the Conference on Comparative Constitutionalism on 12 December 2005, University of Kwazulu-Natal, South Africa.

58 S Fredman, *Human Rights Transformed: Positive Rights and Positive Duties* (Oxford: Oxford University Press, 2008), 1.

from violating them.[59] In the words of Shue: 'taking rights seriously means taking duties seriously'.[60]

These moral claims are hard to refute, and it is not the objective here to take to task those who have proposed them. Even if we do not accept these foundational moral arguments, any analysis of the analytical structure of rights naturally leads us to accept that rights give rise to positive duties. The work on the structure of rights by theorists such as Hohfeld and Jellinek directs us just as comfortably to the conclusion that positive duties are an inevitable consequence of the recognition of a right.[61] So to avoid any doubt on this question, the claim here is not that there is a foundational or analytical problem with the recognition of positive duties arising out of human rights.

Neither is the claim here that positive duties inevitably result in coercion. Many positive duties which relate to the criminal law and criminal justice agencies are not directed towards the coercion of perpetrators of harm. For example, much of the due diligence requirement with respect to gender violence is directed towards systemic reforms required for the sensitive treatment of victims of sexual violence. Moreover, the term 'coercion' can encompass a range of interferences with the liberty of individuals which are not all of equal gravity. A system of taxation that distributes resources within society so as to protect the dignity rights of the worst off necessarily entails some limitations on the property rights of all individuals in that society. This normally involves law enforcement and the coercion of individuals who breach these rules. These kinds of coercive activities which arise indirectly from the assertion of a general human right such as dignity or equality are less the concern here, than those protective duties which arise directly from the assertion of a right which involves the sharp end of the state's criminal law enforcement mechanism or military apparatus. We are concerned here with the forms of coercion directed at perpetrators of harm (or potential perpetrators of harm) which restrict rights and liberties to a far greater extent than the normal general limitations we might experience by living in a fair, socially democratic, and redistributive society.

So what should we call these duties? Many of the duties examined in this essay are well known to human rights lawyers, and even criminal lawyers. But they are not recognized as 'coercive duties'. They are referred to as 'protective duties'[62] or, as

59 D Bilchitz, *Poverty and Fundamental Rights: The Justification and Enforcement of Socio-Economic Rights* (Oxford: Oxford University Press, 2007); A Sen, *Development as Freedom* (Oxford: Oxford University Press, 1999); H Shue, *Basic Rights: Subsistence, Affluence and U.S. Foreign Policy* (2nd edn, Princeton: Princeton University Press, 1996); J Waldron, 'Socio-Economic Rights and Theories of Justice' (Public Law & Legal Theory Research Paper Series Working Paper No 10-79, November 2010).

60 Shue, n 59 above, 167.

61 G Jellinek, *System der subjektiven öffentlichen Rechte* (2nd edn, Tübingen: JCB Mohr, 1905); WN Hohfeld, *Fundamental Legal Conceptions as Applied in Judicial Reasoning* (New Haven: Yale University Press, 1923); R Alexy, *A Theory of Constitutional Rights* (trans J Rivers) (Oxford: Oxford University Press, 2002), 169.

62 A Mowbray, *The Development of Positive Obligations under the European Convention on Human Rights by the European Court of Human Rights* (Oxford: Hart, 2004), 15–22, 127–30, 181; J McBride,

the Germans refer to it, '*Schutzpflicthen*'.[63] This descriptor is incomplete. When the right to life gives rise to a duty on the state it often engages both a protective duty directed towards the individual at risk of harm, and a coercive duty directed at the perpetrator or potential perpetrator of the harm. The duty frequently cuts both ways.[64] While some protective duties give rise to non-coercive duties, such as the training of officers in sensitivity around domestic violence victims, other protective duties *require* the state to coerce individuals who harm or individuals who are at risk of harming, in order to fulfil the duty. To call these duties protective duties alone risks masking the coercive sting in its tail.

Of course, coercive duties are not necessarily a bad thing. Most would argue that they are in fact a very good thing, because they create requirements on the state which are essential to the protection of others. Certainly, coercive duties that are correlative upon rights as fundamental as life or dignity can constitute what we can all comfortably recognize as 'justified coercion'.[65] Moreover, coercive duties are also mechanisms by which the state enforces the correlative duties upon individuals not to breach the rights of others.[66] The state is indeed required to restrain individuals from breaching the rights of others. To this extent, coercive duties can easily be reconciled with Ashworth's 'liberal theory of criminalisation' in that they anchor coercion in relation to the harm to others.

To be clear, the purpose of this essay is not to reject or critique the existence of coercive duties. It is more to name them, and thereby to highlight their existence, rather than sublimating them within the comforting label of 'protective duties'. The motive here is to raise some questions and concerns about how coercive duties may be framed. While we can accept that rights give rise to justified coercion by the state, or that the necessary correlative of a right is a duty on individuals to respect the rights of others and the state is justified in enforcing these, it is crucial that we understand how to shape the scope of coercive duties. The key questions that arise when a coercive duty is established is how much coercion is required to fulfil the right or rights of individuals at harm, or at risk of harm. To put this another way, where the state is under a protective duty as a consequence of a positive right, it is

'Protecting Life: a Positive Obligation to Help' (1999) 24 European Law Review Human Rights Survey HR/43.

[63] *Schutzpflichten* in Germany have commonly been used to justify extension of the criminal law. Most controversially, *Schutzpflichten* have been used to protect the unborn foetus (*BVerfGE* 39, 1). See J Isensee, 'Das Grundrecht als Abwehrrecht und als staatliche Schutzpflicht' in J Isensee and P Kirchhoff (eds), *Handbuch des Staatsrechts der Bundesrepublik Deutschland, Band IV: Allgemeine Grundrechtslehren* (Heidelberg: Müller, 1992), 143. As the FCC is equivocal on this matter, I will not here enter the ongoing debate over whether *Schutzpflichten* should be seen as objective state duties or as correlative duties derived from subjective individual rights to state protection; see Alexy, n 61 above, 301 ff.

[64] This is not to argue that the coercion of a perpetrator or potential perpetrator automatically results in the protection of the subject of the harm. Certainly, in most cases that come to court the harm has already occurred, and where it has not already occurred we cannot be sure that the coercion of potential perpetrators will in fact result in the protection of those at risk of harm.

[65] R Dworkin, *Law's Empire* (Cambridge, MA: Harvard University Press, 1986).

[66] L Lazarus et al, *The Relationship between Rights and Responsibilities*, 18/09 Ministry of Justice Research Series (London: Ministry of Justice, 2009).

critical to establish how much coercion must be exercised in order to fulfil the duty, what form that coercion should take in order to fulfil the duty, what the relation is, and how we strike a balance between the rights of the person subjected to harm (or at risk of harm) and the perpetrator (or potential perpetrator) of the harm.

A short case example may help demonstrate the problem here. The case is *R v G*.[67] G, a 15-year-old boy, had sexual intercourse with R when she was 12. He agreed to submit a guilty plea on the basis that R had willingly agreed to have intercourse with him and that he honestly believed she was 15, as she had told him so. R agreed to G's plea and the prosecutor was invited to drop the charge. G was nevertheless convicted and sentenced under section 5 of the Sexual Offences Act 2003 (rape of a child under 13). G appealed, arguing that he could have been charged with a less serious offence under section 13 of the Sexual Offences Act 2003 (child sex offences committed by children or young persons). Part of G's argument was that his rights under Article 8 ECHR included a right not to be subject to undue stigma and practical interference with his right to private life. G argued that the choice of the more serious offence of rape by the prosecutor and his subsequent conviction was therefore a disproportionate interference with his Article 8 rights. On the other hand, the Supreme Court was aware that the ECtHR has developed a set of positive duties with regard to the protection of rape victims or victims of sexual violence that arise out of Articles 8 and 3.[68] The case involved a number of arguments, some of which veered away from the competing rights arising from Article 8, but the key passage on this question came from Baroness Hale, who had already pointed to the countervailing positive obligations that the ECtHR had developed regarding the state's protection of rape victims or potential rape victims:[69]

> In effect, therefore, the real complaint is that the appellant has been convicted of an offence bearing the label 'rape'. Parliament has very recently decided that this is the correct label to apply to this activity. In my view this does not engage the Art. 8 rights of the appellant at all, but if it does, it is entirely justified. The concept of private life 'covers the physical and moral integrity of the person, including his or her sexual life' (*X and Y v Netherlands* at [22]). This does not mean that every sexual relationship, however brief or unsymmetrical, is worthy of respect, nor is every sexual act which a person wishes to perform. It does mean that the physical and moral integrity of the complainant, vulnerable by reason of her age if nothing else, was worthy of respect. The state would have been open to criticism if it did not provide her with adequate protection. This it attempts to do by a clear rule that children under 13 are incapable of giving any sort of consent to sexual activity and treating penile penetration as a most serious form of such activity. This does not in my view amount to a lack of respect for the private life of the penetrating male.[70]

[67] *R v G* [2008] UKHL 37, [2009] 1 AC 92.

[68] *X and Y v Netherlands* (App no 8978/80) (1986) 8 EHRR 235; *MC v Bulgaria* (App no 39278/98) (2005) 40 EHRR 20. See in general L Lazarus, 'The Human Rights Framework Relating to the Handling, Investigation and Prosecution of Rape Complaints', Annex A to *The Stern Review* (London: Home Office, 2010).

[69] Reference to *X and Y v Netherlands* in *R v G* [2008] UKHL 37, [2009] 1 AC 92 at [41].

[70] *R v G* [2008] UKHL 37, [2009] 1 AC 92 at [54].

Baroness Hale's observations demonstrate the difficulty of framing and balancing the competing rights and duties arising in this case. Article 8 has frequently been deployed to protect the private life or sexual autonomy of individuals. This notion of sexual autonomy cuts both ways. On the one hand, Article 8 was deployed in the decriminalization of homosexuality.[71] On the other hand, Article 8 has been used to require 'practical and effective protection' by the criminal law of those vulnerable to sexual violence.[72] The difficulty that Baroness Hale had to confront was how to reconcile these two parts of the right to sexual autonomy, and to frame the duties on the state in response to these rights. According to Baroness Hale, G's Article 8 rights had almost no countervailing weight against the state's duty under Article 8 to protect potential victims of rape. The justification she provides for her view is shallow. The state was duty bound to protect victims of rape, but this did not in her view 'amount to a lack of respect for the private life of the penetrating male'. The difficulty here was that the duty of general protection against the population at large is being deployed to justify the coercion of a particular individual in a particular way. There was no consideration by Baroness Hale of the individual circumstances of the case, or for that matter of the rights of the individual in question.

To be sure, *R v G* provides a crisp example of the dilemmas and complexity that arise where the state is both under a coercive duty regarding perpetrators of sexual offences, while also subject to their countervailing rights to autonomy. How are we to know whether the choice of the more serious offence in this case constitutes the best balance? Where the court has to take such competing rights and duties into account, the answer can only be found if we understand the contours of the coercive duty to which these rights give rise, and the extent of the countervailing negative rights protections. In the *R v G* decision, the cursory balancing act was insufficient. It rested on broad-brush rhetorical assertions of the protective duties of the state, and included almost no analysis of the content of the competing right.

The rhetorical assertion of coercive duties within the law needs also to be read against the background of an increasing rhetorical use of rights to justify coercive measures by politicians and state actors internationally. As noted earlier, the implications of legal language of this kind cannot be confined to courts of law. We also need to be concerned about the extra-legal implications of broad rhetorical assertions of coercive duties inside the courts, and the concomitant risk of coercive overreach. As I have argued elsewhere in more depth, this has been well demonstrated by the growing rhetoric of the right to security.

6. The Right to Security, Political Rhetoric, and the Risk of Coercive Overreach

Coercive duties are even harder to frame when the right that underpins them is underdetermined, and the potential for their political exploitation is even higher.

71 *Dudgeon v UK* (App no 7526/76) (1982) 4 EHRR 149.
72 *X and Y v Netherlands* (App no 8978/80) (1986) 8 EHRR 235.

The right to security is such a right. In a recent piece, I analyse references to the 'right to security' in the English-speaking press globally over the past ten years.[73] This shows that assertions of the right to security can imply, and have been increasingly politically exploited to mean, increasing police powers, powers of surveillance, powers of pre-trial detention, and pre-emptive measures aimed at risk prevention. This right is also frequently used to legitimate invasions or incursions into countries seen to be a threat to security.[74]

As in South Africa, the right to security is enshrined in a number of domestic constitutions internationally while also being expressed within international law,[75] and the jurisprudence around this right has generated a range of potential claims. Importantly, the right to security has gained an increasing currency in political debate around the world. The political currency of the right to security has not been overlooked by political actors in their quest to legitimate and develop various security measures since 9/11.[76] The rhetoric has been deployed consistently with respect to the Middle East[77] and North Korea.[78] It has also been engaged to justify tightening anti-terrorism measures or even to justify military invasion or responses with respect to Afghanistan,[79] Kosovo,[80] Pakistan[81] and, in Columbia's case, Ecuador.[82] In the war on terror, the language of the right to security is ubiquitous.[83]

[73] L Lazarus, 'The Right to Security—Securing Rights or Securitizing Rights' in R Dickinson et al (ed), *Examining Critical Perspectives on Human Rights* (Cambridge: Cambridge University Press, 2012). See also L Lazarus, 'Mapping the Right to Security' in B Goold and L Lazarus (eds), *Security and Human Rights* (Oxford: Hart, 2007).

[74] Lazarus, 'Mapping the Right to Security', n 73 above; Lazarus, 'The Right to Security—Securing Rights or Securitizing Rights', n 73 above.

[75] eg Canadian Charter, s 7; Constitution of Hungary, Art 55 (1); Northern Ireland Draft Bill of Rights includes a right to be free of violence. See also Art 143 of the United Nations General Assembly 2005 World Summit Outcome Document on 'Human Security'.

[76] Lazarus, 'The Right to Security—Securing Rights or Securitizing Rights', n 73 above.

[77] As George W Bush declared: 'I can understand the deep anger and anguish of the Israeli people. You've lived too long with fear and funerals, having to avoid markets and public transportation, and forced to put armed guards in kindergarten classrooms. The Palestinian Authority has rejected your offered hand and trafficked with terrorists. You have a right to a normal life. You have *a right to security*. And I deeply believe that you need a reformed, responsible Palestinian partner to achieve that security' George W Bush, 'Remarks on the Middle East', speech from the Rose Garden of the White House, 24 June 2002. Full text available at <http://www-cgi.cnn.com/2002/ALLPOLITICS/06/24/bush.mideast.speech/index.html> accessed 17 March 2012) (emphasis added). George Bush has been joined by Barak Obama, Nicolas Sarkozy, Vladimir Putin, Franco Fini, David Milliband, and Colin Powell (amongst others), who have all asserted the collective right to security of the Israeli people.

[78] See *Associated Press,* 'Non-Aligned meeting backs calls for Iraq to disarm; Malaysia warns attack on Iraq would be considered a "War against Muslims"', 23 February 2003.

[79] E Cochrane, 'Troops deserve our support', *Carstairs Courier* (Alberta), 6 November 2007.

[80] *Vancouver Sun*, 'Yeltsin's final fling: The Russian leader, often portrayed in the West as a boorish drunk, had substance that belied his unvarnished style', 27 January 2001.

[81] Press Trust of India, 'Pak should give firm assurance against abetting terrorism', 30 December 2001.

[82] BBC Worldwide Monitoring, 'Colombia defends its incursion into Ecuador', 23 March 2008.

[83] For UK and EU examples, see European Commissioner responsible for Justice, Freedom and Security, 'EU Counterterrorism Strategy', European Parliament, 5 September 2007, Speech/07/505. J Reid, 'Rights, Security Must Be Balanced', *Associated Press Online*, 16 August 2006.

Political rhetoric also manifests in the claim that the right to security, cast as 'the protection of life and limb', is 'the basic right on which all others are based'.[84] These attempts to cast the right to security as a meta-right, and to reorder the priority of rights, hold the risk that rights themselves will be securitized.[85] In other words, rights to autonomy and liberty may themselves be viewed as a product of the meta-right to security. Or as Waldron argues, we may become so preoccupied with delivering security as the precondition to liberty that we end up with perfect security and very little liberty.[86]

Part of the difficulty with the development of the right to security is that it has been taken to mean not just freedom from physical violence in the most core sense,[87] but also a range of other values such as 'personal autonomy', 'physical and psychological integrity and basic human dignity'.[88] The right has also been described by the United Nations as a right to human security, which includes 'the right of people to live in freedom and dignity, free from poverty and despair' and to enjoy 'freedom from fear and freedom from want, with an equal opportunity to enjoy all their rights and fully develop their human potential'.[89] In short, the range of goods and interests that the right to security can protect internationally is now so extensive that it could in theory be deployed to protect most things we want in life. This porous boundary to the right to security leaves open a greater potential for political and state legitimation of coercive overreach where the right is deployed. This is why I have argued strongly for a legal approach to the right to security that restricts the correlative duty to coerce to one that involves 'the development of structures and institutions capable of responding to and minimizing critical and pervasive threats to human safety, namely absence from harm in the most core physical sense of harm to person'.[90]

For the purposes of the argument here, the example of the right to security is raised to demonstrate how particular rights claims may permeate political rhetoric and legitimate strong coercive measures. It is the courts, I argue, that should be tempering broad-brush rhetorical claims made in the name of the right to security, and the potential correlative duties that may flow from them.

7. Rhetoric and the Risk of Coercive Overreach in the Courts

As *R v G* demonstrated above, in cases where the fault of the state is not at issue the duty to coerce is not always adequately restricted. In contrast to the state liability

[84] Full text of speech reported by *BBC News* 'Reid urges human rights shake up',12 May 2007, available at <http://news.bbc.co.uk/2/hi/uk_news/politics/6648849.stm> accessed 17 March 2012.

[85] Lazarus, 'The Right to Security—Securing Rights or Securitizing Rights', n 73 above.

[86] J Waldron, 'Security as a Basic Right (after 9/11)' in *Torture, Terror and Trade-Offs: Philosophy for the White House* (Oxford: Oxford University Press, 2010), 166.

[87] South African Constitution, Art 12; Northern Ireland Draft Bill of Rights.

[88] Canada: *Rodriquez v British Columbia (Attorney General)* [1993] 3 SCR 519.

[89] United Nations General Assembly 2005 World Summit Outcome Document.

[90] Lazarus, 'The Right to Security—Securing Rights or Securitizing Rights', n 73 above.

cases, coercive duties have been broadly framed and deployed to legitimate criminal law measures that are highly coercive, where the rights of offenders are at issue. This is also demonstrated in the South African case of *Chapman*,[91] where an appeal of a 14-year prison sentence of a rapist was based on the fact that the defendant was subsequently brain damaged from a serious head injury. Here the Court framed its duty to coerce as follows:

> The rights to dignity, to privacy, and the integrity of every person are basic to the ethos of the Constitution and to any defensible civilization . . . Women in this country are entitled to the protection of these rights. They have a legitimate claim to walk peacefully on the streets, to enjoy their shopping and their entertainment, to go and come from work, and to enjoy the peace and tranquillity of their homes without the fear, the apprehension and the insecurity which constantly diminishes the quality and enjoyment of their lives . . . The appellant showed no respect for their rights. He prowled the street and shopping malls and in a short period of one week he raped three young women, who were unknown to him. He deceptively pretended to care for them by giving them lifts and then proceeded to rape them callously and brutally, after threatening them with a knife. At no stage, did he show the slightest remorse . . . The Courts are *under a duty* to send a clear message to the accused, to other potential rapists and to the community: We are determined to protect the equality, dignity and freedom of all women, and we shall show no mercy to those who seek to invade those rights.[92]

The questions of whether the appellant deserved his sentence, or whether it was proportionate to the gravity of the crime, or whether the case can be used to imply a harsher sentence for rapists, are not our primary concern here. What is our concern is the mode of legitimation deployed by the Supreme Court. A broad-brush language of rights and duties is harnessed with great effect to legitimate highly coercive measures, which the Court describes itself as *duty bound* to implement. The rights are very broadly framed, as is the correlative duty of the Court, and there is no proper discussion about the nature of the duty, and how it can be framed or narrowed. There is also no consideration of the possibility that coercion in this instance may have a very limited impact on the rights of the victims or potential victims. It cannot be shown that the type and length of sentence (and whether it occurs in a prison or secure hospital) is directly related to the way in which rights of those at risk of harm might be protected. *Chapman* and *R v G* argue that serious criminalization of such harmful acts which result in harsh sentences provide a deterrent effect on potential offenders. But this is an empirical claim about which many criminologists are rightly wary,[93] and which in any event raises serious questions about using the individual offenders in these particular cases as a means to an end.

In the cases where actions are brought regarding state liability, the link between the actions of the state body and the breach of the duty was the primary question:

[91] *S v Chapman* 1997 (3) SA 342 (SCA).

[92] Ibid, 4, emphasis added.

[93] See A von Hirsch, A Bottoms, E Burney, and PO Wickström, *Criminal Deterrence and Sentence Severity* (Oxford: Hart, 1999).

was the state at fault for not coercing the individuals in question? This restricted duty is centred around the question of proximity and reasonableness with respect to the state's assessment of the risk of harm. But in cases like *R v G* and *Chapman*, the idea that the state might be duty bound to protect individuals from the harmful acts of other individuals in clearly defined circumstances, transmutes into a broad-brush legitimation directed at the coercion of the individual offender. These legitimations involve very little rights analysis, and the language in the courtroom sounds not dissimilar to the kind of political rhetoric surrounding the right to security. It is also noteworthy that the coercive duty is far narrower when it applies to the state's wrongdoing, than when it applies to the individual offender's wrongdoing. This suggests that the risk of coercive overreach is higher where the criminal law is applied to individuals, than when the rights are invoked against the state. The risk of coercive overreach is also higher where the reasoning rests on a rhetorical assertion of rights and correlative coercive duties which are not decisive to the resolution of the case, where no countervailing rights are taken into account, and no systematic analysis of the rights and duties in play is undertaken.

8. Balancing Coercive Duties

The ECtHR stipulated in *Osman* that coercive duties had to be balanced against countervailing rights of the accused. But the mechanism by which that balance takes place is opaque, or even non-existent, in the cases discussed where the coercion of the individual is at issue. The matter is not helped by throwaway lines found in *Opuz v Turkey*, where the Court, admittedly facing very extreme circumstances, underlined 'that in domestic violence cases perpetrators' rights cannot supersede victims' human rights to life and to physical and mental integrity'.[94] The balance has to be struck regardless of the gravity of the harm in question. The right cannot merely be suspended in the face of the competing protective duty. It must at the very least receive due regard.

In the *Baloyi* case in the South African Constitutional Court,[95] Albie Sachs was clear that such a balance is unavoidable. This case dealt with the allegation that the Prevention of Family Violence Act 1993 reversed the burden of proof, placing the onus on the accused. The state argued that if the legislative provision in question could be read this way, it was justified as a consequence of the constitutional guarantee of the right to security, as well as international obligations regarding gender violence. Sachs noted that the 'Court faces the novel and complex task of establishing the appropriate balance between the state's constitutional duty to provide effective remedies against domestic violence, and its simultaneous obligation to respect the constitutional rights to a fair trial of those who might be affected

94 *Opuz v Turkey* (App no 33401/02) (ECHR 9 June 2009) at [147]. See discussion of *Opuz* above.
95 *The State v Baloyi* (2000) 1 SACR 81 (CC).

by the measures taken'.[96] When concluding that the legislation in question could not be read to place a reverse burden of proof on the accused, he argued:

The Constitution embodies many enduring common law principles, especially those associated with personal freedom. The Constitution also articulates, however, new values and contains different emphases. As pointed out above, the Constitution and South Africa's international obligations require effective measures to deal with the gross denial of human rights resulting from pervasive domestic violence. At the same time the Constitution insists that no-one should be arbitrarily deprived of freedom or convicted without a fair trial. The problem, then, is to find the interpretation of the text which best fits the Constitution and balances the duty of the state to deal effectively with domestic violence with its duty to guarantee accused persons the protection involved in a fair trial.[97]

Sachs's judgment is an exemplar of the sort of reasoning that needs to be deployed when faced with the competing imperatives of coercive duties on the one hand, and negative rights on the other. But perhaps an even more compelling example of an insistence on the need for a balance between the state's protective duties and the rights of individuals is to found in the German Aviation case.[98] The German Federal Constitutional Court (FCC) struck down powers under the Aviation Security Act to shoot down aircraft which had been hijacked with the intention of using the aircraft 'as weapons in crimes against human lives'. The judges argued that the measures violated the essence of the right to life and human dignity of the innocent passengers on the plane who had been made into mere objects of state action. Importantly, the FCC rejected the government's argument that the relevant powers under the Aviation Security Act could be justified as a consequence of the State's protective duties. It argued thus:

Finally, § 14.3 of the Aviation Security Act also cannot be justified by invoking the state's duty to protect those against whose lives the aircraft . . . is intended to be used. In complying with such duties of protection, the state and its bodies have a broad margin of assessment, valuation and organisation . . . Unlike fundamental rights in their function as subjective rights of defence [against the state], the state's duties to protect which result from the objective contents of the fundamental rights are, in principle, not defined . . . How the state bodies comply with such duties of protection is to be decided, as a matter of principle, by themselves on their own responsibility . . . This also applies to their duty to protect human life. It is true that especially as regards this protected interest, in cases with a particular combination of circumstances, if effective protection of life cannot be achieved otherwise, the possibilities of choosing the means of complying with the duty of protection can be restricted to the choice of one particular means . . . The choice, however, can only be between means the use of which is in harmony with the constitution.[99]

Given the extreme facts of the German Aviation case, and the explicit reasoning deployed by the FCC, this case is a crisp example of both the necessity for, and framework within which, the balance between coercive duties and individual rights

[96] *The State v Baloyi* (2000) 1 SACR 81 (CC) at [1]. [97] Ibid at [26].
[98] *BVerfGE* (2006) 1 BvR 357/05, 15 February 2006, at [120]–[121].
[99] *BVerfGE* (2006) 1 BvR 357/05, 15 February 2006, at [136].

must be struck. Far from the broad-brush approach of *R v G* and *Chapman*, and even the dicta in *Opuz v Turkey*, we see here a court insistent on the necessity of holding both the individual right in play and the protective duty asserted. The case explicitly argues that coercive duties are neither absolute, nor so prescriptive as to require one particular kind of coercion on individuals.[100] On the contrary, protective duties are broadly defined, giving the state a range of alternative routes to their fulfilment, and importantly, must always accord with the values of the Constitution.

9. Conclusion

This is a modest contribution to the question of the relationship between human rights and criminal justice, which builds upon Ashworth's work. It asks for a clearer understanding of positive rights as potentially leading to sharply coercive activity by the state. It also raises some concerns about the rhetorical expression of rights in this context, both within the courts and without. While the case law surrounding the liability of states in respect of their failure to protect individuals from harm by other individuals has managed to contain the reach of coercive duties (or at least the conditions in which a breach of that duty will be found), there are examples of cases like *R v G* and *Chapman* that demonstrate the potential for coercive overreach upon individuals subject to such coercion. We risk overlooking the tensions here if we continue to refer to these positive rights claims only as protective duties. We must not lose sight of the coercive sting in the tail of positive duties, and the necessity of deploying frameworks in which countervailing rights claims can be weighed in the balance. We must also not overlook the potential for rights to intensify and expand criminal law and justice.

[100] See also K Moller, 'The Right to Life between Absolute and Proportional Protection' (2010) *LSE Law, Society and Economy Working Paper Series*, WPS 13-2010.

10

Exploring Entrapment

*Mike Redmayne**

Entrapment is a tactic used by law enforcement agencies whereby a person is encouraged to commit a crime so that he can be prosecuted for it. It is a controversial strategy, because the state seems to be creating the very crime that it then condemns. Courts therefore tend to control entrapment: in the United States entrapment is a defence, while in England and Wales a successful claim of entrapment will lead to a prosecution being stayed for 'abuse of process'. In this essay, I explore the theory of entrapment, taking as a starting point Andrew Ashworth's writings on the topic. I largely agree with Ashworth, both in his reaction to real and hypothetical cases and in his theorization of entrapment. But I want to examine some of the finer details of his account, and ask whether it can be defended against the criticisms raised by some commentators.

Contentious though entrapment is, there may sometimes be good reason to resort to it. Drug dealing is an obvious example. It may be difficult to get convincing evidence that a person is dealing drugs without approaching him and asking for drugs. There is thus a fair degree of consensus, in both doctrine and scholarship, that entrapment is sometimes a legitimate strategy, but that sometimes it is not. If the police have good reason to suspect that D is a drug dealer, but lack the evidence to prosecute him, it might be appropriate for an undercover officer to approach D and ask to buy drugs. But if the police have no reason to suspect D of being a drug dealer and continually pester him to sell them drugs, until D gives in and obtains drugs from a friend in order to sell them on, many would think that a line had been crossed. The difficulty lies in explaining just why the latter scenario is problematic but the former is not, and in proceeding from such explanations to a wider theory of entrapment. This difficulty can be underlined by emphasizing two points. First, if the defendant in the second scenario had been pestered for drugs by a private citizen, there would be little question about the legitimacy of prosecution.[1] Perhaps D gave in to temptation, but it was not temptation by the state.

* I am grateful to Hock Lai Ho for comments on an earlier draft.

[1] There are more qualms where there is private entrapment, ie a non-state actor encourages D to commit an offence and then reports D to the authorities. English courts, however, have not yet allowed claims of private entrapment to be a bar to prosecution: K Hofmeyr, 'The Problem of Private Entrapment' [2006] Crim LR 319. See also *Shannon v UK* [2005] Crim LR 133.

Why, though, should the state's role be so significant? Secondly, there is a sceptical literature on entrapment, which questions whether it is ever appropriate to prevent D's conviction, however much the state lured him into offending.[2] In simple terms, the argument is that we worry about the second scenario because we realize that we all have our price: we ourselves could be tempted into crime if state agents dangled a sufficiently attractive offer in front of us. So while we are happy to see entrapment used against those we regard as a threat to social order, we design the doctrine to protect ourselves. Entrapment thus serves to uphold social inequality.

At the outset, it will be helpful to sketch the law on entrapment in England and Wales, which will form the background to the discussion. In this jurisdiction, entrapment is not a defence as such, which seems appropriate given that entrapment does not affect D's blameworthiness (as can be seen from the contrast with the example where entrapment is by a private citizen: D is equally blameworthy in either scenario).[3] Instead, a successful claim of entrapment will lead a court to stay proceedings for abuse of process, with the effect that the prosecution cannot proceed.[4] The House of Lords decision in the combined appeals of *Looseley* and *Attorney General's Reference No 3 of 2000*[5] gives some guidance on when a claim will be successful. In *Looseley*, undercover police made enquiries in a pub from which they suspected heroin was being sold. They were given Looseley's telephone number, contacted him, and obtained heroin from him on three occasions. Looseley's prosecution was held to be unproblematic. In the *Attorney General's Reference*, undercover officers supplied D with contraband cigarettes. They asked him to obtain heroin for them, which he refused to do. After 'many, many'[6] conversations about cigarettes and heroin, D eventually supplied the officers with the drug. The House of Lords agreed that the trial judge had been entitled to stay the prosecution, with Lord Hutton going further and suggesting that he had been right to do so.[7] At this stage it is worth mentioning two further cases, which fall on different sides of the line. In *Williams and O'Hare* the police mounted a 'mannah from heaven' operation in an area of high vehicle crime, which involved leaving a van parked in the street, with cartons of cigarettes visible through its open back doors.[8] When the

[2] See eg D Squires, 'The Problem with Entrapment' (2006) 26 OJLS 351.

[3] In his first engagement with entrapment, Ashworth did support the creation of a defence of entrapment. At the time, the doctrine of abuse of process was little developed in criminal cases, so it is not surprising that criminal defences provided the analytical framework, as they still do in the USA. But Ashworth's central objection in that short paper does lend itself readily to an abuse of process account: 'is it not arguable that to convict someone for succumbing to temptation from official sources which might otherwise never have been offered is an abuse of the law?' A Ashworth, 'Defences of General Application: The Law Commission Report No 83: (3) Entrapment' [1978] Crim LR 137, 139.

[4] See *R v Looseley; Attorney General's Reference (No 3 of 2000)* [2001] UKHL 53, [2001] 1 WLR 2060. The House of Lords did note, though, that in some circumstances the exclusion of evidence gained by entrapment might be appropriate, such as where evidence of entrapment only emerged at a late stage in the trial: see [42]–[44].

[5] Ibid.

[6] Ibid at [92].

[7] Ibid at [81] (Lord Hoffman); [116] (Lord Hutton); [127] (Lord Scott).

[8] (1994) 98 Cr App R 209.

defendants helped themselves to the cigarettes, they were arrested and prosecuted. In *Looseley* the House of Lords agreed that this was unproblematic. But a later case, *Moon*,[9] was found by the Court of Appeal to involve improper entrapment. Moon frequented an area where heroin was thought to be being sold. She was approached by an undercover officer, who pretended to be suffering the discomforts of heroin withdrawal. While initially reluctant, Moon obtained heroin and supplied it to the officer. The Court of Appeal held that the prosecution should have been stayed.

1. Ashworth's Analysis

Ashworth's account of entrapment is close to that adopted by the Canadian Supreme Court. 'The Supreme Court of Canada surely has it right . . . in requiring proof of reasonable grounds to suspect D of being involved presently in this kind of unlawful activity.'[10] But reasonable suspicion will not license just any degree of pressure being placed on D: 'a line should be drawn between providing the opportunity and encouraging or inducing D to commit an offence'.[11] As Ashworth is aware, notions such as 'encourage' and 'induce' are notoriously problematic. While the English case law at one point favoured a distinction in terms of whether police behaviour was active or passive, Ashworth prefers a test in terms of normality. Thus, with the example of a decoy operation where a police officer dresses up as an old lady in order to attract muggers 'there can surely be no objection: an old lady walking along a street is a perfectly normal occurrence, and no-one other than an intending criminal would treat it as an invitation to commit crime'.[12] But he sees the operation in *Williams and O'Hare* very differently: this was 'a brazen piece of virtue-testing, in that it involved holding out temptation of an unusual kind to which some ordinarily law-abiding people might succumb . . . Leaving cartons of cigarettes unattended in a public place is little different from leaving a wallet on a park bench: neither is normal behaviour, and both represent extraordinary temptation.'[13] As his endorsement of the old lady decoy suggests, Ashworth would, like the Canadian Supreme Court, allow reasonable suspicion to focus on an area, rather than an individual. Thus the old lady decoy would probably only be acceptable if there had been a series of muggings in the area.[14] But Ashworth is certainly cautious about such strategies, and is critical of the House of Lords for not taking a sufficiently critical view of them in *Looseley*.

[9] [2004] EWCA Crim 2872.

[10] A Ashworth, 'What is Wrong with Entrapment?' [1999] Singapore Journal of Legal Studies 293, 305.

[11] Ibid.

[12] Ibid, 301.

[13] A Ashworth, 'Re-Drawing the Boundaries of Entrapment' [2002] Crim LR 161, 174. See also A Ashworth, 'Testing Fidelity to Legal Values: Official Involvement and Criminal Justice' in S Shute and A Simester (eds), *Criminal Law Theory: Doctrines of the General Part* (Oxford: Oxford University Press, 2002), 315.

[14] See Ashworth, 'Re-Drawing', ibid, 174.

Ashworth is also cautious about using the notion of predisposition as part of the test for improper entrapment. His principal concern here is that this would allow the police to target those with previous convictions. But there is a little ambiguity in this aspect of his account. While the quotation above frames the reasonable suspicion test in terms of whether D 'is involved presently in this kind of unlawful activity', at times Ashworth glosses this in terms of whether D is 'ready and willing' to commit an offence.[15] He also refers to 'defendant-centred' elements in the doctrine, 'which refer to the defendant's present dispositions . . . [This] may be regarded as an unusually explicit nod towards the character theory of criminal liability.'[16] Whether D is presently involved in, say, selling drugs, is slightly different from the question whether he has a present disposition to sell drugs (he *is* a drug seller, not just someone with a disposition to do so). In this essay, I shall take the former, narrower test to be the right one. Entrapment is only legitimate where D is currently engaged in offending. This puts less weight on the troubling factors of disposition and character.[17]

For Ashworth, the reason why entrapment is problematic when it crosses the line is, primarily, that 'the function of the police is to prevent and detect crime and not to cause it'.[18] This does not necessarily explain why courts should involve themselves in preventing a prosecution: one might take the view that questions about the proper role of the police are not the court's business.[19] In two of his accounts, Ashworth refers to an integrity theory, along the lines suggested by Gerald Dworkin.[20] The idea is that it is inconsistent for the courts to lend themselves to a process in which they will condemn conduct which D has been encouraged to perform by the state. But in his last substantial engagement with the issues, written in response to the House of Lords decision in *Looseley*, Ashworth also seems to find merit in a protective rationale, under which the entrapment doctrine exists to protect citizens from misuse of state power. 'Ordinary life is full of temptations, some of them temptations to commit crime, and the principle seems to be that citizens should not be at risk of being subjected to deliberate and excessive temptation by officials.'[21] The final view, then, seems to be that protection and integrity offer twin rationales for staying a prosecution based on improper entrapment.

I find Ashworth's account of entrapment, for the most part, very appealing. I also think it accounts for much of the English case law. But, like any theorization of this area of law, it faces some difficult questions. A starting point is to consider the

15 See Ashworth, n 10 above, 305.

16 Ashworth, 'Testing', n 13 above, 322.

17 Of course, to say that someone is a drug seller involves some notion of propensity. This might be thought of as a propensity to engage in a course of conduct, rather than an isolated sale.

18 Ashworth, n 10 above, 298. See also Ashworth, 'Testing', n 13 above, 313. This rationale is also endorsed in *Looseley*, n 4 above, at [59].

19 This was the view of the Court of Appeal in *R v Sang* [1980] AC 402, 408 (CA). The way the courts perceive their role has changed since then: cf *R v Grant* [2005] EWCA Crim 1089, [2006] QB 60.

20 G Dworkin, 'The Serpent Beguiled Me and I did Eat: Entrapment and the Creation of Crime' in *The Theory and Practice of Autonomy* (Cambridge: Cambridge University Press, 1988).

21 Ashworth, 'Re-Drawing', n 13 above, 163.

underlying justifications for entrapment doctrine. As we saw above, Ashworth relies on Dworkin's argument that for the courts to allow certain types of entrapment would be for them to endorse inconsistency. As Dworkin puts it: 'It is certainly unfair to the citizen to be invited to do that which the law forbids him to do. But it is more than unfair; it is conceptually incoherent.'[22] It is not obvious just what Dworkin means here. He admits that there is no literal contradiction, and that such ploys may succeed in deterring crime. Nevertheless, a system whereby the state invites people to commit forbidden acts and then punishes them 'violates elementary standards of coherence and fairness'[23]—at least in cases where D was not already offending. But, as Hock Lai Ho notes, the state's role was hidden and D was given no assurance that his actions were legal.[24] Especially if D is at risk of offending in the future, it is hard to see why it is incoherent to tempt D into crime in order to prosecute him. The better way to ground entrapment doctrine may therefore be to adopt a protective rationale. As we saw above, Ashworth's version of this is that citizens should be protected from deliberate and excessive temptation by the state. But it is not being subjected to temptation that is really objectionable in entrapment;[25] rather, it is being convicted of a crime when one is not a legitimate target for criminalization. As suggested above, a person is not a legitimate target for criminalization—and thus for entrapment—unless he is already committing the relevant crime. To adopt the handy slogan, the state should not involve itself in 'virtue-testing'. If we endorse a protective rationale, entrapment doctrine seems to rest on a political claim about the proper role of the police vis-à-vis the citizen, a claim that is no doubt contestable—especially if it is argued that the state should not pre-empt future crime. I shall say more about the problems of a pre-emptive rationale for entrapment below. Putting pre-emption to one side for the moment, it seems reasonable that, in a liberal polity, the role of criminalization should be constrained so that it is used in response to crimes that have been committed or which are planned, rather than as a means of condemning people who are morally lax but who never have and never will commit crime (other than the one 'created' by the state). It is a separate question, though, whether the courts should involve themselves in keeping the police to such a role—or whether, as suggested above, such things are simply not the business of the courts. My own view is that, while arguments that it is an integral part of criminal adjudication that courts should police the propriety of prosecution face difficulties, it is simply a matter of historical fact that English courts have come to involve themselves in such issues, and that this is largely to be welcomed.[26]

22 Dworkin, n 20 above, 143.

23 Ibid, 144.

24 HL Ho, 'State Entrapment' (2010) 31 Legal Studies 71, 89.

25 See Squires, n 2 above, 370–1, though note the caveat at n 32 below.

26 On this historical shift, see n 19 above, and for further background see A Ashworth, 'Exploring the Integrity Principle in Evidence and Procedure' in P Mirfield and R Smith (eds), *Essays for Colin Tapper* (London: LexisNexis, 2003); A Ashworth and M Redmayne, *The Criminal Process* (4th edn, Oxford: Oxford University Press, 2010), 321–3, 342–69; M Redmayne, 'Theorizing the Criminal Trial' (2009) 12 New Crim LR 287.

2. Retrospective Confirmation

We can now bring the difficulties of entrapment doctrine into sharper focus by considering some hypothetical cases. Suppose that, on the basis of a tip-off from a reliable informer that D is dealing drugs, police approach D and ask him to sell them drugs. D has in fact never sold drugs before—the informer, who has always provided good intelligence on previous occasions, is this time acting on the basis of a grudge against D—but, faced with the undercover officer's proffer of ready cash, D procures drugs from a friend and sells them to the police. Here, the police have acted in good faith (and have not done anything abnormal, such as offering above market price), but D has been tempted into committing a crime that he had not committed before (I shall refer to this case as 'mistaken reasonable suspicion'). Conversely, we might imagine the police acting without reasonable suspicion—an anonymous tip-off that they have no right to believe, given how often such tip-offs are baseless—and approach D, offering to buy drugs. D takes them to his house, where he sells them drugs from a hoard of drugs packaged ready for sale.[27] Here the police operation is not justified, but D was involved in drug dealing, and thus was a legitimate target ('correct unreasonable suspicion'). In a variant on the first case, the police, concerned about a series of sexual assaults in a park, send an undercover female police officer into the park at dusk. D attacks her and is arrested. But DNA analysis reveals that he is not the person who committed the attacks the police were investigating. A legitimate police operation has caught someone whom they did not have reason to suspect ('the second park rapist').

One issue raised by these examples is what Ashworth terms 'confirmation by subsequent facts'.[28] In the case involving correct unreasonable suspicion, the police hunch turns out to be correct. Facts unknown to the police at the time they launch the operation justify it. Ashworth is sceptical of allowing such retrospective justification: if 'the primary rationale of the entrapment doctrine is protection and prevention, law enforcement officers should not be allowed to proceed without reasonable grounds for suspicion'.[29] I am not sure about this. If we are concerned to protect D, surely a pertinent question is whether he deserves protection, whether he is the sort of person the entrapment doctrine is meant to insulate from conviction. Someone who is currently engaged in offending is precisely the sort of person who can be legitimately entrapped, and in terms of the underlying theory adopted here this is not a case where the police have created crime. Further, if we do not allow confirmation by subsequent facts, should we not also rule out retrospective disconfirmation? In the case of mistaken reasonable suspicion, if we think that D is not currently involved in selling drugs, then in terms of the underlying theory this is state-created crime and D is not the sort of person whose conviction should be

[27] *R v Imoro* 251 CCC (3d) 131 (2010) is close to this factual scenario.
[28] Ashworth, 'Re-Drawing', n 13 above, 172.
[29] Ibid, 173.

brought about by entrapment. But if the focus is on reasonable suspicion, D will be properly convicted.

One answer to these puzzles is that entrapment doctrine reflects 'a hybrid model, with official-centred elements that rule out unacceptable conduct by officials and defendant-centred elements which refer to the defendant's present dispositions'.[30] Consequently, a court should stay a prosecution in both the case of mistaken reasonable suspicion and the case of correct unreasonable suspicion. In the former, the reason for a stay is that we have no reason to think that D was offending before the police appeared on the scene, while in the latter it is that the police operation was unjustified. The grounds for ordering a stay in the latter case might be buttressed by imagining how things would look if we imposed no limits on police operations, for then the police would be able to conduct random virtue-testing, securing convictions whenever they got lucky by picking someone who succumbed and who could retrospectively be shown to have already been offending. In the same way, random stop-and-search is objectionable,[31] even if it would lead to some arrests when the police happen to stop someone carrying stolen or prohibited items.

Without denying that there is something to the points just made, it seems to me that this line of argument is slightly evasive. In stop-and-search, the central harm involved is loss of liberty/privacy. But the central harm involved in entrapment is the state creation of crime—something which does not really occur when the person approached either does not respond, or succumbs but is not convicted because he was not already engaged in offending. Random attempts to entrap might be objectionable for other reasons,[32] as they involve a degree of manipulation and might undermine social trust. While it is important to make the point that more than one value is at stake in entrapment,[33] these other harms are not at the core of our objection to entrapment: significantly, while they exist in cases of private entrapment, they have not provoked the courts into staying proceedings in such cases.[34] Further, we could stipulate that in the case of correct unreasonable suspicion the police act in good faith—ie they think they have good reason to suspect D. This would go some way towards blocking worries that by allowing a prosecution to proceed in this case we would be allowing random attempts to entrap. Why not, then, allow confirmation by subsequent facts in such a case?

The foregoing suggests that, in so far as the rationale for entrapment is to confine the state's role to preventing rather than creating crime, there is no reason to frown on confirmation by subsequent facts. The next question I want to raise also involves issues about retrospective confirmation and its relation to reasonable suspicion.

[30] Ashworth, 'Testing', n 13 above, 322.

[31] Which is not to say that it can never be justified.

[32] cf Squires, n 2 above, 370–1, who suggests that it would not be problematic if the police left an unattended wallet on a park bench as part of a research project on the correlation between street lighting and crime. This ignores the elements of deceit and surveillance in the scenario, factors which any research ethics committee would surely consider.

[33] eg, it may undermine trust and breach privacy. In some cases, entrapment involves the manipulation of a person's better nature, as in *Moon*, n 9 above, where the police officer appealed to Moon's sympathy for a withdrawing addict. See further Ho, n 24 above.

[34] See n 1 above.

Ashworth, like the Supreme Court of Canada,[35] favours a dual test: legitimate entrapment must be based on reasonable suspicion and must not amount to inducement—ie the police operation should only involve normal behaviour. One might, though, question the need for the second part of the test. If the police have good evidence that D is a drug dealer, then why not offer to buy drugs from him for above market price to ensure that he goes through with the deal? One response is that the police will rarely be very sure that D is currently engaged in crime—if they were, they might be able to prosecute without engaging in entrapment. The offer made to D and D's response therefore play an evidential role, corroborating the suspicion that D is engaged in crime. But if the police put particular pressure on D, his response will not play this corroborating role: we will be left wondering whether he has been enticed into committing a crime he was not already committing.

D's response can therefore be thought of as a species of retrospective confirmation. As with the analysis above, what is emerging here is that neither reasonable suspicion nor the normality of the temptation held out to D are crucial in legitimating entrapment. While these criteria might be useful guidelines for the police, in terms of entrapment's core rationale what matters is whether we can conclude that D was already engaged in offending, something that may be subject to retrospective confirmation or disconfirmation. The facts of *Looseley* offer a useful illustration of the process involved here, and illustrate how subtle and complex questions about the legitimacy of entrapment can be. While the police had grounds for thinking that heroin was being sold from the pub they targeted, when given Looseley's telephone number they did not have reasonable grounds to suspect him of being a drug dealer: they had no more than a hunch. On being contacted, though, Looseley agreed to 'sort out' the police officer 'a couple of bags'.[36] The officer then met Looseley, who obtained drugs for the police officer from another person (not from a hoard, which would have been better evidence of on-going supply). This process was repeated two more times in the next week. In Lord Hoffman's analysis, which seems correct, once Looseley had responded positively to the first phone call the police had reasonable grounds to suspect him of dealing.[37] While the initial approach can be seen as a process of firming up a hunch, before entrapment proper is attempted, the transaction can also be analysed as a process whereby entrapment occurs without reasonable suspicion, with retrospective confirmation that Looseley is an active dealer coming from his initial reaction and the repeated instances of supply:[38] to have arrested him after just the first episode would have been risky in this respect. A similar process occurred in *Jones*,[39] where the defendant, the owner of a shop selling drug paraphernalia—which is not illegal in itself—was convicted of inciting the cultivation of cannabis after he advised an

[35] See *R v Mack* [1988] 2 SCR 903.

[36] *Looseley*, n 4 above, at [84].

[37] Ibid, at [78]. Cf Squires, n 2 above, 365, who claims that the only evidence that Looseley was an active drug dealer was that the officer obtained his name in the pub.

[38] See also *Looseley*, n 4 above, at [113], where tape recordings of conversations between the officer and Looseley are said to support the view that he was an 'active and current' drug dealer.

[39] [2010] EWCA Crim 925, [2010] 3 All ER 1186.

undercover officer how to use his products to grow 'tomatoes'. While there does not seem to have been any specific reason for suspecting Jones of breaking the law, the police officer was held to have acted like a normal customer interested in drug cultivation. Jones's playing along with the conversation about tomatoes, despite the customer's clear interest in cannabis, can be seen as retrospective confirmation that D was engaged in breaking the law. Given the normality of the officer's conduct in terms of what one would expect of customers in the shop, it seems a fair assumption that this was advice that Jones gave regularly.

3. Present or Future Crime?

In the cases just discussed, D is confirmed to be a legitimate target for entrapment through a process of interaction with the undercover officers. But might it be possible to show that D is currently engaged in offending simply through his reaction to a decoy operation? One criticism of *Williams*, the case involving the van and the cigarette cartons, is that the operation was not a sufficiently demanding test of the defendants' on-going criminality. Perhaps the operation would have been more appropriate had the police left a handbag visible inside a locked car—in Ashworth's terms this would not be such 'extraordinary temptation'. All the same, it is not completely straightforward to infer from D's breaking the window and taking the bag that he is an on-going thief: this might be the first time he has succumbed to temptation. Consider also one of the hypothetical cases sketched above: the second park rapist. This case raises the stakes somewhat, for unless we can fit it into the template of legitimate entrapment, the prosecution will have to be stayed. Most people would be very uncomfortable with that, for it would seem to let a dangerous person go free, yet in this case too it may not be obvious that D has already committed similar offences.[40] Various responses are available. Under the Canadian approach, D's prosecution could easily be sanctioned: the police operation was justified, because the police knew that someone was committing sexual assaults in the area, and, in terms of one of the tests adopted by the Canadian Supreme Court, the temptation would not have caused the average person to commit crime.[41] However, if concern about state-created crime is central to entrapment doctrine, then it is arguable that this analysis does not go quite far enough: we should consider whether D may have been drawn into committing the relevant type of offence for the first time even in cases where the police are right to mount an operation to deal with offending in a particular area. For example, under the Canadian approach, Moon[42] would not necessarily have had her prosecution stayed. After all, the police had grounds to believe that heroin was being dealt in the area they targeted, and the average citizen would not have been tempted to sell

[40] This will tend to be the case with more serious offences, for the simple reason that they are rarer.
[41] *Mack*, n 35 above, at [120].
[42] *Moon*, n 9 above.

drugs as a result of the undercover officer's request.[43] Yet in my view the Court of Appeal was right to hold that Moon's prosecution should have been stayed, for it was entirely plausible that she had not dealt drugs prior to that occasion.

A different way to deal with the case of the second park rapist is to argue that D's conduct shows us that he was in fact a legitimate target for entrapment. If the test is that D is currently engaged in offending, this should not be confined to cases where D has actually committed the crime before. Cases where D is planning to commit a crime—as when he makes enquiries to find a hit-man to kill his wife[44]—should also be included. It might then be argued that in the case of the second park rapist it is likely that D intended to commit a sexual attack before he came across the decoy. A slightly different solution is to expand the test, asking whether D was 'ready and willing' to commit this type of crime. We have already noted that Ashworth may accept this version of the test, and we can now appreciate why it is tempting to do so. Yet once we modify the test in this way we are on less stable ground. Moon and the defendants in *Williams* might be said to have been ready and willing to commit the crimes they committed.

Questions about the proper form of the core of the entrapment test are now surfacing. While so far I have been analysing issues in entrapment in terms of whether D is currently engaged in crime—the test that appears to be favoured by Ashworth and the Canadian Supreme Court—other tests are available. In a sophisticated analysis of entrapment, Ho settles on a test of whether D is likely to commit this type of crime in the future.[45] This more expansive predictive test would easily justify a conviction in the second park rapist case. But, unsurprisingly, the difficulty for such wider tests is that they may also justify the use of entrapment in cases where we are less comfortable about it. Consider an example provided by Ho.[46] Two young men are open to the idea of purchasing heroin. The first, from a stable, middle-class background, simply does not come into contact with people who would provide him an opportunity to experiment with the drug. But the second, from a less privileged background, does, and it is likely that at some point in the future his curiosity will get the better of him and he will purchase heroin. If undercover agents approach both young men and offer to sell them drugs,[47] and both succumb, then under Ho's analysis the entrapment would be justified in the second case, but not the first. This is unsettling, but in terms of Ho's underlying rationale it makes sense. It can be said that the police are intervening to prevent

[43] The facts are close to those in *R v Barnes* [1991] 1 SCR 449, where the Supreme Court held that the police operation was legitimate. In terms of Ashworth's approach, *Moon* might be a close case. While pressure was put on Moon, via appeals to her sympathy for a withdrawing fellow addict, this behaviour is not necessarily abnormal where requests for heroin are concerned.

[44] See *R v Smurthwaite, R v Gill* [1994] 1 All ER 898 (CA).

[45] Ho, n 24 above.

[46] Ibid, 83–4.

[47] I am altering one significant detail in Ho's example. In his second case it is D, rather than the police officer, who makes the first move. It seems appropriate to modify this detail in order to make the only difference between the cases the availability of opportunities to purchase drugs, as this is what is significant in Ho's account.

crime in the second case, but not in the first. In the first case they are creating crime which would not otherwise occur.

Ho's example invites the critique of the sceptics, who claim that entrapment doctrine protects the privileged, but not the less privileged, from virtue-testing. One response is that the differential treatment simply reflects underlying problems of inequality which already pervade the criminal law.[48] Even a more restrictive test for the legitimacy of entrapment, such as the one advocated here, which focuses on whether D is currently engaged in offending, could be said to be tarnished by social inequality: it is just that entrapment becomes justified at a later point in time, after the person from the less privileged background has started to experiment with drugs. Nevertheless, the predictive element in Ho's version of the test is troubling. We are essentially legitimating the use of preventative measures against those who are judged to be dangerous, a policy whose critics include Ashworth.[49] It is true that the problem of predicting the future exercise of free will is not as stark here as in some examples of 'future law',[50] because D's succumbing to the entrapment is good evidence that he would do the same were he to face this temptation naturally. And to predict that D is likely to offend in the future does not, in my view, denigrate D by dismissing his capacity to change.[51] All the same, the open-ended nature of the prediction—the future is a long time—means that there is an unsavoury aspect of social cleansing in allowing the use of entrapment against those whose life chances are thought to be blighted. It is arguably better to let events run their course, and to intervene after the event or when harm is imminent, as under traditional principles of criminal law. Against this remains the fact that D has committed a crime, and one which he would rightly be prosecuted for had the temptation been offered by a private citizen. But so long as we are prepared to stay some prosecutions on the basis of illegitimate entrapment, the whole argument for not doing so in this case is preventative: we think that D is likely to offend in the future. That should not be enough to justify the use of the criminal sanction.

It must be said that Ho's account offers a neat response to some entrapment cases. In *Amin*,[52] undercover police officers flagged down a taxi which was outside the area covered by its licence. The taxi driver was prosecuted for picking them up. Here it is easy to say that D was likely to offend without police intervention. The scenario was likely to recur, and D's response was good evidence of how he would react if it did. But the police did not have reasonable suspicion that D was already offending, and it is not straightforward to say that his reaction is good evidence that

[48] See Ho, n 24 above, 84.

[49] See A Ashworth, 'Criminal Law, Human Rights and Preventative Justice' in B McSherry, A Norrie, and S Bronitt (eds), *Regulating Deviance* (Oxford: Hart, 2009); A Ashworth and L Zedner, 'Just Prevention: Preventive Rationales and the Limits of the Criminal Law' in RA Duff and S Green (eds), *Philosophical Foundations of Criminal Law* (Oxford: Oxford University Press, 2011).

[50] L Zedner, 'Preventive Justice or Pre-Punishment? The Case of Control Orders' (2007) 60 CLP 174, 194.

[51] See M Redmayne, 'The Ethics of Character Evidence' (2008) 61 CLP 371, 385–9.

[52] *Nottingham City Council v Amin* [2000] 1 Cr App R 426.

he was already engaged in breaking the terms of his licence.[53] But there is another way to justify convicting in test purchase cases like *Amin*, which is to argue that the normal rules do not apply when D holds a licence, the terms of which he knows he must comply with. That seems to be a perfectly good analysis, and allows us to account for test purchase cases without widening the normal test for entrapment. Ashworth himself favours this account of cases like *Amin*.[54]

The most difficult problem facing an account of entrapment that is centred on a test of whether D is currently engaged in offending is illustrated by the case of the second park rapist. To respond by modifying the test to whether D is 'ready and willing' to commit the relevant offence risks widening the test too far to include Moon as well as both young men in Ho's example. I have suggested that another way to deal with the case is to argue that the second park rapist was already planning to offend. That may be a way of distinguishing the similar case of *Williams*: we have little reason to think that the defendants were planning to offend until they chanced on the police operation. This analysis seems to me to be preferable to Ashworth's approach to *Williams*, which we noted above: 'Leaving cartons of cigarettes unattended in a public place is little different from leaving a wallet on a park bench: neither is normal behaviour, and both represent extraordinary temptation.'[55] It is not obvious why normality carries normative significance in this context: if leaving unsecured goods in open vehicles becomes common, why should that affect the propriety of convicting D of their theft? In any case, similar behaviour is not that rare: people do forgetful things every day, such as leaving expensive mobile phones in bars or walking away from cash points without taking their money. Most of us will be confronted with a chance to profit from such carelessness at some point. As for extraordinary temptation, that no doubt depends on what is taken as the moral baseline. We know that in *Williams* many people walked past the van without attempting to take the cigarettes.[56] And in terms of the Canadian Supreme Court's test, it is doubtful that the average person would steal the cigarettes. The better argument is that the temptation was one to which 'some ordinarily law-abiding people might succumb',[57] so long as that is interpreted as meaning that the defendants' behaviour gives us little reason to think that they were a legitimate target of entrapment—that they were already engaged in stealing from vehicles.

4. Conclusion

In this essay I have tried to develop an account of entrapment which, while close to Ashworth's, and to which I think he would be sympathetic, differs from his account

[53] While admittedly rather vague, the idea of on-going offending is suggestive of a course of conduct, rather than an isolated incident. Thus it would not be enough if we were sure that D had broken the terms of his licence once before: something more than that is needed.

[54] Ashworth, n 10 above, 300–1.

[55] Ashworth, 'Re-Drawing', n 13 above.

[56] *Williams and O'Hare*, n 8 above, 211.

[57] Ashworth, 'Re-Drawing', n 13 above, 175.

in certain respects. The argument has been that the distinction we draw between legitimate and illegitimate entrapment should focus on whether D is already engaged in offending, or whether, on the contrary, he may have been led into offending by the police operation. It is not enough to say that D was likely to offend in the future, or that he was ready and willing to offend. The account rests on a protective rationale, rather than on arguments based on legitimacy or coherence. On this theory, reasonable suspicion may not be crucial, and confirmation by subsequent facts is justified. Less weight is put on notions such as normality and extraordinary temptation. Predisposition plays no significant role: what matters is whether D is offending, not whether he has a propensity to.

One virtue of this account is that it should be fairly resilient to some of the arguments of the sceptics. If entrapment is only used against those who are already offending, then defendants in entrapment cases are not 'convicted or acquitted by reference to their backgrounds and their character',[58] but on account of what they are doing. The account is vulnerable to a more radical critique, however.[59] By staying prosecutions in cases where there is no evidence that D was already engaged in offending, the courts might be said to be preventing the police from redistributing temptation to crime in a just way.[60] If some people avoid offending only because they are lucky enough to lead relatively privileged lives, why not confront them with the degree of temptation faced by the less privileged? If redistributive taxation is just, why not redistributive entrapment? One answer is that entrapment cannot genuinely redistribute: it might be used to increase temptation for the privileged, but it will not at the same time decrease it for the less privileged (which is surely the strategy to prioritize). To use an analogy: health, like crime, is structured by social inequality, but it would be an odd scheme of social justice that attempted to redress the balance by spreading disease among the well-off.

One aim of this essay has been to suggest refinements to Ashworth's account of entrapment. But I also hope to have highlighted some of the difficulties and subtleties in entrapment doctrine. It is not easy to develop a theory of entrapment that fits our intuitions about key cases and resists the criticisms of the sceptics. And I am not entirely confident that the account sketched here is successful. The case of the second park rapist is a difficult one to deal with without retreating to a 'ready and willing' or 'likely to offend in the future' test—tests that would allow much wider criminalization. I suggested that a conviction might be justified in this case on the argument that D was already planning to commit the offence: it is not likely that the idea of a sexual assault only came into his mind when he saw the undercover officer. That may be a fragile argument, and the line between planning and being ready and willing is hardly clear—thus this argument threatens to undermine any attempt to distinguish the cigarette thieves in *Williams*. Moreover,

[58] Squires, n 2 above, 354. See also L Seidman, 'Entrapment and the Free Market for Crime' in P Robinson, S Garvey, and K Kessler Ferzan (eds), *Criminal Law Conversations* (New York: Oxford University Press, 2009).

[59] See Seidman, ibid.

[60] Or, as Seidman, ibid, puts it, redistributing the costs of deterrence.

it is not obvious that we would want to stay the prosecution even if D convinced us that he had not thought about sexual assault before seeing the decoy. It is therefore perfectly possible that what dominates our intuition in this case is the seriousness of the crime attempted by D.[61] Conversely, in *Williams* it may be the trivial nature of the theft that prompts many to think that the prosecution should have been barred.[62] Some accounts of entrapment do acknowledge the role played by crime seriousness. For example, in the US the Model Penal Code does not allow the entrapment defence to come into play in cases of causing or threatening bodily injury to someone other than the entrapper,[63] and under Duff et al's account claims of illegitimate entrapment can only be raised in the context of victimless crimes (though this would include *Williams*, as there no real harm is done, the property never effectively having left police control).[64] But while concerns about crime seriousness may play some role in our thinking, it is not obvious how they can be incorporated in a theory without making our underlying objection to entrapment look half-hearted.

A concern for principles runs through much of Ashworth's work, and is evident in his writings on entrapment where he tries to develop a coherent theory to limit state creation of crime. In responding to his writings in this area, I have questioned some of his assumptions and suggested ways in which his theory might be fine-tuned. I hope that the account offered here does provide a principled approach to entrapment, one where the focus is confined to the question of whether D was already committing crime. In closing, however, I have allowed some scepticism to emerge. The reason for this is that I find it hard to know what is driving our intuitions in cases such as *Williams* and the second park rapist—whether there really is a difference in these cases in terms of the defendants' commitment to offending, or whether we are influenced more by pragmatism and risk. While it may seem odd to end on a sceptical note, a lingering doubt about the basis for our intuitions is not the only reason for doing so. It is obvious that the courts are influenced by factors such as crime seriousness when considering whether to stay proceedings or exclude evidence.[65] To echo one of Ashworth's most persistent themes: it is only by being aware of the tendency to be influenced by crime seriousness that we are best placed to defend principles as a safeguard against too quick a resort to pragmatism.

[61] And here preventative justice enters the picture again, because when the costs of inaction are sufficiently great, we may think it appropriate to create exceptions to anti-prevention principles: see Ashworth, n 49 above, 103–4.

[62] Ashworth, a critic of *Williams*, certainly seems amenable to the argument that minor theft should not be criminalized: see *Principles of Criminal Law* (6th edn, Oxford: Oxford University Press, 2009), 357–8, 398–402.

[63] American Law Institute, *Model Penal Code* (1980), 2.13. Ashworth describes this limitation as 'contestable': n 10 above, 297.

[64] A Duff, L Farmer, S Marshall, and V Tadros, *The Trial on Trial Volume 3: Towards a Normative Theory of the Criminal Trial* (Oxford: Hart, 2007), 242–7. See also RA Duff, *Answering for Crime: Responsibility and Liability in the Criminal Law* (Oxford: Hart, 2007), 187–91.

[65] For a recent example, see *Warren v Her Majesty's Attorney General of the Bailiwick of Jersey* [2011] UKPC 10. For extended discussion, and defence of principles in such cases, see A Ashworth, *Human Rights, Serious Crime and Criminal Procedure* (London: Sweet & Maxwell, 2002).

11

Excluding Evidence as Protecting Constitutional or Human Rights?

Paul Roberts

1. Introduction: Rewind to 1977

In an article published in the Criminal Law Review in 1977, Andrew Ashworth advanced his 'protective principle' as a novel rationale for excluding improperly obtained evidence from criminal trials.[1] 'Excluding Evidence as Protecting Rights' (EEPR) became an instant classic. Profusely cited ever since, 'the protective principle' soon passed into the terminological canon of criminal procedure scholarship. EEPR anticipates many of the hallmarks of Ashworth's voluminous and enormously influential contributions to the study of criminal law, criminal process, sentencing, and punishment: in emphasizing 'principle and policy';[2] in its appeal to underlying moral values like human dignity;[3] and through its integration of normative theoretical enquiries and detailed doctrinal analysis. Moreover, Ashworth has never wavered from EEPR's substantive thesis. The argument that rights violations should sometimes trigger evidentiary exclusion is reiterated in several recent essays.[4]

In the meantime, the law of criminal procedure in England and Wales has evolved almost beyond recognition from the pre-PACE 1984 patchwork of case law, Judges' Rules, and disparate statutory provisions confronting the legal analyst in the 1970s. After three decades of extensive statutory reform[5] culminating in the

[1] AJ Ashworth, 'Excluding Evidence as Protecting Rights' [1977] Crim LR 723.

[2] Ibid, 723.

[3] Ibid. 726.

[4] See eg A Ashworth, 'The Exclusion of Evidence Obtained by Violating a Fundamental Right: Pragmatism Before Principle in the Strasbourg Jurisprudence' in P Roberts and J Hunter (eds), *Criminal Evidence and Human Rights* (Oxford: Hart, 2012); A Ashworth, 'Exploring the Integrity Principle in Evidence and Procedure' in P Mirfield and R Smith (eds), *Essays for Colin Tapper* (Oxford: Oxford University Press, 2003).

[5] Notably including PACE 1984 and its expanding Codes of Practice; Prosecution of Offences Act 1985; Criminal Justice Act 1988; Criminal Justice and Public Order Act 1994; Criminal Procedure and Investigations Act 1996; Youth Justice and Criminal Evidence Act 1999; Regulation of Investigatory Powers Act 2000; Criminal Justice Act 2003; and Coroners and Justice Act 2009.

Criminal Procedure Rules[6] and the transformation of criminal evidence and procedure into 'a human rights subject',[7] the exclusion of improperly obtained evidence might today be rationalized in terms of protecting *human* or *constitutional* rights. Yet these reinvigorated protective principles themselves pose new questions of conceptual definition and normative analysis. What is a 'human right' in the context of criminal adjudication? How does one identify a 'constitutional right' in the absence of a comprehensive written constitution? And why should these juridical classifications have any bearing on the admissibility of material evidence in criminal trials?

2. Ashworth's Original Argument for the Protective Principle

EEPR begins by observing that '[t]he justifications for excluding involuntary confessions and other improperly obtained evidence have been much debated'.[8] Much debated by scholars, perhaps, but not by English courts. Confessions regarded as 'involuntary' were inadmissible at common law, but voluntariness was largely a practical question of factual classification with minimal jurisprudential interest. As for non-confessional or 'real' (physical) evidence, English courts were strongly influenced by what Ashworth dubbed 'the reliability principle'. This was not so much a genuine 'principle' as a hard-headed pragmatic preference for receiving relevant information bearing on the issues in the trial, almost irrespective of its provenance.[9] '[T]he court is not concerned with how the evidence was obtained', stated Lord Goddard CJ matter-of-factly in a mid-20th-century Privy Council case.[10] According to Ashworth, 'Even in answer to the question "should evidence obtained by torture be admitted?", advocates of the reliability principle stand their ground.'[11] For reliabilists, impropriety in criminal investigations (no matter how serious) is one thing and the admissibility of reliable evidence at trial quite another.

Lined up against the reliability principle, explained Ashworth, is the 'disciplinary principle'. Disciplinarians believe that evidence should be excluded 'even when its

[6] First promulgated in 2005. Now see Crim PR 2011, available at <http://www.justice.gov.uk/guidance/courts-and-tribunals/courts/procedure-rules/criminal/rulesmenu.htm> accessed 19 March 2012.

[7] See B Emmerson, A Ashworth, and A Macdonald, *Human Rights and Criminal Justice* (2nd edn, London: Sweet & Maxwell, 2007); ALT Choo and S Nash, 'Evidence Law in England and Wales: The Impact of the Human Rights Act 1998' (2003) 7 International Journal of Evidence & Proof 31.

[8] EEPR, n 1 above, 723. The textbooks cite cases going back to the 18th century, eg *R v Warwickshall* (1783) 1 Leach 263.

[9] The principle standing behind this pragmatic preference is Bentham's injunction that if 'you exclude evidence, you exclude justice': *Rationale of Judicial Evidence* (1827), quoted by T Anderson, D Schum, and W Twining, *Analysis of Evidence* (2nd edn, Cambridge: Cambridge University Press, 2005), 1.

[10] *Kuruma v R* [1955] AC 197, 203 (PC). Also see Crompton J's notorious remark a century earlier, in *R v Leatham* (1861) 8 Cox CC 498, 501, that '[i]t matters not how you get [relevant evidence]; if you steal it even, it would be admissible'.

[11] EEPR, n 1 above, 724.

reliability is in no doubt, since the court should use its position to discourage improper practices in the investigation of crime'.[12] EEPR's iteration of the disciplinary principle covered two related ideas, neither of which Ashworth himself endorsed. First, that evidentiary exclusion will deter illegality and other investigative impropriety in future proceedings. Secondly, that exclusion would 'punish an errant law enforcement officer'[13] in the instant case. The second rationale for the disciplinary principle is patently dubious. Police officers are 'punished' by excluding improperly obtained evidence only in a highly attenuated sense. Investigators can usually count on a guilty plea to conceal minor procedural irregularities from scrutiny in open court, whilst truly corrupt officers would presumably ensure that cases involving serious police wrongdoing would be prosecuted, if at all, only once their tracks were safely covered.

The deterrence theory of evidentiary exclusion is popular with some courts and commentators in the United States, but vociferously contested by others.[14] The debate rumbles on, inconclusively. English courts have never been much impressed with the disciplinary rationale; though the point might have seemed more arguable in 1977 than hindsight would suggest.[15] Judge Buzzard's first instance ruling in the well-known case of *Sang* encapsulated contemporary orthodoxy: '[T]he object of the rules of evidence and the rules regulating the exercise of discretion is to achieve justice in the instant case, not, for example, to discipline the police or anyone else.'[16] The Court of Appeal has reiterated many times since that 'it is not in general the function of criminal courts to discipline the police'[17] (though the Court's motivation in ruling evidence inadmissible occasionally appears tinged by disciplinary sentiments).[18]

Breaking the deadlock between reliabilists and disciplinarians, EEPR argued that 'a third, "protective" principle provides both a stronger justification for the exclusion of improperly obtained evidence and a plausible explanation of some relevant judicial decisions'.[19] Later in the article Ashworth endorsed the following 'qualified protective principle':

[12] Ibid, 723.

[13] Ibid, n 2.

[14] See eg RM Bloom and DH Fentin, '"A More Majestic Conception": The Importance of Judicial Integrity in Preserving the Exclusionary Rule' (2010) 13 University of Pennsylvania Journal of Constitutional Law 47; D Dripps, 'The Case for the Contingent Exclusionary Rule' (2001) 38 American Criminal Law Review 1.

[15] There is one reported case in which the Court of Appeal mused that 'there may be cases where the exclusion of evidence for disciplinary purposes may be justified': *R v Trump* (1980) 70 Cr App R 300, 304. Eveleigh LJ self-cited this passage in *R v Birtwhistle* [1980] RTR 342, 348 (CA), but no other English court to my knowledge has ever endorsed the disciplinary principle before or since.

[16] *R v Sang and Mangan* (1979) 68 Cr App R 240, 244 (CA).

[17] *R v Grant* [2005] EWCA Crim 1089, [2006] QB 60 at [55]. Also see eg *R v Bailey and Smith* (1993) 97 Cr App R 365, 370 (CA); *R v F* (CA 22 May 2000) at [48]; *R v Oliphant* [1992] Crim LR 40 (CA); *Fox v Chief Constable of Gwent* [1986] 1 AC 281, 292 (HL) (Lord Fraser).

[18] cf *R v Mason* [1988] 1 WLR 139, 144 (CA).

[19] EEPR, n 1 above, 723.

> [E]vidence obtained by means of a departure from a declared standard or procedure should be liable to exclusion, unless the court is satisfied that the accused in fact suffered no disadvantage as a result of the breach.[20]

The protective principle was not to be equated with 'the view that *all* improperly obtained evidence should be peremptorily excluded'.[21] Mindful that 'the prima facie justification for exclusion . . . may occasionally be outweighed by other considerations',[22] Ashworth envisaged his protective principle being applied through judicial discretion. Crucially, however, discretionary exclusion must be structured by a framework of principle, lest 'the unique facts of the case' should become an all-purpose alibi for excessive judicial passivity or lazy reasoning. '[T]he dangers of a wide and unstructured discretion to exclude evidence on grounds of unfairness', Ashworth warned, 'are manifest in the haphazard approach of English courts to improperly obtained evidence.'[23]

The normative rationale for the protective principle was elucidated in the following key passage:

> If a legal system declares certain standards for the conduct of criminal investigation . . . then it can be argued that citizens have corresponding rights to be accorded certain facilities and not to be treated in certain ways. If the legal system is to respect those rights, then it is arguable that a suspect whose rights have been infringed should not thereby be placed at any disadvantage . . . (ie '. . . [E]vidence') obtained by the investigators as a result of the infringement should not be used against the suspect. And the appropriate way of ensuring that the suspect does not suffer this disadvantage is for the court of trial to have the power to exclude evidence obtained by improper methods.[24]

Ultimately, for Ashworth, the question was one of recognizing and protecting suspects' rights without hypocrisy:

> [T]he primary question remains whether we are willing to recognise rights in suspects and to protect them; recognition without any protection would be a pretence.[25]

Modern legal discourse is saturated with rights-talk and criminal procedure is exemplary in this regard, not least because 'the right to a fair trial' has been in the vanguard of the broader human rights revolution in contemporary jurisprudence.[26] It is easy to forget just how recent these profound changes in the legal landscape really are. With his visionary argument for 'protecting rights', Ashworth was taking rights seriously[27] before most British judges and lawyers had read their Dworkin.[28] To assess whether the protective principle is more than just a catchy—and highly successful—slogan, we need to consider what role, exactly, rights do or

[20] EEPR, n 1 above, 729. [21] Ibid, 725 (original emphasis).
[22] Ibid, 725–6. [23] Ibid, 734. [24] Ibid, 725. [25] Ibid, 735.
[26] DJ Harris, M O'Boyle, EP Bates, and CM Buckley, *Law of the European Convention on Human Rights* (2nd edn, Oxford: Oxford University Press, 2009), Ch 6; S Trechsel with SJ Summers, *Human Rights in Criminal Proceedings* (Oxford: Oxford University Press, 2005).
[27] Literally: cf EEPR, n 1 above, 731.
[28] R Dworkin, *Taking Rights Seriously* (rev edn, London: Duckworth, 1978).

should play in arguments about the exclusion of improperly obtained evidence in English criminal trials.

3. Elucidating (and Complicating) the Protective Principle

The deceptive simplicity of the 'protective principle' is belied by the variety of ways in which the principle can be cashed out in theory and practice. Here is the simplest iteration:

PP#1: it is a reason for excluding evidence in criminal trials that the evidence was obtained in violation of the accused's legal rights.

The 'is a reason' formulation preserves the possibility of weighty countervailing reasons which, on balance, demand admissibility in the instant case. This tracks Ashworth's concession that 'the protective principle may occasionally be outweighed by other considerations'.[29] Being tied to legal rights, PP#1 excludes (arguable) moral rights which have not been recognized and enshrined in positive law. This is faithful to Ashworth's stated conditional premiss for the protective principle: '*If* a legal system declares certain standards for the conduct of criminal investigation . . . '.[30]

The following trio specifies textually defensible alternative interpretations of EEPR's protective principle:

PP#2: it is a reason for excluding evidence in criminal trials that the evidence was obtained in violation of one of the accused's substantive legal rights.

PP#3: it is a reason for excluding evidence in criminal trials that the evidence was obtained in violation of one of the accused's criminal process rights.

PP#4: it is a reason for excluding evidence in criminal trials that the evidence was obtained in such a way that the accused has a right that it be excluded, and *that* right would be violated if the evidence were admitted.

An example falling under PP#2 would be evidence procured through violations of the accused's rights to bodily integrity, property, or privacy which exist independently of any criminal investigation or prosecution. These are rights which criminal investigators must work around if they are to conduct lawful investigations. An example falling within the scope of PP#3 would be evidence obtained in violation of criminal process guarantees such as the rights not to be held incommunicado,[31] to receive custodial legal advice,[32] to know the substance of the charge,[33] to be

[29] EEPR, n 1 above, 726.

[30] Ibid, 725 (emphasis added). The legal positivist assumptions of the argument are underlined a few pages later, where Ashworth observes: 'What is essential . . . is that if . . . a right is not protected it should not be proclaimed, and if it is proclaimed it ought to be protected': ibid, 728.

[31] PACE 1984, s 56.

[32] PACE 1984, s 58; Art 6(3)(c) ECHR; *Salduz v Turkey* (App no 36391/02) (2009) 49 EHRR 19.

[33] PACE Code of Practice C, para 16.3; Art 6(3)(a) ECHR.

shielded from forced self-incrimination,[34] and to question or 'confront' incriminating evidence and witnesses adduced by the prosecution.[35] These rights would not exist independently of their distinctive institutional context. They are constitutive features of a system of criminal trial and punishment making certain claims to legitimacy.

Ashworth's own discussion of the protective principle is largely confined to the types of rights violations encompassed by PP#3, deriving from 'certain standards for the conduct of criminal investigations—whether they are enshrined in a constitution, detailed in a comprehensive code or scattered in various statutes and judicial precedents'.[36] However, it is evident that the protective principle was also intended to cover evidence falling within the jurisdiction of PP#2. Even without retrospective reliance on Ashworth's later writings, this inference is confirmed by brief references to torture[37] and arrest powers[38] in EEPR itself. Torture is criminalized in the first instance through the general criminal law of offences against the person,[39] quite apart from whether it is also proscribed by more context-specific constraints on criminal investigations. Arrest powers are obviously part of the law of policing, and their exercise *may*—though in fact it usually does not—lead to criminal charges, prosecution, and trial. However, the law of arrest is not aptly conceptualized as an aspect of the criminal process rights envisaged by PP#3. Arrest powers, properly conceived, constitute an important exception to the right to liberty,[40] which is a general (non-criminal process) right within the bailiwick of PP#2.

PP#4 presents greater analytical difficulties, starting with its apparent circularity: the evidence is to be excluded *because* the accused has a right that it be excluded. However, PP#4 is not tautologous. On any conception of a right which allows for the possibility of conflicting rights (as all the best conceptions do),[41] the accused might have a right to exclusion which is overridden or—in Dworkinian idiom—out-trumped[42] by a competing right, perhaps the right of a deceased murder victim to have his dying accusation read out in court[43] or the right of an abused child to

[34] *R v S (F)* [2008] EWCA Crim 2177, [2009] 1 WLR 1489; *Saunders v UK* (App no 19187/91) (1996) 23 EHRR 313.

[35] *R v Davis* [2008] UKHL 36, [2008] 1 AC 1128; *R v Horncastle* [2009] UKSC 14, [2010] 2 AC 373; Art 6(3)(d) ECHR; *Al-Khawaja and Tahery v UK* (App no 26766/05) (2009) 49 EHRR 1, (2012) 54 EHRR 23 (Grand Chamber).

[36] EEPR, n 1 above, 725.

[37] 'Even in answer to the question "should evidence obtained by torture be admitted?", advocates of the reliability principle stand their ground': ibid, 724.

[38] Characterizing *Scott v Baker* [1969] 1 QB 659 (DC) as an excessively 'rigid application of the protective principle' which 'only tends to bring the law into disrepute': EEPR, n 1 above, 728.

[39] Offences Against the Person Act 1861, ss 18, 20, and 47; Criminal Justice Act 1988, s 134.

[40] Thus, within the framework of the ECHR, arrest powers are subject to Art 5's right to liberty, not to the right to a fair trial under Art 6.

[41] See eg J Waldron, *Liberal Rights* (Cambridge: Cambridge University Press, 1993), Chs 3 and 9.

[42] R Dworkin, 'Rights As Trumps' in J Waldron (ed), *Theories of Rights* (Oxford: Oxford University Press, 1984).

[43] *R v Al-Khawaja* [2005] EWCA Crim 2697, [2006] 1 WLR 1078; *Nembhard v R* (1982) 74 Cr App R 144 (PC).

have the state make serious efforts to bring her abuser to justice.[44] So long as the accused's right to evidentiary exclusion is merely defeasible in particular circumstances and not routinely trumped or traduced, there is no deep conceptual paradox or normative mystery in recognizing such a right.

Another distinctive feature of PP#4 is that a rights violation is not required to trigger it. The evidence must have been obtained '*in such a way* that the accused has a right that it be excluded', but the improper methods in question may or may not have included the infringement of one of the accused's rights. PP#4 stretches Ashworth's original conception of 'corresponding rights' so that the relevant 'standard for the conduct of criminal investigation' just *is* the right to have evidence excluded in certain designated circumstances. I will later explain why this feature of PP#4 is a conceptual and normative strength richly justifying an element of purposive textual construction.

The next step for conceptual elucidation is to perm our first four interpretations to produce new, composite iterations of the protective principle. Combining PP#1 and PP#4 produces:

PP#5: it is a reason for excluding evidence in criminal trials that (i) the evidence was obtained in violation of the accused's legal rights, such that (ii) the accused has a right that it be excluded, and *that* right would also be violated if the evidence were admitted.

PP#5 states a more stringent protective principle with a presumptively narrower field of application. There are now *two* necessary and sufficient preconditions for establishing a reason to exclude evidence. Not only must the accused's rights have been violated, as envisaged by PP#1, but in addition that rights violation should be regarded as triggering a right to exclusion in accordance with PP#4. We could relax the causal relationship between the two triggering factors slightly, to produce:

PP#6: it is a reason for excluding evidence in criminal trials that (i) the evidence was obtained in violation of the accused's legal rights, such that—taking that rights violation in combination with other relevant circumstances—(ii) the accused has a right that it be excluded, and *that* right would also be violated if the evidence were admitted.

On the face of it, interposing a further condition between the initial rights violation and the right to exclusion might be thought to reduce the stringency of PP#6 relative to PP#5. For example, if bad faith on the part of police investigators is regarded as a salient consideration,[45] a rights violation which (let us assume) would not be sufficient in gravity to satisfy the second limb of PP#5 might nonetheless trigger PP#6 if the right were violated deliberately in bad faith. In other words, bad faith would be a 'relevant circumstance', which in combination with the initial

[44] *Judge v UK* (App no 35863/10) (2011) 52 EHRR SE17; J Doak, *Victims' Rights, Human Rights and Criminal Justice* (Oxford: Hart, 2008), Ch 2; A Mowbray, *The Development of Positive Obligations under the European Convention on Human Rights by the European Court of Human Rights* (Oxford: Hart, 2004), 127–30.

[45] Having noted the obvious salience of police bad faith for the disciplinary principle, Ashworth asserts: '[b]ut on a protective principle this factor is irrelevant': EEPR, n 1 above, 731. PP#6 demonstrates why Ashworth's argument does not substantiate his assertion.

rights violation satisfied PP#6. Alternatively, 'other relevant circumstances' could conceivably make PP#6 *more* stringent than PP#5. For example, a breach of a suspect's right, say, to prompt custodial legal advice might be thought sufficient to satisfy PP#5, but might *also* require a showing of bad faith to satisfy PP#6.[46] In that event, police misconduct establishing a reason for excluding evidence under PP#5 would not provide a reason for exclusion under PP#6. In short, the relative stringency of PP#5 and PP#6 pivots on the detailed specification of 'in combination with other relevant circumstances'.

We can be more precise about the meaning of 'the accused's legal rights' in composite, dual-criterion interpretations of the protective principle, just as we were before when considering single-criterion interpretations. Combining PP#4 with PP#2 and PP#3 generates, respectively:

PP#7: it is a reason for excluding evidence in criminal trials that (i) the evidence was obtained in violation of one of the accused's substantive legal rights, such that (ii) the accused has a right that it be excluded, and *that* right would also be violated if the evidence were admitted.

PP#8: it is a reason for excluding evidence in criminal trials that (i) the evidence was obtained in violation of one of the accused's criminal process rights, such that (ii) the accused has a right that it be excluded, and *that* right would also be violated if the evidence were admitted.

Alternatively, PP#2 and PP#3 could in turn combine with PP#6 to produce:

PP#9: it is a reason for excluding evidence in criminal trials that (i) the evidence was obtained in violation of one of the accused's substantive legal rights, such that—taking that rights violation in combination with other relevant circumstances—(ii) the accused has a right that it be excluded, and *that* right would also be violated if the evidence were admitted.

PP#10: it is a reason for excluding evidence in criminal trials that (i) the evidence was obtained in violation of one of the accused's criminal process rights, such that—taking that rights violation in combination with other relevant circumstances—(ii) the accused has a right that it be excluded, and *that* right would also be violated if the evidence were admitted.

In view of the intended scope of Ashworth's original protective principle, PP#5 and PP#6 are probably more interesting and potentially useful interpretations than any of the more particularized variations, PP#7 to PP#10. But all of them are certainly logically possible elucidations of the core principle, with divergent implications for the scope of evidentiary exclusion.

Our inventory of alternative specifications has gone into double figures without yet broaching a vital further question. This concerns the *moral ground* or justificatory rationale of a relevant right, as opposed to its scope, content, strength, or doctrinal legal basis. EEPR advanced several, not entirely consistent, claims bearing on this question. This is Ashworth's most explicit statement of the moral ground of the rights generated by the protective principle:

[46] cf *R v Alladice* (1988) 87 Cr App R 380, 386 (CA); *R v Fulling* [1987] QB 426, 432 (CA).

> A legal system must reach a decision on an acceptable demarcation between permissible and impermissible methods [in the enforcement of criminal law] . . . [O]nce agreement has been reached the rights which flow from it should be respected and protected. An essential part of taking such an agreement seriously is *to protect suspects and accused persons from any disadvantage which results from an infringement of the rights declared or implied.* The relevance of this theory to the law of evidence is that where a legal system lays down certain standards or procedures for criminal investigation, *it is both appropriate and desirable to protect defendants from any disadvantage resulting from the breach of a declared standard or procedure* by excluding evidence obtained as a result of that breach.[47]

Concern with forensic disadvantage suggests an instrumental or consequentialist[48] justification of evidentiary exclusion: unless the evidential fruits of a rights violation are excluded from the trial, the accused will have suffered unfair disadvantage from the violation of his rights; and this is what the protective principle prohibits (albeit defeasibly). Finessing PP#1 with this justificatory rationale leads to:

PP#11: it is a reason for excluding evidence in criminal trials that (i) the evidence was obtained in violation of the accused's legal rights, *and* (ii) exclusion is necessary to prevent the accused from suffering consequential forensic disadvantage.

It would be possible to tack the 'forensic disadvantage' rationale onto each of the variations PP#2 to PP#10, which would give us PP#12 to PP#20. We can skip their exhaustive elaboration, on grounds of economy and tedium.

Ashworth comes closest to propounding a consequentialist conception of the forensic disadvantage rationale in his discussion of the admissibility of confessions at common law.[49] '[B]y concentrating on the *effect on the accused* of the words or conduct of his questioner', Ashworth suggests, 'the courts are in fact recognising the rights of suspects not to be subjected to certain forms of inducement and oppression, and protecting suspects from the disadvantage which might result if evidence obtained through a violation of those rights were admitted at his trial'.[50] The 'effect on the accused' might connote the *actual* effect (if any) on *this* accused in the instant case; or the anticipated effects on the majority of similarly situated defendants in the general run of cases. Applying our now familiar method, this conceptual refinement would contribute PP#21 to PP#30 and PP#31 to PP#40, respectively, to our burgeoning roster of protective principles.

Significantly, only the first set of these latest interpretations is susceptible to case-specific 'harmless error' analysis. Under PP#21 to PP#30, if violation of the accused's rights had no material bearing on the conduct or outcome of the proceedings—say, because the accused is a hardened professional criminal who does not need custodial legal advice[51]—evidentiary exclusion will not be triggered

[47] EEPR, n 1 above, 733 (emphasis supplied).

[48] Though Ashworth is plainly not a consequentialist through-and-through: cf A Ashworth, 'Crime, Community and Creeping Consequentialism' [1996] Crim LR 220; A Ashworth and M Redmayne, *The Criminal Process* (4th edn, Oxford: Oxford University Press, 2010), 45–7.

[49] *DPP v Ping Lin* [1976] AC 574, 606 (HL).

[50] EEPR, n 1 above, 727 (original emphasis).

[51] *R v Alladice* (1988) 87 Cr App R 380 (CA).

by any interpretation of the protective principle rooted in forensic disadvantage. In relation to a search warrant specifying the wrong address, for example, Ashworth explains that 'advocates of the disciplinary principle would look to the source of error, whereas the protective principle might ask whether in fact the accused was misled by the error'.[52] The implication seems to be that the protective principle might not authorize evidentiary exclusion in the absence of tangible forensic disadvantage, either because a relevant right has not been infringed; or because the kind of rights violation involved does not rise to the level of grounding a (defeasible) right of exclusion; or possibly both (these being the dual criteria specified by PP#11 and its more particularized derivatives).

When discussing other examples, however, EEPR intimates a different tack, more in keeping with the second group of forensic disadvantage rationales, PP#31 to PP#40. In the following passage, Ashworth explains how the protective principle would differ from the reliability principle in responding to the argument that investigative impropriety was too trivial to warrant inadmissibility:

> The triviality or seriousness of the breach is measured according to its consequences for the accused, and the reason behind the particular procedure must be examined. If the procedure was intended not to safeguard individual liberty but rather to ensure the accuracy of the evidence collected, the protective principle does not require the exclusion of evidence obtained in contravention of the procedure: its admissibility should depend purely on its reliability. If on the other hand it appears that the procedure was intended as a safeguard for liberty, the court must go on to consider whether the breach actually had the effect of prejudicing that liberty. If it did, the evidence ought to be excluded.[53]

Where the admissibility of evidence would not, in practice, fall to be determined unless the accused necessarily *had been* disadvantaged by violation of his rights (eg a speculative DNA match where the accused's profile was retained illegally),[54] this position would equate to a (defeasible) justification for automatic evidentiary exclusion. As Ashworth adds in a footnote, '[i]f rights are to be taken seriously then any infringement which actually disadvantages the accused would justify the exclusion of evidence gained thereby'.[55] To similar effect but more systematically, PP#31 to PP#40 rationalize presumptive exclusion on the basis of generalized predictions of forensic disadvantage in particular scenarios, eg where interrogators employed tactics known to produce false confessions (irrespective of the truth of the accused's admissions in the instant case).

Yet there is something vitally important missing from the argument here. In the absence of further normative grounding, Ashworth's contention *is* tautologous. Why should evidence be excluded under the protective principle? Because it was obtained by violating the accused's rights. But why should rights violations trigger an exclusionary remedy, rather than providing the accused with direct redress through tort liability, human rights legislation, criminal injuries compensation, or by

[52] EEPR, n 1 above, 731.
[53] Ibid, 731 (footnotes omitted).
[54] *Attorney General's Reference (No 3 of 1999)* [2001] 2 AC 91 (HL).
[55] EEPR, n 1 above, 731.

subjecting individual miscreants to penal or disciplinary sanctions? We have ended up restating the very conundrum which every attempted rationalization of the exclusion of improperly obtained evidence, before and after EEPR, has sought to resolve. In order to break out of this vicious circularity we need to extend and deepen our enquiry into the nature of rights.

4. What's in a Right?

Ashworth's hypothetical illustration introduces a new variable into the discussion—procedures, presumably including procedural rights, 'intended as a safeguard for liberty'. It is unclear how liberty-safeguarding procedural rights are supposed to relate to the protective principle's threshold criterion of forensic disadvantage. Breach of a right designed 'to ensure the accuracy of the evidence', which Ashworth excludes from his principle's protective mantle, could certainly leave the accused at a serious forensic disadvantage, as where the accused's conviction rests on untested hearsay or irrelevant bad character which the Court of Appeal rules improperly admitted at trial but without, on balance, affecting the 'safety' of the accused's conviction.[56] Reliability-based exclusionary doctrines easily lend themselves to harmless error analysis, where the court reasons that, after all, the accused was found guilty on ample evidence and has not suffered any material disadvantage from 'technical' violations of his procedural rights. Indeed, this is exactly the sort of suspiciously convenient rationalization that Ashworth's protective principle was supposed to pre-empt:

> If standards for the conduct of criminal investigation are to be taken seriously, then the reliability principle cannot be an adequate criterion for the admissibility of improperly obtained evidence. It fails to provide any protection for the accused against the disadvantageous consequences of a breach, and therefore subverts the values which the standards and procedures for investigation promote.[57]

Now, 'standards and procedures for investigation' can be regarded as 'promoting' many and diverse values. If we stick with Ashworth's own example of procedures 'intended to safeguard individual liberty', this might suggest:

PP#41: it is a reason for excluding evidence in criminal trials that (i) the evidence was obtained in violation of one of the accused's legal rights; (ii) the right in question was designed to safeguard individual liberty; *and* (iii) exclusion is necessary to ensure that the accused does not suffer any forensic disadvantage from the violation of his rights.

PP#41 reconciles two prominent strands of Ashworth's argument, accommodating both the moral ground of the right (here, liberty) and forensic disadvantage as (part of) the rationale for evidentiary exclusion. Since the liberty ground—part (ii) of

[56] See eg *R v Adams (Ishmael)* [2007] EWCA Crim 3025, [2008] 1 Cr App R 35; *R v Edwards and Rowlands* [2005] EWCA Crim 3244, [2006] 2 Cr App R 4.
[57] EEPR, n 1 above, 729.

PP#41—could be incorporated as a further condition into any of the interpretations of the protective principle previously canvassed, this generates another raft of possible interpretations, PP#41 to PP#80. However, it is evident that EEPR invoked liberty-protecting 'standards and procedures' only by way of illustration and not to define the scope of the protective principle. We can easily think of other important values that procedures and standards in criminal investigations might serve. Non-discrimination on objectionable grounds of nationality, race, gender, sexual orientation, disability, etc, is one obvious candidate, which—on the now well-established formula—could give us PP#81 to PP#120. Standards in criminal investigations also protect bodily integrity and physical security, suggesting PP#121 to PP#160. Ensuring humane treatment is another major institutional concern, producing PP#161 to PP#200, and we certainly must not overlook the special criminal procedure right identified by Dworkin and others[58] not to be exposed to an unreasonable risk of wrongful conviction: PP#201 to PP#240. And so on.

The abiding lesson is that one must pay careful attention to the moral grounding of any salient right. This is usually a significant factor in deciding whether evidentiary exclusion might be an appropriate (defeasible) remedy for rights violations, as PP#41 to PP#240 bring to the fore. Moral and legal rights vary enormously in their importance, depending on the nature of the interests they protect and serve—the ground of the right. Likewise, the strength of the (defeasible) argument for evidentiary exclusion will usually reflect the nature and importance of any right that was breached in order to obtain the evidence. The case for evidentiary exclusion, in other words, is sensitive to the moral ground of the violated right and the importance of the interest(s) that right protects. This supports the assumption, more or less consistently adopted by English courts, that the very fact that a right (any old right) has been violated in the process of obtaining evidence does not, in and of itself, provide a reason for excluding the evidence.[59] Of course, this leaves open the possibility that breaches of *specific* rights might warrant—or even mandate—exclusion, depending inter alia on the nature and importance of the moral grounding of the right and the interest(s) it serves.

Refocusing the inquiry on the moral grounds of rights rather than their scope, structure, or formal pedigree can be pressed still further to produce a second preliminary conclusion, in which rights drop out of the analysis altogether. There may, in short, be important values in criminal investigations that do not ground any rights, or at any rate no rights of the accused. So if evidentiary exclusion supposedly operates as a procedural mechanism for vindicating 'standards for the conduct of criminal investigation', it presumably should not rest content with 'protecting rights', as EEPR's title and analysis strongly implied.

[58] R Dworkin, 'Principle, Policy, Procedure' in CFH Tapper (ed), *Crime, Proof and Punishment* (London: Butterworths, 1981); P Roberts and A Zuckerman, *Criminal Evidence* (2nd edn, Oxford: Oxford University Press, 2010), 240–52.

[59] Perhaps courts always have a rule-of-law reason to vindicate legal rights. Even so, this will not necessarily establish—even a defeasible—reason for excluding probative evidence in criminal trials. For example, rights violations may be clearly justifiable (permitted) or excused in particular circumstances.

Consider the House of Lords' ruling in *A v Home Secretary (No 2)*[60] that evidence probably procured by torture of a third-party non-British national overseas by foreign security agents is never admissible in English courts. The accused in criminal proceedings does not have a right that a third-party non-British national should not be tortured overseas by foreign security agents (although, of course, the torture victim himself has a moral right and a legal right under international law not to be tortured).[61] The House of Lords stated unequivocally that,'[t]orture is not acceptable. This is a bedrock moral principle in this country.'[62] The inherently abominable nature of torture makes its informational fruits inadmissible, irrespective of whether the accused's—or anybody else's—rights under English law have been violated. Whilst torture is an extreme example, the same principle supports a multitude of more prosaic instantiations. Thus, breaches of the PACE Codes of Practice may be sufficiently 'significant and substantial'[63] to warrant exclusion of improperly obtained evidence, even if the provisions in question do not confer legal rights on the accused.[64]

We can now see why the absence of any reference to rights violations in PP#4 should be regarded as a conceptual and normative strength, rather than a weakness. Legal and ethical standards in criminal investigations, in all their normative complexity, cannot be comprehensively vindicated by an exclusionary rule delimited by substantive legal rights, still less by an evidentiary remedy restricted to violations of the rights of the accused (cf PP#2 and PP#3).

5. Constitutional Rights

With relentless tenacity but relatively little imagination, the previous two sections managed to accumulate some 240 different interpretations of Ashworth's protective principle. It would be a simple matter to generate many more conceptual possibilities, by identifying other relevant values and grounds of rights, adding in further circumstantial factors, and recombining all these elements in a spiralling inventory of novel permutations. My intention was to demonstrate the range and variety of considerations bearing on the question whether rights violations should sometimes (always/often/occasionally/never) precipitate evidentiary exclusion. If, as most commentators insist,[65] judicial rulings on the admissibility of improperly obtained evidence are frequently inadequately reasoned, part of the explanation might be found in the geometric complexity and finely nuanced moral discrimina-

[60] *A v Secretary of State for the Home Department (No 2)* [2005] UKHL 71, [2006] 2 AC 221.

[61] A Cassese, *International Criminal Law* (2nd edn, Oxford: Oxford University Press, 2008), Ch 7.

[62] *A v Secretary of State for the Home Department (No 2)*, n 60 above, at [64] (Lord Nicholls).

[63] *R v Keenan* [1990] 2 QB 54, 69–70 (CA).

[64] cf PACE 1984, s 67(10): 'A failure on the part . . . of a police officer to comply with any provision of such a code . . . shall not of itself render him liable to any criminal or civil proceedings.'

[65] See eg D Ormerod and D Birch, 'The Evolution of the Discretionary Exclusion of Evidence' [2004] Crim LR 767; ALT Choo and S Nash, 'What's the Matter with Section 78?' [1999] Crim LR 929.

tions characterizing contextual exercises of judicial discretion. The inherent practical difficulty of the judicial task is compounded by the (largely unexplored) conceptual fecundity of general rationales for evidentiary exclusion, which—as we have seen—can be magnificently protean and malleable.

A promising strategy for alleviating the burdens of judicial decision-making in this context would be to designate a special class of rights which, in view of their moral ground or for some other important reason, should occupy an elevated role in the analysis. Specifically, for our purposes, one might designate a sub-class of rights which always have material implications for the admissibility of evidence obtained through their violation. Though still deliberately vague at the point of application, at least one could now confidently say that violation of *these* particular designated rights, if not others, presumptively provides a reason for triggering evidentiary exclusion in appropriate cases. One way of demarcating this special sub-class of rights, employing terminology which clearly announces their elevated normative status, is to categorize them as 'constitutional' rights.

In a legal system with a comprehensive written constitution, 'constitutional rights' are those rights which are declared in the text of the constitution or elaborated or implied into it through judicial interpretation. Inferring or improvising constitutional rights from a common law constitution is a far more difficult and precarious business.[66] Nonetheless, significant developments in English criminal procedure law during the past 30 years bear out Ashworth's insistence that the common law contains important procedural standards whose vindication should not be left at the mercy of the reliability principle.[67] Reference has already been made to the judgment of the House of Lords in *A v Home Secretary (No 2),* categorically rejecting evidence probably obtained through torture of a third-party witness overseas.[68] Notably, Lord Bingham announced that, '[i]t trivialises the issue before the House to treat it as an argument about the law of evidence. The issue is one of constitutional principle.'[69] Nor was this the first English sighting of self-consciously constitutionalized procedural standards. As long ago as 1979 the House of Lords declared compulsory process, secured through the compellability of witness testimony, a constitutional principle.[70] Subsequently, the absolute nature of legal professional privilege[71] was explicitly singled out for its constitutional pedigree.

It is plausible to suppose that breaches of exceptionally weighty procedural norms might give rise to a defeasible right to evidentiary exclusion, in accordance with:

[66] cf TRS Allan, *Constitutional Justice: A Liberal Theory of the Rule of Law* (Oxford: Oxford University Press, 2001).

[67] '[T]he absence of such declarations from English law no more means that there are no standards of conduct than does the absence of a written constitution or bill of rights mean that Englishmen have no rights or civil liberties': EEPR, n 1 above, 726.

[68] *A v Secretary of State for the Home Department (No 2)*, n 60 above.

[69] Ibid, at [51].

[70] *Hoskyn v Metropolitan Police Commissioner* [1979] AC 474, 484 (HL) (Lord Wilberforce).

[71] *R v Derby Magistrates' Court, ex p B* [1996] 1 AC 487 (HL).

PP#241: it is a reason for excluding evidence in criminal trials that the evidence was obtained in violation of a constitutional right.

The constitutional right in question could be the accused's right, as it is in relation to compulsory process. But it need not be. In *Derby Magistrates, ex p B*[72] the constitutional right of legal professional privilege was invoked to prevent *the accused* from obtaining information that he claimed would help prove his innocence. And in *A v Home Secretary (No 2)*, third-party foreign torture evidence was to be excluded not in virtue of any right of the torture victim himself, but in order to uphold the moral integrity of English law. This example suggests an interesting variation on PP#4:

PP#242: it is a reason for excluding evidence in criminal trials that the evidence was obtained in such a way that the accused has a *constitutional right* that it be excluded, and *that* right would be violated if the evidence were admitted.

This interpretation of the protective principle exploits an important, but little noticed, feature of rights.[73] Whilst the ground of a right is typically some feature of the right-holder's interest sufficient to warrant rights-based protection, the ground of a right may be some other individual's interest (as where parents are afforded rights designed to protect their children's interests) or a collective interest in which the accused herself may or may not have a stake. In *A v Home Secretary (No 2)*, the weighty interest worthy of constitutional protection was safeguarding the moral integrity of British legal proceedings from being corrupted by association with torture,[74] a collective interest in which the applicants shared just in so far as the quality of British justice formed part of their (moral) interests—which, given that the applicants in question were not British nationals, may have been a highly attenuated or possibly non-existent interest.[75] The important idea that the accused might be afforded procedural rights to safeguard interests that are not merely, or at all, personal to him is reflected in the concept of 'private attorneys-general'[76] which has surfaced in US debates surrounding the Fourth Amendment exclusionary rule.

Some version of PP#242 might well be a viable basis for excluding improperly obtained evidence in criminal trials in England and Wales.[77] Indeed, a nascent

[72] Ibid.

[73] But see J Raz, *Ethics in the Public Domain* (Oxford: Oxford University Press, 1994), Ch 2.

[74] 'The use of torture is dishonourable. It corrupts and degrades the state which uses it and the legal system which accepts it': *A v Secretary of State for the Home Department (No 2)*, n 60 above, at [82] (Lord Hoffmann).

[75] The applicants clearly had an instrumental interest in having the evidence excluded if it—rightly or wrongly—was going to incriminate them, but *this* narrowly instrumental interest is not the (moral) ground of the constitutional right to exclusion recognized by English law. Do foreign nationals have *any* interest in the moral integrity of foreign (English) law? If justice is a truly global concern, then we *all* have an interest, no matter how attenuated, in the quality of justice dispensed by *any* legal system anywhere in the world. But that is plainly a controversial, and some will think highly tendentious, proposition that I cannot explore further here.

[76] DJ Meltzer, 'Deterring Constitutional Violations by Law Enforcement Officials: Plaintiffs and Defendants as Private Attorneys General' (1988) 88 Columbia Law Review 247.

[77] There are international and comparative exemplars, eg *People (AG) v O'Brien* [1965] IR 142; Statute of the International Criminal Court, Art 69(7); D Giannoulopoulos, 'The Exclusion of

PP#242 may already be implicit in the precedents just mentioned. Its applications and further development would need to be evaluated contextually, taking account of the generic features and limitations of rights analysis identified in the previous two sections and—especially if the technique is much further expanded—of more general challenges to the legitimacy of common law constitutionalism.[78]

6. Human Rights

EEPR makes fleeting reference to the possibility of 'a constitutional Bill of Rights in England',[79] but never mentions 'human rights' as such. Few if any common lawyers at that time could have envisaged the extent of human rights law's recent influence on criminal proceedings in England and Wales. The advent of the Human Rights Act (HRA) 1998 launches a whole new raft of interpretations of the protective principle, starting with the following elementary variant:

PP#243: it is a reason for excluding evidence in criminal trials that the evidence was obtained in violation of a human right.

PP#243 has one tangible advantage over the constitutional rights-based interpretations of the protective principle canvassed in the previous section. International human rights law has undergone a prolonged period of institutionalization and progressive refinement, in particular through the text of the European Convention on Human Rights (ECHR) (translated into English law by Schedule 1 to the HRA) and the interpretational jurisprudence of the European Court of Human Rights in Strasbourg,[80] to which English courts must have regard pursuant to section 2 of the HRA. Compared with trying to divine from first principles which common law standards, if any, have attained the Olympian heights of constitutional imperative, it is far easier in practice to identify the existence and scope of a 'human right' whose breach might potentially trigger the exclusionary remedy contemplated by PP#243 and its (multifarious) derivatives.

However, the apparent institutional advantage of 'human rights' over 'constitutional rights' is short-lived, for at least two significant reasons. First, the substantive rights specified by the ECHR are not necessarily all of equal importance, and more particularly in the present context, their relation to the exclusionary remedy is far from uniform or self-evident. Secondly, the status of the ECHR as an international treaty and the institutional role and competence of the Strasbourg Court, as a collegiate multinational bench reviewing states parties' compliance with the Convention, introduces further complications with major ramifications for our topic.

Improperly Obtained Evidence in Greece: Putting Constitutional Rights First' (2007) 11 International Journal of Evidence & Proof 181.

[78] See eg T Poole, 'Questioning Common Law Constitutionalism' (2005) 25 Legal Studies 142.

[79] EEPR, n 1 above, 735.

[80] DJ Harris, M O'Boyle, EP Bates, and CM Buckley, *Law of the European Convention on Human Rights* (2nd edn, Oxford: Oxford University Press, 2009).

The structure of the ECHR itself implies that the rights it safeguards are not all of equal importance.[81] Notably, Article 3 is not open to derogation even in times of emergency threatening the life of the nation, whereas Articles 8 to 11 are subject to a range of broadly worded exceptions specified in the text of the Convention. This reflects the point stressed in section 4, above, that the importance of rights can vary enormously depending on the nature of the interest(s) the right is supposed to protect. Even (human) rights with identical grounds may differ greatly in their relative importance. There are material differences of degree and kind differentiating, say, the right to life and the right to respect for one's private life; or the right not to be subject to arbitrary detention without trial and the right to test the evidence for the prosecution in criminal proceedings. There is even scope for debating whether different aspects of the same substantive legal right are of equal importance. For example, is the right not to be tortured of greater importance than the right not to be exposed to 'inhuman and degrading treatment'? What about 'inhuman and degrading' *punishment*? All of these abuses are proscribed by Article 3 ECHR, but is any breach of any part of the provision equally reprehensible? And, crucially for us, should the remedial consequences be identical in every case?

To clarify the potential scope of a human-rights-based protective principle, we also need to link different Convention rights, or particular strands of them, to arguments for the exclusionary remedy. Some of the rights protected by the ECHR, such as the right not to be reduced into slavery,[82] do not have much obvious salience for the exclusion of evidence. Other enumerated rights have more bearing on the substantive criminal law than its enforcement.[83] Issues pertaining to the exclusion of evidence in legal proceedings have predictably revolved around Article 6's fair trial guarantee, and methods of evidence-gathering potentially breaching Article 3 or Article 8. Although the European Court of Human Rights was bold enough to extend the concept of 'fair trial' to cover (pre-trial) investigative techniques where 'from the outset, the applicant was definitively deprived of a fair trial',[84] it is revealing that the Strasbourg Court has balked at pronouncing any comprehensive per se exclusionary remedy covering all the evidential fruits of breaches of ECHR rights, even in relation to Article 3. In *Khan v UK*[85] the Strasbourg Court was not prepared to hold that evidence procured in breach of Article 8 is automatically inadmissible under Article 6. More strikingly still, in the recent case of *Gäfgen*,[86] the Court's Grand Chamber concluded that Article 6 had not been breached by the admission of evidence procured through inhuman or degrading treatment, in violation of Article 3, because '[t]he additional evidence admitted at the trial was not used by the domestic court against the applicant to

[81] Also see Ashworth, n 4 above.

[82] Art 4 ECHR. It is always possible to imagine more or less fanciful hypotheticals, eg the admissibility of a statement made by somebody subjected to forced labour which subsequently becomes material to another person's criminal trial.

[83] eg Art 7's explicit ban on retroactive penal legislation.

[84] *Teixeira de Castro v Portugal* (App no 25829/94) (1998) 28 EHRR 101 at [39].

[85] *Khan v UK* (App no 35394/97) (2001) 31 EHRR 45.

[86] *Gäfgen v Germany* (App no 22978/05) (2011) 52 EHRR 1.

prove his guilt, but only to test the veracity of his confession'.[87] Consequently, the 'impugned real evidence was not necessary, and was not used to prove him guilty or to determine his sentence... [T]here was a break in the causal chain leading from the prohibited methods of investigation to the applicant's conviction and sentence in respect of the impugned real evidence.'[88]

Khan, and still more so *Gäfgen*, were serious disappointments to human rights advocates, and dissenting judicial voices on the Court itself are increasingly being heard.[89] Irrespective of their substantive merits and the quality of the Court's reasoning (which has often been pretty sparse and unpersuasive on any view), these decisions—and others like them—exemplify the inherent moral complexity and associated practical difficulties attending the application of any version of PP#243 to concrete cases. Even a Court whose raison d'être is to apply and develop a pan-European legal framework of fundamental human rights has struggled to trace the logic of protecting the array of diverse interests grounding particular human rights, through to evidentiary exclusion as a presumptive—let alone mandatory—remedy for human rights violations.

These observations hint at a second major obstacle inhibiting the protective principle from hitching an easier ride in the ECHR caravan. The Strasbourg Court is a supra-national tribunal reviewing states parties' compliance with their treaty obligations under the Convention. It has neither the jurisdictional authority nor the jurisprudential competence to interfere directly in the conduct of national criminal proceedings. This is why the Strasbourg Court repeatedly disavows being a 'fourth instance' court of appeal, and frequently (if somewhat misleadingly) asserts that 'Article 6 of the Convention... does not lay down any rules on the admissibility of evidence as such, which is therefore primarily a matter for regulation under national law'.[90] As the Strasbourg Court itself is well aware, its pivotal jurisprudential challenge is to concede to individual states parties an appropriate 'margin of appreciation' in designing their own criminal justice processes in accordance with local procedural traditions whilst still ensuring respect for a floor of minimum human rights in criminal adjudication across the Council of Europe. But even as it clearly recognizes this challenge in abstract terms, Strasbourg jurisprudence interpreting Article 6 has evolved to such a degree of refinement that the Strasbourg Court now not infrequently finds itself embroiled in the technicalities of national law, with predictably uneven and sometimes perplexing results.[91] After all, it is inherently unlikely that an international court comprising 47 national judges working in multiple languages and across different legal and procedural traditions, and approaching the issues from an oblique (human rights, rather than criminal justice) angle, is going to make much headway in prescribing solutions to some of criminal jurisprudence's trickiest and most enduring puzzles.

87 *Gäfgen v Germany* (App no 22978/05) (2011) 52 EHRR, at [179].

88 Ibid, at [180].

89 Also see *Bykov v Russia* (App no 4378/02) (ECHR 10 March 2009).

90 *Schenk v Switzerland* (A/140) (1991) 13 EHRR 242 at [46]. Also see *Teixeira de Castro v Portugal*, n 84 above, at [34].

91 *Al-Khawaja and Tahery v UK*, n 35 above. Cf *R v Horncastle*, n 35 above.

So the promise of fully articulated procedural standards capable of guiding admissibility determinations without needing to reason from first principles, which appeared to be international human rights law's greatest asset in the design and practical implementation of a robust protective principle, turns out to be mostly wishful thinking.

Technical challenges of cosmopolitan adjudication are exacerbated by deeper controversies of political morality. Adducing the statement of a deceased complainant in a criminal trial, for example, might reflect a deeply held conviction that such accusations ought to be given a public hearing, as it were, from beyond the grave.[92] Again, protecting a witness from the risk of violent reprisals engages the witness's rights, and the state's corresponding duties, under Article 8 and even, regarding mortal threats, under Article 2 ECHR. Of course, no defensible system of criminal justice is going to say that these interests should be promoted to the point at which a criminal trial becomes unfair for the accused. However, these countervailing interests might lead one to reappraise just what a fair trial must entail: and this is where the views of the Strasbourg judges and the traditions of domestic legal systems may diverge. In addition to the difficulties already highlighted, the possibility of human rights norms impinging on cherished values embedded in national legal traditions (some of which may have been elevated to constitutional status) is another reason for doubting whether the protective principle can legitimately be invoked to extend the exclusionary remedy to all violations of human rights, even as a defeasible presumption.

7. Conclusion: Fast-Forward back to the Future

This essay's retrospective re-reading of EEPR, more than 30 years after its original publication, celebrates in microcosm the virtues of Andrew Ashworth's peerless scholarship and its extraordinary influence across our discipline. It should be evident that EEPR was a remarkably prescient contribution which anticipated some of the most acute controversies today confronting English criminal procedure law and practice. Its enduring significance and undiminished popularity are attributable to what EEPR can still teach us, through critical engagement with its themes and arguments, about contemporary criminal litigation and its possible futures.

The protective principle's rights-based rationale for excluding improperly obtained evidence is perfectly attuned to the language and judicial culture of the post-HRA era. Recent decades have simultaneously witnessed growing judicial awareness of the self-consciously constitutional dimensions of criminal procedure and evidence. Constitutional rights and European human rights law both present promising opportunities for developing a rejuvenated and super-charged protective principle, albeit with complementary shortcomings. Common law constitutionalism

[92] See eg *Nembhard v R* (1982) 74 Cr App R 144, 146 (PC): '[I]t is important in the interests of justice that a person implicated in a killing should be obliged to meet in court the dying accusation of the victim . . .'.

is securely rooted in indigenous procedural traditions but its doctrinal shape and jurisprudential status are embryonic, contested, and uncertain. Conversely, European human rights law has undergone rapid doctrinal development thanks to the Strasbourg Court's impressive industry, but the fair trial norms that have been elucidated are necessarily pitched at the generic pan-European level and may be somewhat deficient in local suitability, political legitimacy, or professional credibility. Such institutional challenges compound deeper conceptual and normative puzzles about the nature and scope of rights and their moral grounds. In the absence of a tolerably clear, coherent, and normatively defensible conception of rights, it will surely be impossible to specify appropriate legal remedies for their violation.

We have seen how alternative conceptions of the protective principle quickly multiply when this methodological injunction is taken seriously. If the admissibility of improperly obtained evidence is always a function of concatenated and irreducible moral and legal complexity (debatable facts, open-ended norms, *and* contested evidentiary rationales), commentators who hanker after a bright-line exclusionary rule or even any elaborate doctrinal framework articulated beyond the level of flexible general principles seem destined to be forever disappointed. That this essay has presented little more than a preliminary structural survey mapping out this rich seam of theorizing further underlines the enduring salience and robust adaptability of Ashworth's original argument for excluding evidence as protecting rights.

12

Community Sanctions and European Human Rights Law

*Dirk van Zyl Smit**

1. Introduction

Evidence is accumulating that there is a specifically European approach to key aspects of sentencing and punishment. In his wide-ranging career as a criminal justice scholar Andrew Ashworth has made a distinguished contribution to ensuring that the European approach is informed by human rights ideals. Most directly, as chairman of the group that drafted the 1992 Recommendation of the Committee of Ministers of the Council of Europe concerning *Consistency in Sentencing*,[1] he succeeded in the extraordinarily difficult task of rising above the details of diverse national practices in order to define general, human-rights-based sentencing principles that could be accepted by all 47 Member States of the Council of Europe. Whilst such recommendations are often described as 'non-binding',[2] many of them have had considerable long-term impact in Europe on both penal law and policy.

Ashworth's influence on European criminal justice is partly attributable to his rare ability to combine a mastery of sentencing law and other aspects of criminal justice policy with a deep understanding of human rights principles. In recent decades this has been a particularly valuable attribute for an English scholar, for the domestication of the European Convention on Human Rights (ECHR) by the Human Rights Act 1998 has undoubtedly led to human rights concerns playing a much greater role in the development of penal law and policy in the United

* I am indebted to Sonja Snacken for allowing me to use aspects of the conceptual framework that she has developed as a research fellow at the Straus Institute for the Advanced Study of Law and Justice (New York University) as part of our joint project to study the principles on which European policies on non-custodial sanctions and measures are based. I also wish to thank Miranda Boone, Rob Canton, David Hayes, Martine Herzog-Evans, and Paul Roberts for their comments on an earlier draft. Research for this essay was supported by a British Academy Small Research Grant SG102046.

[1] Recommendation No R (92) 17 of the Committee of Ministers to Member States concerning Consistency in Sentencing, adopted 19 October 1992. See A Ashworth, 'Towards European Sentencing Standards' (1994) 2 European Journal on Criminal Policy and Research 7.

[2] P Boillat (ed), 'Foreword' to Council of Europe, *Penitentiary Questions: Council of Europe Conventions, Recommendations and Resolutions* (Strasbourg: Council of Europe Publishing, 2009), 9.

Kingdom. There have also been further explication and development of human rights norms relevant to sentencing and punishment on the European stage, which in turn has made them even more relevant—and often controversial, not only in the United Kingdom, but also in other European countries. Ashworth's scholarship has contributed to both these developments. Not only has he spelt out the general impact of European human rights law for English sentencing law,[3] but he has also used it to critique anti-social behaviour orders and other forms of social control that do not meet the standards implicit in European human rights norms.[4] At the same time much of his work, most notably his book with Ben Emmerson and Alison Macdonald, *Human Rights and Criminal Justice*,[5] can be read as a scholarly contribution to the further evolution of the European human rights law applicable to sentencing and punishment.

This essay builds on this strand of Ashworth's wide-ranging scholarship by exploring the idea of a European approach to punishment. The focus will be on the emergence of pan-European policy and law relating to community sanctions. As will become apparent as comparisons with other forms of punishment are drawn, this is an aspect of European penal policy that has not yet achieved the same binding legal status as the law governing other forms of punishment.

By way of introduction it is worth reviewing the forms of punishment in which strong European legal norms have emerged. The primary example must be the rejection of the death penalty, where abolition at the national level has been reinforced by human-rights-driven abolitionist protocols to ECHR. The European Court of Human Rights (ECtHR) has re-interpreted the Convention itself in a way which effectively reads out the qualified exception to the right to life for a death penalty duly imposed by a properly constituted court.[6] Several scholars and commentators have argued that pan-European opposition to the death penalty goes beyond penal policy or even penal law. This aspect of an idealized penal culture has become a characteristic of the shared European identity.[7] Arguably, there has been a similar evolution in prison law and policy at the pan-European level, which is relatively autonomous of shifts in national penal policy.[8] It has

[3] A Ashworth, *Sentencing and Criminal Justice* (5th edn, Oxford: Oxford University Press, 2010), 68–70.

[4] A Ashworth, 'Social Control and Anti-Social Behaviour: the Subversion of Human Rights' (2004) 120 LQR 263.

[5] B Emmerson, A Ashworth, and A Macdonald (eds), *Human Rights and Criminal Justice* (2nd edn, London: Sweet and Maxwell, 2007).

[6] Art 2 ECHR reinterpreted in the light of Art 3 and Protocols 6 and 13: *Al-Saadoon and Mufdhi v UK* (App no 61498/08) (2010) 51 EHRR 9, which goes further in this regard than the earlier cases of *Öcalan v Turkey* (App no 46221/99) (2005) 41 EHRR 45 and *Soering v UK* (A/161) (1989) 11 EHRR 439.

[7] F Zimring, *The Contradictions of American Capital Punishment* (Oxford: Oxford University Press, 2003); E Girling, 'European Identity, Penal Sensibilities and Communities of Sentiment' in S Armstrong and L McAra (eds), *Perspectives on Punishment* (Oxford: Oxford University Press, 2006), 69; D van Zyl Smit, 'Die Durchsetzung europäischer Prinzipien im Strafvollzug—Parallelen zur Abschaffung der Todesstrafe?' [2008] *Greifrecht* 88.

[8] D van Zyl Smit and S Snacken, *Principles of European Prison Law and Policy; Penology and Human Rights* (Oxford: Oxford University Press, 2009).

resulted in an approach to imprisonment that seeks to guarantee increasingly widely defined legal rights of prisoners across Europe while adopting, as a policy at least, a reductionist approach to the use of imprisonment as a sanction.[9] This approach to the rights of prisoners and the use of imprisonment has near-hegemonic status at the pan-European level, although its impact at national level varies from country to country.

This essay poses two principal questions: (a) Are there similar developments in respect of community sanctions?[10], and (b) If so, what are their implications for the evolution of community sanctions in Europe? In order to address these questions it considers first some of the similarities between the European dimensions of imprisonment and community sanctions and measures. It then turns to the differences, both in law and in policy making, before reflecting on how the human rights element in European law and policy in respect of community sanctions could be strengthened.

2. Similarities between European Approaches to Community Sanctions and to Imprisonment

At the institutional level there are some strong similarities between the approaches to standard setting adopted at the European level to community sanctions, on the one hand, and to imprisonment, on the other. The Committee of Ministers of the Council of Europe has sought to impose its influence on both community sanctions and imprisonment. The most obvious examples are the 1992 European Rules on Community Sanctions and Measures (ERCSM),[11] which were deliberately 'conceived as a parallel to the European Prison Rules' (EPR).[12]

Both the ERCSM and the EPR[13] are comprehensive instruments that set policy on how the respective sanctions should be implemented and specify procedural and substantive safeguards within the European human rights tradition for those subjected to them. On the imposition of sanctions they are complementary, for

[9] See in particular Recommendation No R (99) 22 of the Committee of Ministers to Member States concerning Prison Overcrowding and Prison Population Inflation, adopted 30 September 1999.

[10] The term 'community sanctions' is somewhat difficult to define. Here it is used, following the glossary in the appendix to the ERCSM, n 11 below, to refer to sanctions 'which maintain the offender in the community and involve some restriction of his liberty through the imposition of conditions and/or obligations, and which are implemented by bodies designated in law for that purpose'. The focus is on sanctions which are 'imposed by a court or a judge, as well as ways of enforcing a sentence of imprisonment outside a prison establishment'. As the contrast is with sentences of imprisonment, it is not necessary for present purposes to adopt the formulation 'sanctions and measures' and to include measures 'taken before or instead of a decision on a sanction'.

[11] Recommendation No R (92) 16 of the Committee of Ministers to Member States on the European Rules on Community Sanctions and Measures, adopted 19 October 1992.

[12] Preamble to the ERCSM.

[13] The 1987 European Prison Rules to which the ERCSM refers were replaced by the 2006 European Prison Rules: see the Preamble to Recommendation Rec (2006) 2 of the Committee of Ministers to Member States on the European Prison Rules (EPR), adopted 11 January 2006. All references below to the EPR are to the 2006 version.

they underline the European policy that imprisonment should only be as a last resort and that community sanctions and other alternatives to custody should be developed as independent sanctions in their own right.[14] The underlying idea is that the custody threshold should be raised so that community sanctions can be applied where imprisonment may have been the default sentence in the past.[15]

Both the EPR and ESCRM are supplemented by specialized recommendations that deal with further aspects of imprisonment[16] and community sanctions,[17] but nonetheless remain key sources of principle in their respective areas. Thus, for example, Rule 1 of the EPR states the general principle that '[a]ll persons deprived of their liberty shall be treated with respect for their human rights'. The EPR then spell out in considerable detail what respect for prisoners' human rights requires in terms of substantive conditions of imprisonment. They also include procedural guarantees relating to disciplinary and complaints procedures, for example to ensure that order is maintained in a fair and humane way.

Like the EPR the ERCSM also deliberately set out:

> . . . to furnish members states with basic criteria so that the creation and use of community sanctions and measures may be combined with *guarantees against the danger that the fundamental rights of offenders subject to such sanction and measures are curtailed.*[18]

The ERCSM then spell out detailed protections under the heading 'respect for fundamental rights'. These include a non-discrimination provision[19] and three widely phrased rules relating to human rights:

[14] Preamble to the EPR. See also the Recommendation concerning Prison Overcrowding and Prison Population Inflation, n 9 above.

[15] See also the Recommendation concerning Consistency in Sentencing (n 1 above), s 5a of which encourages the development of criteria for deciding when an offence is sufficiently serious to merit imprisonment, and s 5c of which recommends that legislators should consider introducing non-custodial sanctions rather than imprisonment as the 'reference section' for new offences.

[16] eg, Recommendation No R (98) 7 of the Committee of Ministers to Member States concerning the Ethical and Organisational Aspects of Health Care in Prison, adopted 8 April 1998; Recommendation Rec (2003) 23 of the Committee of Ministers to Member States on the Management by Prison Administrations of Life Sentence and other Long-term Prisoners, adopted 9 October 2003; Recommendation Rec (2006) 13 of the Committee of Ministers to Member States on the Use of Remand in Custody, the Conditions in which it Takes Place and the Provision of Safeguards against Abuse, adopted 27 September 2006.

[17] Recommendation Rec (2000) 22 of the Committee of Ministers to Member States on Improving the Implementation of the European Rules on Community Sanctions and Measures, adopted by the Committee of Ministers on 29 November 2000; Recommendation CM/Rec (2010) 1 of the Committee of Ministers to Member States on the Council of Europe Probation Rules, adopted 20 January 2010. Recommendation CM/Rec (2008) 11 of the Committee of Ministers to Member States on the European Rules for Juvenile Offenders Subject to Sanctions and Measures, adopted 5 November 2008, deals with both imprisonment and community sanctions.

[18] Para b of the Preamble to the ERCSM. Emphasis added. For a detailed analysis of the ERCSM see C Morgenstern, *Internationale Mindeststandards für ambulante Strafen und Maßnahmen* (Mönchengladbach: Forum Verlag Godesberg, 2002); C Morgenstern, 'European Initiatives for Harmonisation and Minimum Standards in the Field of Community Sanctions and Measures' (2009) 1 European Journal of Probation 124.

[19] Rule 20.

Rule 21
No community sanction or measure restricting the civil or political rights of an offender shall be created or imposed if it is contrary to the norms accepted by the international community concerning human rights and fundamental freedoms. These rights shall not be restricted in the implementation of the community sanction or measure to a greater extent than necessarily follows from the decision imposing this sanction or measure.

Rule 22
The nature of all community sanctions and measures and the manner of their implementation shall be in line with any internationally guaranteed human rights of the offender.

Rule 23
The nature, content and methods of implementation of community sanctions and measures shall not jeopardise the privacy or the dignity of the offenders or their families, nor lead to their harassment. Nor shall self-respect, family relationships, links with the community and ability to function in society be jeopardised. Safeguards shall be adopted to protect the offender from insult and improper curiosity or publicity.

These rules are combined with others designed to ensure legal certainty. Rule 3 provides that community sanctions shall be defined by law and that the law should also govern their adoption and application. Definitions of sanctions should include a clear legal framework specifying the limitations and obligations that such sanctions may entail and the consequences of failing to observe them[20] and 'any instructions of the implementing authority, including, in particular, those relating to control requirements shall be practical, precise and limited to what is necessary for the effective implementation of the sanction'.[21] The ERCSM also attempted to ensure further legal certainty by requiring that 'no community sanction or measure shall be of indeterminate duration'.[22] However, this requirement was amended and made less strict by the subsequent Recommendation on Improving the Implementation of the European Rules on Community Sanctions and Measures, which allows for indeterminate community sanctions to be imposed on offenders 'who by reason of a serious prior or current offence in combination with a specific personal characteristic manifestly pose a continuing threat to life, health or safety in the community'.[23]

The ERCSM also seek to guarantee due process in the imposition and implementation of community sanctions by providing that the decision to impose or revoke a community sanction or pre-trial measure shall be taken by a judicial authority[24] and guaranteeing to offenders the right to make a complaint to a higher authority against a decision subjecting them to a community sanction or modifying or revoking such a sanction.[25] There is also provision for an appeal to a judicial authority concerning the implementation of a community sanction or measure, 'whenever the offender wishes to complain that a restriction of his liberty or the decision is unlawful or contrary to the content of the imposed sanction or measure',[26] and for complaints about the actions of the implementing authority.[27]

[20] Rule 4. [21] Rule 24. [22] Rule 5.

[23] Recommendation Rec (2000) 22 of the Committee of Ministers to Member States on Improving the Implementation of the European Rules on Community Sanctions and Measures, adopted 29 November 2000.

[24] Rule 12. [25] Rule 13. [26] Rule 14. [27] Rule 15.

It is notable that in their guarantees the ECSRM are more precise and go further than the United Nations Standard Minimum Rules for Non-custodial Measures (Tokyo Rules),[28] which were adopted two years earlier. Although the Tokyo Rules do contain some protections, they are more loosely phrased and focus more on the propagation of this form of sanction.[29] Arguably this is also true of the EPR, which are more explicit in terms of human rights than the United Nations equivalent, the 1955 Standard Minimum Rules for the Treatment of Prisoners.

The symmetry between the rules of the Council of Europe in respect of community sanctions and imprisonment is reflected at EU level. In 2008, in response to the challenges of moving sentenced offenders around the European Union (an element in the joint criminal justice policy that is slowly emerging), two key Framework Decisions were adopted by the Council of the European Union dealing with the transfer of sentenced prisoners[30] and the transfer of offenders subject to community sanctions,[31] respectively. As Hanna Kuczyńka has explained:

> Together these two framework decisions form a coherent area of legislation in the field of recognition of final judgments, regardless of their nature: either related to the deprivation of liberty or to alternative solutions.[32]

In practice the Framework Decisions are binding on all Member States of the European Union, which from 6 December 2011 (the date both come into effect for all EU states except for Poland, which has negotiated a five-year opt out with respect to sentenced prisoners) are to implement them as mechanisms for the transfer of foreign sentenced prisoners and offenders subject to community sanctions to their countries of origin, where they will be required to serve the remainder of their sentences.

These legal parallels are complemented by a parallel in practice. Both the abolition of the death penalty and the acceptance of 'European' standards of imprisonment were among the requirements set explicitly for Central and Eastern European states who wished to join both the Council of Europe and the 'more exclusive' European Union, after the collapse of the Soviet Union. In the course of making this demand, European standards in respect of imprisonment were clarified and support for their implementation in new Member States of the Council of

[28] GA res 45/110, annex, 45 UN GAOR Supp (No 49A), 197, UN Doc A/45/49 (14 December 1990).

[29] D van Zyl Smit, 'Legal Standards and the Limits of Community Sanctions' (1993) 1 European Journal of Crime, Criminal Law and Criminal Justice 309.

[30] 'Council Framework Decision on the Application of the Principle of Mutual Recognition to Judgments in Criminal Matters Imposing Custodial Sentences or Measures involving Deprivation of Liberty for the Purpose of their Enforcement in the European Union', 2008/989/JHA of 27 November 2008.

[31] 'Council Framework Decision on the Application of the Principle of Mutual Recognition to Judgments and Probation Decisions with a View to the Supervision of Probation Measures and Alternative Sanctions', 2008/947/JHA of 27 November 2008.

[32] H Kuczyńka, 'Mutual Recognition of Judicial Decisions in Criminal Matters with Regard to Probation Measures and Alternative Sanctions' (2009) 1–2 Eucrim 43, 45. See also D O'Donovan, 'Transfer of Probation Supervision between Member States: An EU Initiative' (2009) 6 Irish Probation Journal 77.

Europe was provided not only by the Council itself but also by the European Union and individual Western European states.[33]

Although the introduction or reform of community sanctions was not an explicit part of the initial requirements, similar practical initiatives in this respect soon materialized. Canton identifies membership of the Council of Europe as a direct driver of an initiative taken by Ukraine to seek assistance for the introduction of community sanctions in the late 1990s.[34] And this tendency has continued. Consider, among other examples, the depiction of a recent British-run project to develop a probation service in Turkey. A report of the CEP (the European Organization for Probation) explains:

> The development of the Turkish probation services was seen in the light of Turkey's wish to join the EU and was therefore funded within the EU Instrument for Pre-Accession Assistance (IPA). In 2005, the UK had assisted Turkey in properly establishing probation services in a separate project. Subsequently, from January 2009 until October 2010, the goal was to develop working, training and other materials for the probation workers and staff. 60 European experts from—and research trips to—England, Northern Ireland, Austria, The Netherlands, France, Germany, Hungary, Czech Republic and Catalonia became valuable sources of information.[35]

But why are probation services significant in an instrument of accession to the European Union? The project description provided by the European Union leaves little doubt about the underlying motives:

> In the course of progress towards accession to the European Union and in response to the obligations of the *acquis* of the EU and its Member States, the Turkish government is actively following a National Programme for the Adoption of the Acquis. However the objective of the process of law approximation is to not only implement the relevant amendments to existing legislation but as importantly, to strengthen those institutions responsible for the enforcement or implementation of the new procedures and processes.[36]

The report goes on to explain that, although historically there has been a probation service in Turkey, a process of further 'institution building'[37] to enhance administrative capacity is seen as crucial in ensuring the successful transition for Turkish institutions to the standards, norms, and achievements of EU Member State administrations. The Turkish Penal Code and related laws are to be amended specifically to make provision for community sanctions. Note the reference to the *acquis* of the European Union in the quotation above: the *acquis* (*communautaire*) is the accumulated legislation, legal acts, and court decisions which constitute the

[33] Van Zyl Smit and Snacken, n 8 above, Chs 1 and 9.

[34] R Canton, 'Taking Probation Abroad' (2009) 1 European Journal of Probation 66.

[35] CEP, 'British–Turkish Twinning Project Successfully closed in Ankara' (22 October 2010). Available at <http://www.cep-probation.org/news/65/322/british-turkish-twinning-project-successfully-closed-in-ankara> accessed 20 March 2012.

[36] See European Union, *Development of Probation Services in Turkey* (2004), 2, section 3.1. Available at <http://ec.europa.eu/enlargement/fiche_projet/document/TR%200404.02%20Establishment%20of%20a%20national%20probation%20service.pdf> accessed 20 March 2012.

[37] Ibid.

body of EU law. A French term of art, *acquis* means that which has been acquired. The suggestion is that alternatives to imprisonment, that is, community sanctions and a probation service to administer them, have become part of the constitutive institutional framework of the European Union.

The overall conclusion to be drawn from these normative and institutional developments is that, as in the case of imprisonment, community sanctions are of growing importance at the European level, both in terms of explicit policies and in practice. Their place in the *acquis* is an indication that they have made it into the collective European penal culture too. Operating a developed system of community sanctions is what a 'good' European country does. The parallel with the requirement that candidate countries modernize their prison systems is clear.

3. Differences between European Approaches to Community Sanctions and to Imprisonment

Similarities at the European level between the attitude to the death penalty and a human-rights-based approach to imprisonment, on the one hand, and the approach to community sanctions, on the other, are tempered by some significant differences. The most striking difference between community sanctions and imprisonment lies in the legal backing that the policies relating to them have at the European level. The human rights mentioned in the EPR are complemented by human rights protections for prisoners in the European Convention for the Prevention of Torture (ECPT) and the ECHR, both treaties that have been ratified by all European states, except Belarus, while the ERCSM are not legally supported in the same way.

The ECPT's stated purpose is to prevent torture and inhuman or degrading treatment or punishment of all persons who are deprived of their liberty in Europe. Its brief does not extend to those whose liberty is merely restricted without confinement. Its executive arm, the Committee for the Prevention of Torture (CPT), is a Europe-wide inspection mechanism which operates by inspections and reports and has developed its own standards for all institutions in which people are deprived of liberty: prisons being the most prominent of these institutions. In reporting on prisons and in developing standards the CPT regularly refers to the EPR and occasionally also to other recommendations of the Council of Europe relating to prisons. The CPT is not only based on a legally binding treaty, but is in practice one of the most effective pan-European criminal justice bodies. There is no parallel inspection mechanism for those whose liberty may be restricted to a very significant extent by a community sanction.

The approach to the ECHR is radically different, too. In literally hundreds of cases the ECtHR has referred to the reports of the CPT and the standards developed by it, as well as, particularly since 2006, to the EPR. The ECtHR has done so while interpreting the prohibition on cruel and inhuman treatment as well as rights to private and family life, that are contained in the ECHR, and then applying them to the position of prisoners. In contrast, the judgments of the ECtHR contain to my knowledge only five references to the ERCSM or to the Recommendation made in 2000 on Improving the Implementation of the European Rules on Community Sanctions and Measures. They were all instances where the Court relied on the ERCSM to support arguments for the use of alternatives to continued imprisonment.[38] In no case have the ERCSM been used directly to protect the substantive or procedural human rights of persons subject to community sanctions.

Underlying these formal legal constraints is a subtle yet persistent difference in perception. To a great extent imprisonment continues to be seen as the 'real' punishment, with community sanctions as alternatives granted as a favour to deserving offenders. Changing this perception is a major project that requires nothing less than the social reconstruction of the public image of these sanctions.[39]

This battle for the acceptability and legitimacy of community sanctions is also reflected in the social forces involved in propagating them at the European level. The protagonists of community sanctions differ significantly from those involved in promoting other penalties. Abolition of the death penalty, in recent years, has been the product of a wide European political movement that stretches far beyond criminal justice professionals. At the European level intervention in prison matters has also been driven largely by idealistic reformers. Admittedly, there has been a series of Council of Europe-sponsored Conferences of National Directors of Prison Administration, who might be thought of as constituting a group with strong collective self interests, but suspicions that it functions to increase or even consolidate the use of imprisonment in Europe are misplaced. If anything, it supports a mildly reductionist agenda and is not averse to the recognition of the human rights of prisoners, while mostly leaving direct advocacy to others.[40]

In these respects the role of the CEP is very different. It is an independent organization, which includes both public- and private-service providers, and which aggressively argues for the extension of 'probation', or more precisely the establishment, defence, and development of probation bureaucracies. '*Be evangelical* in reaching out to those countries in the Council of Europe which do not yet have

[38] *Kafkaris v Cyprus* (App no 21906/04) (2008) 49 EHRR 35 at [72]; *Mouisel v France* (App no 67263/01) (2002) 38 EHRR 34 at [30]; *McGlinchey v UK* (App no 50390/99) (2003) 37 EHRR 41 at [5]; *Hüseyin Yildirim v Turkey* (App no 2778/02) (ECHR 3 May 2007) at [57]; *Matencio v France* (App no 58749/00) (ECHR 15 January 2004) at [36]; *Tekin Yildiz v Turkey* (App no 51479/99) (ECHR 10 November 2005) at [49].

[39] JV Roberts, 'Public Opinion and the Nature of Community Penalties: International Findings' in JV Roberts and M Hough (eds), *Changing Attitudes to Punishment* (Cullompton: Willan, 2002), 33; S Maruna and A King, 'Public Opinion and Community Penalties' in A Bottoms, S Rex, and G Robinson (eds), *Alternatives to Prison* (Cullompton: Willan, 2004), 83.

[40] This may change. In 2011 a new organization, *Europris*, the European Organisation of Prison and Correctional Services, was established by the heads of a number of prison services in the EU. It may well become the functional equivalent of the CEP in respect of the implementation of the Framework Decision relating to the transfer of sentenced prisoners in the EU. See <http://europris.org/> accessed 20 March 2012.

developed probation systems',[41] exhorted John Scott, a past president of the organization, at its conference in Malaga in 2010. Another Board member saw a key advantage of the Turkish project discussed above as usefully strengthening the reach of the CEP and the network it represents.

The CEP successfully lobbied the Council of Europe to develop a new set of Rules, which emerged in 2010 as the Council of Europe Rules on Probation.[42] In reality, they are mostly not rules on probation, for they define probation simply as the 'implementation of community sanctions and measures' and largely follow the ERCSM on substantive points. Fundamentally they are a set of European recommendations on probation agencies. One of the 'basic principles' of the new Rules provides that: 'Probation agencies shall be accorded an appropriate standing and recognition and shall be adequately resourced.'[43] Note, not 'community sanctions or measures' or even 'probation' shall be adequately resourced, but 'probation agencies'. Moreover, there are indications that administering community sanctions is to be reserved exclusively to such agencies. This is illustrated by Rule 47, which deals with one of the most important community sanctions:

> Community service is a community sanction or measure *which involves organising and supervising by the probation agencies* of unpaid labour for the benefit of the community as real or symbolic reparation for the harm caused by an offender.[44]

The italicized words make clear that community service has to be both organized *and* supervised by probation agencies. In other words, community service, even if it is organized by a probation agency, will not be a recognized sanction for the purpose of these Rules if it is not also supervised by such an agency. Other organizations that may not fit within the definition of 'probation agencies' are apparently excluded and implicitly delegitimized.[45]

It should be emphasized that there is nothing improper about interest groups seeking to enhance their European position by having the standards for their work specified in a recommendation of the Council of Europe. Nor is there any suggestion that the new 2010 Council of Europe Rules on Probation undermine human rights standards established by the ERCSM. The 2010 Rules contain the general proviso that 'nothing in these rules should in any way be interpreted as

[41] J Scott, 'Summary of Conclusions', at the CEP Conference 'Probation Works' in Malaga, 28–29 May 2010, 4. Emphasis added. Available at <http://www.cepprobation.org/uploaded_files/John%20Scott.pdf> accessed 20 March 2012.

[42] Recommendation CM/Rec (2010) 1 of the Committee of Ministers to Member States on the Council of Europe Probation Rules, adopted 20 January 2010.

[43] Ibid, Rule 10.

[44] Ibid. Emphasis added.

[45] The ERCSM define 'probation agency' formally as any body designated by law to implement the tasks and responsibilities associated with probation. Probation in turn 'relates to the implementation in the community of sanctions and measures, defined by law and imposed on an offender'. However, one can imagine an organization that would be asked to supervise community service and would be competent to do so but would be excluded because it lacks legal powers to supervise the tasks and responsibilities associated with probation. The effect of these Rules could be to increase the need for probation bureaucracies, rather than focusing directly on what is required to meet standards necessary to ensure that a particular form of community sanction is implemented humanely.

precluding the application of any relevant international human rights instruments and standards that are more conducive to the treatment of offenders'. The 2010 Rules also state that they 'need to be read together with Recommendation No. R (92) 16 on the European rules on community sanctions and measures'.

Furthermore, the 2010 Rules on Probation restate many of the earlier rules and, in some respects, develop them further.[46] However, if one steps back and examines this development from the perspective of the sociology of the professions, one may discern a relatively new grouping exploring fresh opportunities at the European level to defend and indeed improve its own professional status. It may do so by lobbying aggressively and by using the framework of Council of Europe-generated rules and recommendations to campaign for the organizations and members that it represents to be given increased control over the implementation of a key penal policy; recommending the use of community sanctions to the authorities and implementing them when imposed. This is not necessarily 'good' or bad' for those subject to such sanctions. However, targeted intervention by the organized probation profession marks a significant departure from the role played hitherto by practitioners in sponsoring other forms of punishment that have achieved hegemonic status in Europe.[47]

There is a further and more subtle danger in having a group that aspires to improve its professional status making much of the running. The sociology of the professions teaches us that professional groups seek to identify a body of knowledge, which gives them expertise and sets them apart from the wider public. The history of probation itself illustrates how the case work method seemed, from the 1930s onwards, to provide one such resource. It is noticeable that the CEP places strong emphasis on accredited programmes and on 'what works', as the special area of expertise of probation professionals.[48] The CEP has suggested that European co-operation in this area, which arguably will be required more frequently when the framework decision on the transfer of probation comes into force, should be based on the use of similar techniques and reinforced by similar training programmes for probation officers across Europe.

Does this imply that the recognition of mutually acceptable human rights criteria may end up taking second place in practice? In fairness to the CEP, it should be noted that in November 2010 it also issued a 'statement on probation values and principles'.[49] Although this statement is preoccupied with matters of professional

[46] S Snacken, 'The Impact of the Criminal and Social Context on Probation Systems in Europe: The Council of Europe Probation Rules in Context', unpublished paper available in outline at <http://www.cepprobation.org/uploaded_files/Sonja%20Snacken.pdf> accessed 20 March 2012.

[47] Arguably some parallel in respect of prisons is to be found in the International Corrections and Prisons Association (ICPA), but its focus is not specifically European. In the USA a similar role is played by the American Correctional Association (ACA).

[48] See eg the presentation by F Lösel, 'What Does the Evidence Tell Us?: (with Particular Reference to the Importance of Applied Research)' at the CEP conference 'Probation Works' in Malaga, 28–29 May 2010, available at <http://www.cepprobation.org/uploaded_files/Friedrich%20Lösel.pdf> accessed 20 March 2012.

[49] Available at <http://www.cep-probation.org/default.asp?page_id=157&map_id=55> accessed 20 March 2012.

status and the need for funding of probation services, this statement affirms that community sanctions should be enforced in a manner compatible with the ECHR and includes a commitment to facilitating, as a matter of social justice, the social inclusion of offenders who are subject to such sanctions. There is clearly enough flexibility in the approach adopted by the CEP for European policy on community sanctions to develop in different ways, and its interaction with other policy-makers at the European level requires further analysis than is possible here.

4. Strengthening European Human Rights Protections for Offenders Subject to Community Sanctions

If we accept that, as in the case of imprisonment, there is growing European influence over developments in the sphere of community sanctions (even if the forces involved are somewhat different), what is to be done to ensure positive protection and promotion of the substantive human rights of all Europeans who may be subject to such sanctions? This is a large question to which I can give only some preliminary answers.

One point of departure, which crosses the boundary between law and sociology, is to be found in the work of the Utrecht School of Criminal Justice, which from the 1970s onwards adopted what van Swaaningen has identified as an approach of 'legal guaranteeism' within the wider framework of European critical criminology.[50] Key to the work of this School is an attempt to link the legal principles associated with imposition and implementation of punishment systematically to both human rights norms and to penal practice. In the area of imprisonment Kelk has been a towering figure in advancing the *Rechtsburgerschap* (legal citizenship) of prisoners and for insisting that, when one considers the social reality of imprisonment, only an approach that attempts to recognize prisoners' rights fully has the possibility of having any real impact on how imprisonment is implemented.[51]

Kelk's approach has been developed and applied systematically to community sanctions by Boone in an important book, *Recht voor commuun gestraften,* which appeared in 2000.[52] Boone argues that much could be gained by constructing a legal position for persons subject to community sanctions, in the same way as Kelk has done to recognize the rights of prisoners. When doing so, she found that community sanctions and measures, at least as implemented in the Netherlands at the turn of this century, could be construed in this way. If reference were made to the wider rights that all citizens had in the spheres of labour and welfare, for example, these legally guaranteed rights could easily be extended to offenders

[50] R Van Swaaningen, *Critical Criminology: Visions from Europe* (London: Sage, 1997), Ch 10.

[51] C Kelk, *Recht voor gedetineerden: een onderzoek naar die beginselen van het gevangenisrecht* (Alphen aan den Rijn: Samsom, 1978). For a summary of Kelk's position in English, see Van Zyl Smit and Snacken, n 8 above, 69–72.

[52] M Boone, *Recht voor commuun gestraften* (Deventer: Gouda Quint, 2000).

subject to community sanctions who had the same needs for legal protection as other members of society.

Boone noted also that the blurring of the boundaries between imprisonment and community sanctions and measures was increasing as prison sentences became more relaxed, while community sanctions and measures were being enforced more strictly. She warned that the potential harshness of community sanctions and measures might pose a growing threat to persons subject to them if steps were not taken to enhance the protection of their rights. It was complacent to assume that 'anything is better than imprisonment'.

This is truer than ever. The tendency towards blurring has increased over the past decade, resulting in penal systems where the distinction between imprisonment and community sanctions becomes a question of degree: 'degrees of freedom' as it has been called.[53] On the one hand, prisoners may be granted greater contact with the outside world. The majority of European countries now allow conjugal visits for prisoners, a tendency that has been encouraged by the ECtHR.[54] Prisoners may also be allowed to leave prison for short periods, to undertake outside work, for example. Indeed, imprisonment itself may be redefined. In some European countries electronic monitoring is seen merely as a device for monitoring the implementation of community sanctions, while in others it is regarded in law as a form of imprisonment. This allows the authorities to claim that they are implementing court-imposed prison sentences while reducing the number of people housed in expensive and overcrowded prisons.[55] At the same time, there is a tendency to increase the punitive nature of sentences imposed specifically to be served in the community. In England, for example, not only does an offender sentenced to a community sanction of unpaid work have no choice on whether to accept community work, but he may be compelled to do it while wearing an orange jacket with 'community payback' emblazoned on it.[56]

How is one to respond at the European level to these developments? In my view a conventional human rights law-based approach may still contribute to the protection of offenders subject to community sanctions. The ECHR remains a largely untapped resource. It is only a matter of time before the extreme forms of community punishments (particularly those of the 'community payback' variety with the public shaming this entails[57]), are challenged directly in the ECtHR on

[53] H Tulkens, *Graden van Vrijheid: Over hervormingsmogelijkheden van de vrijheidsstraf* (Arnhem: Gouda Quint, 1988); D van Zyl Smit, 'Degrees of Freedom' (1994) 13 Criminal Justice Ethics 31.

[54] However, the ECtHR has not yet recognized a right to such visits: *Aliev v Ukraine* (App no 41220/98) (ECHR 29 April 2003) at [189].

[55] S Snacken, K Beyens, and M-A Beermaert, 'Belgium' in N Padfield, D van Zyl Smit, and F Dünkel (eds), *Release from Prison: European Policy and Practice* (Cullompton: Willan, 2010), 70.

[56] For details see Ministry of Justice, 'First Birthday for Offender Community Payback Jackets', 1 December 2009. Available at <http://www.wired-gov.net/wg/wg-news-1.nsf/0/6510A51C10E169AC8025767F00405FF4?OpenDocument> (accessed 16 April 2012); see also Ministry of Justice, 'Offenders to Wear High-Visibility Jackets on "Payback" ', 1 December 2008, available at <http://www.cjp.org.uk/news/archive/offenders-to-wear-high-visibility-jackets-on-payback-01-12-2008/> (accessed 16 April 2012).

[57] For a potentially more benign interpretation of 'payback', from a Scottish perspective, see F McNeil, 'Probation, Rehabilitation and Reparation' (2009) 6 Irish Probation Journal 5. See also

grounds that public humiliation is degrading to the human dignity of offenders subject to such sanctions and therefore infringes Article 3 ECHR.[58]

Even where such penalties are not so degrading that they infringe human rights norms directly, the 'pains of probation'[59] (analogous to the 'pains of imprisonment' which sociologists have long recognized) are increasingly being studied. Their accurate description may provide a basis for an extension of the prohibition on inhuman or degrading punishment or treatment contained in Article 3 ECHR as the recognition grows that community sentences inevitably involve some measure of degradation. This would contribute to the further evolution of the 'standards of decency' which underpin the analysis by the ECtHR of what must be tolerated before Article 3 can be invoked. Other Convention rights, particularly the right to respect for privacy and family life protected by Article 8, may come into play too. Against this background, the general test developed by von Hirsch for the 'acceptable penal content' for community sanctions—that they should be 'of the kind that can be endured with self-possession by persons of reasonable fortitude'[60]—will require further refinement.

There is growing recognition that when individuals are subject to community sanctions imposed for an excessively long period, for example, that too may be regarded as a human rights infringement, both because the burden of sentence may become intolerable and because grossly disproportionate sentences are inherently degrading and thus in contravention of the ECHR.[61] Disproportionate sentences are also outlawed directly by the EU Charter of Fundamental Rights, which has been incorporated into the Treaty of Lisbon and is thus of increasing salience and legal effect within the European Union.

The principle of legality has an important part to play in safeguarding the human rights of those subjected to community sanctions. Ashworth has highlighted the dangers that anti-social behaviour orders pose to the due process protections of Article 6 ECHR, by making a criminal conviction a consequence of the breach of a civil order.[62] There is also the risk that penalties may be presented as mere preventative orders and thus be imposed in breach of the prohibition on retrospective punishment in Article 7 ECHR.[63] In addition, there is the danger that community penalties may not be defined precisely enough. In *Hashman and Harrup v UK*,[64] for

A Bottoms, 'The Community Dimension of Community Penalties' (2008) 47 Howard Journal of Criminal Justice 146.

[58] See also Rule 47 of the Council of Europe Probation Rules: 'Community service shall not be of a stigmatizing nature and probation agencies shall seek to identify and use working tasks which support the development of skills and the social inclusion of offenders.'

[59] I Durnescu, 'Pains of Probation: Effective Practice and Human Rights' (2011) 55 International Journal Offender Therapy and Comparative Criminology 530.

[60] A von Hirsch, 'The Ethics of Community-Based Sanctions' (1990) 36 Crime and Delinquency 163, 167. See also A von Hirsch, *Censure and Sanctions* (Oxford: Clarendon Press, 1993), Ch 9.

[61] D van Zyl Smit and A Ashworth, 'Disproportionate Sentences as Human Rights Violations' (2004) 67 MLR 541.

[62] Ashworth, n 4 above, 273.

[63] Ibid, 279–80.

[64] *Hashman and Harrup v UK* (App no 25594/94) (1999) 30 EHRR 241.

example, the ECtHR held that an order 'binding over' hunt protesters 'to be of good behaviour' in the community, was too imprecise to be regarded as a limit on their right of freedom of expression that had been properly 'prescribed by law' as required by Article 10 ECHR.

Although the framework decision on the transfer of persons subject to community sanctions is based on the mutual recognition of national laws governing such sanctions, the trans-border enforcement will require, at the very least, clarification of operative legal definitions and requirements. This will present an additional opportunity to test whether community sanctions are compliant with substantive human rights standards. As the Framework Decisions are enactments of the European Union, this means that the substantive standards of the EU Charter of Fundamental Rights will also be relevant and the European Court of Justice in Luxembourg may well become involved in determining whether the requirements of the Charter have been met, particularly where an EU framework directive has been used to transfer offenders from one state to another.

Such interventions at a European level may offer valuable legal safeguards to individual offenders subject to community sanctions, who may be exposed to the risks of oppression through degrading treatment and the arbitrariness of vaguely defined punishments and procedures for their implementation. These safeguards might be strengthened by the fuller incorporation of the specific requirements of the ERCSM into the jurisprudence of the European courts. However, valuable as that may be, focusing only on these safeguards runs the risk that they will be limited to the assertion of civil and political rights. The true battle will be to assert successfully that a wider approach is required that stresses the social dimension of community sanctions and the rights that follow from it.

Here, there are suggestive parallels with imprisonment. The emphasis on a right to resocialization in modern Dutch and German prison law has had a strong impact on developing wider positive rights of prisoners—a development that is also emerging at the European level, where it has been characterized as a right to opportunities for social reintegration.[65] This approach is still best expressed in the classic 1973 decision of the German Federal Constitutional Court in the *Lebach* case:

> As bearer of guaranteed fundamental rights to human dignity the convicted offender must be given the opportunity, after the completion of his [prison] sentence, to establish himself in the community again. From the point of view of the offender, this interest in resocialization develops out of his constitutional rights [to develop his personality freely in conjunction with the protection of human dignity]. Viewed from the perspective of the community, the principle of the *Sozialstaat* requires public care and assistance for those groups in the community who, because of personal weakness or fault, incapacity or social disadvantage, were retarded in their social development: prisoners and released prisoners also belong to this group.[66]

[65] Van Zyl Smit and Snacken, n 8 above, 105–8.

[66] BVerfG 35, 203 at 236, my translation. On the basis of this analysis, the Court found that a television station should not broadcast a programme on the details of a prisoner's crime at the time of

The last sentence is a statement of legal principle reflecting a particular view of the state as a provider of social welfare to an individual offender. It embodies a wider social view of enforceable human rights. This approach could also be applied to convicted offenders on whom community sanctions have been imposed directly, and who, accordingly, could assert that the state has a wider duty to organize the implementation of their punishment in a way that would facilitate their 'resocialization'. Used in this sense, resocialization inevitably has a social rights dimension. If anything, this dimension is even more strongly present in the case of community sanctions; for while prisoners are withdrawn from the community, offenders on whom community sanctions are imposed are kept in the community into which they should be reintegrated. Their successful reintegration depends on 'public care and assistance' in a free society that would enable them to overcome the barriers that 'retarded their social development'.

At the European level there is little doubt that human rights protection has focused on the civil and political rights of sentenced persons, rather than on their economic, social, and cultural rights. Relatively little attention has been paid to the European Social Charter[67] and the impact that it should have when practical ideas such as the 'social inclusion' of offenders subject to community sanctions are considered.[68] An exception is Rule 28 of the ERCSM, which provides that 'rights to benefits in any existing social security system shall not be limited by the imposition or implementation of a community sanction or measure', but the full legal implications of enforcing such rights have yet to be considered.[69]

Finally, it is worth noting that the passage quoted from *Lebach* recognizes the agency of the sentenced offender in any process of resocialization. As a matter of human rights, the offender must be 'given the opportunity', rather than compelled to take part in this aspect of the sentence. Such opportunities are essential if offenders are to build up the 'social capital' that will enable them to desist from criminal conduct.[70] Even if the socio-economic circumstances are satisfactory, it remains up to the sentenced offender to take advantage of what is on offer.

The sanction of imprisonment does not depend on the co-operation of the offender for it to be carried out. Where loss of liberty is the sanction, the sentenced prisoner can be held against his will and the core implemented in that way. Lack of co-operation is not fatal. However, it is often essential for the implementation of the restrictions of liberty which form the core of community sentences that the

his release, as it might hamper his reintegration into the community. In the circumstances the prisoner's right to resocialization outweighed the right to freedom of expression of the media.

[67] CETS No 35 (1961).

[68] For a fuller analysis of the potential significance of the Social Charter and of the importance of social inclusion in Europe, see S Snacken, 'Resisting Punitiveness in Europe?' (2010) 14 Theoretical Criminology 273.

[69] cf M Boone, 'Zacht als boter, hard als steen. Het juridisch gehalte van het recht op maatschappelijke opvang' [2005/6] Process 232, who considers the potential role in this regard of internationally derived 'social human rights' in the Dutch context.

[70] For an overview of the literature on desistance and social capital, see F McNeil and B Weaver, *Changing Lives? Desistance Research and Offender Management* (Glasgow: The Scottish Centre for Crime and Justice Research, 2010).

offender chooses to co-operate. Community sanctions also contain restrictions on liberty which are imposed on offenders and which in part can be implemented against their will. Even where such impositions are technically possible, they may still be controversial: for example, in the case of electronic monitoring.[71] However, where the core of the sanction is community work or some other activity requiring the active co-operation of the offender, it cannot be implemented if the offender objects. Moreover, the sanction is likely to be most effective, in the sense of the offender desisting from criminal conduct during the course of the sanction and in the future, if the offender co-operates in its implementation.

In the case of electronic monitoring, national practices vary considerably. In some countries, the consent of the offender, or even of his housemates, is required on the grounds that electronic monitoring is particularly invasive and affects co-residents in a way that custody does not.[72]

Most controversial, however, is the question of whether a community sanction can include a compulsion to work.[73] Part of the debate is about whether the offender subject to such a sanction is being subjected to a prohibited form of forced or compulsory labour. Although the wording of the general prohibition in the ECHR creates an exception only where work 'is required to be done in the ordinary course of detention . . . or during conditional release from such detention',[74] it has been argued that the exception can be extended by analogy to include an unpaid work requirement imposed directly as part of a community sanction.[75] The ECHR has not directly considered a case where the compatibility of a community sanction with the ECHR has been challenged on this ground. However, the argument by analogy overlooks the positive aspects of consent in respect of community sanctions, namely that the offender who consents is taking the first step in participating in his own sentence in a way that is more likely to lead to a positive outcome in terms of an offender's successful reintegration. Even though consent may be cynically dismissed as unlikely to be freely given where the alternative may be a period of incarceration, it is important to do everything possible to encourage the active participation of offenders in their own 'rehabilitation'. Consent serves to keep compulsion to a minimum in accordance with the wider human rights objective of recognizing the human dignity and autonomy of offenders, while at the same time promoting the effectiveness of community sanctions.

A promising recent indication of the importance placed on co-operation by persons subject to community sanctions is that the EU Framework Decision that regulates their transfer between EU Member States, which puts considerable emphasis on what it calls 'social rehabilitation' through community sanctions,

[71] cf M Nellis, 'Surveillance and Confinement: Explaining and Understanding the Experience of Electronically Monitored Curfews' (2009) 1 European Journal of Probation 41.

[72] Snacken et al, n 55 above.

[73] For an overview of the debate see C Morgenstern, 'The Requirement of the Offender's Consent to Community Service' in M Groenhuijsen, T Kooijmans, and T de Roos (eds), *Fervet Opus; Liber Amicorum Anton van Kalmthout* (The Netherlands: Maklu, 2010) 151.

[74] Art 4(3)(a) ECHR. Other exceptions listed in Art 4(3) are clearly not in point.

[75] Emmerson, Ashworth, and MacDonald, n 5 above, paras 16–63 and 16–64.

does not allow for persons sentenced to community sanctions to be returned against their will to the Member State where they 'lawfully and ordinarily' reside, unless they 'want to' return.[76] In this respect it differs from the parallel Framework Decision governing the transfer of sentenced prisoners, which allows for such prisoners to sent back, whether they want to or not. It remains important, however, that sentenced persons are fully informed about how the community sanction that has been imposed on them will be implemented if they choose to return, so that the expression of the desire to return can legitimately be regarded as fully informed. By indicating in this way that they want to return, persons subject to a community sanction that has an element, such as community work, for which consent may be required in the state in which they are sentenced but not in the state to which they may sent are in fact consenting to that element too. It may be that this practice will lead to the reconsideration of the lack of a consent requirement for others on whom the non-consensual work requirement may have been imposed directly in the same jurisdiction.

5. Conclusion

While at the European level recognition of the human rights of offenders subject to community sanctions has not hitherto been as prominent as that accorded to offenders sentenced to imprisonment, a range of legal arguments can and should be advanced to bolster such recognition. The importance of using human rights in this way cannot be underestimated. There can be little doubt that human rights values may be compromised by the implementation of community sanctions in ways that emphasize their punitive aspects and their potential for limiting the risk posed by the offenders subject to them.[77] The challenge is to ensure that those seeking to shape the European dimension of community sanctions are confronted by these arguments when there may be apparent short-term advantages in ignoring them. By placing human rights concerns at the centre of his criminal justice scholarship, Andrew Ashworth has indicated how this can be accomplished and given us much on which to build.

[76] Art 5(1) of the Framework Decision on the Application of the Principle of Mutual Recognition to Judgments and Probation, n 31 above.

[77] B Hudson, 'Human Rights, Public Safety and the Probation Service: Defending Justice in the Risk Society' (2001) 40 Howard Journal of Criminal Justice 103.

13

A System of International Criminal Justice for Human Rights Violations: What is the General Justification for its Existence?

*Andreas von Hirsch and Vivian C Schorscher**

We wish to address, in this chapter, the justification for the existence of a system of international criminal justice. For present purposes, we will consider a hypothetical penal system akin to (albeit not necessarily identical to) the International Criminal Court, established under the Rome Treaty in 1998.[1] Such a system (which we term 'ICrJ') would deal with serious human rights violations, and have international jurisdiction. Its governing statute or treaty would define and proscribe such crimes, and establish an international court with authority to prosecute these offences and impose punishment of those convicted. Its sanctions would be guided by principles of individual culpability; and also of proportionality with respect to the seriousness of the crimes involved. There would be explicit standards or guidelines concerning the scaling of punishments. Our question for this essay is whether, in principle, the establishment of such a system of international criminal justice is justifiable, and why. This search for the relevant justifying principles will require us to address both deontological and consequentialist grounds (including those of crime prevention) for ICrJ's existence.

In what follows, we shall direct our attention to bringing to justice the principal perpetrators of mass atrocities. It is here that the case for an international scheme of punishment seems the strongest, as the intended injurious consequences of the perpetrators' conduct is the greatest. The further issues of dealing with the subordinate perpetrators (from foot soldiers and camp guards through middle-ranking officials) will be deferred.

* The authors are grateful for extensive and most helpful comments by Jakob von Holderstein Holtermann, Antje du Bois-Pedain, Andrew Simester, Massimo Renzo, Alexander Hevelke, and the two editors of this volume. We are thankful, also, for comments on an early version of this analysis, received at a conference on human rights and the philosophy of criminal law. The conference was organized by Professor Jesper Ryberg of Roskilde University, Denmark, and was held at the Carlsberg Academy in Copenhagen on 5–6 October 2010.

[1] G Werle, *Principles of International Criminal Law* (The Hague: TMC Asser Press, 2005), 34–42.

It is a great pleasure for us to participate in this essay collection in honour of Professor Andrew Ashworth. Across the past four decades, he has undertaken a major reconceptualization of criminal law in this country—bringing to it, as never before, an articulation of principles essential for understanding and interpreting the law. Our pleasure is all the greater because one of us (von Hirsch) has collaborated extensively with Andrew in exploring a variety of issues concerning criminal law theory. The present essay, indeed, draws extensively from an account of the general justification of punishment in the domestic context, that Andrew Ashworth and Andreas von Hirsch wrote together as part of a 2005 co-authored volume.[2]

1. Censure and Crime Prevention?—Arguing by Analogy from Domestic Criminal Law Conceptions

In his textbook on international criminal law, Gerhard Werle asserts that the aims of a system of international criminal justice should be those of retribution and deterrence.[3] However, the use of the term 'retribution' raises the question of retribution of what kind, and for what reasons. Citing both retribution and deterrence as justifying aims calls also for an explanation of how those conceptions should relate to one another. However, the basic idea seems to be a useful starting point: that the aim should be to punish deservedly, and also to help discourage such conduct.

Andreas von Hirsch and Andrew Ashworth, as just noted, have developed a general justification for the existence of the penal system in a domestic context. Their argument relies on the two main themes of penal censure and crime prevention.[4] The institution of punishment, the authors assert, should exist to serve the dual aims of conveying authoritative disapprobation for the wrongdoing in criminal behaviour, and of helping to prevent such conduct from occurring in future.

On von Hirsch's and Ashworth's account, the institution of criminal punishment needs to be supported by both deontological and consequentialist reasons. Punishment's censuring feature, of visiting the offender with a sanction expressing disapprobation for his criminal conduct, involves a moral appeal that cannot be reduced purely to the preventative effects of threatened unpleasant consequences.[5] The criminal sanction's other, hard-treatment element, however, is crime preventative at least in part: to help induce people to desist from injurious conduct.[6]

The von Hirsch/Ashworth account is of, course, not the only general justification model that gives a central role to notions of penal censure. A major alternative

[2] A von Hirsch and A Ashworth, *Proportionate Sentencing: Exploring the Principles* (Oxford: Oxford University Press, 2005), Ch 2.

[3] Werle, n 1 above, 30–1; see also S D'Ascoli, *Sentencing in International Criminal Law* (Oxford: Oxford University Press, 2011), 135–7.

[4] von Hirsch and Ashworth, n 2 above, Ch 2.

[5] Ibid, 17–21.

[6] Ibid, 21–4.

is Antony Duff's account, which draws likewise on communicative conceptions of censure. In lieu of crime prevention, however, Duff invokes the conception of the penance to explain punishment's other element: the hard treatment of punished offenders.[7] The relative merits of these competing models have been debated elsewhere, including by those authors,[8] and need not be rehearsed here. We will content ourselves with examining whether an account combining censure with prevention may properly be extended to help justify the existence of a system of international criminal justice concerned with major human rights violations. By doing so, we hope to bring out how the arguments concerning penal censure and crime prevention would alter when such an extension is attempted.

2. The Censure Element in ICrJ's General Justification

Punishment, according to the von Hirsch–Ashworth model, should have *censure* as a central characteristic. But censure of what character and for what reasons?

Censure, according to von Hirsch's and Ashworth's account, has its ultimate justification in normative reasons. It serves as a public valuation of the wrongfulness of the conduct, and constitutes an appeal for desistance on the part of actors and potential actors, viewed as agents capable of moral deliberation. Through that valuation, the actor's status as a moral subject is affirmed, as one capable of assessing and recognizing normative reasons for desistance. Through the criminal law's prohibition, the actor is called upon to desist in virtue of the conduct's reprehensible character, and not purely for instrumental reasons of crime prevention. It is this censuring feature that can provide the basis for requirements of wrongdoing in criminalization theory,[9] of fault in substantive criminal law doctrines,[10] and of proportionality in sentencing.[11]

With major human rights violations of the kind that ICrJ should address, the case for such a censuring response becomes particularly strong, in view of the egregious nature of the conduct. The offences involved here are purposeful in character, and have a greatly enhanced degree of injuriousness: consider the horrific character of the ethnic cleansing campaigns in Bosnia or the genocide in Rwanda in the mid-1990s. The perpetrators, moreover, tend to act less from immediate pressure by superiors than do foot soldiers.[12] Characteristically, the most funda-

[7] RA Duff, *Punishment, Communication and Community* (Oxford: Oxford University Press, 2001), Ch 3. His penance-orientated conception emphasizes inducing the offender to recognize the wrongfulness of his conduct, and to experience remorse on its account.

[8] Ibid; von Hirsch and Ashworth, n 2 above, 17–21.

[9] See A Simester and A von Hirsch, *Crimes, Harms, and Wrongs: On the Principles of Criminalisation* (Oxford: Hart Publishing, 2011), 10–11.

[10] See von Hirsch and Ashworth, n 2 above, 20–1.

[11] Ibid, Chs 2 and 9.

[12] JH Holtermann, 'A "Slice of Cheese"—a Deterrence-based Argument for the International Criminal Court' (2011) 11 Human Rights Review 289, esp 306–7.

mental norms of decent treatment of other human beings are grossly and systematically infringed.[13]

In ordinary domestic contexts, the criminal law's disapprobation of the conduct is supported by everyday moral and social norms. Acts of violence are not only condemned by the criminal law but also by ordinary citizens' informal ethical norms. In the area of serious human rights violations, however, the role of such informal moral standards may be compromised. A variety of mechanisms may serve to undermine citizens' beliefs concerning the blameworthiness of such conduct. These include denial of the wrongfulness of the conduct: victims are deemed, for example, to be of little or no intrinsic worth, or to have provoked the conduct through their own misbehaviour.[14] In such a context, the need for a clear and authoritative condemnation of the conduct and its perpetrators becomes particularly urgent.[15]

3. The Crime Prevention Element: Deterrence

Censure of misconduct might be accomplished purely by formal symbolic condemnation, or else it can be conveyed through the means of hard treatment. Punishment takes the latter form: it expresses the censure through penal deprivation. The von Hirsch–Ashworth model argues in favour of this 'hard treatment' element in punishment, on the grounds of its supplementary *preventative* function, of providing a disincentive against criminal behaviour.

The deprivation element in punishment, according to this view, is also an integral feature of the criminal sanction. It is the means through which penal censure is expressed. However, it serves also as a prudential disincentive against offending that operates within a censuring framework. Having such a prudential disincentive—rather than a purely symbolic censuring response—helps human beings (as moral agents but fallible ones) to resist the temptation to offend.[16] The model thus makes use of notions of crime prevention (particularly deterrence) to explain why the censuring response should be expressed through the medium of penal deprivations, instead of purely through symbolic means.[17] Because punishment still centrally involves the element of censure, however, that censuring feature serves as an essential constraint on why, whether, and how much to punish.

[13] It is sometimes asserted that human rights violators are less culpable than ordinary criminals, because their conduct may be deemed more acceptable in their own social and political environments—thus reducing their consciousness of wrongdoing; see M Drumbl, *Atrocity, Punishment and International Criminal Law* (Cambridge: Cambridge University Press, 2007). For a contrary view, that ignorance of wrongdoing in criminal law should not be judged purely by such a subjective standard, see D Husak and A von Hirsch, 'Culpability and Mistake of Law' in S Shute, J Gardner, and J Horder (eds), *Action and Value in the Criminal Law* (Oxford: Oxford University Press, 1993), 157–74.

[14] S Cohen, *States of Denial: Knowing about Atrocities and Suffering* (Cambridge: Polity Press, 2001), Ch 4.

[15] See further, sections 4 and 5, below.

[16] von Hirsch and Ashworth, n 2 above, 22–4.

[17] Ibid, 22–6.

By prohibiting conduct through the criminal law, the state instructs citizens to refrain from it, and warns them of unwelcome treatment if they do commit it. This threat is made in order to help induce them to desist. The disincentive or deterrent is thus firmly built into the structure of the criminal law.[18] It needs to be considered, however, whether this preventative aim can succeed in the context under discussion. To what extent are ICrJ prohibitions likely to be capable of influencing the behaviour of potential violators?

In domestic criminal law, the penal sanction's preventative function operates against a background of continuous enforcement: the police, prosecution, and courts remain on hand to seek out, apprehend, try, and punish offenders. The continued risk of apprehension and punishment is an important feature in the system's deterrent effect: it gives potential offenders reason to believe that they may face bad consequences should they offend. With human rights violations, however, this feature of continued enforcement tends to be diluted or absent. The principal perpetrators often have control of the state's apparatus, and thus may feel confident (at least, so long as they can retain control) that they will not be called to account. While Charles Taylor held power as head of state in Liberia, for example, he had little reason to fear being prosecuted for his misdeeds by local criminal justice authorities.

An international criminal court for human rights violations is designed expressly to address this difficulty, because its authority is constituted outside national borders. However, enforcement remains more difficult than in the domestic context. Thus Charles Taylor was not arrested and brought to face trial before an international tribunal (the Special Court for Sierra Leone) until after he had lost his authority as Liberian head of state. Persons who are charged with human rights violations by an international court but who succeed in preserving their political authority (such as Sudan's President Bashir) are unlikely to be brought effectively to justice so long as they hold power. Impunity thus remains a more realistic possibility for human rights violators than for ordinary miscreants.

Deterrent effects, however, can still function by indirection. Many brutal regimes operate in unstable political environments, where leaders need to take seriously the possibility of being dislodged from power, and must ask, 'What happens to me then?'. In former days, such individuals could look forward to comfortable exile in another country.[19] Now, if charged with major human rights crimes, they may face the much less comfortable possibility of a life on the run; and of the risk of eventual discovery, extradition, and prosecution. Taylor himself discovered this to his cost: after losing power in Liberia and having taken refuge in nearby Nigeria, he was compelled eventually to return to Liberia at the behest of

[18] See Simester and von Hirsch, n 9 above, 14–16.

[19] But not always. Talaat Pasha, a member of the triumvirate governing the Turkish Empire during its final years before the end of World War I, was one of the chief instigators of the Armenian genocide. After the Empire's defeat and dissolution, he moved to what he imagined would be safe and comfortable retirement in Berlin. While never tried for his atrocities, however, his retirement proved far from safe: he was assassinated by agents of an Armenian resistance organization in 1922.

that country's new President, and was turned over to a special tribunal at The Hague for trial on human rights charges.

Can ICrJ function as a deterrent, then? Deterrence, it should be borne in mind, operates only partially and selectively. Many political leaders refrain from committing serious human rights violations because they would find such conduct abhorrent. Others might be inclined to engage in such behaviour (for ideological reasons, political advantage, or even personal preference) notwithstanding the existence of substantial penal sanctions. Between these two groups is a third, consisting of those who would consider committing the conduct or desisting from it, depending on the incentives or disincentives for doing so.[20] It is chiefly the members of this third group that a deterrence rationale seeks to address. By removing impunity, ICrJ may motivate some persons in the latter category to desist.

The foregoing suggests that an international system for punishing human rights violators should be capable, in principle, of providing potential human rights violators with prudential reasons for desistance. However, the question remains of what empirical confirmation, if any, can be provided that deterrent effects actually can be achieved.

Deterrence research, in a domestic context, operates ordinarily by examining rates of offending before and after a given penal measure has been enacted. The research compares rates of offending before and after the adoption of the measure—say, a new criminal prohibition, or an increase in levels of sentence severity. If crime rates fall significantly after the measure's adoption, and if that effect cannot plausibly be accounted for by other seemingly germane factors (say, economic or demographic variables), that would furnish *pro tanto* evidence of a deterrent effect.[21] The available research suggests that introduction of a new criminal prohibition may be capable of reducing the incidence of the undesired behaviour, although changes in sentence severity for already prohibited conduct tend to have little or no apparent impact on crime rates.[22]

Such a before-and-after model for assessing deterrent effects is not well suited, however, to addressing a penal system's general justification. With the domestic penal system, the problem derives from the difficulty of identifying and obtaining data for the 'before' stage. In modern Western countries, penal systems have always existed, and few would have wish their temporary abolition or suspension for experimental research purposes. However, certain 'natural experiments' are suggestive of deterrent effects. A notable example is an episode in Copenhagen near the end of World War II, when the German occupiers arrested and deported the city's

[20] AE Bottoms and A von Hirsch, 'The Crime-Preventive Impact of Criminal Sanctions' in P Cane and HM Kritzer (eds), *Oxford Handbook of Empirical Legal Studies* (Oxford: Oxford University Press, 2010), Ch 4, 99–100.

[21] Ibid, 100–2.

[22] Ibid, 103–6. With behaviour subject already to significant criminal penalties, the most risk-averse (hence easily deterred) persons would already have been induced to desist from offending, leaving a residue of those least readily intimidated, who continue to commit crimes. It is thus not surprising that increased penalties—applying as they do only to that residual, less risk-averse group—will have reduced deterrent effect.

entire police force, replacing it with an ineffective watch corps. With the resulting practical immunity from arrest and prosecution, crime rates for robbery and theft rose sharply.[23]

When the focus shifts to a system of international criminal justice for human rights violators, there is also an impediment, but of a different character. As such schemes are of relatively recent origin, a 'before' stage can readily be identified: namely, at a time when there was no such special penal system. The difficulty, however, arises regarding the 'after' phase: namely, in assessing the rate of human rights violations after ICrJ's introduction. Domestic offending constitutes a continuing phenomenon, so that deterrence research can identify any reduction in crime rates that occur after the introduction of a new penal measure. However, the occurrence and incidence of major human rights violations are highly discontinuous and episodic. These phenomena depend on certain special political and social constellations—for example, the occurrence of a major political crisis, and the seizure of power by a nationalist elite espousing an ideology of suppression of ethnic minorities.[24] In the absence of such special circumstances, the incidence of serious human rights violations may be low even without the creation of any special penal system. In Bosnia, for example, relations between Serbs, Croats, and Muslims had been improving over several decades before the 1990s. In that decade, it was the breakup of the multinational Yugoslav state, the outbreak of civil conflict among its constituent national groups, and the coming to power of certain extremist nationalist leaders (eg Karadzic and Mladic) that led to the atrocities.[25] Such dramatic discontinuities and dislocations greatly complicate the task of identifying deterrent effects through fluctuations in the rate of human rights offences.

It may, however, be possible to provide indirect evidence. One kind of evidence, cited by Holtermann,[26] relates to perpetrators' efforts at concealment. During the last months of the Third Reich, when defeat was imminent and Allied leaders had declared their intention to bring perpetrators to justice, the Nazi authorities went to considerable efforts to raze extermination camp facilities and conceal evidence of mass killing. Similarly, there were systematic efforts at concealment by Bosnian-Serb forces, after the 1995 Srebrenica massacre. Indeed, some months after that event, the Bosnian-Serb military authorities ordered the exhumation and reburial of large numbers of victims' bodies, in order to impede discovery.

What do such efforts at concealment suggest? Deterrence consists of the avoidance of prohibited conduct through fear of its legal consequences.[27] The desired form of avoidance is, of course, compliance with the legal norm. Another form of avoidance, however, consists of concealment efforts: the perpetrators commit the prohibited conduct, but then seek to hide the evidence. With large-scale human

[23] See Holtermann, n 12 above, 296.

[24] An example of such an occurrence is the coup d'état in 1994 by ultranationalist Hutu officers in Rwanda, leading to the genocide of a substantial portion of the Tutsi population.

[25] For a fuller analysis of these developments, see M Biondich, *The Balkans: Revolution, War and Political Violence since 1878* (Oxford: Oxford University Press, 2011), Ch 4.

[26] Holtermann, n 12 above, 305–6.

[27] See Bottoms and von Hirsch, n 20 above, 98.

rights violations, however, concealment may become a less promising strategy. This will especially be case when the system for prosecuting human rights violations includes systematic forensic anthropology programmes aimed at disclosing evidence of violations—such as those undertaken by investigatory authorities subsequent to the Srebrenica massacre.[28] If concealment has diminished apparent prospects of success, the risk of discovery, prosecution, and punishment increases.

Why, then, are concealment efforts suggestive of deterrence? A threatened sanction can deter only if two conditions are satisfied.[29] First, the perpetrator (or potential perpetrator) must be aware of the potential for being punished. If he is unaware, the penal threat cannot induce him to desist. Critics of international criminal justice sometimes claim that human rights violators (even their leaders) seldom have any such real awareness. Concealment efforts, however, clearly do suggest knowledge of potential legal consequences. Secondly, potential violators must consider the threatened sanctions worth avoiding, in terms of their subjective utilities and disutilities. Some potential perpetrators thus may think the threatened penalty is worth avoiding, but yet wish to engage in the conduct nevertheless. For those persons, concealment efforts may be an appealing alternative. Here, however, the deterrence mechanism would continue to operate. The smaller the prospects of successful concealment become, the less attractive the conduct will be—at least, to those potential offenders concerned at all with avoiding legal consequences. If they are wholly unconcerned, however, the question would recur: why would they bother with concealment?

Our claims about deterrence address the general justification for the existence of a system of punishment—here, of an international system of criminal justice for serious human rights violators. Invoking deterrence for this purpose would not warrant carrying its use over to sentencing: that is, taking the further step of relying on deterrent effects in determining sentence severity. Indeed, we would oppose that latter approach. Once a penal system has been established, it is the severity of punishment that conveys also the implied degree of censure for the criminal conduct. Therefore, the criterion for determining comparative sentence severity should be focused on censure and blameworthiness (that is, on the seriousness of the criminal conduct), and not on deterrence as well.[30]

4. The Crime Prevention Element: 'Positive' General Prevention

European criminal law scholars have also explored another crime prevention mechanism, beyond deterrence. This calls attention to punishment's role in reinforcing citizens' internal inhibitions against crime. The criminal sanction,

[28] The International Commission on Missing Persons identified the remains of more than 6,000 individual victims at Srebrenica in 1995, on the basis of DNA profiles extracted from the burial sites.

[29] See Bottoms and von Hirsch, n 20 above, 99.

[30] This thesis has been developed more fully by von Hirsch and Ashworth in their discussion of determining sentence severity in a domestic context. See von Hirsch and Ashworth, n 2 above, 134–41.

according to the Norwegian penal theorist Johannes Andenaes, 'is a concrete expression of society's disapproval' of criminal acts, which creates 'conscious and unconscious inhibitions against crime'.[31] German penologists have termed this strategy 'positive general prevention'.[32] The criminal law, through its censuring features, is said to constitute an authoritative expression of social disapproval of the behaviour; and hence to reaffirm, reinforce, or stabilize the informal norms of conduct among citizens that restrain the commission of predatory conduct. Positive general prevention thus may be conceived as an alternative way (beyond straightforward deterrence) of achieving crime prevention.

In domestic legal contexts, positive general prevention is often difficult to ascertain, because the classic criminal prohibitions against theft, force, and fraud already reflect strong social norms discouraging such behaviour. Ordinarily, it will not be easy to determine how much those informal norms have been influenced by the criminal law's prohibitions. There are, however, certain contexts where the existence of a positive general preventative effect might more plausibly be inferred. Consider, for example, criminal prohibitions against drinking and driving. When drink-driving statutes were originally adopted, compliance seems to have occurred initially mainly for deterrence reasons, from fear of apprehension and punishment. Over time, however, the prohibition appears to have altered moral attitudes toward the conduct, at least to some extent. This may have occurred because the legal norm prohibiting drinking and driving appears to comport with citizens' more fundamental normative beliefs. Most people probably have always thought it wrong to engage in conduct that risks others' lives. The hazards of drink-driving, however, were not well understood by ordinary motorists. The drink-driving prohibition, and the publicity accompanying it, may have had its preventative impact through focusing public attention on the conduct's dangers.[33] However, such contexts, where positive general preventative effects have at least some empirical confirmation, tend to be rare.[34]

Could positive general preventative effects carry over to the protection of human rights? Human rights violations are facilitated in places where significant segments of the population believe that the conduct is morally permissible, or even desirable. Can prohibitions of human rights violations, with their features of authoritative censure, help alter such attitudes and thus possibly generate or reinforce social norms discouraging such behaviour?

[31] J Andenaes, 'General Prevention: Illusion or Reality?' in J Andenaes (ed), *Punishment and Deterrence* (Ann Arbor, MI: University of Michigan Press, 1974), 3–33, and esp 7–8.

[32] For fuller discussion of positive general prevention in German criminal law theory, see B Schünemann, A von Hirsch, and N Jareborg (eds), *Positive Generalprävention: Kritische Analysen im deutsch-englischen Dialog* (Heidelberg: CF Müller Verlag, 1998).

[33] See more fully, A von Hirsch, AE Bottoms, PO Wikström, and E Burney, *Criminal Deterrence and Sentence Severity* (Oxford: Hart Publishing, 1999), 11.

[34] For German-language surveys of the available evidence, see KF Schumann, *Positive Generalprävention* (Heidelberg: CF Müller, 1989); KF Schumann, 'Empirische Beweisbarkeit der Grundanahmen von Positiven Generalprävention' in Schünemann, von Hirsch, and Jareborg (eds), n 32 above, 17–28.

Major human rights infringements typically involve conduct (eg, murder, torture, rape, and forcible mass-expulsions) which, if perpetrated against those deemed ordinary citizens, would be perceived as morally outrageous. However, it is ethnic, religious, or political minorities that tend to be targeted—concerning whom much antipathy exists, or has been fostered, in the general population. A variety of mechanisms exist that facilitate attitudes of denial of wrongfulness in such contexts. These include:

- denial of the actual occurrence of the violations, on grounds that victims' ('those people's') reports of flagrant mistreatment are untrustworthy, and that 'our' people or soldiers or government officials would never be capable of committing such vile deeds;[35]
- perceptions of the targeted groups and their members as undeserving of protection because they are inferior, worthless, or have brought their sufferings on themselves;
- perceptions of the victim groups as being especially threatening to the interests of ordinary citizens—thus making violence against that group seem justifiable as a matter of purported self-defence;
- perceptions of the conduct as being exempt from moral or legal scrutiny—for a variety of reasons, including sovereign immunity, national security, or political 'realism'.

Might a system of punishing human rights violations be helpful in counteracting these mechanisms of denial? In principle, it could. First, a formal criminal trial provides a forum for challenging claims that the human rights infringements never occurred. A large body of evidence can be presented and scrutinized in detail, showing that the conduct in fact did take place, and showing how extensive and aggravated it was. That evidence can also establish that 'our' officials or paramilitaries were fully capable of such acts and had actually committed them on a large scale. Secondly, punishment for such rights violations (through its censuring implications) conveys in dramatic fashion that the conduct is profoundly reprehensible. It thus signifies that the rights of the persecuted group *are* to be taken seriously; and that the victims have human status and are not fair game for gross mistreatment or extirpation. Thirdly, the proceedings against perpetrators also demonstrate that politically motivated brutalities should not be exempt from challenge on political grounds such as sovereign immunity or national security.

The trial and punishment of human rights violators, with its censuring implications, should thus arguably be capable of helping to convey a sense of the wrongfulness of the conduct—and thus might help reinforce moral inhibitions against such behaviour. But to what extent are there grounds for believing that these mechanisms actually do operate in this fashion? Here, valid empirical evidence will not be easy to supply. We have noted above[36] the difficulty of

[35] Cohen, n 14 above, Ch 5.   [36] See text at n 34 above.

confirming positive general preventative effects empirically, even in the domestic context. Here, the relevant factors would be still more complex and difficult to assess.

Could there, at least, be historical support for this positive general prevention thesis? Perhaps, but the case is not easily made. Consider the case of Germany and Russia during World War II. At that time, both countries had totalitarian governments that perpetrated some of the worst and most extensive human rights abuses in history. In both countries, those regimes fell. In Germany after the war, a substantial effort was made to confront such atrocities, including numerous prosecutions of Nazi war criminals over several decades—first, by special international tribunals and, after the end of the Allied occupation, by German courts. In Russia since the fall of the Soviet system in 1989, no such effort has been made. Virtually no prosecutions or other efforts to uncover the Soviet era's mass human rights violations have been undertaken. The eventual attitudinal differences are notable. German public opinion now largely views Nazism and its crimes with abhorrence. In Russia, however, Stalin's reputation as a great leader has been revived (with the present regime's enthusiastic concurrence), and the mass human rights violations by the Soviet regime are seldom mentioned in Russian media. Why this difference? A variety of factors might be cited. Nazism was discredited through its catastrophic military defeat in World War II, whereas the Soviet regime gained credit from having repelled the German invaders. Germany had a substantial tradition of a *Rechtsstaat* before the Nazi period, which was revived after the war, whilst Russia has scarcely had any such tradition. But Germany's willingness after the war to confront the Nazi regime's massive human rights abuses, as opposed to Russia's unwillingness to do so, might arguably be said to have made a difference.

Providing adequate empirical confirmation of such effects would, however, be fraught with difficulty. The question of ascertaining the direction of causality, for example, would remain troublesome. The causal nexus might well have run in the reverse direction: that it has been the development of critical attitudes toward human rights abuses that led to a willingness to call violators to account, rather than the reverse. Germany became more willing to proceed with its own prosecutions of Nazi war criminals, on this hypothesis, because its post-war political leadership had developed such antipathy to the country's recent fascist past. The Russian complacency about Soviet human rights abuses may well derive from the authoritarian and nationalist character of its present political leadership. Positive general preventative effects thus remain more of a plausible scenario than an empirically confirmable effect.

5. Positive General Prevention: Justifying Element or Aspiration?

Given this uncertain state of the evidence concerning positive general prevention, how important is that conception to the rationale for ICrJ? To respond to that question, it might be helpful to take another look at that idea, and at how it relates to the other elements of ICrJ's general justification.

Censure, on our analysis, is a way of addressing offenders and potential offenders as agents capable of moral deliberation. This constitutes a first element in our case for ICrJ's existence (see section 2 above). Deterrence, the second element (section 3), is explicitly crime preventative: it concerns how the threat to punish provides potential offenders with prudential reasons for desistance.

What of positive general prevention? This seems to be an odd hybrid. Like deterrence, its ultimate aim is crime preventative. Yet it derives not from punishment's hard treatment aspect, but from its censuring character. It is the censure that provides authoritative expression of social disapprobation of the conduct; and it is that disapprobation which is said to help reinforce or stabilize citizens' moral inhibitions against grossly wrongful behaviour.

Positive general prevention is also a more demanding aim. Unlike deterrence, it does not just involve giving potential offenders prudential reasons for desistance, but rather bringing about attitudinal change. What matters is reinforcing people's *internalized* norms discouraging criminal conduct. Whether and to what extent that phenomenon occurs depends not only on punishment's censuring message, but on other (typically quite complex) social and political background factors.

Must we, then, treat positive general prevention as a third essential justifying element? We think not. The two other elements, censure and deterrence, would suffice to provide a case for the existence of ICrJ. Punishing human rights violators does, and should, convey disapprobation of criminal conduct; and a system of penal sanctions, when institutionalized, should be capable of deterring potential violators at least to some extent (see sections 2 and 3). With these two elements in place, there would be a prima facie reason for establishing such a penal system. That would be the case whether or not there was adequate confirmatory evidence of positive general preventative effects.

This conclusion is supported by another consideration. This concerns the differing character of the two principal justifying grounds, deterrence and censure, and the manner in which censure is linked with positive general prevention. Deterrence is essentially teleological: its point is to induce people to desist. Consequently, if the penal system yields no significant deterrent effects, a rationale for that system based in part on deterrence would fail. This explains why we have been so concerned about the state of the evidence of deterrent effects (see section 3 above). The evidence we were able to supply was only partial and indirect—for example, that concerning efforts of concealment by perpetrators. But the latter is, in our view, *some* evidence. Had we been unable to adduce any evidence, the deterrence element in our case for ICrJ would not have been sustainable.

However, positive general prevention is not so straightforwardly teleological. True, the ultimate aim is crime preventative: reinforcing or altering addressees' internalized norms, so that they become less inclined to offend. But this is to be achieved by means of penal censure, and censure is *not* mainly consequentialist in character. To censure conduct is to treat it as *misconduct*—to convey that it is wrong. That judgement of wrongfulness implies a moral appeal: that people ought to desist because the conduct is wrong. Positive general preventative effects are mediated yet further: the moral appeal embodied in the penal law's prohibitions must be capable of influencing the targeted audience's own set of moral standards.

These more complex linkages become more easily disrupted than is so for simple deterrence, as so much depends on the people's own moral attitudes and on the character of their social environment. With deterrence, what matters chiefly is that the sanctions are unpleasant and hence thought worth avoiding. (True, the deterrent effect still depends on addressees' personal utilities and disutilities: for example, the extent to which the person actually does or does not fear a prison sentence. But at least, it is not necessary to persuade the person of the wrongfulness of the conduct.) With positive general prevention, this kind of persuasion is essential, and that makes the aim so much more difficult to achieve. Crucial to its achievement would be the moral reasoning process of members of the targeted audience, as they must be willing to internalize the law's judgment of the conduct's wrongfulness. That makes that achievement depend on the moral psychology of the targeted audience—its ethical, political, and social assumptions.

What, then, should be the role of positive general prevention? It should, we think, be an important aspiration of ICrJ. An international system of criminal sanctions, we have suggested, might well be capable (at least in certain contexts) of helping to change attitudes concerning people's fundamental rights, in a manner that reinforces their moral inhibitions against perpetrating politically motivated atrocities. The extent to which it succeeds in doing so will depend, however, on the historical background and the social and political environments within the countries affected. With propitious background conditions, such attitudinal changes may well occur to some degree and that should count as an important success. With unpropitious background factors, such success may well elude us, and that is reason for regret. But it is desirable nevertheless—for reasons outlined in sections 2 and 3—to have an international penal system that can testify to the wrongfulness of the conduct, and can provide some disincentive against its commission.[37]

6. Concluding Thoughts

The present essay has examined the general justifying aims of an international system of criminal sanctions for dealing with serious human rights violations.

[37] Another problem may arise, moreover, from the normative 'remoteness' of an international criminal tribunal. In a domestic context, it is the affected country's own state institutions that enact and enforce the criminal prohibitions. The state's putative moral authority may impart to those prohibitions—and their implied censure—a degree of credibility that could matter for the achievement of positive general preventive effects. With ICrJ, it is an extraterritorial international body that is responsible for the prohibitions and their enforcement, and that body's normative judgments may well carry less weight with a country's citizens. However, the extent to which this 'remoteness' effect operates will depend on the social and political situation of the particular country involved. Moreover, returning sole responsibility for dealing with major human rights violations to the state may not be a satisfactory alternative, to the extent that states themselves are responsible for serious human rights violations.

Taking as our starting point the idea that such a system should help prevent such conduct and express public recognition of its wrongfulness, we have tried to spell out with greater specificity what those aims should involve. We have thus taken a closer look at the role of such a system in deterring such conduct and in acknowledging its wrongfulness through penal censure. We have also discussed the system's possible role as 'positive general prevention'—as helping to reinforce citizens' own moral norms against gross violations of others' rights.

Our analysis remains, nevertheless, one of modest scope. We have not endeavoured to examine ostensibly non-punitive approaches to mass human rights violations, such as restorative justice[38] or amnesty[39] schemes. We also have not addressed the issues of political legitimacy, or legal standing and accountability,[40] that a system of international criminal justice will inevitably raise. We deferred considered questions of possible counterproductive effects: whether, and under what circumstances, prosecuting human rights violators might interfere with achieving political settlement in troubled areas.[41] Ours is thus a discussion of limited scope. But we hope it has some usefulness in its own terms, as an analysis of some of the principal justifying aims of a system of international criminal justice.

[38] For an analysis of restorative justice approaches in this area, see JH Holtermann, 'Outlining the Shadow of the Axe—On Restorative Justice and the Use of Trial and Punishment' (2009) 3 Criminal Law and Philosophy 187.

[39] See A du Bois-Pedain, *Transitional Amnesty in South Africa* (Cambridge: Cambridge University Press, 2007).

[40] RA Duff, 'Authority and Proportionality in International Criminal Law' in S Besson and J Tasioulas (eds), *The Philosophy of International Criminal Law* (Oxford: Oxford University Press, 2010), Ch 29.

[41] See Holtermann, n 12 above, 308–9.

PART III

SENTENCING

14

Equality Before the Law and Equal Impact of Sanctions: Doing Justice to Differences in Wealth and Employment Status

Kate Warner

The principle of equality before the law requires that sentencing decisions should treat offenders equally irrespective of wealth, race, colour, sex, employment, or social status; and the principle of equal impact requires that sentences should be calibrated to create an equal penal impact on offenders subject to them. Like cases should be treated alike and different cases differently. However, sentencing law has grappled with the problem of which differences are to be considered relevant, while theorists have debated about how the principles of equality before the law and equal impact can be accommodated within retributive or consequential theories and reconciled with the principle of parsimony and issues of efficiency in the administration of criminal justice.

1. Overview

This essay seeks to explore the tensions between the principles of equality before the law and equal impact in the context of financial penalties and employment status. While it is acknowledged that the criminal justice system, and sentencing in particular, can do little to address social inequalities, it will be argued that by failing to adopt a day or unit fine system, the United Kingdom, Australia, and other common law countries have lost an opportunity of doing justice to difference. However, in the case of employment status, it is argued that to allow employment to count in an offender's favour is contrary to the principle of equality and discriminatory; it is to do injustice to difference.

2. The Principles of Equality and Equal Impact

The principle of equality has its foundations in the common law. Dicey treated it as an aspect of the rule of law—its consequence was that everyone from the Prime

Minister to a police constable was subject to the rule of law.[1] The limits of formal equality as a principle of fairness are illustrated by the often-quoted words of Anatole France: 'The law, in its majestic equality, forbids the rich and the poor alike to sleep under the bridges, to beg in the streets and to steal bread.' In human rights instruments and constitutional documents the principle is commonly expressed as a principle of non-discrimination. Article 26 of the International Covenant on Civil and Political Rights (ICCPR) provides that: 'All persons are equal before the law and are entitled to equal and effective protection against discrimination.' The European Convention on Human Rights (ECHR) has a more restrictive right not to be discriminated against in the exercise of another Convention right. However, a broader protection against discrimination is included in Protocol 12 to the Convention, and the Equality Act 2006 has established a general legal anti-discrimination framework in English law.[2]

Two sentencing principles derive from the general principle of equality before the law.[3] The first is a principle of non-discrimination. Sentencing decisions should treat offenders equally and not discriminate against them on the basis of their wealth, race, gender, sexual orientation, employment, or social status. This is reflected in the principle that offenders with wealth are not allowed to 'buy themselves out of prison' by paying large fines or compensation.[4] As the Court of Criminal Appeal of Western Australia put it, 'courts should avoid giving the impression that a rich person can purchase absolution for cash'.[5] However, as a principle of non-discrimination, it is not purely a principle of formal equality. Both direct and indirect discrimination are covered. Unintentional direct discrimination derives from stereotypical views about different kinds of people. In the sentencing context, von Hirsch, Ashworth, and Roberts use Hudson's example of gender stereotypes in the sentencing context 'whereby "employment for men and domestic responsibilities for women operate as constraints on imprisonment" but greater punishment is likely to flow from the opposite characteristics'.[6] Examples of indirect discrimination in the sentencing context include the discount for guilty pleas, which leads to more severe sentences for black offenders because they are less likely to plead guilty,[7] and the disproportionate impact of mandatory penalties for second and third offences on indigenous offenders in Australia because they are more likely to have prior convictions. As a principle of non-discrimination, the principle of equality demands equality of treatment for similarly serious offences. The offender is not a variable and the impact of punishment or the punitive bite of the sanction is assumed to be the same for all offenders.

[1] AV Dicey, *Introduction to the Law of the Constitution* (10th edn, London: Macmillan, 1959), 202.

[2] A Ashworth, *Sentencing and Criminal Justice* (5th edn, Cambridge: Cambridge University Press, 2010), 239.

[3] A von Hirsch, A Ashworth, and J Roberts, *Principled Sentencing: Readings on Theory and Policy* (3rd edn, Oxford: Hart, 2009), 344.

[4] *Markwick* (1953) 37 Cr App R 125 (CCA).

[5] Wickham, Wallace, and Pidgeon JJ in *Cobby* (unreported, CCA, WA, No 19 of 1983, cited by Malcolm CJ in *Sgroi* (1989) 40 A Crim R 197, 200).

[6] von Hirsch et al, n 3 above, 344.

[7] Ibid.

The second principle is the principle of equal impact. It recognizes that the punitive bite of a sanction of a particular length or value is not necessarily the same for all offenders. Bentham, for example, argued that 'individual sensibilities' should be taken into account in calculating punishment.[8] In Ashworth's words, negatively phrased, the principle of equal impact requires 'that the system should strive to avoid grossly unequal impacts on offenders with differing resources and sensitivities, because that would be unjust'.[9] In the context of fines, this means that the amount of the fine should be adjusted to reflect the means of the offender. Reconciling the competing demands of these two principles can create difficulties. In the case of employment, for example, the principle of equality suggests that loss of employment should not be taken into account as personal mitigation because by allowing a source of mitigation not open to the unemployed it is discriminatory. On the other hand, the principle of equal impact and the principle of parsimony would favour taking into account loss of employment as a mitigating factor. Similar issues arise in relation to the effect of imprisonment on the elderly or the very young. Custody is likely to have a disproportionately severe impact on an elderly offender with limited life expectancy and to be more onerous for a teenager than an adult because of its impact on opportunities for education and personal development and because of the reduced psychological resilience of younger offenders.[10]

The principle of equality has similar roots to the principle of proportionality—both seek to ensure fair treatment. By ignoring the impact of a particular punishment on an individual offender, strict proportionality and formal equality can lead to unequal and unfair outcomes. If strict proportionality is modified to require the same sentence not only for similarly serious offences but also for similarly situated offenders, the question is what factors are to count as dissimilar in offenders' situations for which due allowance can be given. If equality of treatment includes equality of impact, the question is which personal/offender factors should be taken into account to determine impact. Ashworth has given detailed consideration to the questions raised by the principle of equal impact, how it can be reconciled with the principle of equality or non-discrimination, and how it can be integrated into a system of proportionate sentencing. This has stimulated debate about a principled and coherent approach to personal mitigation, including 'equity factors' which are unrelated to offence seriousness and so do not fit comfortably within a desert framework.[11]

[8] JH Burns and HLA Hart, *The Collected Works of Jeremy Bentham: An Introduction to the Principles and Morals of Legislation* (London: Athlone Press, 1970).

[9] Ashworth, n 2 above, 100.

[10] Ashworth, n 2 above, 185; A von Hirsch and A Ashworth, *Proportionate Sentencing: Exploring the Principles* (Oxford: Oxford University Press, 2005), 41–3.

[11] See eg C Piper, 'Should Impact Constitute Mitigation? Structured Discretion versus Mercy' [2007] Crim LR 141; S Easton, 'Dangerous Waters: Taking Account of Impact in Sentencing' [2008] Crim LR 105; A Kolber, 'The Subjective Experience of Punishment' (2009) 109 Columbia Law Review 182, who argues that the severity of punishment should be assessed in subjective rather than objective terms by punishment theorists; compare von Hirsch and Ashworth, n 10 above, 41.

3. Fines and Means

The common law approach to calculating the amount of a fine requires the court to determine the level of fine that reflects the seriousness of the offence and the culpability of the offender and then to make an appropriate adjustment downwards if the offender is unable to pay. If an offender lacks any means to pay, a fine should not be imposed,[12] even if default only leads to civil enforcement rather than imprisonment[13] or if imprisonment is very much a last resort in enforcing payment.[14] Nor should courts impose a more severe penalty on an offender who is unable to pay what is regarded by the court as an adequate fine.[15] In such a case, the proper course is to move down the sentencing hierarchy to a conditional discharge, for example.[16] And it should not be possible to impose a prison sentence on 'a man of means' to whom a fine would mean 'virtually nothing'.[17] Where a fine is the appropriate sanction, imposing a more severe sanction either on a person unable to pay or on a person for whom a fine would be meaningless would clearly infringe the principle that no one should be sentenced more severely on account of their wealth, race, colour, gender, employment status, sexual orientation, and so on.

Reducing a fine on account of an offender's means is an uncontroversial example of the principle of equal impact. However, the English common law did not permit the amount of the fine to be inflated on the grounds of the affluence of the offender, although that was changed by the Criminal Justice Act 1991.[18] Similarly, Canadian and New Zealand courts have treated ability to pay as a mitigating rather than an aggravating factor.[19] In contrast, in a Scottish case where four equally culpable co-accused had been fined varying sums equivalent in each case to five weeks' income, the fines were held to have been correctly assessed.[20] English legislation now makes it clear that financial circumstances should be taken into account to increase as well as reduce the amount of a fine.[21] Legislation in many jurisdictions provides that courts should take into account the offender's financial circumstances before imposing a fine.[22] While such a requirement is broad enough to allow courts to

[12] *Young v Geddie* (1978) 22 ALR 232.

[13] *Rahme* (1989) 43 A Crim R 81 at 86.

[14] *Nandan v Tasmania* [2009] TASSC 75.

[15] *Ball* (1981) 3 Cr App R (S) 283 (CA); nor can it refuse to impose a fine on the grounds that the maximum fine would have little impact on an affluent offender: *Rose v Howard*, unreported, Supreme Court of Tasmania, Serial No 36/1981.

[16] Ashworth, n 2 above, 328.

[17] *Johnson* (1971) 5 CCC (2d) 541; *Rose v Howard*, unreported, Supreme Court of Tasmania, Serial No 36/1981.

[18] *R v Wallace* [1969] Crim LR 211 (CA); *R v Tao* [1977] QB 141 (CA); *R v Fairbairn* (1980) 2 Cr App R (S) 315 (CA).

[19] *Wells* (1977) 15 AR 606 (DC), where a fine based on the daily earnings of an offender was set aside; *Woroby* (2003) 174 CCC (3d) 128, where a fine of $10,000 was held to be excessive because it was based on the offender's income; *Ministry of Transport v Graham* [1990] 3 NZLR 249.

[20] *Scott v Lowe* 1990 SCCR 15.

[21] Criminal Justice Act 2003 (UK), s 164(4).

[22] eg Fines Act 1996 (NSW), s 6; Sentencing Act 2002 (NZ), s 41; Criminal Code (Can), s 734(2).

impose a heavier fine on the grounds of an offender's wealth, in the absence of a clear mandate to increase the amount of the fine, such provisions are unlikely to be interpreted as authorizing this. In Canada, in refusing to treat the ability to pay as an aggravating factor, the Court of Appeal of Manitoba said 'if Parliament had intended to make fines proportional to the offender's wealth or lack thereof, Parliament could have specifically indicated this, as has been recently done in England'.[23]

Fixed penalty fines

The principle that a fine must be within an offender's reasonable capacity to pay must yield to a statutory provision which requires a court to impose a fine of a minimum amount.[24] Mandatory minimum fines are not uncommon in many jurisdictions for a wide range of offences, particularly driving-related crimes, including breathalyser offences. Increasingly popular are on-the-spot-fines—fixed financial penalties imposed by the issue of a penalty or infringement notice which, if accepted and paid, is an alternative to prosecution. Initially introduced for parking infringements in the United Kingdom and Australia, many offences are now resolved in this way. The range of offences covered extends well beyond traffic matters and covers offences such as stealing property under $300 in value and offensive conduct and language.[25] In England and Wales, Penalty Notices for Disorder (PNDs) can now be issued to offenders who admit to offences such as criminal damage, shop theft, or possession of cannabis, as well as many motoring offences. In Scotland too, fixed penalty notices (FPNs) apply to a range of low-level anti-social and nuisance offences, as well as motoring offences.[26] Scotland also allows 'fiscal fines' which give a procurator fiscal the discretion to make an offer of a fixed penalty instead of being prosecuted.[27] The level of fiscal fine offered is set and is determined solely by the nature of the offence.[28]

While in theory offenders may have the option of going to court or applying to a state agency for review or relief rather than accepting the penalty notice or fiscal fine, there are uncertainties in, and disincentives for choosing to do so. For marginalized groups, lack of literacy can present an obstacle to contesting the offence or obtaining time to pay. These penalties clearly impact unequally on economically disadvantaged and marginalized groups. An on-the-spot fine of a modest amount can represent a significant proportion of weekly income for a low-income earner, but only a small percentage of the average take-home weekly wage.

[23] *Woroby* (2003) 173 CCC (3d) 128, 137.

[24] *Davies v Deverell* (1992) 1 Tas R 214, 217–18.

[25] Criminal Procedure Regulation 2010, Sch 3. Notices for these offences are known in New South Wales as Criminal Infringement Notices (CINs).

[26] Antisocial Behaviour etc (Scotland) Act 2004, s 128; Road Traffic Offenders Act 1988, s 34.

[27] Criminal Procedure (Scotland) Act 1995, s 302.

[28] Sentencing Commission for Scotland, *Basis on which Fines are Determined* (Edinburgh: Sentencing Commission for Scotland, 2006), 11.

When default leads to driver licence sanctions the problems for defaulters escalate, particularly for those in regional areas lacking in public transport.[29] While avoiding the stigma and trauma of court proceedings (and acquiring a conviction) have been used to justify expansion of the penalty notice system,[30] saving the criminal justice system time and money is clearly the principal motivation. In this situation the principle of equal impact is compromised by considerations of administrative efficiency.

4. Unit Fines in Europe

European countries which have adopted day or unit fines systems take the principle of equality of impact more seriously. Unit fine systems require the amount of the fine to be calculated as a proportion of the disposable income of the offender. Fines are assessed in two steps. First, a decision is made as to the number of fine units that should be imposed. Secondly, the actual monetary amount involved per unit is assessed on the basis of the offender's income less certain allowed deductions. So instead of merely permitting means to reduce the amount of the fine, the fine can be increased in proportion to the financial means of the offender. Sweden has had a day fine system since 1932. However, it does not apply to minor offences because of the administrative burden of calculations and because the imposition of very large fines was thought to be out of place for petty offences.[31] Similarly, in Germany, minor offences are excluded from the day fine system. In Finland, while minor traffic offences do not attract the day fine system, the range of offences caught by the system is very broad. For certain petty offences prosecutors also have the power to order day fines. In Denmark day fines are also used, but for more serious offences and only by the courts.[32]

Clearly allowing the amount of a fine to be increased as well as reduced helps to ensure that the imposition of a fine on an affluent offender achieves the principle of equal impact. It helps ensure that the 'penal bite' of the fine is the same for all offences to which the system applies. Arguably also, setting fairer fining levels has other advantages, such as encouraging the use of fines, particularly in higher courts where fining levels are low, raising revenue, and facilitating enforcement because fines are better calibrated to the offenders' means.

[29] Some jurisdictions, such as New South Wales, suspend licences until fines are paid. Drivers who then drive whilst disqualified face mandatory disqualification and further serious penalties.

[30] New South Wales Law Reform Commission, *Sentencing*, Report No 79 (Sydney: New South Wales Law Reform Commission, 1996), 76.

[31] Advisory Council on the Penal System, *Report on Non-Custodial and Semi-Custodial Penalties* (London: HMSO, 1970), para 20.

[32] E Zedlewski, *Alternatives to Custodial Supervision: The Day Fine*, National Institute of Justice Discussion Paper, NCJ 230301 (Washington, DC: National Institute of Justice, 2010), 4. This paper also reports that many Latin American countries use day fines and the Dominican Republic claims to have done so since 1884.

5. Flirting with Unit Fines in Common Law Jurisdictions

United Kingdom

England and Wales experimented briefly with the idea of unit fines between 1991 and 1993. A unit fine system together with a statutory provision empowering courts to vary fines according to means was proposed by the government as part of a just deserts framework for sentencing reform in 1990.[33] The government claimed that 'it is in the interests of justice that offenders should be fined according to their means, otherwise fines have a different impact on offenders, according to their means and not the seriousness of their offences'.[34] It was claimed that experiments with unit fines in four magistrates' courts had led to increased confidence about using fines and that setting fairer fine levels should lead to their greater use and to fewer difficulties with enforcement.[35] A unit fine scheme was introduced by the Criminal Justice Act 1991. It came into operation in October 1992 but was abandoned seven months later.

Ashworth has succinctly documented the reasons for the demise of the scheme. The following two explanations seem to be the most salient.[36] First, the scheme for assessing means was flawed in its emphasis on income to the exclusion of other indications of wealth and in its complexity for calculating weekly disposable income. Secondly, a lack of public education about the goals of the scheme exposed it to attack by a media campaign which highlighted high fines for middle-class motoring offenders and inconsistent fines for similar offences, without explaining that inconsistencies were attributable to differences in income.[37] Publicity given to cases such as that of a man who was fined £1,200 for dropping a potato crisp packet in the street contributed to the discrediting of the scheme, even though the reason for the high fine was due to the offender's failure to appear and disclose his income. He successfully appealed the amount of the fine, which was reduced to £48.[38] So not only were the procedures for implementing the scheme poorly designed, it was not well explained to the public and the press were able to ridicule it.

The unit fine concept was revived in 2004 with the release of the Carter Report, which recommended that fines for a range of offences be linked to income.[39] To avoid excessive fines for low-level crime, it was recommended that fixed penalty and low-level fines should be excluded. A Bill to amend section 164 of the Criminal Justice Act 2003 to fix fines in accordance with daily disposable income was

[33] Home Office, *Crime, Justice and Protecting the Public* (Cm 965, 1990), 7, 25–6.

[34] Ibid, 26.

[35] Ibid, 25.

[36] Ashworth, n 2 above, 330–1.

[37] Ashworth, n 2 above, 331; see also J Greene, 'The Unit Fine: Monetary Sanctions Apportioned to Income' in A von Hirsch and A Ashworth (eds), *Principled Sentencing: Readings on Theory and Policy* (2nd edn, Oxford: Hart, 1998), 268, 270.

[38] M Tonry, *Sentencing Matters* (New York: Oxford University Press, 1996), 127.

[39] P Carter, *Managing Offenders, Reducing Crime: A New Approach* (The Carter Report) (London: TSO, 2003).

introduced in 2005 but lapsed when Parliament was prorogued.[40] In 2006 the UK Labour government reaffirmed its intention to introduce day fines.[41] The current Conservative/Liberal Democrat government does not appear to have a policy on day fines.

Unit fines have been considered in Scotland. In 1990 a Bill with provisions authorizing an experimental scheme was introduced but the provisions were dropped from the Bill before it was passed.[42] Most recently, the Sentencing Commission for Scotland considered but rejected the concept.[43] Providing access to centrally held information to verify the financial status of the offender was seen as essential for a unit fine system and the cost of providing the technology to do so prohibitive. The Commission was 'uncomfortable' with the alternative of requiring a defendant to provide financial information prior to conviction and requiring this post conviction was regarded as leading to unacceptable delays. The issue of disproportionate penalties for minor offences committed by those with higher incomes and the fact the scheme could not apply to fixed penalty notices and fiscal fines were seen as drawbacks.

Other common law jurisdictions

The idea of day or unit fines has been floated from time to time in Australia by various bodies including a Western Australian committee inquiring into imprisonment rates,[44] the Australian Law Reform Commission, the New South Wales Law Reform Commission, the Tasmanian Law Reform Commission and its successor, the Tasmania Law Reform Institute, and the New South Wales Sentencing Council. In each case the issue has been rejected or deferred. Day fines have also been considered but rejected in New Zealand. The Criminal Justice Working Group was concerned by the potential for such a scheme to increase the disparity between court-imposed fines and infringement notices.[45]

In the 1980s and 1990s there was considerable interest in the possibility of introducing structured or day fines in the United States. Over a decade, trials or demonstrations were conducted or assisted by the Vera Institute, first in Staten Island, New York and later in Arizona, Connecticut, Iowa, and Oregon.[46]

[40] S Easton and C Piper, *Sentencing and Punishment: The Quest for Justice* (2nd edn, Oxford: Oxford University Press, 2008), 225.

[41] Home Office, *A Five Year Strategy for Protecting the Public and Reducing Reoffending* (Cm 6717, 2006), 19.

[42] Sentencing Commission for Scotland, n 28 above, 28–9.

[43] Ibid, 36–7.

[44] OF Dixon, *Report of the Committee of Inquiry into the Rate of Imprisonment* ('the Dixon Report') (Perth: Committee of Inquiry into the Rate of Imprisonment, 1981), 169.

[45] New Zealand Criminal Justice Working Group, *Review of Monetary Penalties in New Zealand* (Wellington, NZ: Ministry of Justice, 2000), 173.

[46] Vera Institute of Justice, *Structured Fines: Day Fines as Fair and Collectable Punishment in American Courts* (New York: Vera Institute of Justice, 1995) and US Bureau of Justice Assistance, Justice Management Institute and Vera Institute of Justice, *How to Use Structured Fines (Day Fines) as an Intermediate Sanction* (Washington DC: The Bureau of Justice Assistance, 1996).

Considerable academic interest was also shown in the subject.[47] A few states introduced legislation allowing the imposition of day fines.[48] Interest in the idea seems to have waned, although recently the Justice Policy Institute suggested unit fines as part of a strategy to reduce incarceration rates,[49] and the National Institute of Justice has published on day fines with suggested strategies to deal with the administrative difficulties which led to the termination of efforts to adopt them.[50] Canada too has considered the concept but has not got beyond recommending further study on ways of maximizing equity of impact of fines on offenders of varying means.[51]

6. Why have Common Law Jurisdictions Failed to Embrace Day/Unit Fines?

Is inflating a fine on grounds of an offender's wealth unfair?

The strongest argument in favour of day fines is fairness. Time is a much more egalitarian measure than money in that everyone has exactly 24 hours in a day.[52] Prison terms, community service orders and, in part, probation orders,[53] are measured in time. While the issue of unequal impact can also arise in relation to punishments measured by time, particularly in the case of the imprisonment of elderly offenders who stand to lose a greater proportion of their remaining days,[54] the unequal impact of financial penalties is particularly stark. Ordinary fines are inherently unfair. Whilst in some cases they may be adjusted downwards if the offender is unable to pay, for mandatory minimum fines and for fixed fines imposed by infringement or penalty notices, no such adjustments are possible. Moreover, a fine of the same amount can be burdensome for the poor but hardly felt by the rich. It may even be paid by someone other than the offender. However, the fairness argument has not gone unchallenged. In opposing the Carter Report's recommendation for unit fines in England and Wales, the Shadow Secretary for State for Constitutional Affairs is reported to have said:[55]

[47] GM Friedman, 'The West German Day-fine System: A Possibility for the United States?' (1983) 50 University of Chicago Law Review 281; ST Hillsman, 'Fines and Day Fines' (1990) 12 Crime and Justice 49.

[48] Zedlewski, n 32 above, 6.

[49] Justice Policy Institute, *Finding Direction: Expanding Criminal Justice Options by Considering Policies of Other Nations* (Washington, DC: Justice Policy Institute, 2011), 23, 59.

[50] Zedlewski, n 32 above.

[51] Canadian Sentencing Commission, *Sentencing Reform: A Canadian Approach* (Ottawa: Ministry of Supply and Services Canada, 1986), Recommendation 12:19.

[52] L Eriksson and RE Goodin, 'The Measuring Rod of Time: The Example of Swedish Day-fines' (2007) 24 Journal of Applied Philosophy 125.

[53] The conditions of a probation order contribute to its penal bite and can be quite onerous.

[54] Ashworth, n 2 above, 185.

[55] *The Times*, 7 January 2004.

This latest policy will strike many people as deeply unfair. It combines taxation and injustice in a single Act. Surely the punishment should fit the crime, not somebody's bank balance. It is right to use discretion when people can't pay fines, but it is wrong to inflate fines simply because somebody is wealthy.

Underlying this view of unfairness is the perception that increasing fines on the basis of means would penalize those who have escaped poverty through prudence. However, in striving to achieve fairness through equality of impact, courts cannot be involved in value judgements that examine the reasons for affluence or poverty in an attempt to distinguish between those who are wealthy or poor through luck, inheritance, prudence, or ability. Achieving fairness in the criminal justice system in an unjust world will always be aspirational and never perfect. The criminal justice system should at least aim to ensure that financial penalties, which are easily adjustable, impose the same punishment on differently circumstanced offenders for the same offence. As Rawls argues, social institutions should be arranged so that inequalities of wealth and income work to the advantage of those who are worse off, rather than those who are better off.[56]

If the system is properly implemented, the argument that adjusting fines upwards is unfair or disproportionate is hard to sustain. If the number of units or days is determined on the basis of harm and culpability and only then the amount of each unit calculated according to means, there can be no issue of a disproportionate fine. As Ashworth points out, there is no conflict between the principle of equal impact and the proportionality principle. Proportionality only has a role in relation to estimating the gravity of the offence and culpability of the offender, taking account of relevant aggravating and mitigating factors.[57] This is made quite clear where the fine is announced in terms of the number of 'units' or 'days'. Indeed, if only the number of days (or units) is announced, the issue of apparently disproportionate fines is avoided.[58] In Sweden, day fine sentences are reported in newspapers in terms of the numbers of days only. This has been explained on the grounds that the monetary amount is seen as an uninteresting administrative detail or is treated as confidential to avoid violating the offender's privacy.[59] Adopting a unit measure for fines which uses a unit of income or financial deprivation also avoids any conflict between the principles of equality and equal impact. By reframing the punishment in unit terms it becomes possible to assert that the same punishment is being imposed irrespective of the wealth of the offender.

Reporting only the number of units or days would also address the problem of very low fines for poor offenders being seen as a meaningless or insufficient sanction. If the possibility of disproportionately heavy sanctions for minor offences is seen to be a problem, it can be addressed by excluding minor offences from the

[56] J Rawls, *Justice as Fairness: A Restatement* (Cambridge, MA: Harvard University Press, 2001), 42–3.

[57] Ashworth, n 2 above, 253.

[58] In Sweden it seems that only the number of days is reported and not the amount of the fine: Eriksson and Goodin, n 52 above, 131. In Germany both the number of units and the amount of the fine must be published in the court's decision: Criminal Code, StGB § 40(4).

[59] Eriksson and Goodin, n 52 above, 131.

day fine system—as is the case in Germany, Sweden, and Norway. Imposing an upper limit on the amount that can be awarded per unit can also avoid fines which may appear preposterous for a minor transgression. Commentators have suggested that the maximum unit amount in the abandoned English system was too high and considerably higher than the maximum in the successful pilot projects. However, such concessions compromise the principle of equality. The system in Finland has survived publicity given to fines imposed which appear to be very high for traffic offences. For example, a Formula 1 driver was given 12 day fines which translated to €30,000 for illegally transporting snowmobiles in 2005 and a speeding fine of €40,000 was imposed on a 23-year-old heir to a family fortune in 2000. In 2009 a company owner was fined almost €112,000 for travelling at 82 kilometres per hour in an area with a 60 kilometres per hour limit.[60]

These fines seem to be accepted by the public in Finland without protest, although the International Press has reported the cases with headlines such as 'Highway Robbery' and 'Fineland'. A study in 2002 found that four out of five respondents regarded the day fine system as fair and just and only 17 per cent considered day fines for traffic violations to be too severe.[61] In Finland the minimum amount of a day fine is €6 but there is no upper limit. The day fine system applies to a wide range of offences. Not all minor offences attract a day fine, some attract a fixed 'petty fine', but the range of offences that attract day fines is nevertheless broad. Speeding, for example, attracts a petty fine if the offender exceeds the speed limit by up to 20 kilometres per hour but a day fine if the limit is exceeded by 20 kilometres per hour. The anomalies this can cause could give rise to criticism. It is answered by the argument that it is fairer for at least part of the system of fining to have equal impact on offenders than for none of it to do so.

Day/unit fines unduly restrict discretion

An argument sometimes advanced against day fines is that they place too great a restriction on the discretion of the court to impose a sentence that is appropriate given all the circumstances of an individual case.[62] This argument is hard to follow. The discretion as to the number of day fines appropriate to the particular offence remains. The system merely constrains the value of each unit in accordance with the principle of equal impact. Similarly, an objection to the abandoned English scheme was the lack of flexibility because of the relatively few number of units available. This could be remedied by a higher maximum number of units and is not a principled objection.

[60] Examples taken from *Helsingin Sanomat*, International Edition.

[61] T Lappi-Seppala, 'Crime Prevention and Community Sanctions in Scandinavia', Resource Material Series No 74 (Tokyo: United Nations Asia and Far East Institute for the Prevention of Crime and Treatment of Offenders (UNAFEI), 2008), 29.

[62] New South Wales Law Reform Commission, n 25 above, para 3.14.

The two issues that appear to present the greatest obstacles to the adoption of unit fines are first, problems of implementation and means assessment, and secondly, privacy. Another issue relates to the difficulty in sentencers accepting fines as an intermediate sanction for a wider range of offences than is currently the case and as an alternative to imprisonment. However, this is a reservation about the potential of unit fines to reduce incarceration rates for reasons such as public perception, rather than a principled objection to such an approach.

Assessing means and administrative problems

There are many issues to be resolved in designing a day or unit fine system including the proportion of an offender's disposable income or degree of economic deprivation that a unit should represent. In Sweden, the degree of economic deprivation imposed is relatively modest. In Germany it is harsher.[63] The scale of day fine units available is another issue, while in Sweden, day fine sentences are intended for use for less serious offences than is the case in Germany. The range of day fine units is therefore limited to from 1 to 120 (180 for multiple offences). The scale is the same in Finland. In Germany the scale is from 1 to 360 (and up to 720 days in the case of exceptional and serious offences and aggregate offences) because of the wider range of offences covered by the system.[64]

Any day or unit fine system also faces the issue of accurately assessing means. The difficulty and the expense of administering such a scheme are seen as major obstacles. This is exacerbated by the absence of readily available information about means. In Europe there are two approaches to this. In Sweden and Finland assessing the means of the offender is facilitated by access to income tax returns. The calculation is dauntingly complex in Sweden, but possible because courts have legal access to income and tax records.[65] The calculation is based on gross annual income, with deductions for business expenses and living expenses, dependants, and partner's income. Adjustments are also made for capital wealth and for significant debts.[66] In Finland the day fine is usually one-half of daily disposable income. Daily disposable income is considered to be 1/60th part of the person's mean monthly income after taxes, social security payments, and a basic living allowance have been deducted. Income is calculated on the basis of the latest taxation data. Information for Finnish citizens and permanent residents can be accessed by data-link. While the courts can access income tax information, it seems, in Sweden at least, that this is rarely invoked. Day fine units are routinely valued according to self-reported income information.[67]

Courts in Germany have no access to an offender's income or tax records. The day fine value is the net daily income which is not discounted for financial

63 Hillsman, n 47 above, 81.
64 § 40, 54 StGB (Criminal Code).
65 Hillsman, n 47 above, 80.
66 Ibid, 81.
67 J Greene, 'The Staten Island Day-fine Experiment' in DC McDonald, J Greene, and C Worzella (eds), *Day Fines in American Courts: The Staten Island and Milwaukee Experiments* (Washington, DC: National Institute of Justice, 1992), 25.

responsibilities. It is taken to be equivalent to the daily net income that the offender would have forfeited had she been imprisoned instead. Courts rely upon information from the police on employment status, occupation, and living circumstances, supplemented by a brief oral investigation by the judge. Judges have the power to best guess the offender's income, an outcome which is subject to appeal.[68]

The discussion of the European systems demonstrates that the administrative burden of assessing disposable income is considerable and for this reason exempting minor offences is attractive. However, in jurisdictions like England and Wales and Australia where fines are predominantly used for regulatory and minor infringements, this is the area where inequity is most pronounced. Flat-rate penalties imposed by penalty or infringement notices also have an inequitable impact on low-income and disadvantaged offenders. And there is also the problem of the disparity between court-imposed fines and fixed fines imposed by penalty or infringement notices if only the former are subject to a unit fine system. A compromise would be to adopt a more streamlined approach for penalty and infringement notices rather than exempting them from the system altogether. One suggestion has been to set the standard fixed penalty for an offence on the basis of average annual earnings. In accepting an infringement notice, offenders would have to nominate their income on a progressive scale. The rate would then be reduced or increased based on the ratio of the offender's income to average income so that offenders earning half the average income would be half the standard penalty and those earning double would pay double the standard penalty.[69] Another suggestion, which is being considered by the New South Wales Law Reform Commission, is to provide a concession rate for penalty notice fines for people on low incomes, which is either fixed or determined by a formula.[70]

It has been suggested that the main problem encountered in administering a day fine system in the United States was not in assessing means to compute fine amounts. The courts had little difficulty with this. Rather, the problem lay in monitoring and enforcing fine collections.[71] Zedlewski's suggested solution is to move the collection process out of the courts. In Australia, at least, considerable efforts have been made in recent years to overhaul the fine collection processes and collection rates have improved. Fine collection is unlikely to be a significant obstacle to implementing a day fine scheme.

Privacy

The privacy objection to unit fines is often raised as an obstacle to implementing a unit or day fine system. Disclosing income tax data in particular may be seen

[68] Hillsman, n 47 above, 82.

[69] This suggestion has been advocated by the Tasmanian Council of Social Security (TasCOSS) and the Greens: Tasmanian Social Policy Council, Discussion Paper towards the Development of Formal TasCOSS Policy in Relation to Income Based Monetary Penalties, July 2006.

[70] New South Wales Law Reform Commission, *Penalty Notices*, Consultation Paper 10 (Sydney: New South Wales Law Reform Commission, 2010), 131–3.

[71] Zedlewski, n 32 above, 10.

as an invasion of privacy. However, whilst information privacy is undoubtedly a well-recognized human right, it is not an absolute right. The right to privacy in Article 17 ICCPR, Article 8 ECHR, and in the Victorian Charter and Australian Capital Territory Human Rights Act is a qualified right. Interference with privacy is justified if it is in accordance with the law, is necessary in a democratic society for the pursuit of legitimate aims, and is not disproportionate to the object pursued. Legislation disclosing income tax data to courts for the purpose of facilitating the imposition of fines of equal impact could be regarded as a sufficiently important aim to justify the interference. Even if the commission of very minor offences requires access to income data, the law could be said to be proportional and parsimonious if the number of units rather than the monetary value of the fine was published by the court.

Personal information held by governments, such as income tax data, is commonly protected by privacy or data protection legislation.[72] But there are exemptions for disclosures required by or made in connection with legal proceedings or for law enforcement purposes.[73] In Australia, taxation legislation protects the confidentiality of taxpayer information, but there are exceptions which are designed to reflect the principle that disclosure should be permitted if the public benefit derived from the disclosure outweighs privacy.[74] A specific exception for disclosure to courts and law enforcement agencies would conform to this principle.

Whilst interference with the right to privacy by providing courts with access to income tax records can be justified under human rights principles, this may not protect it from popular criticism. As mentioned above, one way of addressing public concern with disclosing the income of defendants who are fined would be to announce the fine in units only. In Australia, where the legislation in most jurisdictions specifies the maximum fine for an offence in units rather than dollars, expressing fines in units is already familiar. Rather than accessing income tax records, courts could direct the offender to make a declaration as to his financial capacity, as is done in New Zealand for fines of $100 or more where the court is uncertain of capacity to pay. The declaration requires offenders to list all sources of income and assets as well as outgoings.[75]

7. A Comprehensive Unit Fine System

The fairest way of imposing fines that impact equally on offenders of differing means is to adopt a unit fine system which covers a broad range of offences. While England has abandoned the old rule that fines should not be increased for the rich, the English experience suggests that allowing fines to be increased is not as effective at ensuring equality of impact as a unit fine system. After the abolition of unit fines

[72] Data Protection Act 1998 (UK); Privacy Act 1988 (Cth).
[73] Data Protection Act 1998 (UK), s 35; Privacy Act 1988 (Cth), s 14.
[74] See eg Taxation Administration Act 1953 (Cth), Sch 1, Division 355, s 355–1.
[75] Sentencing Act 2002 (NZ), s 42.

in 1993 the level of fining not only declined but the average fine rose for the unemployed and decreased for the employed.[76] Moreover, there is evidence that magistrates differ in their willingness to increase fines for the wealthy—with the result that there are disparities in fining wealthy offenders. Since 2008 the Magistrates' Court Sentencing Guidelines have introduced much more structure into fining by requiring fines to be first calculated as a percentage of weekly income before turning to the financial circumstances of the offender to determine weekly income and the amount of the fine.[77] It is not yet clear how effective these guidelines are in fostering a common approach and ensuring equal impact. The guidelines do not apply to the Crown Court or to fines imposed by means of a fixed penalty notice.

8. The Relevance of Employment

Imposing fines in units rather than in money avoids infringing the principle of equality before the law and, at the same time, it satisfies the principle of equal impact. But the two principles cannot so easily be reconciled in relation to the relevance of employment status. Taking employment status into account contradicts the principle of equality while satisfying the principle of equal impact.

There are three ways in which employment status can be used to reduce sentence:

- a good employment record can be regarded as a mitigating factor;
- loss of career can be regarded as a collateral consequence of the offence justifying a reduced sentence; and
- employment status may result in a lesser sentence to avoid loss of employment and hardship to the offender's family.

A good employment record is commonly relied upon in pleas in mitigation. In their empirical study of personal mitigation Jacobson and Hough found that having a steady job was one of the more influential mitigating factors, although interviews with judges showed that they were divided on the issue.[78] Some judges who scored a steady job as 'minimal/no impact' in a burglary scenario suggested that this factor made the offender more culpable as there was little reason or excuse for committing an acquisitive crime. In contrast, those who scored the employment factor highly reasoned that a good employment record was an indication they were less likely to re-offend. Comments suggesting a steady job is mitigating because it demonstrates responsibility and organisation carry an inference of the moral or social superiority of a person with a good employment record. This involves the same kind of social accounting

[76] A Ashworth, *Sentencing and Criminal Justice* (4th edn, Cambridge: Cambridge University Press, 2005), 307.

[77] Ashworth, n 2 above, 333.

[78] J Jacobson and M Hough, *Mitigation: The Role of Personal Factors in Sentencing* (London: Prison Reform Trust, 2007), 17–18, 37.

reasoning that is criticized in the context of giving credit to offenders for worthy social contributions. As Ashworth argues, such 'social accounting' is not the role of the courts, whose task is to impose sentence for the particular crime committed.[79] Moreover, treating a good employment record as mitigating clearly provides a source of mitigation that is not open to the unemployed and is therefore discriminatory and objectionable.[80]

Loss of profession or career is sometimes regarded as a mitigating factor. In Sweden, the Criminal Code expressly provides that loss or likely loss of employment can qualify as a mitigating factor,[81] apparently because this itself is a form of punishment. English decisions suggest that this may be the case when the crime is unrelated to the offender's employment. But where the offence arises out of employment and is a breach of trust, no allowance should be made for such collateral matters.[82] In Australia the High Court has accepted that it is legitimate to take into account collateral consequences such as loss of employment.[83] However, as with giving credit for a good employment record, to do so is discriminatory because it operates in favour of professional classes particularly and is not a form of mitigation available to the unemployed or those whose criminal record is no barrier to employment.[84]

Courts commonly try to impose a sentence that ensures an offender with a job is able to keep it to avoid hardship to the offender's family.[85] Being employed may also be seen as positive in terms of rehabilitation prospects. An offender with a job may be regarded as a better risk. Again, the consequence is that offenders convicted of exactly the same offence may be treated differently on the basis of their employment status—the unemployed offender will not have access to this source of mitigation. Tonry and Morris[86] have argued that disallowing mitigation for loss of employment on grounds of the principles of equality and proportionality is applying a principle of equality of suffering. They argue that the principle of parsimony should be given greater weight than the principle of proportionality. Proportionality should only be a limiting principle, one that sets loose upper and lower limits. The principle of parsimony justifies reducing a sentence to preserve employment when the reduced punishment is as likely to be no less effective than the greater punishment.

Ashworth, on the other hand, while alert to the claims of equal impact and parsimony, argues that the principle of equality before the law is fundamental and should prevail over the principle of parsimony in individual sentencing decisions

[79] Ashworth, n 2 above, 182.
[80] Ibid, 184.
[81] Swedish Criminal Code, Ch 29, para 5, cited by Ashworth, n 2 above, 183.
[82] Ashworth, n 2 above, 184, citing Sentencing Guidelines Council, *Theft and Burglary other than in a Dwelling* (London: Sentencing Guidelines Council, 2008), 11.
[83] *Ryan* (2001) 206 CLR 267 at [54] (McHugh J).
[84] Ashworth, n 2 above, 185.
[85] Ibid, 98.
[86] N Morris and MH Tonry, *Between Prison and Probation: Intermediate Punishments in a Rational Sentencing System* (New York: Oxford University Press, 1990).

and that no weight should be given to employment status.[87] In weighing the two principles he argues that their wider social effects should be considered, as well as their intrinsic strengths:[88]

> Discrimination in the criminal justice system may alienate sections of the community and contribute to racial tensions or class divisions, as well as undermining respect for the administration of justice. Moreover, Morris and Tonry's approach is not the only possible one. They seem to assume the principle of parsimony entails the reduction of individual sentences wherever possible; another interpretation is that it requires a general lowering of punishment levels and expansion of community sanctions, and not discriminatory distinctions between individual offenders.

9. Conclusions

The above discussion of financial circumstances and employment status focuses very narrowly on two factors of personal mitigation. Ashworth's contribution to this debate has been much wider. He has, for example, considered the importance of how 'equity factors', namely personal mitigation, which is unrelated to the culpability of the offender or the seriousness of the offence, can be taken into account in a principled manner. Factors such as old age, disability, ill-health, social deprivation, financial circumstances, employment status, and impact of the sanction on dependants all have an intuitive claim to sentence reduction. However, as Ashworth argues, if they are to be recognized as mitigating factors, there should be a principled and coherent basis for doing so. Mercy is an unsatisfactory justification because it is discretionary and therefore uncertain.[89] One principle that he has developed over a number of years to justify personal mitigation is the principle of equality of treatment. In recognition of the fact that the same sentence may have a disproportionately severe impact on certain offenders, the principle of equal impact requires that the quantum of punishment should be adjusted where inequalities in impact are clear, such as in the case of severe illness or pregnancy and where prison conditions fall below minimum standards. Just as the principle of proportionality can be accommodated by announcing a fine in penalty units, in the case of severe illness for example, Ashworth and Player have argued that the court should announce both the proportionate sentence and the adjusted sentence in a particular case.[90] Selecting financial circumstances and employment status as a focus for discussion has demonstrated how Ashworth has developed the principle of equal treatment and attempted to reconcile and balance differing conceptions of the principle of equality with other principles such as proportionality and parsimony.

[87] Ibid, 250–1, 256.

[88] Ibid, 258.

[89] von Hirsch and Ashworth, n 10 above, Appendix 1.

[90] A Ashworth and E Player, 'Sentencing, Equal Treatment and the Impact of Sanctions' in A Ashworth and M Wasik (eds), *Fundamentals of Sentencing Theory* (Oxford: Clarendon Press, 1998), 272.

Arguing for a unit fine system that allows financial circumstances to increase the amount of a fine, and against taking a good employment record or loss of employment into account in imposing sentence can be criticized on the basis that it is engaging in social engineering and that unequal distribution of wealth and employment opportunities should be tackled by means other than sentencing. Ashworth's response does not contest this, but he argues that it is inappropriate for the criminal justice system to exacerbate social injustices and that moderating inequalities is a worthy goal. Similarly, in defending socially sensitive sentencing, Zedner points out that there is a significant difference between insisting that criminal justice should aspire to social justice and the unrealistic claim that criminal justice has the potential to become an engine of social justice.[91]

Wherever one stands on the issues of unit fines or the relevance of employment status to sentencing decisions, Ashworth has unquestionably made an important contribution to such debates by clarifying the issues and advocating a principled approach to the sentencing task. Using equality principles and the principle of proportionality, he has argued that a unit fine system is a much fairer system of imposing financial penalties.[92] This essay has endeavoured to examine the obstacles to the adoption of a unit or day fine scheme, or in the case of England and Wales, the obstacles to reversing the 1993 decision to abandon them. It is argued that the three main objections to a unit fine system—unfairness, privacy, and cost and inefficiency—are unfounded. The claim that it is unfair to inflate fines for the wealthy because this penalizes the prudent is countered by the point that perfect fairness is unattainable and in seeking to ensure equal impact of a financial penalty, courts cannot look behind the causes of poverty or wealth. Privacy considerations can be alleviated by a unit fine system which only announces the number of units in court and not the amount of the fine. And in so far as allowing courts access to income tax information and financial circumstances infringes the right to privacy, this is a justifiable infringement to facilitate the imposition of financial penalties of equal impact.

Arguably the greatest stumbling block to the introduction of a unit fine system is the problem of assessing means and the time and cost of doing so. Problems with accurately assessing means are commonly raised as an objection to unit fine schemes. The ability of the wealthy to hide financial circumstances and the difficulty of assessing the means of those who derive their income from illicit means are raised as obstacles. Administrative efficiency is the reason some unit fine systems exempt court-imposed fines for minor offences from the scheme. And administrative efficiency is the justification for fixed penalties imposed by penalty notices. But the principle of equality before the law is a fundamental principle which should not 'simply be traded for gains in efficiency and so forth . . . This is

[91] L Zedner, 'Reflections on Criminal Justice as a Social Institution' in D Downes, D Hobbs, and T Newburn (eds), *The Eternal Recurrence of Crime and Control: Essays in Honour of Paul Rock* (Oxford: Oxford University Press, 2010) 69, 90.

[92] Ashworth, n 2 above, 253, 331.

not to say it should be regarded as absolute and inviolable.'[93] As Ashworth recognizes, compromises are necessary. The standardized nature of calculations in any unit fine system to achieve relatively rapid processing of large numbers of cases in the lower courts is necessary. In Ashworth's words: 'Such systems can therefore claim greater equality of impact, not perfect equality. So long as the compromise is relatively generous to those least able to pay, it may be acceptable.'[94]

In the case of penalty units, Ashworth argues there is a case for re-examining the impact of fixed penalties on the economically disadvantaged.[95] Given that an increasing number of offences are dealt with in this manner, this is particularly important. Worthy of consideration are the proposals discussed above for a system of income-based fixed penalties, or at least concessions for people on low incomes.

The difficulties in implementing a unit fine scheme in common law countries are not insurmountable. Unit or day fines work successfully in countries such as Germany, Sweden, and Finland. By not embracing the concept, the opportunity of doing justice to difference and rebuilding fines as a credible punishment has been lost.

[93] Ibid, 258. [94] Ibid, 254. [95] Ibid.

15

Sentencing Women: Towards Gender Equality

Elaine Player

1. Overview

Discussion about the sentencing of women has tended to focus on the fact that they appear to be treated less severely than men and to question whether this reflects a degree of leniency by the courts or is a consequence of their less serious offending, fewer previous convictions, and greater likelihood to plead guilty. Thirty years of empirical research has revealed a relatively complex picture in which sentencers take account of different considerations and give different weight to mitigating factors when sentencing men and women. More recently, the legitimacy of these differential practices has been brought sharply into focus by the passage of the Equality Acts of 2006 and 2010 which impose a Gender Equality Duty (GED) on all public authorities, requiring them to be proactive in eliminating discrimination and harassment and to promote equality of opportunity between men and women. This GED applies to the work of all criminal justice agencies and the Ministry of Justice has pledged to move beyond minimal compliance. The criminal justice context into which it has been introduced has increasingly recognized gender differences in offenders' pathways to crime, risks of re-offending and resettlement needs, and distinct policies for women have developed to take account of this and to address problems that arise as a result of their minority status. But the implications of the GED for sentencing have received scant attention.

Andrew Ashworth's substantial contribution to contemporary debates on sentencing has, however, identified some important questions that arise when considering how the principle of equality before the law can be applied within a statutory sentencing framework that pursues a number of potentially competing objectives and accords sentencers considerable discretion.[1] He considers what weight should be given to the principle of non-discrimination in relation to other relevant principles, and whether the GED requires sentencers to avoid discrimination only in relation to their own decisions or whether it summons a broader approach that attempts to counteract inequalities emanating from other social institutions

[1] A Ashworth, *Sentencing and Criminal Justice* (5th edn, Cambridge: Cambridge University Press, 2010), 240.

and practices. These and other questions provide a starting point for the development of discussion in this important area of sentencing policy and practice.

This essay opens the debate to expose what are potentially radical implications for sentencing policy and practice. Specifically it argues that, within the current policy framework, the GED can be used to justify changes that incorporate an unequivocal commitment to concepts of social justice. Whilst this depends in large measure upon a more equitable allocation of punishments and rehabilitative opportunities to men and women, equality in sentencing cannot be achieved by focusing solely on matters of fair distribution. It must also embody a critical awareness of how conceptions of fairness and just treatment are shaped and rationalized by prevailing cultural norms and values that support and legitimize certain institutional rules and outcomes rather than others.

2. Legislating Equality

The Equality Act 2006 imposed specific equality duties on public authorities in relation to groups who share the following characteristics: age, disability, gender, gender reassignment, race, religion, and sexual orientation.[2] It differed from earlier equality legislation in two important respects: by requiring public authorities to be proactive in eliminating discrimination and harassment, rather than reacting to complaints brought by individuals; and by requiring public authorities to promote equality of opportunity as well as avoid discrimination. The GED came into effect in April 2007 and imposed a *general duty* on all public authorities to adopt a proportionate approach to the promotion of equality, prioritizing actions that address the most significant inequalities and which deliver the most effective outcomes. Listed public bodies also had *specific duties* that were intended to assist them in carrying out the general duty; such as the requirement to consult with staff and stakeholders in developing a gender equality scheme for their institution, monitoring change and publishing progress reports, and conducting and publishing gender impact statements on new legislation and policies. Statutory enforcement was provided by the creation of a single Commission for Equality and Human Rights whose mandate suggests that the concept of equal opportunities should be interpreted widely.[3] In relation to the GED the Equal Opportunities Commission made clear that this was to extend beyond procedural fairness to include equality in the delivery of certain outcomes, 'specific identifiable improvements in policies, in the way services are delivered, in the exercise of public functions and in outcomes for employees and service users'.[4]

[2] Equality Act 2006, s 10(2).

[3] Ibid, ss 4–12.

[4] Equal Opportunities Commission, *Developing Gender Equality Objectives and a Gender Equality Scheme: Guidance for GB Public Authorities* (London: Equal Opportunities Commission, 2007), 3.

The Equality Act 2010 consolidated what had become a fragmented body of equality legislation, and introduced a new Public Sector Equality Duty[5] that covers all the protected characteristics:[6]

A public authority must, in the exercise of its functions, have due regard to the need to:

(a) eliminate discrimination, harassment, victimisation and any other conduct that is prohibited by or under this Act;
(b) advance equality of opportunity between persons who share a relevant protected characteristic and persons who do not share it;
(c) foster good relations between persons who share a relevant protected characteristic and those who do not share it.[7]

The duty to advance equality of opportunities requires public authorities to:

(a) remove or minimise disadvantages suffered by persons who share a relevant protected characteristic that are connected to that characteristic;
(b) take steps to meet the needs of persons who share a relevant protected characteristic that are different from the needs of persons who do not share it;
(c) encourage persons who share a relevant protected characteristic to participate in public life or in any other activity in which participation by such persons is disproportionately low.[8]

In achieving these objectives it is permissible to treat some parties more favourably than others.[9] What is referred to as 'positive action' can be taken if any of the following circumstances exist: first, if individuals suffer a disadvantage that is connected to a protected characteristic; secondly, if those who share a protected characteristic have different needs from other groups; and finally, if the level of participation in an activity is disproportionately low amongst those who share a protected characteristic.[10] The positive action taken should be a proportionate response that is directed to overcome or minimize the disadvantage, meet the identified needs, or enable and encourage participation in previously under-represented activities.[11]

These measures have potentially radical implications for sentencing practice. In relation to the sentencing of women they require the courts to avoid discrimination on grounds of sex and to advance equality of opportunity by responding to gender-specific disadvantages experienced by women and by meeting their gender-specific needs.

[5] Equality Act 2010, Sch 19 specifies government departments (with limited exceptions) as public authorities subject to the Duty.

[6] The characteristics protected by the equality duty are: age, disability, gender reassignment, pregnancy and maternity, race, religion or belief, sex, sexual orientation. Equality Act 2010, s 149(7).

[7] Equality Act 2010, s 149(1).

[8] Ibid, s 149(3).

[9] Ibid, s 149(5)–(6).

[10] Ibid, s 158(1).

[11] Ibid, s 158(2).

3. The Sentencing Framework in England and Wales

The constitutional position in England and Wales is that Parliament determines sentencing policy, within a regulatory framework set by the European Convention on Human Rights and European Community law, and the judiciary apply the legal principles to individual cases. The principle of equality is deeply embedded in concepts of fairness in English sentencing, upholding rule of law values that ostensibly apply to everyone irrespective of their sex, race, religion, sexual orientation, or social class.[12] This concept of universality is supported by a commitment to impartial and consistent decision-making, embodied in the claim that like cases should be treated alike. The English judiciary has, however, insisted that rigid rules are incapable of taking account of the complex combination of facts that arise in individual cases and that a degree of judicial discretion is essential for the just application of legal rules and principles. Consistent sentencing has consequently been defined and pursued in relation to a conformity of approach, rather than a conformity of outcome. In recent years, however, the exercise of individual discretion has been increasingly shaped by the development of sentencing guidelines, initially by the Court of Appeal and more recently by statutory bodies, currently the Sentencing Council.[13] The past 20 years have also witnessed an unprecedented level of legislation that has politicized sentencing policy and brought the senior judiciary into open conflict with government ministers.[14]

These developments have revealed sentencing practice to be a normative as well as an instrumental or technical process, expressing cultural values and legal principles that are pursued and given meaning within a specific political context. Nowhere is this more clearly illustrated than in the shifting priorities accorded to the social purposes of sentencing that were pursued in successive legislation between the Criminal Justice Acts of 1991 and 2003. In 1991 retributive desert or proportionality was established as the primary sentencing rationale, which could only be replaced by incapacitation in cases of sexual or violent offences if it was deemed necessary to protect the public from serious harm.[15] During the 1990s, however, increasingly punitive populist strategies narrowed the reach of proportionality and severely restricted judicial discretion by introducing mandatory and

[12] See Ashworth, n 1 above, Ch 7.

[13] The Sentencing Advisory Panel established under the Crime and Disorder Act 1998, ss 80–1, initially advised the Court of Appeal on the formulation of guidelines for specific types of case; the Sentencing Guidelines Council created by the Criminal Justice Act 2003 took over the function of establishing sentencing guidelines from the Court of Appeal, advised by the Sentencing Advisory Panel; the Sentencing Council was created under the Coroners and Justice Act 2009 and replaced both the Sentencing Advisory Panel and Sentencing Guidelines Council.

[14] See most notably response to proposals for mandatory and minimum sentences in Crime (Sentences) Bill by Lord Taylor, 'Continuity and Change in the Criminal Law' (1996) 7 King's College Law Journal 1; Lord Bingham, 'The Courts and the Constitution' (1996) 7 King's College Law Journal 12; also comments by Lord Taylor and Lord Williams of Mostyn in Hansard, HL vol 572, cols 1025–33 (23 May 1996).

[15] Criminal Justice Act 1991, ss 1(2)(b) and 2(2)(b).

minimum sentences in the Crime (Sentences) Act 1997.[16] The Labour government that won office later that year did nothing to arrest this process and over the next 13 years sentencing objectives were increasingly focused on public protection and the problem of persistent offending. The Criminal Justice Act 2003 expanded the range of mandatory and minimum sentences for serious and persistent offenders, and whilst the principle of proportionality remained an important consideration it was no longer statutorily defined as the primary sentencing rationale. Instead, sentencers were now required to have regard to the full range of sentencing purposes:

(a) the punishment of offenders,
(b) the reduction of crime (including its reduction by deterrence),
(c) the reform and rehabilitation of offenders,
(d) the protection of the public, and
(e) the making of reparation by offenders to persons affected by their offences.[17]

Ashworth described this as 'a major step backwards' that would lead to chaos, and roundly criticized the government for returning to 'the worst of "pick and mix" sentencing'.[18] He warned that, in the absence of a primary rationale, section 142 represented an invitation to inconsistent decision-making and undermined the point of having guidelines. The guidance issued to the courts by the Sentencing Guidelines Council confirmed that the legislation did not specify any one purpose as being more important than any other and stated that it was for sentencers to decide 'the manner in which they apply'.[19] Although this appears to allow judges and magistrates a free rein to follow their own philosophical preferences, the Sentencing Guidelines Council issued a clear instruction in the next paragraph—'[t]he sentencer must start by considering the seriousness of the offence'[20]—which was followed immediately by a similarly prescriptive direction:

A court is required to pass a sentence that is commensurate with the seriousness of the offence.[21]

The guideline therefore established that offence seriousness should be the starting point and that the principle of proportionality should set the parameters of the sentence. This is consistent with provisions in the legislation that restrict the use of custodial and community penalties, requiring the courts to be satisfied that the

[16] Crime (Sentences) Act 1997, ss 2–4.
[17] Criminal Justice Act 2003, s 142.
[18] A Ashworth and E Player, 'Criminal Justice Act 2003: The Sentencing Provisions' (2005) 68 MLR 822, 825; Ashworth, n 1 above, 74.
[19] Sentencing Guidelines Council, *Overarching Principles—Seriousness* (London: Sentencing Guidelines Secretariat, 2004), para 1.2. Available at <http://www.sentencingcouncil.org.uk/docs/web_seriousness_guideline.pdf> accessed 21 March 2012.
[20] Ibid, para 1.3.
[21] Ibid, para 1.4.

offence is sufficiently serious to warrant such a sentence, rather than a lower tariff penalty:

> A court must not pass a community sentence on an offender unless it is of the opinion that the offence, or the combination of the offence and one or more offences associated with it, was serious enough to warrant such a sentence[22] . . . the restrictions on liberty imposed by the order must be such as in the opinion of the court are commensurate with the seriousness of the offence, or the combination of the offence and one or more offences associated with it . . .[23]
>
> The court must not pass a custodial sentence unless it is of the opinion that the offence, or the combination of the offence and one or more offences associated with it, was so serious that neither a fine alone nor a community sentence can be justified for the offence[24] . . . [T]he custodial sentence must be for the shortest term (not exceeding the permitted maximum) that in the opinion of the court is commensurate with the seriousness of the offence, or the combination of the offence and one or more offences associated with it.[25]

Sentencing women

It is well documented that the criminal justice system is predominantly concerned to regulate the criminal behaviour of the male majority of offenders and that women comprise only a small proportion of those arrested, prosecuted, convicted, and sentenced.[26] Currently women represent around one in five defendants sentenced by the courts in England and Wales, and this figure has remained relatively stable over time. Compared with men, women are more likely to receive sentences at the lower end of the tariff and this has raised questions as to whether they enjoy a degree of chivalrous leniency that is not extended to male offenders. Empirical enquiries have consistently thrown doubt on this conclusion, arguing that differential sentencing decisions owe much to the fact that women tend to be convicted for less serious offences than men, possess fewer previous convictions, and are more likely to plead guilty and accept trial in the magistrates' courts where sentencing powers are limited.[27] However, research has also revealed that the courts take account of different factors, and give them different weight in mitigating sentence severity, when the defendant is female rather than male. Studies have repeatedly shown that sentencers selectively focus on the social and domestic circumstances of female defendants, to an extent unmatched when sentencing men, and rely upon stereotypical assumptions about female behaviour in reaching their judgments.[28]

[22] Criminal Justice Act 2003, s 148(1). [23] Ibid, s 148(2)(b).

[24] Ibid, s 152(2). [25] Ibid, s 153(2).

[26] Ministry of Justice, *Statistics on Women and the Criminal Justice System* (London: Ministry of Justice, 2010). Available at <http://www.justice.gov.uk/downloads/publications/statistics-and-data/mojstats/statistics-women-cjs-2010.pdf> accessed 21 March 2012.

[27] See A Morris, *Women, Crime and Criminal Justice* (Oxford: Basil Blackwell, 1987); C Hedderman and L Gelsthorpe (eds), *Understanding the Sentencing of Women*, Home Office Research Study 170 (London: Home Office, 1997); L Gelsthorpe and A Morris, 'Women's Imprisonment in England and Wales: A Penal Paradox' (2002) 2 Criminology and Criminal Justice 277.

[28] See P Carlen, *Women's Imprisonment* (London: Routledge and Kegan Paul, 1983); F Heidensohn, *Women and Crime* (London: Macmillan, 1985); M Eaton, *Justice for Women* (Milton Keynes:

Some of the early studies found that in cases where women's criminality can be understood as compliant with traditional female roles, such as aspiring to be a good mother, the courts treat them less severely than when their crimes fail to fit conventional categories of gender-appropriate behaviour.[29]

A particularly prominent theme that has been challenged in this literature is the notion that criminal behaviour is unnatural for women and reflective of an underlying pathology. A common finding has been that women offenders are repeatedly perceived as lacking agency and often denied full responsibility for their behaviour. This has directed the courts to favour sentences that address the welfare needs of women, rather than those that adopt a primarily retributive response. Research by Gelsthorpe and Loucks[30] revealed how magistrates tend to categorize women offenders as 'troubled' rather than 'troublesome' and how their sentences are principally shaped to respond to their criminogenic 'needs', rather than to deliver a proportionate punishment. Dowds and Hedderman[31] also found that the courts were particularly reluctant to fine women in cases where they would have fined a male offender. Magistrates were concerned that the women's limited resources rendered them incapable of paying an appropriate financial penalty and they feared that the imposition of a fine could have detrimental consequences for the women's domestic situation and especially for any dependent children. As a result, while many women were sentenced below the tariff to a discharge, others were shifted up to a community penalty, particularly where it was felt that the woman could benefit from the supervision and assistance provided by probation. An unintended and harmful consequence of this is that some women have been propelled up the sentencing scale and, in the event of subsequent offending, are at a higher risk of imprisonment because they are perceived to have exhausted the non-custodial options.

Since the publication of Hedderman and Gelsthorpe's[32] research, sentencing trends have shown an increased punitiveness in the sentencing of women which has outpaced a similar trend for men. The use of fines for women has continued to decline, but so too have absolute and conditional discharges, whilst the use of community sentences and imprisonment has grown. There is broad consensus in the research literature that the growth of custodial sentences for women has not

Open University Press, 1986); A Worrall, *Offending Women* (London: Taylor and Francis, 1990); A Wilczynski, 'Mad or Bad? Child-Killers, Gender and the Courts' (1997) 37 British Journal of Criminology 419; L Gelsthorpe and N Loucks, 'Magistrates' Explanations of Sentencing Decisions' in C Hedderman and L Gelsthorpe (eds) *Understanding the Sentencing of Women*, Home Office Research Study 170 (London: Home Office, 1997).

[29] See DP Farrington and A Morris, 'Sex, Sentencing and Reconviction' (1983) 23 British Journal of Criminology, 229; SSM Edwards, *Gender, Sex, and the Law* (London: Croom Helm, 1985). Heidensohn, n 28 above; Morris, n 27 above.

[30] n 28 above.

[31] L Dowds and C Hedderman, 'The Sentencing of Men and Women' in C Hedderman and L Gelsthorpe (eds), *Understanding the Sentencing of Women*, Home Office Research Study 170 (London: Home Office, 1997).

[32] n 27 above.

been caused by a commensurate rise in the seriousness of their offences.[33] Instead, inflationary sentencing practice, and the specific failure of the courts to replace short prison sentences for women with community penalties, appears to have been driven by a number of competing factors that influence judicial reasoning. First, the continued emphasis upon proportionate sentencing may encourage sentencers to be wary of the potential for discrimination that attaches to decisions which rely on the differential qualities of offenders. Secondly, the contemporary politics of criminal justice have promoted a generalized intolerance of crime, supported by legislative change that has increasingly focused on protective sentences and the precautionary management of criminal risk. The inclusion of female criminality within this punitive framework has been supported by media constructions of a new breed of female offender who is portrayed as increasingly mimicking male delinquency and crime.[34] Thirdly, pre-existing equality legislation in the United Kingdom has been designed to prohibit discrimination, rather than confer positive rights to equal treatment.[35] Although anti-discrimination principles have applied to both men and women, the principal 'mischief' the legislation intended to redress has been the discriminatory treatment of women. Sex equality has consequently been understood in terms of women being given access to benefits already enjoyed by men, and frequently its achievement has been conceived in terms of men and women being treated in the same way. Given this heritage, it is perhaps unsurprising that the growth of human rights principles in criminal justice and their inherent commitment to equal treatment has coincided with an increasing convergence in the severity of sentences imposed on men and women. Evidence of increased punitiveness in the sentencing of women has not been restricted to England and Wales but has occurred in other common-law jurisdictions such as the United States and Australia. Meda Chesney-Lind has described this phenomenon as 'vengeful equity' whereby the equal treatment of women has been interpreted as requiring criminal justice responses that are equally punitive to those imposed on men.[36]

[33] Gelsthorpe and Morris, n 27 above; C Hedderman, 'Why are More Women Being Sentenced to Custody?' in G McIvor (ed), *Women Who Offend* (London: Jessica Kingsley, 2004); C Hedderman, 'Government Policy on Women Offenders: Labour's Legacy and the Coalition Challenge' (2010) 12 Punishment and Society 485.

[34] A Hough, 'Judge: "ladette binge-drinking culture" to blame for "plague" of alcohol fuelled violence', *Daily Telegraph*, 28 May 2010, available at <http://www.telegraph.co.uk/news/uknews/crime/7770832/Judge-ladette-binge-drinking-culture-blame-for-plague-of-alcohol-fuelled-violence.html> accessed 21 March 2012; R Ford, 'Ladettes push girl violence to new high: sharp rise in assaults and public disorder', *The Times*, 30 January 2009; M Hickley, 'Rise of the thugettes: quarter of ALL violent assaults in Britain are now carried out by women', *Daily Mail*, 26 May 2009, available at <http://www.dailymail.co.uk/news/article-1187531/Rise-thugettes-Quarter-ALL-violent-assaults-Britain-carried-women.html#ixzz0gMLW02K5> accessed 21 March 2012; G Wilson, 'Shock rise in women who batter men', *The Sun*, 14 September 2009, available at <http://www.thesun.co.uk/sol/homepage/news/2635618/Shocking-400-percent-rise-in-women-who-batter-men.html> accessed 21 March 2012.

[35] See Married Women's Property Acts 1870 and 1872; Representation of the People Act 1928; Equal Pay Act 1970; Sex Discrimination Act 1975.

[36] M Chesney-Lind, 'Patriarchy, Crime and Justice: Feminist Criminology in an Era of Backlash' (2006) 1 Feminist Criminology 6, 17.

Over the past decade a separate policy stream for women has developed in England and Wales that aims to address the 'needs' of women offenders, together with those of women who are at risk of offending, by adopting a holistic approach to their complex problems. As part of the government's wider policy towards gender equality, the Women's Offending Reduction Programme (WORP) was established in 2004 to co-ordinate work across government departments. The *Together Women* programme was launched the following year in five centres in the North of England, with the primary aim of reducing female crime by addressing the needs of female offenders and those at risk of offending. Multi-agency services in these centres target a wide range of problems related to social exclusion, including advice and assistance on housing, debt, training and employment, domestic violence, substance misuse, parenting, and issues concerning low confidence and self-esteem.

A specific scheme to divert women from the criminal process has been piloted as part of the national conditional cautioning framework, enabling women offenders to be steered at an early stage towards a community centre for a full needs-assessment and from there to cross-departmental projects offering personalized support for women with multiple needs.[37] At the other end of the criminal process, the government broadly accepted the recommendations of the Corston Report[38] on vulnerable women in custody. The published response to the report promised a co-ordinated approach to women prisoners that would respond to the disadvantage and adversity that characterized their life experiences and pathways into crime.[39] Yet, despite this degree of cross-departmental commitment, the use of imprisonment for women has continued to rise and to do so at a faster rate than for men. For example, between 1999 and 2009 the number of women entering prison under sentence increased by 66 per cent, compared with 8 per cent for men; and over the decade 2000 to 2010 the female prison population increased by 44 per cent, while the number of male prisoners increased by only 26 per cent.[40]

4. Towards Gender Equality in Sentencing

Sentencing guidance

In its published advice to the Sentencing Guidelines Council on the overarching principles of sentencing, the Sentencing Advisory Panel, chaired by Ashworth,

[37] H Easton, M Silvestri, K Evan, R Mathews, and S Walklate, *Conditional Cautions: Evaluation of the Women Specific Condition Pilot* (London: Ministry of Justice, 2010). Available at <http://www.justice.gov.uk/downloads/publications/research-and-analysis/moj-research/evaluation-women-specific-condition-pilot.pdf> accessed 16 April 2012.

[38] J Corston, *Review of Women with Particular Vulnerabilities in the Criminal Justice System* (London: Home Office, 2007).

[39] Ministry of Justice, *Government Response to the Report by Baroness Corston of a Review of Women with Particular Vulnerabilities in the Criminal Justice System* (Cm 7261, 2007). Available at <http://www.official-documents.gov.uk/document/cm72/7261/7261.pdf> accessed 16 April 2012.

[40] Prison Reform Trust, *Bromley Briefings: Prison Factfile* (London: Prison Reform Trust 2011).

provided a specific briefing on the sentencing of women.[41] In this it argued that the GED introduced by the Equality Act 2006 required the same principles of sentencing to apply to both men and women. However, it qualified this by stating that the ways in which these principles should be put into effect would be likely to vary given the different profiles of male and female offenders. The Panel took the view that many of the concerns that had been expressed about the sentencing of women related to the influence of offender mitigation in reducing culpability. It argued that, in principle, these factors could affect men as well as women, and should therefore be addressed by framing recommendations that were essentially 'gender-neutral'.[42] It emphasized that male and female offenders should not be sentenced on the basis of their sex and that where mitigating factors applied equally to men and women they should have a similar impact on the sentence.

However, it was acknowledged that the incidence of these generic mitigating factors lowering culpability was typically higher when the offender was female, rather than male. As a consequence, the Sentencing Advisory Panel concluded that the existing sentencing framework, when applied to women, generally directs the courts to consider sentences in the lower range of the offence-specific guidelines. Nonetheless, it also recognized that a sentencing system set up primarily to process male offenders may lack sufficient sensitivity to the vulnerabilities and needs of many women offenders and result in unfair treatment and outcomes. The report made reference to a wealth of empirical research that reveals how female offenders are more likely than men to have a history of mental health problems and, most significantly, to be the primary or sole carer of children or other relatives. It also acknowledged that a disproportionate number of women appearing before the courts have suffered physical, sexual, and mental abuse and that such victimization can have significance for sentencing:

> Although there may not be a direct causal link between victimisation and crime, a more constructive response to offending, based on an appreciation of the impact of victimisation on a woman's circumstances and behaviour, may be justified.[43]

So, in addition to the so-called generic factors of mitigation that affect offender culpability, the Sentencing Advisory Panel urges the courts to consider the differential *impact* of sentences on women. Historically, where these considerations have been taken into account they have formed part of the offender's personal mitigation and have not been regarded as categorical factors affecting female offenders as a distinct group. As a consequence the role of impact mitigation has been viewed as problematic in a sentencing framework that prioritizes a retributive rationale.[44] The Panel, however, does acknowledge the collective vulnerability of all female

[41] Sentencing Advisory Panel, *Advice to the Sentencing Guidelines Council: Overarching Principles of Sentencing* (London: Sentencing Advisory Panel, 2010).

[42] Ibid, 68.

[43] Ibid, 73.

[44] Ashworth and Player, n 18 above; S Easton, 'Dangerous Waters: Taking Account of Impact in Sentencing' [2008] Crim LR 105; C Piper, 'Should Impact Constitute Mitigation?: Structured Discretion Versus Mercy' [2007] Crim LR 141.

offenders that arises from their minority status within the criminal justice system. For example, when considering the appropriateness of a prison sentence the Panel advises the courts to take account of the fact that women will generally be held further from their homes than men, due to the small size of the female prison estate and its wide geographical distribution. The impact of this 'will limit family visits and increase the chance of family breakdown and mental depression and isolation for the offender'.[45] The court should also consider that mothers in prison are less likely than fathers to have a partner in the community to look after their children and homes and, as a result, are at greater risk of losing both and face complex problems in relation to resettlement following release. Similarly, the Panel advises that the high incidence of self-harm amongst female prisoners and their heightened risk of suicide should also be factored into the sentencing equation as, again, they reveal the disproportionate and unintended penal impact that imprisonment imposes on women. The Panel recommends that the statutory requirement under section 153 of the 2003 Criminal Justice Act, that a prison sentence should only be imposed if a financial or a community penalty is inappropriate, should be given 'special force in relation to women offenders because of the multiple harms that are likely to result from incarceration'.[46] In order to encourage restraint, it also recommends that when a court is considering a prison sentence for a woman it should always obtain a pre-sentence report and that a defendant should normally be granted bail whilst this is produced.[47]

Similar concerns are acknowledged about the equal impact of non-custodial penalties. Again, women's minority status has resulted in a lack of specialized community provision tailored to their specific needs.[48] The Panel recognizes that in cases where the custodial threshold is met but where a prison sentence is not essential, the courts have more restricted opportunities to find suitable community sentences for women than for men, and that this may result in the courts concluding that a prison sentence is the only realistic option in these circumstances. The Panel's guidance unequivocally states that where a community sentence is deserved, 'the court must not impose a custodial sentence because of a perceived lack of community sentence provision or difficulty in identifying suitable community order requirements'.[49] The Panel also address the risk of 'up-tariffing' that can result from the avoidance of financial penalties for women. It reminds the courts to hold on to the principle of proportionality and recommends that where an offence committed by a woman is insufficiently serious to justify a community order 'the

[45] Sentencing Advisory Panel, n 41 above, 74.

[46] Ibid, 75.

[47] Ibid, 76.

[48] Social Exclusion Task Force, *Short Study on Women Offenders* (London: Ministry of Justice/Cabinet Office, 2009). Available at <http://library.npia.police.uk/docs/cabinetoffice/setf-shortstudy-womenoffenders.pdf> accessed 21 March 2012; Centre for Crime and Justice Studies, *Crime, Courts and Confidence: Report of an Independent Inquiry into Alternatives to Prison* (London: Esmée Fairbairn Foundation, 2004).

[49] Sentencing Advisory Panel, n 41 above, 79.

appropriate sentence is a fine or a discharge' and an offender's low income 'should not prevent the court from imposing a fine'.[50]

The Panel's advice on sentencing women has responded to the weight of research evidence that shows how male and female offenders follow distinctive pathways into crime, present different criminogenic needs, and have different experiences in the criminal justice system. It aims to give effect to the GED by recommending that the same principles of sentencing should apply with equal force to men and women. However, this does not call for a uniformity of treatment, but guides sentencers to adopt practices that treat men and women differently. In particular, gender differences are to be taken into consideration in relation to three specific areas of decision-making: in the identification and meaning attributed to personal mitigation in assessing culpability; in considering the differential punitive impact of sentences; and in responding to the differential provision of services for men and women in both custodial and non-custodial penalties. The focus of this guidance continues to sustain the principle of proportionality, and its recognition of gender diversity is predominantly concerned to avoid discrimination, both in relation to procedural fairness and greater equality of outcomes. However, the Panel's advice is less well-defined in relation to the more innovative elements of the GED, which concern the promotion of equal opportunities and which are unrelated to achieving an equivalence of punitive impact. Although the Panel invites the courts to consider a 'more constructive response to offending' by taking account of indices of social exclusion and personal vulnerability, it is not clear how these factors are to be given meaning and incorporated into a sentencing framework that continues to be dominated by the retributive principle of desert.[51] The high incidence of sexual and violent abuse experienced by female offenders, their caring responsibilities for dependent children and other family members, and the impact their sentence is likely to have on these innocent third parties 'may' be considered relevant, but a principled justification for doing so is not articulated in the Panel's guidance. Those who support 'desert' as the primary sentencing rationale have argued that broader ambitions to moderate the impact of a sentence on offenders or their families should be pursued through means outside the sentencing framework. For example, Sue Easton suggests that the hardship suffered by prisoners' families would be more effectively dealt with by the introduction of more 'family-friendly' policies in relation to visiting arrangements in prison and more generous allowances of home leave.[52]

A different argument was made by the Wedderburn Committee, which argued for criminal justice policies to be consistent with other social policy objectives.[53] The Equality Duty introduced in the 2010 Equality Act requires public authorities to remove or minimize disadvantages associated with a protected characteristic and

[50] Sentencing Advisory Panel, n 41 above, 80.
[51] Sentencing Advisory Panel, n 41 above, para 234.
[52] Easton, n 44 above, 5.
[53] Prison Reform Trust, n 40 above, 78.

to take steps to meet their specific needs.[54] Arguably, this duty requires criminal courts to pursue a concept of justice that enables proportionate sentences to be mitigated in order to serve other statutory purposes of sentencing that advance equality of opportunity. The Ministry of Justice has made clear that sentencers should place greater emphasis upon the prevention of reoffending through rehabilitation, yet the small scale and wide geographical dispersal of women's prisons means that opportunities for skills training and education are more limited and barriers to resettlement are more intractable than in the male system. Under these circumstances, a proportionate sentence of imprisonment upon a female offender could justifiably be replaced by a community penalty in order to facilitate her equal access to rehabilitative services. In this endeavour the sentencing process can be understood as extending beyond the narrow remit of proportionate punishment to become an integral part of a broader system of distributive social justice.

Gender equality and distributive justice

The application of the GED in sentencing requires the courts to adopt a form of distributive justice that actively promotes gender equality and revises the principles that guide decision-making. Dominant in sentencing is the principle of 'desert', but it will be argued that the GED demands that the courts give greater weight than before to the 'needs' of individual offenders in order to facilitate equal treatment. David Miller[55] has defined the concept of desert as a fitting response to an individual performance. In the context of contemporary sentencing a 'fitting response' has been interpreted primarily in relation to retributive values that construe desert as a response that imposes censure and harsh treatment in proportion to the seriousness of the offence. But what is 'deserved' need not be defined solely in retributive terms. Where high levels of social deprivation and exclusion have placed a female offender at an increased risk of offending, it could be argued that she 'deserves' to have her criminogenic needs addressed and be given access to rehabilitative opportunities. Exactly which needs are relevant to sentencing decisions, however, is not clear. One approach is to focus only on those factors that have been identified as predictive of offending, specifically: 'poor cognitive skills, anti-social attitudes and feelings, strong ties to and identification with anti-social/criminal models, weak social ties, difficulty with self-management, dependency on drugs and alcohol, adverse social or family circumstances, unemployment and literacy problems'.[56] But adopting this line of action conflates the concept of need with that of risk and, within the current protective framework of criminal justice policy, tends to lead sentencers to preventative strategies of risk management and an interpretation of equality based upon impartial procedures and universal treatment. Ashworth has been particularly critical of this approach to equal treatment, claiming that it can lead to 'the imposition of more onerous sentences on the

[54] Equality Act 2010, s 149(1).
[55] D Miller, *Principles of Social Justice* (Cambridge, MA: Harvard University Press, 2003), 133.
[56] Gelsthorpe and Morris, n 27 above, 289.

disadvantaged' and 'tends to scapegoat a vulnerable group rather than to seek a longer-lasting solution'.[57]

It is beyond the remit of this essay to explore the gendered nature of risk management in contemporary criminal justice, but it is noteworthy that feminist challenges have successfully questioned the presumption of gender neutrality in the assessment of criminal risk and the consequent over-classification of women offenders.[58] Even when risk factors are 'women centred' their assumed objectivity remains problematic not least because, as Kelly Hannah-Moffat has argued, the calculation of risk rests on untested assumptions and value judgements on the part of officials responsible for completing the evaluations.[59]

An alternative conceptualization of need as a distributive principle looks beyond criminogenic risk factors toward the experience of social harms. David Miller has suggested that the deployment of 'need' as a distributive principle might be defined as that which is minimally necessary to avoid being harmed, and that harm occurs when human experience falls below what is socially defined as a minimally decent life.[60] Recognizing that minimal standards of decency are socially contingent, subject to variation over time and place, it is nonetheless argued that the life experiences of many women offenders, including de facto their offending behaviour, have been harmful to them in ways that fall short of accepted standards of a minimally decent life and consequently create needs to which the state has an obligation to respond. Taking account of offenders' needs is already entrenched in English sentencing, particularly when responding to female crime. As discussed earlier, a separate policy stream has developed to address the needs of women offenders and women at risk of offending. The principal arguments supporting this are contained in a short study by the Social Exclusion Task Force, in which a case is made for a differentiated response to female offenders that is justified in terms of their 'multiple needs' that arise from their 'complex problems':

> Women offenders experience high rates of mental health disorders, victimisation, abuse, and substance misuse, and have low skills and rates of employment. Their specific needs are distinct from those of male offenders.[61]

It argues for the adoption of a broader social-harms approach and supports the conclusions reached by Hedderman et al in their review of the first year of the *Together Women* programme:

> . . . it is possible that adverse experiences, such as childhood abuse, may interact with other areas of criminogenic need. It may be that a history of abuse in itself is not a powerful

[57] Ashworth, n 1 above, 241.

[58] J Belknap and K Holsinger, 'The Gendered Nature of Risk Factors for Delinquency' (2006) 1 Feminist Criminology 48; K Hannah-Moffat, 'Pandora's Box: Risk/Need and Gender Responsive Corrections' (2006) 5 Criminology and Public Policy 183; M Shaw and S Dubois, *Understanding Violence by Women: A Review of the Literature* (Ottawa, Correctional Service of Canada, 1995).

[59] K Hannah-Moffat, 'Moral Agent or Actuarial Subject: Risk and Canadian Women's Imprisonment' (1999) 3 Theoretical Criminology 71.

[60] Miller, n 55 above, 206–7.

[61] Social Exclusion Task Force, n 48 above, 3.

dynamic risk factor for offending in adult life, but if the abuse interacts with other psychological and social processes then the risk of re-offending increases. Thus the conceptual issue with regard to women offenders lies in the question of how adverse life events interact with each other and how, in turn, this interaction relates to offending.[62]

To fulfil the GED it is argued that the courts, as public authorities, must pursue sentencing objectives in ways that extend beyond a formal consistency of procedure and avoidance of discrimination, and engage more directly with a form of distributive justice that is designed to promote equality of opportunity. It requires sentencers to respond to the gendered needs of female offenders and possibly to construe the concept of 'desert' from this perspective.

Beyond distributive justice

Arguments in favour of the redistribution of material resources to address the needs of offending women are clearly central to understanding the implications the GED has for the development of justice in sentencing policy and practice. But arguably there are other implications that the GED has for achieving equality in sentencing which extend beyond material distributions. In relation to social justice more generally, critical theorists such as Michael Walzer[63] and Iris Marion Young[64] argue that focusing exclusively on the distribution of goods and services can effectively obscure the social structures and processes that actually generate unequal opportunities and disadvantage. Conceptualizing social justice in sentencing solely in distributive terms leads to a focus on the patterns of court disposals and overlooks the institutionalized rules that produce these outcomes and the social values that define their content. Barbara Hudson argues that even when the same circumstances inform the construction of each offender's culpability, they are likely to be given different meanings and significance according to the 'woman's race, sexual status, appearance, demeanour and lifestyle'.[65]

Young is also critical of the ways in which the distributive paradigm has been over-extended to include the disposition of not only material resources but also non-material goods such as power, rights, duties, and opportunities.

> Applying a logic of distribution to such goods produces a misleading conception of the issues of justice involved. It reifies aspects of social life that are better understood as a function of rules and relations than as things.[66]

In relation to equality of opportunities, Young argues that it makes no sense to speak of opportunities as possessions because the concept of opportunity is one of enablement rather than possession. A person has opportunities if she is 'not

[62] C Hedderman et al, *Implementing Services for Women Offenders and Those 'at Risk' of Offending: Action Research with Together Women* (London: Ministry of Justice, 2008), 8.

[63] M Walzer, *Spheres of Justice* (New York: Basic, 1983).

[64] IM Young, *Justice and the Politics of Difference* (Princeton, NJ: Princeton University Press, 1990).

[65] B Hudson, 'Gender Issues in Penal Policy and Penal Theory' in P Carlen (ed), *Women, Punishment and the Struggle for Justice* (Cullompton: Willan, 2002), 40.

[66] Young, n 64, above, 25.

constrained from doing things and lives under the enabling conditions for doing them'.[67] Although having opportunities may be dependent upon material possessions, their realization also depends upon social processes and relations which include 'the rules and practices that govern one's actions, the way other people treat one.... and the broader structural possibilities produced by the confluence of a multitude of actions and practices'.[68]

> Evaluating social justice according to whether persons have opportunities, therefore, must involve evaluating not a distributive outcome but the social structures that enable or constrain the individuals in relevant situations.[69]

Applied to the achievement of equal opportunities in sentencing, this calls for an awareness of, and attention to, not only the distribution of resources to address the needs of women offenders, but also the institutional conditions and social processes that enable or inhibit their operational effectiveness. For Young, injustice exists when opportunities cannot be realized because a group or individual is oppressed or dominated by others. She defines oppression as 'the institutional constraint on self-development' and domination as 'the institutional constraint on self-determination'.[70] These concepts overlap, in that oppression frequently embodies domination, but it may also entail inhibiting factors that are not directly the result of the dominance of one group over another. Similarly, Young argues that 'not everyone subject to domination is also oppressed'.[71] Oppression, she claims, exists when a group is subject to any one of the following five conditions: exploitation, marginalization, powerlessness, cultural imperialism, and violence. It will be argued below that the context in which female offenders are exposed to services that define and address their needs is one characterized by oppression and that this can seriously inhibit the objectives of sentencing and the achievement of justice as defined in the government's policy for female offenders.

Empirical research has accumulated compelling evidence of the oppression experienced by female offenders and especially female prisoners. Most recently, the Social Exclusion Task Force[72] has detailed the economic marginalization of offending women, revealing not only their lack of participation in the labour market but also their preceding histories of failure and exclusion within the education system. The Social Exclusion Task Force calculated that almost six out of ten female offenders identified unemployment and skills deficits as factors that contributed to their offending.[73] Earlier in 2002, the Social Exclusion Unit had found that more than 70 per cent of women in prison had no educational qualifications, one in three had been excluded from school, and more than eight out of ten left school at or below the minimum school-leaving age.[74] Similarly, the

[67] Young, n 64, above, 26. [68] Ibid. [69] Ibid.
[70] Ibid, 37. [71] Ibid, 38.
[72] Social Exclusion Task Force, n 48 above.
[73] Ibid, 11.
[74] Social Exclusion Unit, *Reducing Re-Offending by Ex-Prisoners* (London: Office of the Deputy Prime Minister, 2002), 44. Available at <http://www.thelearningjourney.co.uk/file.2007-10-01.1714894439/download> accessed 21 March 2012.

Chief Inspector of Prisons reported in 2005 that half of the female prison population had the reading skills, and three quarters the numeracy skills, at or below the level expected of an 11-year-old child.[75] The damage these women are caused by their limited participation in economic production extends beyond material deprivation to experiences that are characterized by exploitation and dependency:

> Long term poverty, debts and loans with high interest are the reality for many women offenders. In addition, the family finances may have been managed by the partner with the women not even having a basic bank account.[76]

According to Iris Marion Young 'the provision of welfare itself produces new injustice by depriving those dependent on it of rights and freedoms that others have'.[77] Reliance on state welfare marginalizes women offenders from full citizenship by exposing them to an invasive authority exercised by state agencies that undermines individual claims to privacy and autonomy.[78]

Their status of powerlessness, however, is not limited to conditions of economic exchange, but is broadly reflected in the ways social norms and values define and determine gendered relations of dominance and subordination. Opportunities for self-determination are severely impaired for women offenders who are disproportionately victimized by male violence and sexual assault.[79] Domestic violence and childhood histories of physical and sexual abuse inflict harms beyond their immediate injuries, lowering women's self-confidence and self-esteem and their capacity to exercise choice.[80] The widespread misuse of illicit drugs, alcohol, and prescribed medication amongst women offenders creates its own culture of dependency and reinforces their marginal status as citizens. This is intensified by the high incidence of mental health problems experienced by women offenders, which are both shaped by and shape their social isolation and low self-esteem.

The concept of cultural imperialism was developed by Young to refer to the ways in which dominant groups establish their own interests and perspectives as universal norms, projecting 'their own experience as representative of humanity'.[81] The injustice inherent in this is:

> ... that the oppressed group's own experience and interpretation of social life finds little expression that touches the dominant culture, while the same culture imposes on the oppressed group its experience and interpretation of social life.[82]

[75] HM Inspector of Prisons, *Women in Prison* (London: HM Inspectorate of Prisons, 2005), 15. Available at <http://www.justice.gov.uk/downloads/publications/hmipris/thematic-reports-and-research-publications/womeninprison-rps.pdf> accessed 16 April 2012.

[76] *Offender Management Guide to Working with Women Offenders*, cited in Social Exclusion Task Force, n 48 above, 11.

[77] Young, n 64 above, 54.

[78] Young, n 64 above; N Fraser, 'Women, Welfare and the Politics of Need Interpretation' (1987) 2 Hypatia 103.

[79] Social Exclusion Task Force, n 48 above; Social Exclusion Unit, n 74 above.

[80] See End Violence Against Women, <http://www.endviolenceagainstwomen.org.uk/pages/the_facts.html> accessed 21 March 2012; United Nations, 'Violence Against Women', <http://www.un.org/rights/dpi1772e.htm> accessed 21 March 2012.

[81] Young, n 64 above, 59.

[82] Ibid, 60.

The criminal law and the criminal justice system have been developed predominantly by men and with a male subject in mind. Ostensibly universal and impartial in their functioning, legal rules and institutional norms assert a position of neutrality, typically expressed as 'gender blindness', which renders invisible the specifically gendered experiences of female offenders and victims. Illustrations include the repeated failure of the criminal law to accommodate women's experience of domestic violence within the defences to murder; the decision to model the female prison system on that provided for men, regardless of the detrimental consequences it has for women's geographical displacement, their adaptations to prison regimes, or opportunities for resettlement; and sentencing policies and guidelines that claim to treat like cases alike but fail to take account of the differential impact a sentence may impose on men and women.

Young's conception of the injustice caused by systems of domination and oppression is not necessarily the product of a deliberate coercive discrimination but can emerge from 'the everyday practices of a well-intentioned liberal society'.[83] The GED requires the courts to avoid discrimination and pursue equality of opportunity, developing policies that respond to diversity by distributing resources to meet the gender-specific needs of women. But, as Young points out, oppression cannot be eliminated simply by introducing new laws. The potential of the GED to achieve equality as a condition of justice in sentencing is dependent only in part upon the distribution of material resources. Its practical realization in addressing the distinctive needs of women offenders depends also upon the extent to which sentences passed by the courts can address gendered patterns of domination and oppression that are constituted by the normal processes of everyday life and systematically reproduced in major social institutions:

> [O]ppression refers to the vast and deep injustices some groups suffer as a consequence of often unconscious assumptions and reactions of well-meaning people in ordinary interactions, media and cultural stereotypes, and structural features of bureaucratic hierarchies and market mechanisms.[84]

Put simply, there would be little point in providing educational programmes to counter skills deficits if the oppressive conditions that affect offenders' incentives to engage with these facilities and their ability to exercise choice and control over their lifestyles are ignored. Recent government policy has demonstrated some sensitivity to these issues by emphasizing the complexity of women's needs and the importance of personalized programmes to break cycles of disadvantage.[85] Reports on the delivery of services to women offenders demonstrate an implicit awareness of how social structures and social action are co-constitutive:

> Bristol Court Assessment and Referral Service (CARS), responsible for mental health assessments, found that a high proportion of women refused to take up psychiatric

[83] Young, n 64 above, 41. [84] Ibid.

[85] Ministry of Justice, *A Report on the Government's Strategy for Diverting Women Away from Crime* (London: Ministry of Justice, 2009). Available at <http://www.swdc.org.uk/silo/files/a-report-on-the-governments-strategy-for-diverting-women-away-from-crime.pdf> accessed 16 April 2012.

assessment. It was discovered that this was due to a misperception by women that the assessment could lead to their children being removed from their care. Therefore the mental health worker position was widened to become a more generic women's worker role. So now women are assessed for health and wellbeing, including employment, housing, and benefits advice. This has led to an increase in the uptake of the service.[86]

Ashworth has drawn attention to the complexities of applying the principle of equality before the law to sentencing decisions, particularly since the passage of the Criminal Justice Act 2003.[87] He identifies important conflicts that exist between the pursuit of equality and the achievement of other legitimate goals. The efficiency of the criminal justice process, for example, tends to be compromised by the expenditure of time and money necessary to generate information to enable the courts to attend to issues of equality. Another conflict is said to exist between equal treatment and the principle of parsimony in sentencing, particularly in the use of imprisonment. Ashworth questions whether a sentence should be reduced for one offender on grounds of personal mitigation if it effectively discriminates against those who do not have access to such claims. Arguing principally from a retributivist perspective, he challenges the conclusions of Norval Morris and Michael Tonry,[88] who weigh parsimony above equality, and claims that both principles should be considered in relation not only to their intrinsic merits but also to their wider social effects. In doing so, he concludes that sentencing practices that advantage some offenders and discriminate against others are at risk of alienating sections of the public and undermining respect for the administration of criminal justice. Rather than introducing categorical reductions for some offenders such as women, Ashworth prefers to pursue the principles of parsimony and equality through a general lowering of punishment levels and by sentencers paying attention to equality of impact.

However, Ashworth has highlighted another, more intransigent conflict of principle which represents a significant and growing threat to equal treatment and the avoidance of discrimination. Risk-based sentencing has emerged as part of a 'new penology' that is focused on actuarial assessments of criminal risk and the management of specific groups of offenders. Although traditionally used to distinguish a sub-sample of dangerous offenders in order to protect the public from grave crimes, the principle of risk management has been applied to a wider range of decisions in the criminal justice system. As noted earlier, Ashworth has warned of the dangers of risk-based sentencing, and has been particularly critical of its reliance on 'non-legal' variables causing direct and indirect discrimination:

The direct discrimination would be against the poor and unemployed. The indirect discrimination would be against those who fall disproportionately within the categories of high risk, such as certain ethnic minorities and single mothers.[89]

[86] Ibid, 12. [87] Ashworth, n 1 above.

[88] N Morris and M Tonry, *Between Prison and Probation* (New York: Oxford University Press, 1990).

[89] Ashworth, n 1 above, 259.

The growth of mandatory sentences, in particular the introduction of the Indeterminate Sentence for Public Protection (IPP), has required the courts to apply identical criteria with equal force to men and women in order to determine their dangerousness to the public.[90] There is evidence that particularly vulnerable women have been disproportionately affected by this sentence. HM Inspector of Prisons and Probation has reported the prevalence of mental health needs amongst female IPP prisoners, together with additional needs, including learning difficulties, alcohol dependency, and a history of self-harm.[91] The Inspectorate expressed concern that 'nearly all' of the pre-sentence reports on the female IPP prisoners were 'deficient in some respect' and in more than half the cases studied 'the level of risk was overestimated'.[92] Their offence profile was found to be different to male IPP prisoners in that 'far fewer were convicted of sexual offences and far more of arson, even in circumstances that did not appear to endanger others'.[93] The Prison Reform Trust has drawn attention to the Inspectorate's finding that 'nearly 80 per cent of IPP sentences for women surveyed . . . were for offences of arson, which is often an indicator of serious mental illness and self-harm'.[94] In his written evidence to the Home Affairs Select Committee, Simon Creighton detailed the disadvantages experienced by women serving IPP sentences both in relation to their access to offending behaviour programmes and their transfer to prisons located long distances from their homes.

> The prison system has not been in a position to invest in the specialist assessment, treatment and support necessary for women serving life sentences. The direct consequence is that women who receive IPP sentences with short tariffs are the group least likely to be released on tariff expiry.[95]

The application of the GED to risk-based sentencing should tackle not only issues of distributive justice but non-distributive issues that affect the ability of female offenders to make use of opportunities that aim to reduce their likelihood of reoffending and inhibit their own exposure to social harm. In this way, the equality legislation could exercise an important restraining influence over the tyranny of risk

[90] Criminal Justice Act 2003, s 225 requires the courts to impose an IPP on any offender aged 18 or over, who is convicted of a serious specified violent or sexual offence committed on or after 4 April 2005, for which the maximum penalty is ten years or more; and who, in the court's opinion, poses a significant risk of harm to the public. Amended by Criminal Justice and Immigration Act 2008, s 47 and Sch 8. IPP sentences may only be imposed where the offender would be required to serve at least two years in custody. The Act also removes the presumption of risk (requirement for judges to conclude that the offender is dangerous) where there is a previous conviction for violent or sexual crime.

[91] HM Inspector of Prisons and HM Inspector of Probation, *The Indeterminate Sentence for Public Protection: A Thematic Review* (London: HMIP and HMIP 2008). Available at <http://www.justice.gov.uk/downloads/publications/hmipris/thematic-reports-and-research-publications/ipp_thematic_2008-rps.pdf> accessed 16 April 2012.

[92] Ibid, 7.

[93] Ibid, 13.

[94] Prison Reform Trust, n 40 above, 27.

[95] House of Commons, *Home Affairs Select Committee, Written Evidence submitted by Simon Creighton,* Memorandum 5, Session 2006–07, para 14. Available at <http://www.publications.parliament.uk/pa/cm200607/cmselect/cmconst/467/467we06.htm> accessed 21 March 2012.

assessment and the increasing punitiveness of sentences deemed necessary for public protection. The implications of these issues for preventative sentencing practice have, however, received little attention.

But non-distributive issues of justice also have relevance to at least two other types of decisions taken by sentencers. The first issue arises where the courts deal with women who are in breach of a court order. A constructive response must take account of any socio-cultural factors that inhibit a woman's compliance and her ability to benefit from rehabilitative opportunities. The second concerns the ways in which sentencers respond to persistence. Currently there is a statutory duty under section 143 of the Criminal Justice Act 2003 to treat relevant previous convictions as factors that aggravate seriousness and justify the imposition of incrementally severe sentences. The realization of the GED, however, requires desert to be viewed in the context of an offender's need which is shaped, at least in part, by the structural conditions that enable or inhibit her capacity for self-development and self-determination. From this perspective, the courts are required to ask different questions in deciding upon sentence. Rather than routinely increasing the punitive value of the sentence in response to persistence, the judiciary must develop a more problem-solving approach that considers not only those factors that appear to exacerbate a woman's risk of reoffending, but also those circumstances that limit her ability to engage effectively with rehabilitative interventions. To make this operationally effective, however, demands a great deal from sentencers, requiring them to take account not only of differences in the life experiences of men and women, but also differences that exist within gender groups. Given that the application of supposedly 'neutral criteria' has not protected black ethnic minorities from cumulative disadvantage in the criminal justice system,[96] it is crucial for sentencers to have some awareness of the ways in which the dominance and oppression of women are mediated by other cultural variables such as race and social class.

5. Conclusion

The published equality objectives of the Ministry of Justice for 2012–2016 reaffirm that 'equality remains at the heart of what we do. This includes how we design and deliver our policies and services to the public, how we procure and commission from others and how we act as an employer.'[97] In pursuing gender equality in criminal justice, and specifically in sentencing practice, the duty implies that men and women should be treated in ways that facilitate equal autonomy, equal access to justice, equal protection from criminal harms, and equal rights and responsibilities. Yet it is clear from recent policy statements concerning the treatment of women

[96] B Bowling and C Phillips, *Race, Crime and Criminal Justice* (Harlow: Pearson, 2002).

[97] Ministry of Justice, *Ministry of Justice Policy Objectives 2012–2016* (London: Ministry of Justice, 2012), 3. Available at <http://www.justice.gov.uk/downloads/publications/corporate-reports/MoJ/2012/moj-equality-objectives.pdf> accessed 16 April 2012.

offenders,[98] and from the full equality impact assessment of the Green Paper, *Breaking the Cycle: Effective Punishment, Rehabilitation and Sentencing of Offenders*,[99] that equal treatment in this context does not mean identical treatment of men and women, but depends crucially on recognizing the specific and complex needs of women offenders.

Andrew Ashworth's approach to equality in sentencing emphasizes the recognition of individual differences and engages with questions about the role that sentencing can play in achieving social justice. However, he cautions against expecting too much, correctly pointing to the structural nature of social inequality, and the fact that the sentencing system is limited in its reach, dealing only with those offenders who are prosecuted and convicted. Nonetheless, he appeals for 'greater recognition of the skewed nature of the sample of offenders who appear before the courts'[100] and for the courts to give greater attention to equality of impact.[101] As discussed earlier, his approach to resolving conflict between the principle of equal treatment and other sentencing goals is to consider not just their intrinsic merits but also their wider social impact. Under his chairmanship, the Sentencing Advisory Panel has emphasized the importance of avoiding discrimination by striving towards an equivalence of impact in sentencing, even though it has been more reserved on the subject of equality of opportunity. Although the Panel is not unsympathetic towards the multiple disadvantages that characterize the life experiences of many women offenders, it is wary of allowing these to challenge the principle of proportionality beyond its commitment to equal impact. However, without directly addressing the question of equal opportunities, it does leave open the possibility of sentencers exercising their discretion on whether and when to take account of socio-cultural variables, including the women's histories of abuse, their caring responsibilities within the family, and the effect their sentence could have on innocent third parties.

Since the election of the coalition government, the stated rationale for sentencing has shifted increasingly toward rehabilitation and the prevention of reoffending. In response to the consultation following the Green Paper, *Breaking the Cycle: Effective Punishment, Rehabilitation and Sentencing of Offenders,* the government concluded that:

> Our priorities are to get offenders off drugs and alcohol for good; address offenders' mental health problems; get offenders into work; and reduce barriers to resettlement. We will take into account the different profile of women's offending in achieving this.[102]

Operating within this context, the GED obliges the courts to promote equal opportunities for women in accessing, and benefiting from, resources designed to

[98] Ministry of Justice, n 85 above; Social Exclusion Task Force, n 48 above.

[99] Ministry of Justice, *Breaking the Cycle: Government Response. Full Equality Impact Assessment* (London: Ministry of Justice, 2011). Available at <http://www.justice.gov.uk/downloads/consultations/full-eia.pdf> accessed 21 March 2012.

[100] Ashworth, n 1 above, 259.

[101] Ashworth and Player, n 18 above.

[102] Ministry of Justice, n 99 above, 6.

achieve these ends. It requires sentencing to be seen as part of a wider process of social justice that operates across government departments and challenges the case for judicial decisions to be driven predominantly by retributive concepts of desert. The GED directs attention to the needs of women offenders and construes the notion of a deserved sentence as one that directly addresses underlying social harms. Whilst embedded in a system of distributive justice, the GED also has the potential to facilitate a more radical approach to sentencing, in which equal opportunities are conceived not only in terms of material distribution but also in relation to the means of enablement. In practice this calls for sentencers to be aware of the operational context in which individual sentences must function, and particularly those rules and values that can enable or constrain an equality outcome.

16

Proportionate Sentencing and the Rule of Law

*Malcolm Thorburn**

It is no easy thing to maintain a clear focus on both the forest and the trees. In the study of criminal justice, most writers restrict themselves either to the study of the detailed operation of particular systems or to a theoretical engagement with the foundational issues in the field. But over a career of many years, Andrew Ashworth has been a leader in criminal justice studies of both sorts. Indeed, it is a hallmark of Ashworth's scholarship that even in his treatment of the most apparently narrow and technical topic, he makes clear the deep issues of principle that are at stake and how those principles ought to guide our thinking on the issue at hand.

In this essay, I focus my attention on two of Ashworth's most cherished principles of criminal justice: first, what Michael Tonry calls the 'strong proportionality principle'[1] and secondly, what I call the 'state monopoly principle'. I argue that, taken together, these two principles set out a *jurisdictional* conception of criminal sentencing. That is, unlike most of his contemporaries, who have jumped immediately to the question of how best to justify the punishment of criminal offenders, Ashworth has seen (correctly, in my view) that such questions may only be asked meaningfully once we have settled two conceptually prior questions: (1) 'Who has jurisdiction to impose criminal punishment?', and (2) 'What, specifically, do criminal punishers have the jurisdiction to do?' That is, rather than moving directly to the abstract question 'What do criminal wrongdoers deserve?', he begins by asking 'What role may the state legitimately play in setting and enforcing criminal norms within a legitimate constitutional order under the rule of law?' Stated in this fashion, Ashworth's position might not seem to be a startlingly novel approach to

* Canada Research Chair in Crime, Security and Constitutionalism, Faculty of Law, Queen's University, Canada. Thanks to the Social Sciences and Humanities Research Council of Canada for financial support and to Professor Bernd Schünemann and his Institut für die gesamten Strafrechtswissenschaften, Rechtsphilosophie und Rechtsinformatik at Ludwig-Maximilians-Universität, Munich for providing a stimulating research environment in which to write this paper. Thanks to the participants in the All Souls Criminology Lecture at the University of Oxford, where I presented an earlier version of this paper. Thanks also to Larissa Katz, Arthur Ripstein, and Lucia Zedner for valuable comments and discussion. Responsibility for any errors is mine alone.

[1] M Tonry, 'Proportionality, Parsimony and Interchangeability of Punishments' in RA Duff, SE Marshall, RE Dobash, and RP Dobash (eds), *Penal Theory and Practice* (Manchester: Manchester University Press, 1994).

criminal justice. But as I shall endeavour to show in this essay, it holds a deep and important lesson that most of Ashworth's contemporaries have ignored.

1. The Two Principles Stated

The strong proportionality principle

Andrew Ashworth[2] has long been a champion of what Tonry calls the 'strong proportionality principle' in criminal punishment. This is a considerably more subtle and nuanced principle than is sometimes recognized. First, it is to be distinguished from the ancient idea of *lex talionis* that the harm visited on the offender should be the same (in kind or in degree) as the harm he visited on his victim. Indeed, Ashworth has consistently opposed such a view, insisting that it is up to each system of criminal justice to determine absolute levels of punitiveness based on a variety of local factors. 'There seems to be no crime,' Ashworth writes, 'for which one can readily perceive a specific quantum of punishment as the uniquely deserved one.'[3] Ashworth's concern is not to ensure that offenders suffer punishment that is *the same as* the harm they impose on others; rather, it is to ensure that the punishment they suffer is *proportionate to* the wrong for which they are being punished. Ashworth's focus is on the relative treatment of offenders across a system of criminal justice. As a matter of justice among offenders, Ashworth insists, each offender should receive an equally severe sentence as those who committed offences of equal seriousness (the principle of parity); it should be more severe than those who committed less serious offences and less severe than those who committed more serious offences (the principle of rank ordering); and it should be more or less severe than other sentences in proportion to the degree of seriousness of the offence (the principle of spacing).[4]

Secondly, Ashworth's 'strong proportionality principle' is not even the idea that proportionality must be the only factor the sentencing judge considers when determining the appropriate severity of sentence. Although Ashworth has done more than most to show the relevance of a great variety of factors to individual desert, he has also made clear in his recent work that sentencing judges may deviate from the proportionate sentence by as much as 15 per cent for reasons other than individual desert.[5] With the addition of this wrinkle, it becomes clear that

[2] In many of my references to Andrew Ashworth, I am actually referring to works co-authored with others—usually Andreas von Hirsch, but sometimes others as well. I indicate co-authorship in footnotes where appropriate.

[3] A Ashworth and A von Hirsch, *Proportionate Sentencing: Exploring the Principles* (Oxford: Oxford University Press, 2005), 142. They add that there are strong reasons to favour reductions in overall severity so that 'lengthy prison terms would be reserved only for the most serious violent offences' (143).

[4] Ashworth and von Hirsch, n 3 above, 139.

[5] For detailed description of the changes in Ashworth's arguments on this topic, see M Thorburn and A Manson, 'The Sentencing Theory Debate: Convergence in Outcomes, Divergence in Reasoning' (2007) 10 New Criminal Law Review 278.

Ashworth's conception of criminal sentencing is not as different in the outcomes generated from its main rival, limiting retributivism, as one might have thought at first.[6] For whereas Ashworth insists that sentencing judges must determine the precisely proportionate sentence and then may deviate from it by up to 15 per cent for non-desert-based reasons, limiting retributivism holds that proportionality only sets upper and lower limits to the range of acceptable sentences and the choice within that range may be determined by reference to non-desert-based reasons. So why does Ashworth insist so strongly on the superiority of his own 'strong proportionality' principle to the theory of limiting retributivism? The main reason, I believe, is not primarily the difference in outcomes (for these may quite often be the same); rather, the superiority of Ashworth's model lies principally in the way that it ties the structure of judicial reasoning in the process of determining criminal sentences to the grounds of the state's role in imposing criminal punishment.

It is perhaps most fruitful to think of the distinction between Ashworth's strong proportionality principle and Tonry's limiting retributivism as answers to two quite different questions. Michael Tonry, like most writers of his generation, is concerned with generating defensible sentencing *outcomes*. On this score, it is not implausible to say that sentences that are not severely disproportionate and that are also designed to do some good (through rehabilitation, deterrence, etc) are justifiable. By contrast, Ashworth's project is squarely focused on the sentencing judge's obligation to provide the right sort of justification for the sentence she imposes in the particular case. Her first obligation is to determine what justice requires by way of a proportionate sentence, for it is a matter of 'common-sense notions of justice, that how severely a person is punished should depend on the degree of blameworthiness of his conduct'.[7] Once the judge has determined precisely what this just sentence must be, she may then consider whether there are any grounds upon which to justify deviating from the deserved sentence. And, of course, in so far as she deviates from the proportionate sentence, it is up to the sentencing judge to articulate her reasons for deviation quite clearly to the offender and to the polity more generally. Although there might be some (very limited) room for sentencing judges to consider other factors, they must give proportionality what Rawls calls 'lexical priority',[8] and any deviation from it must be underwritten by strong and clearly articulated justification.

But why? Why couldn't it be open to the sentencing judge to consider a variety of important factors all together in her response to the offender's wrongdoing? As John Gardner reminds us, justice is but one of many virtues that the law (or institutions or individuals) can have; to say that something is a requirement of justice is not necessarily to say that it must be given priority over all other considerations. 'Naturally the law should be just,' Gardner writes, 'but it should

[6] Norval Morris, Michael Tonry, Richard Frase and others have pursued the 'limiting retributivist' line of argument for many years. For more on the differences (and similarities) between their view and Ashworth's 'strong proportionality' view, see Thorburn and Manson, n 5 above.

[7] Ashworth and von Hirsch, n 3 above.

[8] John Rawls made this expression famous in *A Theory of Justice* (Cambridge, MA: Harvard University Press, 1971).

also be honest, humane, considerate, charitable, courageous, prudent, temperate, trustworthy, and so on.'[9] What gives questions of justice this lexical priority in criminal sentencing?

In this respect, it seems that Ashworth thinks of criminal sentencing as different in kind from punishment in the private realm, where there is no strict division between matters of individual desert and other factors. Take the case of a parent who is punishing her child. Although proportionality should probably play some role in her thinking when determining the appropriate punishment, this seems to be just one element in the mix. We normally think that the parent's choice of appropriate punishment should involve a consideration of a wide variety of factors right from the start. Will the punishment strengthen or undermine the child's relationship with his parents? Will it reinforce or distract the child from other lessons that the parent is trying to instil? Will non-punitive measures be more effective in providing for the child's moral education? And so on. Why should we think that criminal sentencing is any different? Before looking any further here, let us now turn to the second jurisdictional principle in Ashworth's account of criminal sentencing: the state monopoly principle. For on my account, at least, these two principles stand or fall together.

The state monopoly principle

As we have just seen, the strong proportionality principle seems to be at work on only one side of a fairly sharp distinction between sentencing judges (who are required to respect this principle) and private citizens (who are not). In this way, the argument for the strong proportionality principle is closely connected to Ashworth's 'state monopoly principle'. This is the claim that the administration of criminal justice should be controlled exclusively by state officials and should never be outsourced to private parties. It is on this basis that Ashworth has argued vigorously and repeatedly against the claims of restorative justice that the parties themselves should be in charge of the process through which the offender's sentence is determined.

Ashworth's version of the state monopoly principle is a considerably stronger one than that which is invoked by most other criminal law writers today. His view is not merely that the state should monopolize the administration of criminal justice because it is a superior instrument for punishing wrongdoers (because of the considerable expertise of judges in matters of criminal sentencing or because the state is bigger and better resourced than private actors and can therefore provide a more predictable and systematic response to crime). Rather, he argues that irrespective of the relative abilities of state and private parties to administer criminal justice, only the state has the standing to do so. 'Although the list of failures of state justice is a lengthy one,' he writes, 'the state must, as the primary political authority,

[9] J Gardner, 'The Virtue of Justice and the Character of Law' (2000) 53 CLP 1, 29.

retain control over criminal justice and its administration.'[10] Clearly Ashworth is not just making an empirical claim about the state's ability to do the job best; he is insisting that such questions are simply beside the point because it is not even open to us to consider handing over the job of administering criminal justice to a private party.

2. The Jurisdiction of Sentencing Judges

Taken together, Ashworth's two principles articulate what I call a *jurisdictional* account of criminal sentencing. By this, I mean to say a good deal more than just that Ashworth takes account of questions of jurisdiction in his account of criminal sentencing. Of course, virtually any model of sentencing must take account of jurisdictional questions at some point: no matter what we might like sentencing judges to do, it is clear that as a matter of positive law they do not have the legal jurisdiction to do whatever we might like them to. I call Ashworth's account a jurisdictional one because it gives conceptual pride of place to matters of jurisdiction in a way that most of his contemporaries do not. The state monopoly principle (which determines who has the jurisdiction to administer criminal justice) and the strong proportionality principle (that sets important constraints on the jurisdiction of officials in the administration of criminal justice) are the starting-points for Ashworth's account of criminal sentencing. They do not merely recognize *ex post facto* constraints on our pursuit of independently valuable objectives in criminal sentencing; rather, these principles of jurisdiction frame our enquiry into what sentencing judges have reason to do in the first place. The very idea of criminal punishment, on Ashworth's account, is an expression of what state officials have the jurisdiction to carry out. This is an important contrast, but it is also perhaps a rather obscure one. In order to make clear what makes Ashworth's account of criminal justice 'jurisdictional', it might be helpful to set it in contrast to what has become the standard view on this question—a view that Alon Harel calls 'state instrumentalism'.[11]

State instrumentalism and the state monopoly principle

State instrumentalism about punishment, Harel says, is the view that 'punishment serves important societal goals that could in principle be realized by other nonstate agents'.[12] According to this doctrine, the fundamental questions of punishment theory are set out in the passive voice: who should be punished and how much should they be punished? Only after these questions have been answered do state

[10] A Ashworth, 'Responsibilities, Rights, and Restorative Justice' (2002) 42 British Journal of Criminology 578, 581.

[11] A Harel, 'The Vices of State Instrumentalism' (2009) 42 Israel Law Review 464. For a fuller treatment of state instrumentalism in punishment theory, see A Harel, 'Why Only the State May Punish: Against Privately Inflicted Criminal Sanctions' (2008)14 Legal Theory 113.

[12] Harel, n 11 above, 118.

instrumentalists then turn to the secondary question of 'policy instrument choice': that is, the choice of who is best placed to carry out a pre-determined task. The status of the punishing agent as a public official is assumed to be (as a matter of principle, at least) neither here nor there.[13] All three of the dominant theories of punishment today—utilitarian, retributivist, and communicative—proceed in this two-step way, treating the question of who should carry out the punishment as a secondary and quite separate one to be answered simply by reference to considerations of expedience. John Gardner captures this idea neatly in the following terms:

> What we face here is . . . mainly a question of the efficient use of rational energy. It may not be my place (my role) to extract justifications and excuses [or to punish]. It may be the law's place, or the place of the person who was wronged, or the place of the wrongdoer's friends and family, etc. But where this is so, this is mainly (not only, but mainly) because and to the extent that this person with *locus standi* is the one who is best placed to do the extracting, i.e. who will do the best job of conforming to the reason that we all have in common to see to it that the wrongdoer answers for her wrongs.[14]

Harel calls this position 'state instrumentalism' because it treats the state as just one possible instrument through which offenders may be held accountable and suffer the appropriate punishment. There is nothing in the nature of criminal punishment, in this view, that requires that it be state officials who administer it. If some private actors (whether they are corporate prison operators and security firms, or just particularly thoughtful victims in a restorative justice process) are able to carry out the task more cheaply and more effectively, then state instrumentalists are generally quite open to the possibility of giving them the job of administering some aspect of the criminal process.

Utilitarian accounts of punishment adopt the state instrumentalist position quite naturally. For them, we may determine when it is appropriate to impose punishment fairly straightforwardly by comparing costs and benefits: if punishment is able to prevent more societal harm than it causes (whether through the mechanism of deterrence, offender rehabilitation, incapacitation, or otherwise), then it is justified.[15] Who should carry out the punishment is (in principle) quite immaterial to the question of whether it should be carried out.[16] Of course, there might be pragmatic reasons to prefer the state as enforcer of the criminal law (say, because its *ex ante* threats of punishment are more credible than those of individuals or small

[13] John Gardner makes this claim explicit—and broadens it to cover all of criminal justice—insisting that 'it is . . . true that occasionally people have additional legal powers by virtue of being public officials . . . But although these additional powers are the powers of public officials, nothing turns, for the criminal law, on the fact that they are the powers of public officials.' J Gardner, 'Justification under Authority' (2010) 23 Canadian Journal of Law and Jurisprudence 71, 97.

[14] J Gardner, *Offences and Defences* (Oxford: Oxford University Press, 2007), 278.

[15] Paul Robinson is perhaps the best-known contemporary exponent of this view. See P Robinson, 'A Theory of Justification: Societal Harm as a Prerequisite for Criminal Liability' (1975) 23 UCLA Law Review 266.

[16] As Bernard Williams pointed out many years ago, this instrumentalist attitude is a pervasive aspect of utilitarianism generally. Williams argued that utilitarianism views each moral agent merely as 'a janitor of [its] system of values'. B Williams, 'Critique of Utilitarianism' in JJC Smart and B Williams, *Utilitarianism: For and Against* (Cambridge: Cambridge University Press, 1973), 116–17.

private organizations or because it is better able to co-ordinate the activities of people across society) but there is no reason in principle why utilitarians should insist on state control of the criminal justice system. Utilitarianism tells us simply to prefer whichever punishment provider can effectively minimize socially undesirable conduct at minimum cost.

It is somewhat more surprising to find that the same is also true of most modern retributive accounts of criminal punishment. According to Michael Moore's influential brand of retributivism, for instance, the central questions of punishment theory are once again posed in the passive voice: who should be punished and how much? Moore sets out his answer in agent-neutral terms: it is moral wrongdoers who should be punished, and they should be punished in proportion to their wrongdoing.[17] There are important differences between Moore's retributivism and utilitarian accounts of punishment, of course: whereas utilitarians take punishment to be a necessary evil—causing harm in the hopes of maximizing aggregate welfare—Moore takes the punishment of wrongdoers to be an intrinsic good to be pursued for its own sake. But on the question of state instrumentalism, they are *ad idem*: we can decide who should be punished and how severely they should be punished prior to any consideration of who should carry out the punishment. So long as *someone* brings about this good (and, presumably, does it effectively and efficiently), it is a matter of indifference to both utilitarians and retributivists that someone might be. Moore seems to favour state control of the criminal justice system for reasons of efficiency, but others who are committed to retributivism need not share this view. Indeed, some writers such as Doug Husak suggest that there might be good reason to prefer non-state actors to administer punishment in at least some cases.[18]

Finally, many 'expressive'[19] or 'communicative'[20] accounts of criminal punishment also embrace state instrumentalism. According to these accounts of criminal justice, punishment is best understood as a communicative act by the punisher conveying moral censure of the wrongdoer for his wrongdoing. Even though the 'grammar'[21] of communication is necessarily relational (for there must be both someone to communicate the message and someone to whom it is communicated), most communicative theories of punishment are also indifferent (on the level of

[17] MS Moore, *Placing Blame: A General Theory of the Criminal Law* (Oxford: Oxford University Press, 1997), 153 ff.

[18] DN Husak, 'Why Punish the Deserving?' (1992) 26 Nous 447.

[19] J Feinberg, 'The Expressive Function of Punishment' (1965) 49 The Monist 397.

[20] Gardner, n 14 above. By contrast, although Antony Duff is one of the best-known exponents of a communicative theory of punishment, he does not fall prey to state instrumentalism in the same way. He makes this clear as follows: 'An essential dimension of a political theory that is going to make sense of punishment is the matter of agency: when an offender is punished, by whom is he punished? If we begin, as theorists and preachers often seem to begin, with an impersonal demand from heaven or from justice that "the guilty must be punished" (the passive voice is significant), we must still ask who, if anyone, has the standing to meet that demand.' RA Duff, 'Retrieving Retributivism' in MD White (ed), *Retributivism: Essays in Theory and Policy* (Oxford: Oxford University Press, 2011), 6.

[21] I use the term 'grammar' here in the technical sense introduced by Ludwig Wittgenstein in L Wittgenstein, PMS Hacker ,and J Schulte (eds and trans) *Philosophical Investigations* (4th edn, Oxford: Wiley-Blackwell, 2009).

principle) as to the identity of the party communicating the moral censure. Although *someone* must communicate censure to the wrongdoer, there is no principled reason why it must be one party rather than another. As John Gardner points out: 'We each have reason to see to it that people in general answer for their wrongs.'[22] Although the law typically identifies someone as the person who has the legal standing to administer communicative punishment, that legal standing is allocated for reasons of practical efficiency and not for reasons of principle.

Once we set Ashworth's state monopoly principle in contrast to state instrumentalist accounts, the depth of Ashworth's commitment to that principle becomes apparent. He does not think of the state's jurisdiction over the administration of criminal justice to be a question merely about the 'efficient use of rational energy' (as John Gardner calls it); rather, it is a matter of principle—a fixed point in his account of criminal sentencing. There is something in the nature of criminal sentencing that requires that it be administered by state officials and not by private actors. Although we have not yet identified the grounds for Ashworth's deep commitment to the state monopoly principle, it is clear that his reasons are quite distinct from the instrumental considerations that guide most of his contemporaries.

The analogy to parental discipline and the strong proportionality principle

The state monopoly principle is only one half of what I am calling Ashworth's jurisdictional account of criminal sentencing. The other half—the strong proportionality principle—is an equally important part of the story. Ashworth's account is not merely that state officials are the only ones with the jurisdiction to administer criminal justice; he goes further and insists that the terms of their jurisdiction impose further limits on how they may act when administering criminal punishment. To see the significance of this second move, it is useful once again to contrast Ashworth's view with those of some of his contemporaries.

Among those who recognize the state monopoly principle, most theorists assume that the job of administering criminal justice can be understood fairly well by appeal to our extra-legal moral intuitions. The job of the sentencing judge, they often assume, can be understood best by way of analogy to the punishment of children by their parents. Accounts built on this analogy usually recognize (as state instrumentalist arguments do not) that punishment is legitimate only within the context of an on-going relationship of authority:[23] just as we might insist that parents (and only parents) are the ones to discipline their children, even if they do

[22] Gardner, n 14 above, 278.

[23] This is in contrast to those who, like John Gardner, see the possibility of punishment in almost any sort of relationship. In his introduction to the new edition of *Punishment and Responsibility*, he suggests that this is possible within the context of a relationship between equals, such as spouses: 'It is very common for one estranged spouse to punish the other, for example, by preventing him or her from spending time with his or her children, fully intending that this should be a terrible experience. I know of no reason to think that such punishment is "sub-standard or secondary" as compared with, say,

not have as much expertise or effective power as a stranger, so we can insist that it is the state (and only the state) that is entitled to punish criminal wrongdoers, even if some well-run corporation or thoughtful victim might do it more cheaply and more effectively. Writers such as Neil MacCormick, Anthony Bottoms, and Alon Harel, for instance, seem ready to recognize that only those with the appropriate standing are entitled to administer punishment, criminal or otherwise. In so far as a non-parent is entitled to punish a child at all, it is only in so far as he is acting *in loco parentis*—either officially sanctioned by the parent or taking on the role in circumstances of emergency.

The analogy of criminal punishment to parental discipline of children is both helpful and misleading. It is helpful because (unlike the state instrumentalist view), it makes clear that one must have the proper standing to punish—it is not enough just to be the most effective policy instrument for the job. But the analogy is also misleading, for there are dynamics at work in the state–citizen relationship that do not exist in the parent–child relationship. Neil MacCormick insists that parents and children are no less paradigmatic of the punisher–punishee relationship than are states and citizens—they are both equally significant examples of the same basic phenomenon.[24] Anthony Bottoms argues that any account of punishment must be able to explain the structure of punishment in the family context in the same way as it can explain state-administered criminal punishment. He writes:

> Inclusion of an actual incident of punishing [of a child by his parent] at an early stage of the argument may therefore serve the dual purpose of first, reminding those of a theoretical bent that their theories need to be translatable to, and make sense in, the real world; and, secondly, reminding penal practitioners that even the most trivial incidents in daily life can produce rich data for theoretical reflection upon what exactly we think we are doing when we punish someone.[25]

The trouble is that the analogy to parental discipline jumps too quickly to its conclusion: although the parental case and the criminal case might both be examples of punishment[26] carried out by a party with the appropriate jurisdiction

imprisonment by the courts.' HLA Hart and J Gardner, *Punishment and Responsibility* (2nd edn, Oxford: Oxford University Press, 2008), 1.

24 'We ought to reflect carefully how deep or essential the differences are [between state punishment and private "punishment"]. For it has become a commonplace in discussions of punishment to treat the panoply of the criminal law, with formal accusations, pre-announced laws, trials by due process of law, formal sentence, and enforced execution of the sentence, as the paradigm for punishment, while every other instance of "punishment" is seen as counting only to whatever degree it appears analogical with the paradigm case. But this may surely be doubted. For there is a kind of natural authority of parents, and more generally of concerned adults, over children . . .' N MacCormick and D Garland, 'Sovereign States and Vengeful Victims: The Problem of the Right to Punish' in A Ashworth and M Wasik (eds), *Fundamentals of Sentencing Theory* (Oxford: Oxford University Press, 1998), 23.

25 A Bottoms, 'Five Puzzles in von Hirsch's Theory of Punishment' in Ashworth and Wasik, n 24 above, 55.

26 Indeed, one might put the point even more strongly and say that parental discipline is not really punishment at all in the sense understood by criminal justice theorists. It is not the infliction of hard treatment against fully responsible agents. Rather, it is the use of coercive force for the education of minors.

to do so, it does not necessarily follow that the grounds of their jurisdiction to do so are the same. And if the normative grounds for their jurisdiction are different, we have reason to expect that the scope of that jurisdiction would be different, as well. This is a point that Ashworth—who argues for special jurisdictional constraints of 'strong proportionality' on state officials administering criminal punishment but not on parents punishing their children—seems to recognize, but these other writers do not.

3. Jurisdiction, Political Theory, and the Rule of Law

Ashworth's wavering commitments

So far I have argued that, taken together, Ashworth's two principles form an account of criminal justice that puts matters of jurisdiction front and centre. Unlike state instrumentalists, Ashworth recognizes that it is simply not open to us to allocate jurisdiction over the administration[27] of criminal justice to whoever might carry out the task most efficiently in the circumstances; something deeper is at work here that constrains us in the allocation of jurisdiction from the very beginning. And unlike those who draw a fairly straightforward analogy between parental discipline and criminal sentencing, Ashworth recognizes that the normative grounds of the state's jurisdiction to punish criminal offenders is different from the grounds of parents' jurisdiction to discipline their children; this is why the jurisdiction of criminal justice officials to punish offenders is different from that of parents to punish their errant children.

Ashworth's insistence on the strong proportionality principle and the state monopoly principle strongly suggest that he is committed to a particular conception of the role of criminal sentencing within a larger constitutional order. Further, the place of criminal justice officials within that constitutional order imposes *ex ante* limits on the jurisdiction of criminal justice officials that it is simply not open to us to revisit. Unfortunately, a clear articulation of this underlying political theory of sentencing is very hard to find in Ashworth's writings.[28] Instead, when it comes to the foundations of the state's jurisdiction to punish, Ashworth often turns to the writings of criminal law theorists who are not at all sympathetic to the jurisdictional account. Most troublingly, Ashworth has repeatedly invoked John Gardner's 'displacement' argument for why the state is in control of criminal justice, rather

[27] For the purposes of my argument here, I am focused on the allocation of punishment by courts. I have argued elsewhere that different considerations will apply when we consider the application of punishment: M Thorburn, 'Why Only the State May Decide When Sanctions are Appropriate' in P Robinson, S Garvey, and K Ferzan (eds), *Criminal Law Conversations* (Oxford: Oxford University Press, 2009), 140–2.

[28] The closest he has come is in his recent work on the preventative function of criminal justice. See A Ashworth and L Zedner, 'Just Prevention: Preventive Justice and the Limits of the Criminal Law' in A Duff and S Green (eds), *Philosophical Foundations of Criminal Law* (Oxford: Oxford University Press, 2011).

than private actors.[29] This is troubling in two ways. First, Gardner's writing is at odds with Ashworth's clear commitment to a non-instrumentalist account of the state's role in the administration of criminal law. Gardner suggests that one of the most important reasons why the state has a role to play in criminal justice is because it is best equipped to do a pre-determined job (displacing the private desire for revenge by being just harsh enough to satisfy the thirst for revenge while simultaneously civilizing the response by reference to principles of justice and humanity). This argument, which turns on a judgment about who is best qualified to carry out a pre-determined task, is based on the assumption that private parties could carry out the task of punishment if they were better qualified in the appropriate way. That is, it embraces state instrumentalism and undermines Ashworth's claim that 'the state *must*, as the primary political authority, retain control over criminal justice and its administration'.[30]

Secondly, if Ashworth truly endorses Gardner's 'displacement' argument, he should also embrace Gardner's instrumentalist argument about the constraints on the reasoning of sentencing judges. Consistent with his state instrumentalism, Gardner argues that Ashworth's strong proportionality principle is just a policy choice we have made (rather than a requirement imposed upon us *ex ante* by our conception of the very foundations of the state's power to punish). He writes:

> The just person . . . artificially blinds herself to some qualities of people and aspects of their lives . . . It leads to . . . a remote and sometimes callous disinterest in people's well-being . . . [T]he courts of law . . . should normally keep their distance from us in precisely this way. Courts are law-applying institutions, and it is in the nature of modern law, with its 'Rule of Law' aspiration to apply more or less uniformly to all those who are subject to it, that questions of how people are to be treated relative to one another always come to the fore at the point of its application.[31]

Thus, for Gardner, the strong proportionality principle is little more than a stipulation: the law courts must live up to special rule of law demands because that is in the nature of modern law. Gardner himself concedes that 'this line of thinking . . . of course calls for much more detailed elaboration'. But in fact it needs more than that: it requires a normative argument as to why it is appropriate—or perhaps even necessary—for law courts to give this special regard to proportionality in punishment in a way that private actors need not (and indeed *should* not) do. What is this rule of law aspiration Gardner mentions and why does it have such a pull on us? We will need to look elsewhere to find the answers to these questions.

The rule of law foundations of Ashworth's principles

If we want to explain an intuition such as Ashworth's about matters of jurisdiction—why we insist that only the state may carry out criminal punishment and

[29] eg, Ashworth and von Hirsch, n 3 above, 28, citing Gardner, n 14 above.
[30] Ashworth, n 10 above, 581 (emphasis added).
[31] Gardner, n 14 above, 219.

why the jurisdiction of state officials to administer criminal punishment is constrained in certain crucial ways *ex ante*—it behoves us to look beyond punishment theory to the foundations of the state's authority over its subjects more generally. For no matter what we might want to do to wrongdoers (because it would promote utility, because it would give them what they deserve, because it would communicate the right message, or for some other reason), there are limits on our jurisdiction to do so that are imposed by our understanding of the state's jurisdiction over its subjects more generally. I take it that Ashworth's jurisdictional account of criminal sentencing is gesturing in the direction of this sort of account of the political foundations of criminal sentencing.

There is an account of the foundations of the state's authority over its subjects that seems to fit quite neatly with Ashworth's conception of criminal sentencing and, indeed, with the structure of much of contemporary criminal law doctrine, as well. As Alan Norrie has recently pointed out, 'there is something essentially Kantian about the criminal law, and . . . it is enshrined in the historical structure of modern legal form'.[32] That is, although Norrie is no friend of the liberal legal order established by Kantian political theory, he recognizes that as a descriptive matter, at least, our criminal justice system is best understood as the institutional manifestation of Kantian liberal ideals: the best explanation for why criminal justice officials give considerations of proportionality lexical priority comes from the Kantian obsession with the limited jurisdiction of state officials, and the best explanation for the insistence that criminal justice must be administered only by public officials also comes from the Kantian insistence on a firm distinction between public and private. If we mean to understand the workings of the criminal justice system as we know it—whether to criticize it or to vindicate it on its own terms—it behoves us to see it in the context of these political ideals.

What does such a Kantian account tell us about the nature and limits of the state's legitimate coercive power over its subjects and how might this provide stronger arguments for Ashworth's two principles? We are getting ahead of ourselves. Before we can answer these questions, we need first to make clear the normative starting-point from which the Kantian liberal account begins. We begin with each person's claim to freedom simply in virtue of being human. Contrary to some liberal accounts, the sort of freedom that is of interest to Kantians is not something that individuals can enjoy outside civil society.[33] Freedom as independence is best understood in contrast to slavery: it is the freedom to be one's own master, rather than being subject to the arbitrary will of anyone else. The trouble is that in a state of nature, we are always unfree in this sense, for we are always liable to arbitrary interference from others. And this problem is a good deal deeper than we usually assume. It is not just that as a descriptive matter, we need a

[32] A Norrie, 'Alan Brudner and the Dialectics of Criminal Law' (2011) 14 New Criminal Law Review 449, 451.

[33] It is typical of Lockean accounts, for example, to talk of individuals 'giving up' some of their pre-political freedom in exchange for security and other benefits of civil society. J Locke, *Second Treatise of Government* (1690), XX. This view is also shared by JS Mill, J Raz, GA Cohen, and many others.

powerful state to protect us from interference at the hands of others. Our problem is the normative one that in the state of nature, we have no claim of right against others that they should forbear from interfering with us. For unless others have some assurance that they, too, will be free from domination by others, their unilateral forbearance is simply an act of self-abnegation, rather than an obligation of right. In the state of nature, not only are we unable to demand that others refrain from interfering with us and with our things, we are also unjustified in making that demand.

The state can allow us to escape this predicament not simply because it has the power necessary to resist those who would try to interfere with us, but (more importantly) because it has the unique moral standing that enables it to change our moral position in such a way that we are entitled to demand that others forbear from interfering with us. Waldron puts the point in the following terms:

> The state [is] important from a moral point of view because its presence and operations make a significant difference to ordinary moral reasoning or to our sense of what it is reasonable or right to do . . . [B]y showing that the state makes a moral difference that no other institution can make, the [Kantian liberal] theory may be able to show that these risks [of abuse of power by the state] are worth taking or—more interesting still—that they are risks we are morally *required* to incur because we are not free to turn our backs on the moral possibilities that the existence of the state opens up.[34]

The Kantian liberal state's claim to legitimacy is that, unlike all private actors, it has no partisan will of its own. Instead, it exists merely as the servant (or, as I have called it elsewhere, the fiduciary)[35] of its subjects and their claims of freedom. The state's legitimate role, on this account, is simply to constitute the institutional framework necessary to ensure the freedom of all its subjects. Once this institutional structure is in place, then our moral position vis-à-vis all others is changed forever: now we are all under a genuine obligation of right to forbear from interfering with others (for we are simply granting the same freedom to others that the law grants to us, as well). This requires institutions to demarcate clear boundaries to each person's claim of freedom, it requires institutions to resolve disputes about the scope of each person's freedom, and it requires institutions that vindicate the state's own claim of supremacy in all these matters. Although the officials who administer the state's affairs will inevitably make mistakes along the way, they deserve deference nonetheless because without the state we quickly fall into a situation that is morally intolerable—where our very claim of individual freedom is meaningless.

The institutions and the principles according to which they must act constitute the basic requirements of the rule of law. On the side of private right, this means a respect for the independence of each person (as manifest in their rights to bodily integrity, property, contract, and so on) in so far as this is compatible with equal

[34] J Waldron, 'Kant's Theory of the State' in P Kleingeld (ed), *Toward Perpetual Peace and Other Writings on Politics, Peace and History* (New Haven: Yale University Press, 2006), 183.

[35] See M Thorburn, 'Justifications, Powers, and Authority' (2008) 117 Yale Law Journal 1070 and M Thorburn, 'Criminal Law as Public Law' in A Duff and S Green (eds), *Philosophical Foundations of Criminal Law* (Oxford: Oxford University Press, 2011).

respect for the independence of all others; and on the side of public right, this means that public officials must act in a way that is consistent with the normative grounds for positing the existence of a public power in the first place—acting without partisan interest, refraining from arbitrariness in the exercise of public power, and acting only for the purpose of putting in place the conditions of equal freedom for all its subjects.[36]

The state monopoly principle

Within this Kantian liberal framework, criminal punishment appears as an essential part of the state–citizen relation under the rule of law; and the two features of criminal justice that are so important to Ashworth—strong proportionality and state control—appear as essential features of that institution. A criminal justice system controlled by anyone other than the state would undermine the most basic promise of the liberal state: the guarantee that it will ensure that we are always our own masters, never answerable to any private power. Seen in this way, the reason why criminal justice must remain the state's monopoly is not merely an instrumental one; rather, it flows from the fact that only the state has the standing to act in the name of the system of rights itself rather than in some narrower, partisan interest.

Because the Kantian argument is focused on the question of standing, it is able to answer those who suggest that private actors should be allowed to administer some aspect of the criminal justice system so long as they are subject to the same procedural rules as public officials.[37] The point is not simply that public officials are, in fact, subject to a great many procedural rules to which private actors are not. The deeper concern is that private actors are *private*: no matter how scrupulously they might observe the requirements of procedural fairness, equal treatment and so on, they remain private, partial actors who can only ever have the standing to act in their own name. Making and enforcing the law are acts of self-government that are legitimate only when undertaken by the state on behalf of the people as a whole. Although it is often a difficult task in practice to draw the line separating state employees who act on behalf of all from independent contractors who merely do

[36] This last claim in particular is liable to be misinterpreted. The Kantian claim is not the libertarian one that the state is limited simply to vindicating private rights in one's person, property, contract, etc. Most importantly, it also requires the state to set in place institutions that will ensure the empirical conditions of equal freedom for all. Thus, it is not only an option for the state but a requirement that it should put in place public roads, public education, basic health care, and other institutions that ensure that everyone can remain independent in the requisite sense. For more on this, see E Weinrib, 'Poverty and Property in Kant's System of Rights' (2002–2003) 78 Notre Dame Law Review 795 and A Ripstein, *Force and Freedom: Kant's Legal and Political Philosophy* (Cambridge, MA: Harvard University Press, 2009).

[37] M Trebilcock and E Iacobucci, 'Privatization and Accountability' (2003) 116 Harvard Law Review 1422 argue that private providers of public services might actually be held accountable more effectively than public officials in many instances. But on the question of standing, this is beside the point.

what they are paid to do,[38] we can still maintain our confidence that the line itself is of great significance.

The strong proportionality principle

We saw earlier that the strong proportionality principle applies to criminal justice officials but not, it seems, to private actors such as parents disciplining their children. What does the Kantian liberal account have to say about this distinction? The crucial difference between the two cases, on this account, is the normative ground of the authority the punisher holds over the punishee. Liberals generally accept that parents are legitimately charged with ensuring the welfare of their children, broadly understood. And they accept that the authority of parents over children is consistent with a liberal respect for individual autonomy because minor children are unable to make meaningful choices about virtually all aspects of their lives. The role of fiduciary exists in order to deal with precisely this sort of problem:[39] because minor children are not competent to take charge of their own welfare, we recognize their parents as having standing to make those decisions for them, but only in so far as they take those decisions in the best interests of the children broadly understood. Because parents hold this broad fiduciary power over their children, it is appropriate for them to consider a wide variety of factors related to the children's welfare broadly understood when punishing them. But the situation is rather different when we consider the situation of competent adults—the usual objects of criminal punishment. Criminal offenders generally *are* able to make decisions for themselves about virtually all aspects of their own lives. Accordingly, it would be inappropriate for a liberal state to take over decision-making for such competent adults on all these questions where those adults can decide for themselves.

In an important way, then, the liberal state's legitimate coercive power is different in kind and much narrower in scope than parental power to discipline children, for it is consistent with a liberal respect for individual autonomy in only the narrowest of cases. The state's authority over its subjects is consistent with their autonomy only when it is carrying out a morally necessary task that competent adults cannot carry out on their own: setting out and administering the institutions necessary to establish and vindicate the free and equal moral status of all persons under the rule of law. That is, the liberal state has no business using coercive power to maximize aggregate (or even individual) welfare or to bring about some sort of cosmic retributive justice. In so far as state officials may deviate from the

[38] Indeed, there is an enormous literature and even larger jurisprudence on this topic in the USA, Canada and other countries where the significance of the public–private distinction is made explicit. The *locus classicus* of this discussion is Charles L Black's 1967 essay 'The Supreme Court, 1966 Term—Foreword: "State Action," Equal Protection, and California's Proposition 14' (1967) 81 Harvard Law Review 69.

[39] I set out this fiduciary conception of state authority in greater detail in M Thorburn, 'Criminal Law as Public Law' in A Duff and S Green (eds), *Philosophical Foundations of Criminal Law* (Oxford: Oxford University Press, 2011), 39 ff.

proportionate sentence at all, it must be for a very narrow set of reasons concerned with the preservation of the system of rights itself. Although these reasons go beyond a narrow consideration of individual desert, they do not include the pursuit of instrumental objectives such as specific deterrence or rehabilitation for their own sake. It goes beyond the scope of this essay to determine precisely how this Kantian liberal account narrows the freedom of sentencing judges to consider instrumental factors such as deterrence, rehabilitation, etc in every case. An example will have to suffice for now. If the sentencing judge were to deviate from the proportionate sentence on grounds of rehabilitation, this could be justified on Kantian liberal grounds if this were part of a larger argument concerning the necessary conditions for ensuring the independence of the offender. In so far as the state takes coercive measures toward one of its subjects, that action must be taken in such a way as to ensure that the individual is capable of living independently. Like Ashworth himself, the Kantian liberal account is reluctant to admit considerations other than proportionality at all, but it provides a conceptual apparatus within which both to explain that reluctance and yet to allow for limited deviations from proportionality in certain cases.

4. Conclusion

In this essay, I have sought to vindicate two of Andrew Ashworth's core claims about the criminal justice process—the 'strong proportionality principle' and the 'state monopoly principle'—by means of a rather different set of arguments than the ones he deploys in their defence. Given the overwhelming influence of state instrumentalism in criminal justice theory today, it is not surprising that Ashworth has sometimes relied on arguments of this sort in support of his principles from time to time. But his principles are most compelling and their proper normative grounding is clearest when they are set out in the context of a Kantian liberal account of state authority more generally.

17

Concurrent and Consecutive Sentences Revisited

*Martin Wasik**

1. Introduction

This essay will consider an issue of great practical importance in sentencing, but one which has been sadly neglected in the academic literature. Thousands of sentencing cases each year involve the sentencing of multiple offenders. Offenders are often sentenced on one occasion for two, three, or perhaps many more offences. Often these are in the form of several counts relating to a similar form of offending, but sometimes they cover completely unrelated offences, committed at different times and in different places, which for various reasons now fall to be sentenced together. With the possible exception of the principles relating to a reduction for a plea of guilty, this is the most frequently encountered sentencing issue in practice. It might therefore be expected that the principles which govern it are well known and understood, but in fact they are obscure and unsatisfactory. Until very recently, no sentencing guideline in England and Wales addressed this generic issue. The offence guidelines have been built on the 'artificially pristine model'[1] of sentencing an offender for a single offence, and the problem of multiple offending has been almost entirely ignored.[2]

Offences which are sentenced on the same sentencing occasion are called 'associated offences'. This does not require that all, or indeed any, of the crimes were committed against the same victim, or were spatially, temporally, or in any other way connected. It just means that they fall to be sentenced together.[3] There is

* I am grateful to the editors, and to Antony Duff, Nicola Lacey, and Sotirios Santatzoglou for their helpful comments on earlier drafts.

[1] KR Reitz, 'The Illusion of Proportionality: Desert and Repeat Offenders' in JV Roberts and A von Hirsch (eds), *Previous Convictions at Sentencing: Theoretical and Applied Perspectives* (Oxford: Hart, 2010), 137.

[2] In order to keep this essay within reasonable bounds the focus is on concurrent/consecutive determinate *custodial* sentences. The similar, but not identical, issues arising in relation to financial or community penalties are omitted. Nor are the special rules relating to the imposition of a custodial sentence on a serving prisoner, or on a prisoner who has been released on licence, discussed here.

[3] Powers of Criminal Courts (Sentencing) Act 2000, s 161(1).

a duty on lawyers and judges to ensure that, so far as possible, all outstanding matters against the defendant are dealt with at the same time.[4] A separate and distinct sentence must be passed for every offence which is to be dealt with on each sentencing occasion.[5] When a court is sentencing for associated offences, this affects the overall seriousness of the case, and whether the statutory custody threshold is passed. Statute requires that the court must consider all the associated offences to decide whether the offending is so serious that a custodial sentence is justified.[6] If custody is indeed required, then the duration of the custodial term will also be affected by the presence of associated offences, because the overall sentence must be for the 'shortest term . . . that in the opinion of the court is commensurate with the seriousness of the offence, or the combination of the offence and one or more offences associated with it'.[7] Two or more custodial sentences can be imposed so as to run *concurrently*. Concurrent sentences run at the same time, so in effect the longest custodial sentence imposed on the relevant sentencing occasion is the total sentence. Or the offences may be dealt with by *consecutive* sentences, which run one after the other. The judge must explain, for each sentence passed, whether it is to run concurrently or consecutively. It is not possible for two sentences to 'overlap' by being partly consecutive.[8]

Whether the final sentence comprises concurrent or consecutive terms (or some mix of the two), the total length of the custodial term is said always to be subject to 'totality'. The 'totality principle' was first identified by David Thomas in the 1970s, in his path-breaking analysis of sentencing decisions of the Court of Appeal.[9] He found that when sentencing multiple offenders the proper approach (according to the decisions of the Court at that time) was, first, to impose appropriate sentences for each of the associated offences. Then, these sentences were imposed to run consecutively or concurrently in accordance with certain principles—in particular that offences which arose from a 'single transaction' should (with certain specified exceptions) be sentenced concurrently.[10] Finally, the whole sentence had to be adjusted 'for totality' to ensure that the overall punishment imposed on that sentencing occasion was not too severe. A court 'must not content itself by doing the arithmetic and passing the sentence which the arithmetic produces—it must look at the totality of the criminal behaviour and ask itself what is the appropriate

[4] *Bennett* (1980) 2 Cr App R (S) 96 (CA). Indeed, a defendant sentenced more severely by virtue of being dealt with on two sentencing occasions, rather than one, has a ground of appeal: *Watts* [2000] 1 Cr App R (S) 460 (CA).

[5] Save for any offences taken into consideration, for which a global additional punishment is given. Sometimes an offence is dealt with by marking it with 'no separate penalty'.

[6] Criminal Justice Act 2003, s 152(2).

[7] Ibid, s 153(2).

[8] *Salmon* [2002] EWCA Crim 2088, [2003] 1 Cr App R (S) 414.

[9] D Thomas, *Principles of Sentencing*, (2nd edn, London: Heinemann, 1979), 52–61. This principle is a creation of case law, but has been recognized in the Criminal Justice Act 2003, s 166 (3)(b), which provides that nothing shall prevent a court 'in the case of an offender who is convicted of one or more other offences, from mitigating his sentence by applying any rule of law as to the totality of sentences'. In fact, it is not clear whether the 'totality principle' is a rule of law or a sentencing convention.

[10] Considered further below.

sentence for all the offences'.[11] The totality principle will result in some degree of scaling back of the overall sentence where the overall sentence simply 'looks wrong'.[12] It is clear that many, if not most, criminal justice systems take a similar approach to England and Wales, and accept that total sentences must be scaled back for multiple offenders, but there are some American decisions in which totality is ignored and custodial terms amounting to hundreds of years, far in excess of any person's natural life, are imposed.[13]

2. The Problem with Sentencing Multiple Offences

It is clear that the multiple offender will receive a shorter (perhaps much shorter) sentence if he is dealt with for several offences on a single sentencing occasion than if he is sentenced for those same offences on two or more separate sentencing occasions. This peculiar 'discount for bulk offending' creates problems for sentencing theorists of all shades. The discount seems to undermine the deterrent effect of the law, both for the defendant and for others. If the defendant has committed one offence, the totality principle certainly seems to reduce the disincentive from committing a second, third, and fourth offence. Indeed, offenders might see the 'bulk discount' as an encouragement to spree offending. Bottoms[14] considers the deterrence argument, but dismisses it as fanciful, citing the empirical research on deterrence which shows that, apart from some special cases, adjustment of sentence length to achieve a deterrent effect is unlikely to have much effect in practice.[15] Nils Jareborg[16] also dismisses it, for the same reason. I have no reason to doubt the empirical evidence either, but this does not entirely dispose of deterrence in the present context, and we return to this issue later. Bottoms himself suggests a 'mercy-based' approach to sentencing multiple offenders, designed to avoid a total sentence which is inappropriately severe.[17] Thomas also noted that avoiding a 'crushing' sentence was part of the Court of Appeal's rationale for the totality principle.[18]

The totality principle also creates problems for desert theorists such as Andrew Ashworth. For the desert theorist, of course, the central concern is upon proportionality between seriousness of offence and severity of punishment. This focus has been almost entirely on proportionality between a single offence and a single

[11] Thomas, n 9 above, 57, citing *Barton*, unreported, 1972.

[12] Ibid, 56.

[13] See eg the sentence of 431 years imposed by a Californian court on Philip Garrido for the abduction, false imprisonment, and repeated rape of Jaycee Dugard over a period of 18 years.

[14] A Bottoms, 'Five Puzzles in von Hirsch's Theory of Punishment' in A Ashworth and M Wasik (eds), *Fundamentals of Sentencing Theory* (Oxford: Clarendon Press, 1998), Ch 3.

[15] See A von Hirsch, A Bottoms, E Burney, and P-O Wikström, *Criminal Deterrence: An Analysis of Recent Research* (Oxford: Hart, 1999).

[16] N Jareborg, 'Why Bulk Discounts in Multiple Offence Sentencing?' in Ashworth and Wasik (eds), n 14 above, Ch 5.

[17] Bottoms, n 14 above, 64.

[18] Thomas, n 9 above, 57–8.

punishment. At face value this suggests that for multiple offenders each offence should receive its appropriate sentence and it is simply a matter of adding up the individual terms. Yet desert theorists maintain that the total sentence must be scaled back. Why should there be what Reitz calls 'collapsing desert for multiple convictions'?[19] Ashworth's answer is to say that adding up individual sentences will result in a total term which is disproportionate to the *type of offence* which is being sentenced so that, for example, a defendant being sentenced for numerous counts of theft from shops would attract punishment at a similar level as the rapist or armed robber. The serious sexual or violent offender deserves a higher overall sentence, it is argued, irrespective of the number of offences for which the shoplifter is being sentenced. So, when sentencing an offender for multiple offences the focus of proportionality moves away from the single offence to a broader assessment of the kind of criminality engaged in by this offender. This move is under-explored in desert theory,[20] but its importance in practical sentencing has long been recognized by the Court of Appeal. In the old case of *Holderness*,[21] the Court of Appeal said, when reducing a total sentence of four years on an offender for a variety of motoring offences, that the trial judge had clearly failed to 'take the step . . . of standing back and looking at the overall effect of the sentences . . . if he had done so he would have at once appreciated that he was imposing the kind of sentence which is imposed for really serious crime'.

This approach to the totality principle has been endorsed and restated by Ashworth, although he prefers to talk about 'overall proportionality' rather than totality. He says that where there is a choice between two applications of proportionality—strict offence-by-offence proportionality (resulting in cumulative sentences) and overall proportionality—'the principle of restraint in the use of custody should be applied'[22] and 'overall proportionality' should be preferred. Ashworth's account is a more convincing explanation than the rehabilitative need to avoid a 'crushing' sentence. As Ashworth himself points out, not all cumulative sentencing would produce such a sentence, and a single very long determinate sentence may be 'crushing' for an offender, so this seems to be a rehabilitative objection to very long sentences in general, rather than something confined to multiple offence cases.[23] Ashworth's support for overall proportionality, persuasive though it is, cannot deal with the fundamental, and probably intractable, problem that the total sentence received by a multiple offender depends crucially upon the number of sentencing occasions over which his offences are dealt with. This peculiar phenomenon, which is the product of a range of prosecution and charging practices, including the policy of bringing all outstanding matters against the defendant before a court at the same time, is clearly a system-wide issue that cannot

[19] Reitz, n 1 above, 141.

[20] It runs close to asking 'what kind of offender' we are dealing with, which is hardly a desert-based approach to sentencing.

[21] Thomas, n 9 above, 58.

[22] A Ashworth, *Sentencing and Criminal Justice* (5th edn, Cambridge: Cambridge University Press, 2010), 276.

[23] Ibid.

be resolved at the sentencing stage.[24] However, whenever an offender does fall to be sentenced for several offences on the same occasion, the tools which are available to the judge to ameliorate some of the worst of the anomalies are concurrent and consecutive sentences and totality. It is to these important practical matters that we now turn.

3. Concurrent and Consecutive Sentences, and Totality, Explored

The totality principle applies to all multiple offence cases, whatever combination of concurrent and/or consecutive sentences a judge imposes. Two different judges might impose a different mix of sentences on the same multiple offender but, whatever the individual sentences passed, the totality (or 'overall proportionality' as Ashworth puts it) should be the same. This is a fundamental point. Suppose that the offender is being sentenced for two offences. He might receive four years for offence A and one year concurrent for offence B or, alternatively, three years for offence A and one year consecutive for offence B. Both these formulations comply with a totality of four years, and are identical in their practical outcome, in the sense that both offenders will be eligible for release from prison at the same time. Since the overall outcomes are the same, it can be seen that under these conditions *no proportionality issue arises over the choice between concurrent and consecutive sentences.* The choice between concurrent and consecutive sentences is, rather, to do with the manner, or style, in which the overall sentence is *presented* by the judge.

It will also be appreciated from this simple example that concurrent sentences carry what can be described as a greater *internal sum* than consecutive sentences with the same totality (in this example, an internal sum of five years as against four years). The difference between the internal sum on one hand, and totality on the other, becomes more pronounced as more offences are dealt with. If the offender is being sentenced for three offences he might receive four years for offence A, one year concurrent for offence B, and one year concurrent for offence C (an internal sum of six years as against a totality of four years). The implications are very different for consecutive sentences. In the simple two-offence example, to include the consecutive sentence of one year for offence B while retaining a totality of four years, offence A has to be *under-sentenced* (by reducing it from four years to three years). This is even clearer in the three-offence example. If the judge passes three sentences consecutively, *at least one of the other offences will have to be under-sentenced.* It follows that concurrent sentences are more in tune with proportionality principles than are consecutive sentences, because concurrent sentences allow a judge to pass custodial terms which are proportionate to the individual offences dealt with, whilst also complying with totality. An offender's criminal record lists the sentences passed for *every* offence, and so indicates *both* the internal sum and the

[24] Reitz, n 1 above, 157 suggests that the 'discount for bulk offending' must be linked to broader issues of incarceration rates and cost. He says that 'resource constraints [limit] ultimately what can be done in individual cases'.

totality. Concurrent sentences, therefore, provide a fuller and more accurate indication of multiple offence criminality than do consecutive sentences. These are good reasons in principle why concurrent sentences are preferable when sentencing multiple offenders, unless some overriding reason can be found to use consecutive ones. Students coming to the subject of sentencing for the first time often ask: 'What's the point of concurrent sentences?' The better question, it seems, is: 'What's the point of consecutive ones?' Other jurisdictions have come to this conclusion already. In France consecutive sentences are prohibited for multiple current offences.[25] In the State of Victoria in Australia consecutive sentences are permitted but there is both a common law and a statutory presumption in favour of concurrent sentences.[26]

4. Totality and Sentencing Guidelines

According to Thomas's account of multiple offence sentencing, the sentencer is first required to determine the sentences for all the individual offences and only later, towards the end of the sentencing exercise, to 'step back' and, if necessary, adjust for totality. The obvious question, then, is: how should the form and extent of that adjustment be determined? At this point, Thomas identifies a further principle, which is that:

> [T]he aggregate sentence should not be longer than the upper limit of the normal bracket of sentences for the category of cases in which the most serious offence committed by the offender would be placed.[27]

This looks like a crucial principle, with great potential value for the practical business of sentencing. The difficulty is that it runs against Thomas's general account of totality. It now seems, from this further principle, that the approach cannot be as Thomas originally described it—determining all the individual sentences first, and then scaling back for totality—but the other way round. Instead, an early task in the sentencing exercise should be to identify the appropriate range for the 'lead' sentence (to be imposed for the most serious of the offences), and then to fit the other sentences in and around it, using concurrent or consecutive sentences as appropriate, while ensuring that the total sentence remains within that range. Totality then becomes not a limiting principle but a determining principle for sentencing the multiple offender.

In his account of multiple offence sentencing, Ashworth refers to the possibility that totality might come *first* in the sentencer's chain of reasoning, but he does not

[25] RS Frase, 'Comparative Criminal Justice as a Guide to American Law Reform: How Do the French Do it, How Can We Find out, and Why Should We Care?' (1990) 78 California Law Review 539, 618–19.

[26] R Fox and A Freiberg, *Sentencing: State and Federal Law in Victoria* (2nd edn, Melbourne: Oxford University Press, 1999), para 9.603.

[27] Thomas, n 9 above, 9.

appear to endorse the idea.[28] There is empirical evidence from Australia that judges have adopted 'a top-down approach which starts with totality rather than ending with it'.[29] There are some decisions of the English Court of Appeal which also seem to support the earlier consideration of totality, argued for above. In the old case of *Smith*,[30] Scarman LJ said that 'the overall sentence should reflect the total appropriate to the course of criminal conduct . . . but . . . it is fairer . . . to impose the total sentence in respect of one, perhaps the most grave of the offences, and then to impose lesser sentences in respect of the other(s)'. More recently, Hughes LJ said in *Round*[31] that 'the natural structure of a sentence will normally, though not always, be to pass the principal (and thus usually the longest) term first'. If, as I suggest, totality should be regarded as a determining principle, then it is probably best to think of it as a reference point for the judge *throughout* the whole sentencing exercise, rather than as something that comes just at the beginning, or just at the end. Some may object that the problem with employing totality as a determining, rather than a limiting, principle, as is proposed in this essay, is that totality is too loose an idea to be serviceable. However, sentencing guidelines offer a suitable way forward.

When Thomas wrote the second edition of his work in 1979 there were no appellate sentencing guidelines, and certainly nothing like the multitude of definitive guidelines issued under statutory authority since the turn of this century. The new Sentencing Council (which replaced the Sentencing Guidelines Council in 2010) is charged with the responsibility of producing new sentencing guidelines, and updating old ones and, in particular, has a statutory duty[32] to prepare guidelines to take account of the 'totality principle'. The Council has very recently published a guideline on this issue,[33] and has already issued offence guidelines (on assault, burglary, and drug offences), all of which endorse the idea that totality should be considered by the sentencer towards the end of the sentencing exercise, rather than at the beginning.[34] However, the structure of all the offence guidelines so far produced, whether under the current or previous regimes, relies upon the setting out of sentencing 'ranges' and 'starting points' for individual offences. The Sentencing Council offence guidelines specify a very wide 'offence range' to cover all manifestations of the offence in question, and a number of more specific 'category ranges', each appropriate to a particular form of the offence. Each category range has within it a starting point. None of the existing guidelines deal with the

[28] Ashworth, n 22 above, 274–5.

[29] Ibid, 274, referring to M Wells, *Sentencing for Multiple Offences in Western Australia* (Nedlands, WA: University of Western Australia Crime Research Centre, 1992); and A Lovegrove, *Sentencing the Multiple Offender: Judicial Practice and Legal Principle* (Canberra: Australian Institute of Criminology, 2004).

[30] *Smith* (1975) CSP A5-3F01.

[31] *Round* [2009] EWCA Crim 2667, [2010] 2 Cr App R (S) 45 at [41].

[32] Coroners and Justice Act 2009, s 120.

[33] Sentencing Council, *Totality Guideline* (London: Sentencing Council, 2012).

[34] Sentencing Council, *Allocation, Offences Taken into Consideration, and Totality, Consultation Guideline* (London: Sentencing Council, 2011), 17: 'the consideration of totality should be a "stand back and look" test that is applied towards the end of the sentencing decision-making process'.

multiple offence problem (and they were not designed to do so), but if totality is indeed a determining principle, then there is clear potential for the sentencing guidelines structure to be built upon to provide a proper framework for sentencing multiple offences too.[35]

If we take seriously (as I wish to do) Thomas's principle that the overall sentence for the multiple offender should not exceed the upper limit of the category range for the most serious offence committed by that offender, this raises some immediate questions. One issue is whether the category ranges in existing sentencing guidelines are suitable for extension in this way to multiple offence sentencing, or whether they are too narrow, or too broad. When sentencing for an individual offence it is well understood that a judge may sometimes pass a sentence above the category range, provided that good reasons are given for doing so. It is never permissible, however, to pass a sentence which is above the *maximum* for the offence. How tight a constraint should the category range for the lead sentence provide in cases of multiple offending, and when should a sentencer be permitted to exceed that range? More specifically, should it be possible, as the law currently allows,[36] for the total sentence passed on a multiple offender to exceed the maximum available for the lead offence? These are issues which the Sentencing Council should address, but it has declined to do so in its Consultation Paper and resulting Guideline. The Council says that it does not want to be 'mathematical', or to 'provide strict guidance', given the wide variety of circumstances in which the totality principle needs to be applied.[37] I think it should have gone further.

The Sentencing Council might have made a start by endorsing Ashworth's contention that, no matter how many offences of a particular kind an offender is found to have committed, the total sentence should remain within the range appropriate to that type of offence, although of course the total sentence will be higher in that range than would have been the case for a single offence. This seems a promising approach as far as it applies to the 'specialist' offender (such as the persistent thief), but other examples are not so clear. Few offenders are specialists, and a court may well be sentencing a multiple offender for different sorts of offences. Reitz has looked at this issue, and he rejects the suggestion that 'one robbery plus ten burglaries cannot surpass the maximum seriousness threshold of one robbery'.[38] In response to Reitz's example we can note that, for a street robbery in which a weapon is produced but not used, the current starting point is four years within a category range of two to seven years.[39] If we assume that four years is

[35] See further JV Roberts and A Rafferty, 'Sentencing Guidelines in England and Wales: Exploring the New Format' [2011] Crim LR 681.

[36] The classic example is the case of *Prime* (1983) 5 Cr App R (S) 127 (CA), where a total sentence of 38 years was upheld for espionage (consecutive terms of 14, 14, and 7 years, 14 years being the maximum sentence), plus 3 years consecutive for unrelated sexual offences against young girls.

[37] Sentencing Council, n 34 above, 19.

[38] Reitz, n 1 above, 146.

[39] These figures are taken from the Sentencing Guidelines Council's Definitive Guideline on *Robbery*, and assume that the defendant is a first offender who has been convicted after a trial. One-third reduction from the indicated sentence is recommended where the offender has admitted guilt 'at the first reasonable opportunity'.

suitable for our particular robbery, it allows an upward revision of three further years to deal with the burglaries before the sentencer needs to consider going above the category range. The seriousness of the particular robbery must make a difference. If that offence alone justifies a sentence at or near the top of the category range, then the pressure to exceed the category range to accommodate the additional offences will be greater. Exceeding the maximum sentence is, however, another matter. The maximum sentence for robbery is life imprisonment, and so, in this particular example, could not be exceeded. But suppose the maximum for robbery was 14 years.[40] Perhaps such a maximum would provide ample headroom to deal with the multiple offender in Reitz's example, and still preserve overall proportionality. The issue of exceeding the maximum sentence is returned to later.

5. Is Totality All that Matters?

The process of sentencing might aptly be compared to setting out on a journey. Before embarking it is helpful to decide where one is going. Having settled on the destination, one then determines the route to get there. The most important aspect of any sentence is totality—the 'bottom line'—the decision which the defendant is waiting to hear. As the Court of Appeal noted in *Whitehead*:[41] 'The primary focus of any sentencing judge will be on what the appropriate total is, however it is rationalised or reasoned.' Provided that the total sentence complies with totality, it seems that different judges might take somewhat different approaches in their use of concurrent and consecutive sentences. As Lord Lane CJ said in *Lawrence*:[42]

> . . . the problem is really one of determining what sentence is appropriate to the offences taken as a whole . . . Whether that is done by imposing shorter sentences to run consecutively or longer sentences to run concurrently does not really in the end make any difference.

The Court of Appeal often deals with appeals against sentence by multiple offenders. The relevant ground of appeal is that the sentence was 'wrong in principle or manifestly excessive'[43] or, in the case of an Attorney General's Reference, that the sentence was 'unduly lenient'. A failure by the trial judge to adjust (or adjust enough) for totality will result in a finding by the Court that the sentence was 'manifestly excessive'. One way in which this may be remedied is by changing consecutive sentences to concurrent ones. Such an adjustment provides a convenient way to achieve the necessary overall reduction. If, however, the overall

[40] Which in practice is the highest maximum sentence laid down by Parliament short of the life sentence.

[41] [2010] EWCA Crim 3252, [2011] 2 Cr App R (S) 16.

[42] (1989) 11 Cr App R (S) 580 (CA).

[43] Other grounds for adjusting sentence are (i) sentence unlawful; (ii) sentence passed on wrong factual basis; (iii) some matter improperly taken into account, or some fresh matter to be taken into account; and (iv) failure to honour a legitimate expectation: JF Archbold and PJ Richardson, *Archbold: Criminal Pleading, Evidence and Practice* (London: Sweet & Maxwell, 2012), para 7–136. These grounds are not relevant to this essay.

sentence cannot be impugned in terms of totality, it is very rare indeed for an appeal to succeed in a case where totality has been respected by the judge but the offences might have been sentenced consecutively rather than concurrently or vice versa.[44]

Ashworth, as we might expect, seeks to impose order out of the myriad reported cases that deal with multiple offenders, and hence concurrent and consecutive terms. He insists that the wide range of circumstances in which these issues arise, and the manifest practical difficulties, 'should not be allowed to stifle the search for some general principles'.[45] We need now to take a step back, and examine the principles which are said to underpin the use of concurrent and consecutive sentences. It may seem strange that we have not considered these earlier in this essay, but my suggestion is that these principles actually have very little importance in driving sentence outcome but, rather, provide judges with options within which multiple offence sentencing can be *presented within totality*. The word 'presented' is chosen carefully here, and is not meant to imply a cosmetic exercise. 'Presentation' involves the careful, sympathetic, nuanced delivery of a sentence, and is an aspect of judge-craft. A judge is required not just to announce the total sentence to the defendant, but also to explain what sentence has been passed for each offence, and whether these sentences are to run concurrently or consecutively. There is a statutory duty to explain not just the reasons for the overall sentence, but its practical effect.[46] Communication is with the defendant and with others present in the courtroom, including the victim(s), but also with the wider public through media reports of the decision.[47] Ordering sentences to run consecutively instead of concurrently, though not impacting on overall proportionality, can sometimes be useful as a way of communicating a message. That message has traditionally been expressed in deterrent terms.[48] The judge may wish to stress to all concerned that an *additional* punishment has been imposed for one of the offences, and to demonstrate that by passing a consecutive term. One does not need to believe in the efficacy of deterrence to understand the value of clear and forceful presentation of this kind. As we have seen, however, this does require a degree of sleight of hand, since totality requires that for every consecutive punishment for a multiple offender there must be an equivalent reduction in punishment elsewhere.

6. Sentencing Principles and Sentencing Presentation

Concurrence and the 'single incident'

The first and most prominent principle said to be applicable to concurrent/consecutive sentencing is that where two or more offences are committed in the

[44] For a rare contrary example, see *Wacker* [2002] EWCA Crim 1944, [2003] 1 Cr App R (S) 92, discussed below.

[45] Ashworth, n 22 above, 263.

[46] Criminal Justice Act 2003, s 174(1).

[47] RA Duff, *Punishment, Communication, and Community* (Oxford: Oxford University Press, 2001), esp Ch 3.

[48] Ibid, 82 ff: 'Communication, Deterrence, and Prudential Supplements'.

course of a *single incident* the sentences for those offences should be concurrent. This principle was identified by Thomas, and has been referred to in the sentencing texts ever since. The Magistrates' Courts Sentencing Guidelines state that: 'While concurrent sentences are generally to be preferred where the offences arose out of a single incident, consecutive sentences may be desirable in some circumstances.'[49] At first sight concurrent sentences for a single incident is indeed a plausible idea, and the Sentencing Council also takes it to be the central issue.[50] The single incident idea does reflect the important point that, whether a particular piece of criminal conduct is charged as one, or more than one, offence, the difference in charging practice should not affect the overall sentence. The problem, however, is that what constitutes the 'same' or a 'different' criminal incident is dependent upon a range of contingent considerations of time, space, identity of victim, as well as variation in charging practices. Jareborg says that:

> ... it is in practice very difficult to handle concepts like 'same act', 'continuous criminality' and 'same transaction'. To use them is an invitation to endless argument, and the response from the courts may well be a formalism that draws attention away from the real issues.[51]

This is surely right, and is borne out by the appellate decisions being very hard, if not impossible, to reconcile. Let us take just a few examples.

According to the Court of Appeal in *Tamby*,[52] where the defendant penetrated the victim's vagina with his finger, and then his penis, that is a single incident (requiring concurrent sentences). This seems to be because here we have two offences against the same victim within a short time frame. But it was held in *Cosco*[53] that if the defendant indecently exposes himself to three different women in the course of an afternoon, that is also a single incident (concurrent). Here we have three different victims, and a broader time frame, so now it seems to be the similarity of the offending that makes it a single incident. In *RC*[54] there were three separate offences of rape committed by the offender on his sister, two when she was under 13, and one when she was over 13. The judge passed three consecutive sentences of six years, making a total of 18 years. The Court of Appeal varied that to a total of 12 years, with the first two prison terms consecutive and the third concurrent. So here it seems that the offending is neither one incident, nor three, but two which, with respect, makes no sense at all. If the defendant drives dangerously for some time and then crashes the car, causing serious injury to a passenger in that car, the driving offence and the assault are part of the same incident (concurrent).[55] We

[49] Sentencing Guidelines Council, *Magistrates' Court Sentencing Guidelines: Definitive Guideline* (London: Sentencing Guidelines Council, 2008), 147.

[50] Sentencing Council, n 34 above, 18: 'The general approach ... is that offences that arise out of the same incident or facts should be served concurrently, whilst offences that arise out of unrelated facts or incidents should be served consecutively.'

[51] Jareborg, n 16 above, 131.

[52] *Tamby* [2008] EWCA Crim 207, [2008] 2 Cr App R (S) 366. Ashworth regards this as a 'clear case', n 22 above, 266, but see further, below.

[53] [2005] EWCA Crim 207, [2005] 2 Cr App R (S) 405.

[54] [2011] EWCA Crim 1872.

[55] *Bain* [2005] EWCA Crim 7, [2005] 2 Cr App R (S) 319.

have two different crimes, factually linked, within a relatively short time frame. If the victim of the assault had been a pedestrian struck by the speeding vehicle, rather than a passenger in the car, might that have made a difference to whether this would be seen as one incident or two? In *Edwards*[56] the Court of Appeal upheld consecutive sentences for assault and theft, where the defendant punched the victim to the floor, briefly left the scene but then returned and stole the victim's wallet. Why is this not a single transaction, since the offences involved the same victim and occurred within a very short time frame?

The corollary of the 'single transaction' principle, then, is that where offences arise from separate incidents, sentences may (and in some cases should) be consecutive. In *Worrell*[57] the Court of Appeal approved consecutive sentences for an offence of terrorism and an offence of racially aggravated harassment. The choice of consecutive sentences seems to reflect the fact that the two matters were factually unconnected and were being sentenced together simply for convenience. Intuitively it does seem right that such entirely separate matters should attract consecutive sentences but, as we have seen, it is common in multiple offence sentencing for a judge to be dealing with an offender for factually unrelated crimes. No clear rule emerges from the cases that consecutive sentences should be imposed for separate incidents, or even for offences on separate indictments. In *Jamieson*[58] the defendant was dealt with for nine thefts. In four of those he sprayed security guards with acid, giving rise to four offences of administering a noxious substance with intent. In another of the thefts he punched a security guard, so there was a further count of assault. There was also an unrelated offence of burglary, sent up from the magistrates' court. The Court upheld a total sentence of nine years, comprising four consecutive sentences of two years for each of the noxious substance offences, six months for each of the nine offences of theft, to run concurrently but consecutively to the eight years, six months consecutive for the assault, and finally 12 months concurrent for the burglary. Leaving aside the burglary, how many 'incidents' were there? The thefts were committed in 2006 and 2007, so the time frame is presumably too great for these to be seen as a single transaction (cf *Cosco* above). The number of consecutive sentences upheld on appeal suggests five incidents, but there were nine thefts in total. Why does this case add up to five incidents, rather than nine? Also, should not the burglary, which was an entirely separate matter, have attracted a consecutive term?

Other examples might be given, but enough has been said to show that the 'single incident' principle is too malleable and vague to form a useful basis for distinguishing concurrent from consecutive sentencing. As Fox and Freiberg say, 'for every case that can be cited to illustrate the rule, another can be found that provides an exception, or effectively negates it'.[59] The single incident principle is taken seriously by Ashworth, but he accepts that there are problems with it, and he

[56] [2009] EWCA Crim 602.
[57] [2009] EWCA Crim 1431, [2010] 1 Cr App R (S) 27.
[58] [2008] EWCA Crim 2761, [2009] 2 Cr App R (S) 26.
[59] Fox and Freiberg, n 26 above, 715.

says that often 'it seems to be little more than a pragmatic device for limiting overall sentences'.[60] This observation is surely correct. It will be recalled from the earlier discussion that there were sound reasons why sentences for multiple offences should run concurrently. The 'concurrent sentences for a single transaction' notion adds little or nothing, and is only likely to create confusion. Jareborg notes that the 'single transaction' principle has been abandoned in Swedish law, and it is submitted that the same course should be adopted here.

Consecutive sentences required

Next, we need to examine the situations in which the courts have said that sentences *should* be imposed consecutively. There is statutory provision making it clear that where an offender commits a new offence in breach of a suspended sentence, and receives a prison sentence for it, the suspended sentence should normally be activated in full,[61] and normally consecutively to the new term.[62] The case law on breach of other court orders, such as a community sentence or a conditional discharge, by commission of a fresh offence, permits a consecutive sentence for the breach but there is no presumption. In practice the breach is often treated as aggravating the new offence, and the new offence is given a higher sentence in consequence.[63] The original order may be revoked in light of a custodial sentence for the new offence, and breach of the order then sentenced concurrently, or with 'no separate penalty' ordered. There is some authority that a consecutive sentence should be passed where the offender commits an offence while on bail for another offence,[64] but again this is often not applied in practice. There is a statutory provision that breach of bail must be treated as an aggravating factor,[65] and these rules cannot *both* be applied, as this would double-count the same feature. Another group of authorities deals with cases where an offender commits an offence against justice (such as perjury, perverting the course of justice, or failing to attend court) in an attempt to avoid conviction for another offence. Most of the decisions say that the two matters should receive consecutive custodial sentences, but again there are exceptions. Relying on the 'single incident' idea, Ashworth says that this 'may also not be regarded as a true exception'[66] because there will often be a clear time difference between the two offences. This was true in *Atkinson*,[67] where the offender was facing trial for indecent assaults on a young boy and, while on remand in custody, he sent a letter to the boy which was designed to discourage him from

[60] Ashworth, n 22 above, 266.

[61] Criminal Justice Act 2003, Sch 12, para 8(2) This course should be taken unless 'unjust to do so'.

[62] Sentencing Guidelines Council, *New Sentences: Criminal Justice Act 2003* (London: Sentencing Guidelines Council, 2004), para 2.2.21.

[63] 'Failure to respond to previous sentences' is a standard aggravating factor: Sentencing Guidelines Council, *Overarching Principles: Seriousness* (London: Sentencing Guidelines Council, 2003), para 1.22.

[64] *Whittaker* [1998] 1 Cr App R (S) 172 (CA), considered further below.

[65] Criminal Justice Act 2003, s 143(3).

[66] Ashworth, n 22 above, para 8.2.3.

[67] *Attorney General's Reference (No 1 of 1990)(Atkinson)* (1992) QB 630 (CA).

giving evidence. The Court of Appeal said that the concurrent sentence imposed for the perversion of justice offence had been incorrect, and stressed the separate nature of the two offences. But it is surely not the *separateness* that makes the difference here. The common feature in all the examples in this paragraph, where consecutive sentences have often (though not always) been endorsed, is that the defendant has compounded his criminality by flouting a court order, or by attacking the justice system.[68] The traditional language of judges when recommending consecutive sentences in these cases is *deterrence*. The suspended prison sentence is classically rooted in deterrence and, if the offender commits a further offence in breach, a consecutive sentence at least gives the impression that an extra punishment has been given for it. If an offence is committed on bail, a consecutive sentence 'makes it absolutely clear to all those concerned that once you have committed offences and are on bail you do not have a free run to commit other offences'.[69] Similarly, when a further offence has been committed in breach of an earlier court order, 'it is most important that offenders should be made to realise . . . that a subsequent offence . . . will involve punishment for the crime for which the offender was originally given the benefit of this lenient treatment'.[70]

There are a couple of other situations in which there has been judicial support for the use of consecutive sentences. The first is where the offender is convicted of an offence against the person and possession of a weapon[71] and the second is where an offender has been interrupted while committing an offence and has used force against a member of the public, or a police officer, in trying to get away.[72] Ashworth says that the first example is generally followed, at least where a firearm is involved but less predictably if the weapon is a knife,[73] but the second example is unpredictably applied. Charging practice is a key variable here. In the first situation the offender may be convicted of a single offence of assault or robbery (aggravated by the presence of the weapon), or of two offences. The carrying of a weapon is a prominent aggravating factor in the robbery guidelines[74] and, as with the bail example given above, there is a risk of double-counting the same feature. In the second situation often no separate assault charge will be brought, and the assault will be treated as an aggravating feature of the property offence. If the police officer or member of the public suffers significant injury the offences are more likely to be the subject of separate charges. But whichever approach is taken to charging, the offender's total conduct is the same, and the total sentence should be the same. So why bother with consecutive sentences? Again, the traditional reason is deterrence or, as I would prefer to put it, presentation. So, if an offender carries a weapon when

[68] For an exceptional case where the sentence for escape from custody was ordered to run concurrently with the sentence for the original offence see *Patmore* [2010] EWCA Crim 2887, [2011] 2 Cr App R (S) 21.

[69] *Hunnybun* (1979) CSP A5-2F02.

[70] *Webb* (1953) 37 Cr App R 82 (CCA).

[71] *Faulkner* (1972) 56 Cr App R 594 (CA).

[72] *Kastercum* (1972) 56 Cr App R 298 (CA).

[73] Ashworth, n 22 above, 267.

[74] Sentencing Guidelines Council, *Robbery: Definitive Guideline* (London: Sentencing Guidelines Council, 2006), 6.

committing another offence, a consecutive sentence should be imposed to 'discourage such conduct'.[75] While the presentational value of an additional punishment in some of these cases is clear, the use of consecutive sentences carries the risk that overall proportionality will be lost. The only way to safeguard totality is to under-sentence elsewhere.

7. Some Illustrative Cases Revisited

The bail case

The case generally cited as authority for the principle that offending in breach of bail should produce a consecutive sentence is *Whittaker*.[76] It is submitted that this is a simple case masquerading as a complex one, in which the Court of Appeal was led into error. The offender was convicted at trial of four burglaries, all targeted at elderly householders. The latter two offences had been committed after the defendant had been released on bail awaiting trial on the first two. The judge imposed five years on each of the first two burglaries, concurrent, and five years on each of the latter two burglaries, concurrent, but with the two five-year terms to run consecutively because of the breach of bail. The Court of Appeal was clearly concerned that ten years was 'a very severe total sentence' but, with some misgivings, upheld the judge's approach. It is submitted that the Court fell into error by allowing the breach of bail to drive consecutive sentences, and thereby to breach totality. Surely this is a case of four serious residential burglaries, the latter two carrying an additional aggravating factor (they were committed on bail). Five years is probably too short for any one of the burglaries, but ten years is too long in total. An alternative sentence construction would have been, say, seven years concurrent on each of the two later burglaries, six years concurrent on each of the two earlier ones, those terms to run concurrently making seven years in all. This change would reduce totality from ten to seven, but increase the internal sum from 20 years (2 x 5) + (2 x 5) to 26 years (2 x 7) + (2 x 6).

Multiple death cases

The interplay of totality, concurrent, and consecutive sentences is critical in a case where several deaths have occurred. *Wacker*[77] involved multiple counts of manslaughter by gross negligence. The defendant was convicted of conspiracy to facilitate the entry into the United Kingdom of illegal immigrants, and 58 offences of manslaughter relating to the victims who had asphyxiated in the back of his lorry. The judge imposed eight years for the conspiracy, and six years on each count of manslaughter concurrent, those sentences to run consecutively, totalling 14 years.

[75] *Faulkner* (1972) 56 Cr App R 594 (CA).
[76] *Whittaker* [1998] 1 Cr App R (S) 172 (CA).
[77] [2002] EWCA Crim 1944, [2003] 1 Cr App R (S) 92.

The Court of Appeal of course considered the central issue of whether 14 years was manifestly excessive for what the defendant had done, and concluded that it was not—the total sentence 'fairly reflected the seriousness of the matter'. As we have seen, in the great majority of cases that would have been enough to dismiss the appeal. However, Kay LJ said that: 'There are cases *where the way in which the total sentence is composed* may cause public concern, and diminish the faith of the public in the criminal justice system as a whole.'[78] The issue, then, is now one of presentation of multiple offence sentences within totality. The Court substituted 14 years on each manslaughter count, all concurrent, and upheld eight years for the conspiracy, also to run concurrently. Kay LJ was explicit in his reasoning: 'this method of sentencing . . . will be more readily understood by the public. It will not give the appearance, as may have occurred in this case, of devaluing the loss of life.'[79] This, with respect, is correct. The overall sentence was unaffected by the adjustment, but the way the sentence is now presented contains within it an important message about the relative seriousness of the counts. The Court incidentally adjusted the consecutive sentences to run concurrently without referring to the question whether this case involved a 'single incident' or not. The Court was concerned with how the sentence looked, and the message it communicated to the defendant, to the relatives of the victims, and to the wider public. The final sentence observed totality and was elegantly structured. While totality was unaffected, the internal sum increased from 356 years (8 + (6 x 58)) to 820 years (8 + (14 x 58)).

Another illustrative case is that of *Noble*,[80] a notorious example of multiple deaths caused by dangerous driving. The judge passed sentences totalling 15 years—three concurrent terms of five years for the deaths of the offender's three friends who were in the car with him, plus three concurrent terms of ten years for the deaths of the three other entirely innocent victims, these to run consecutively to total 15 years. This was a lawful sentence, despite the judge exceeding the maximum sentence of ten years (as it was at the time) since, as explained above, where consecutive terms are ordered the total sentence may exceed the maximum which could have been imposed for any one of the offences. The Court of Appeal allowed the appeal against sentence. First, the Court preferred to sentence within the permitted maximum for the offence, and this was achieved by adjusting all the sentences to ten years and ordering them to run concurrently, totalling ten years. The case is said by David Thomas to involve the principle that 'consecutive terms should not be imposed in respect of offences which arise out of a single incident'.[81] On my account, however, the adjustment by the Court of Appeal is not about this being a single incident, but is all about presentation and communication. It is submitted that the better way to understand the case is to say that the sentencer should be loyal to the maximum sentence, and in this case the maximum sentence

78 [2002] EWCA Crim 1944, [2003] 1 Cr App R (S) 92, at [45].
79 Ibid, at [53].
80 [2002] EWCA Crim 1713, [2003] 1 Cr App R (S) 312.
81 Thomas, Current Sentencing Practice, A5-2.

was justified, it being the worst conceivable example of such an offence.[82] This was partly because of the number of deaths, but also because of many other aggravating features—the offender was very heavily intoxicated, was already disqualified from driving, he fled the scene, and by contesting the case he forfeited the discount for plea. The Court of Appeal said that 'the fact that multiple deaths had been caused was not in itself a reason for imposing consecutive sentences'. I agree with that result, but the way to arrive at it is to impose the maximum sentence to reflect overall proportionality and then, for presentational reasons, to reflect the multiple deaths by passing the equivalent number of concurrent sentences. Some might say that using concurrent sentences here implies that it is no worse to kill six people than to kill one, but the better argument is that the total sentence is clearly and distinctively associated with each death.[83] It will be noted that the Court (wisely in my view) did not adopt the judge's approach of drawing a distinction in the punishment for the deaths of the offender's companions and the deaths of the other victims. This point is not mentioned in the judgment, but Keene LJ quietly equates the sentences for all of the deaths, lest the message go out that some lives are worth more than others. In this interesting case totality was reduced (from 15 to 10 years) but the internal sum was increased, from 45 years (3 x 5) + (3 x 10) to 60 years (6 x 10).

Assaults on the same victim

A different kind of case is *Tamby*,[84] where the offender was convicted of assault by penetration and rape in respect of the same victim on the same occasion. He was sentenced to two years for the former offence and eight years for the latter, consecutive. The appeal to the Court of Appeal was on the basis that totality had been infringed. That argument was accepted, and the total sentence was reduced to eight years. That result was reached by ordering the two terms to run concurrently. The case is cited by Thomas as another example of the principle that consecutive sentences should not be imposed for offences arising out of a single incident. I am not convinced that the case really is authority for that point. Indeed, Underhill J in the Court of Appeal specifically said that the passing of consecutive sentences 'would not matter if the overall term were fair'. The crucial point is that the overall sentence was disproportionate. Given that, how should the sentence have been restructured? The most convenient way for the Court to achieve that was to order the existing sentences to run concurrently, rather than consecutively—a reduction in totality from ten years to eight, but with the same internal sum (ten years). An alternative would have been to reduce both sentences (say, to one year

[82] According to Keene LJ, this was 'a case which comes at the very top of the range'. The maximum for the offence has since been increased to 14 years.

[83] Hughes LJ in *Round* [2009] EWCA Crim 2667, [2010] 2 Cr App R (S) 45 at [8], said that 'consecutive sentences may properly be passed in order to make clear to individual victims that the offence concerning them has been met by an individual sentence', but it submitted that in multiple death cases this is better achieved by concurrent sentences.

[84] [2008] EWCA Crim 207, [2008] 2 Cr App R (S) 63.

and seven years) but still to run consecutively (both totality and internal sum of eight years). The Court probably demurred from that approach because it would have required a double reduction and, presentationally, would have resulted in lenient sentences for each offence.

Robbery with a weapon

As we have seen, one of the examples where consecutive sentences are said to be appropriate is that of robbery committed with a weapon. Lord Judge CJ in *Ralphs*[85] said that was an 'obvious' example because 'distinct offences are committed' albeit on a single occasion. With great respect, this is not 'obvious', and there is a clear division in the sentencing authorities as to whether robbery with a weapon should be sentenced concurrently or consecutively. In *Greaves and Jaffier*[86] Lord Woolf CJ was in no doubt that the correct principle was to impose a consecutive sentence, for the familiar deterrent reason that this 'gives a clear message to those who commit crimes of this nature that if they carry a weapon when committing a robbery they will receive an additional sentence'. In *Hahn and Webster*,[87] however, where the Court of Appeal considered in some detail the best way to approach sentences in such cases, Potter LJ said that if:

> ... the judge has in fact imposed a sentence appropriate to the overall criminality of the enterprise before him, including the possession of a firearm, then the fact that he has allotted that sentence entirely to the charge of robbery and has imposed a concurrent sentence in respect of the firearms charge will not afford grounds for interference by this court.

That is surely right. If the offence of robbery *simpliciter* is charged, and possession of the weapon is relied upon as an aggravating feature, then the matter is simply one of passing a proportionate sentence. If the robbery and possession of the weapon are separately charged, again the crucial issue is overall proportionality—there can be no justification for arriving at a different total sentence by virtue of different charging practices. More generally, if the total sentence for the offending should be five years, then it is a presentational matter whether the sentence is better expressed as five years and one year concurrent or four years and one year consecutive.[88] It is submitted that this issue cannot be resolved by asking whether the robbery with a weapon was one incident or two.[89] In other decisions of the Court of Appeal the Court has striven to uphold consecutive sentences in cases involving weapons, but

[85] *Attorney General's Reference (No 57 of 2009) (Ralphs)* [2009] EWCA Crim 2555, [2010] 2 Cr App R (S) 30.

[86] [2003] EWCA Crim 3229, [2004] 2 Cr App R (S) 10.

[87] *Attorney General's Reference Nos 21 & 22 of 2003 (Hahn and Webster)* [2003] EWCA Crim 3089, [2004] 2 Cr App R (S) 13.

[88] In *Greaves and Jaffier*, Lord Woolf said that the length of the consecutive sentence for the weapons offence 'should be apparent' to the offender and to others. Of course the countervailing aspect of this is that the sentence for the robbery count must be shorter to achieve the same overall sentence.

[89] There are some other issues here. Conviction and sentence for a separate weapons offence may confer the benefit that the weapons offence shows clearly on the offender's criminal record. But, again, that should not affect the overall proportionality.

of course, has been unable to do so without significantly reducing the overall sentence. In *Kent*,[90] Hedley J said that the trial judge had been right to pass a consecutive sentence for carrying a firearm, but that as a result 'the sentence was, in its totality, rather longer than it should have been'. The sentence for the weapons offence was therefore cut from five years to two years.

Maximum penalty problems

A difficult issue arises in cases where the offender is convicted of offences carrying relatively low maximum penalties. Having regard to the totality of the offending, the court may be tempted to impose consecutive sentences in order to reach what it believes to be an appropriate figure, where concurrent sentences are not enough to do the job. In the oft-cited case of *Wheatley*[91] the defendant, a persistent motoring offender, pleaded guilty before the magistrates to driving while disqualified, driving with excess alcohol, and driving without insurance. In the Crown Court he received 12 months for the first of these offences, six months consecutive for the second, and a fine for the third. The custodial offences were then the maximum available penalties. The defendant appealed, but the Court of Appeal upheld the sentence, saying that concurrent sentences were inappropriate since 'otherwise this man would have a licence to drive[92] with excess alcohol without any added penalty':[93] the usual deterrent rationale for consecutive sentencing. *Wheatley* is used as authority that, sometimes, consecutive sentences can be passed for two offences arising out of the 'same incident', but the case is really about permitting a sentencer in a multiple offence case to circumvent statutory maxima. It is striking how often difficulties over concurrent/consecutive sentences derive from maximum penalty problems. This arose in *Edwards*.[94] The offender was a resident in a hostel. He went to the room of another resident, who was physically frail, knowing that that man had cash on his person or in his room. The offender punched the victim to the floor, picked up the victim's wallet which contained £1,000 and took it away with him. The victim remonstrated with the offender, who returned and hit him again. The offender pleaded guilty to assault occasioning actual bodily harm and theft. The judge imposed three years for the assault and two years for the theft, consecutive. The Court of Appeal said that the overall sentence was appropriate, but there was a problem because the two offences did seem to arise from the same incident and should therefore have received concurrent sentences. In the end, however, the Court upheld the consecutive sentences, relying on *Wheatley* for the vague proposition that there could sometimes be exceptions to the 'single incident' principle. The problem lay with how to reach a total of five years by using concurrent sentences for the assault (maximum five years) and the theft (maximum seven

[90] *Kent* [2004] EWCA Crim 407, [2004] 2 Cr App R (S) 67.
[91] (1983) 5 Cr App R (S) 417 (CA).
[92] No pun, presumably, intended.
[93] (1983) 5 Cr App R (S) 417, 419 (CA).
[94] [2009] EWCA Crim 602.

years) while giving proper allowance for plea.[95] The Court was highly critical of the prosecution for not charging robbery, on which basis a sentence in the order of five years could have been reached more easily.

The Sentencing Council has recently proposed that 'courts should not structure sentences consecutively in order to evade the statutory maximum penalty',[96] but it is not clear if that means that a court should *never* exceed the statutory maximum for the lead offence when sentencing a multiple offender. That is because the Sentencing Council cites *Ralphs*,[97] in which case Lord Judge CJ says that exceeding the maximum is permissible if the court is dealing with distinct and separate incidents, but not if the offences arose out of the same incident. It will be clear from the above discussion that I am sceptical about the value of such a distinction, and would abandon it.

8. Conclusions

(i) In this essay I have sought to demonstrate that, in concurrent sentencing, additional offences are accommodated by increasing the internal sum but retaining totality (or overall proportionality). In consecutive sentencing, however, additional offences can only be accommodated by under-sentencing one or more of the offences. Whether sentences are imposed concurrently or consecutively, or in some mix of the two, the total sentence must be the same. It follows that there is no proportionality issue in the choice between concurrent and consecutive sentences. Since concurrent sentences better reflect the sentences for each of the individual offences, as well as overall proportionality, there should be a clear presumption in favour of employing concurrent sentences in multiple offence cases.

(ii) The 'single incident' rationale for distinguishing between cases suitable for concurrent as against consecutive sentences is unworkable, and should be abandoned.

(iii) The choice between concurrent and consecutive sentences can sometimes have presentational importance. Concurrent sentences have greater presentational value, such as in the multiple death cases considered above, where the total sentence is explicitly linked to each of the deaths. Sometimes, however, the court may find it useful to announce that an additional offence has been punished by a consecutive sentence, but the judge will at the same time have to reduce at least one other sentence to accommodate it. Further thought needs to be given to the question of in which (if any) categories of case the presentational value of using a consecutive sentence

[95] At least the Court gave an appropriate reduction. No reduction at all was given in *Wheatley*, even though the defendant pleaded guilty to all the offences.

[96] Sentencing Council, n 34 above, 19.

[97] *Attorney General's Reference (No 57 of 2009) (Ralphs)* [2009] EWCA Crim 2555, [2010] 2 Cr App R (S) 30.

outweighs the normal preference for concurrence. My provisional view is that such an argument might be made out for breach of a suspended sentence, and perhaps also in cases where the defendant has compounded his criminality by an attack on the criminal justice system, such as by committing perjury or perverting the course of justice in relation to a charge against him.

(iv) The totality principle should be regarded as a determining principle, rather than a limiting principle. This can be made reality by the appropriate development of sentencing guidelines for individual offences, so as to extend their application to multiple offence cases. This is a challenging task, but feasible and well worth doing. It is disappointing that the Sentencing Council has not chosen to go down that road, and is content merely to restate what it takes to be existing practice.[98] It has been argued in this essay that the crucial principle should be that the lead sentence for the most serious offence should normally fall within the category range for that offence. Other offences should be sentenced concurrently (or, exceptionally, consecutively) but so as normally not to exceed the category range for the lead sentence. Sometimes it will be necessary to exceed the category range. Judges are permitted to exceed the category range when sentencing a single offence, so the same must apply in multiple offence cases. By how far it is exceeded will depend, inter alia, on where the lead sentence falls within the category range, and the seriousness and number of the additional offences. Very occasionally it may be necessary to exceed the maximum sentence for the lead offence, such as where the top of the applicable category range coincides with the maximum for the offence.[99]

[98] Sentencing Council, n 34 above, 15: 'The Council has sought to reflect current law and sentencing practice . . . it is not seeking to bring about any change . . .'

[99] In fact there is often a gap between the top of the highest category range and the maximum sentence for the offence. The maximum penalty for assault occasioning actual bodily harm, for example, is five years, but the highest category range in the Sentencing Council's guidelines for that offence is one to three years' custody.

18

'Wrongful' Acquittals and 'Unduly Lenient' Sentences—Misconceived Problems that Provoke Unjust Solutions

*Michael Tonry**

Several years ago, I made an off-hand remark in an academic meeting that I did not understand why people care about wrongful acquittals. 'Just a matter of luck,' I said. People are born gifted or win lotteries or are hit by trucks or fall prey to cancer, good and bad things that they in no moral sense deserve. If we have views on such matters we typically say how fortunate they are, or what a pity. 'Why,' I rhetorically asked, 'do we not react the same way to wrongful acquittals?' In moral and legal senses, a conviction would have been justified but—lucky fellow—it didn't happen. That defendant won this particular one of life's lotteries. No doubt he has lost many others. Every other person in the room appeared to disagree with me. I suspect that most were expressing an intuition they had not thought through, as I was. I expect their intuitions included some notion of symmetry: if wrongful convictions are unjust, and warrant efforts to remedy them, surely wrongful acquittals also are and do. The consequences for individuals, and the interests at stake, however, are fundamentally different.

'Wrongful acquittals' in at least one sense is a term of art dating from the build-up to enactment of the Criminal Justice Act 2003 in England and Wales. The putative aim of the Act's abrogation of the centuries-old double jeopardy rule was to permit retrial of acquitted offenders who were widely believed to be factually guilty. OJ Simpson in the United States and the alleged killers of Stephen Lawrence in England might be thought of as paradigm cases. My argument in this essay—that beneficiaries of 'wrongful' acquittals, in that sense, should be left alone to enjoy their good luck—is at odds with Andrew Ashworth's views on a related subject. He has several times written about unsuccessful completed attempts, the legal treatment of people who take the last step to commit a crime but through happenstance

* Michael Tonry is professor of law and public policy and director, Institute of Crime and Public Policy, University of Minnesota. He is grateful to Antony Duff, Douglas Husak, Oren Gross, Gregory Shaffer, and the editors of this volume for comments on earlier drafts.

fail.[1] His argument is that they should be considered no less culpable than offenders whose attempts are successful, and that their offences should be classified and they should be punished in the same way. To my knowledge, Ashworth does not favour abrogation of the double jeopardy doctrine, but the logic of his views on unsuccessful completed attempts might be extended by some to treatment of wrongful acquittals.

Despite the verbal parallels, wrongful convictions and wrongful acquittals raise fundamentally different issues. Wrongful convictions provoke sympathetic reactions from almost everyone. Those we hear and read about usually involve serious violent and sexual crimes and feature near-irrefutable DNA or other evidence that someone did not commit the crimes of which he or she was convicted or that someone else did. Sometimes the convictions appear to have been entirely innocent: judges, prosecutors, defence counsel and, where they were involved, juries did their work competently and in good faith and made at-the-time understandable but in retrospect terrible mistakes. Often such cases feature police or prosecutorial misconduct, incompetent defence counsel, erroneous eyewitness testimony, shabby forensic procedures, coercive interrogations, or a combination of several of these factors.

Wrongful convictions are plainly wrong. Each is a tragedy. They attribute moral wrongdoing to individuals, stigmatize them, unjustifiably intrude into and diminish the quality of their lives, and alter their and their loved ones' life chances. Mechanisms are needed for identifying them and, inevitably inadequately, remedying them. Technical legal and procedural issues such as deadlines for filing appeals should never be allowed to stand in the way.

In England and Wales, a few notorious acquittals of apparently guilty people were in recent years reified into the seemingly parallel construct of the 'wrongful acquittal'. Controversial, seemingly slight sentences in other cases came to be characterized as wrongful acquittal's little sister, the 'unduly lenient sentence'. Both are unexceptionable inventions as a rhetorical or polemical matter—if they enable people to express strong emotions or sell newspapers, so much the better. Unlike wrongful convictions, however, they should be allowed to rest where they fall.[2] No one should have to face twice the awesome power of the state in a criminal prosecution for a single offence—in the case of serious crimes a life-changing, psychically damaging, and soul-chilling experience. That is why common law jurisdictions since Magna Carta have recognized a double jeopardy rule. The stakes

[1] A Ashworth, 'Criminal Attempts and the Role of Resulting Harm under the Code, and in the Common Law' (1988) 19 Rutgers Law Review 725; A Ashworth, 'Taking the Consequences' in S Shute, J Gardner, and J Horder (eds), *Action and Value in Criminal Law* (New York: Oxford University Press, 1993).

[2] My concern is the vast run of ordinary cases. Some people, even if my arguments persuaded them about those cases, would want to disregard double jeopardy and related concerns (eg, limitations periods) for crimes against humanity such as genocidal killings or killings of American civil rights activists in the 1960s that led to racism-contaminated acquittals. Maybe such exceptions could be justified—because the stakes are so high—but even for these cases the better course is probably to initiate criminal charges concerning related wrongdoing (eg, perjured testimony, bribed jurors, racially biased officials) or to pursue other, separate criminal charges that could have been filed but were not.

may be less but the issues are the same concerning sentencing. And that is why, until recently, in the United States and England and Wales, prosecutorial appeals of sentences were not allowed.

Wrongful acquittals and unduly lenient sentences should not be vulnerable to reconsideration or alteration. Those outcomes do not cancel out wrongdoing or bestow moral approbation. They do not exculpate; like the Scottish 'not proven' verdict, an acquittal does not imply innocence and a 'lenient' sentence does not imply that a harsher one could not have been justified. They have no implications concerning community and social judgements about the occurrence, commission, or degree of wrongdoing, or concerning social labelling and stigmatization. All that happens is that individuals are serendipitously spared the burdens of convictions or punishments they appear to have deserved.

It happens every day. The vast majority of people who commit crimes and could be convicted and punished, are not. Some crimes are never discovered or reported, some are never solved, some are committed by people too young or mentally handicapped to be held legally responsible,[3] and some result in arrests that cannot be prosecuted for lack of admissible evidence. Some cases that are prosecuted are later dismissed for prudential, policy, or resource-allocation reasons. Some result in acquittals because of evidentiary problems or because defence counsel are especially artful. Most defendants plead guilty and receive sentences less severe than if they had been tried. In England, guilty pleas are rewarded with explicit, publicly acknowledged, and officially sanctioned reductions in sentence. Most convicted offenders in America receive lesser sentences as a result of plea bargains. Unless the harsher penalty after a trial is conceptualized as legitimately encompassing an increment of additional punishment for exercising the constitutional right to trial, punishments imposed after trial are the appropriate ones. By that standard upwards of 90 per cent of convicted offenders receive lenient sentences.[4]

There may be persuasive reasons to consider wrongful acquittals and unduly lenient sentences as something different from or more important than these vastly more numerous occasions on which people are not charged, prosecuted, convicted, and punished as they might deserve to be. I have not been able to figure out what those reasons are.

The three sections of this essay explain why. The first provides a recitative of recent developments in England and Wales and the United States concerning 'wrongful acquittals' and 'unduly lenient sentences'. Policy-makers' arguments usually focus on public opinion, unfavourable or demagogic media attention, threats to the legitimacy of state institutions, vindication of victims, and the moral need for penal consequences to be apportioned to culpability. Opponents

[3] At risk of warranted accusations of pedantry: defendants deemed incompetent to stand trial or below the age of criminal responsibility cannot be convicted, but it would be difficult and slightly perverse to explain to the victim of, eg, a rape or assault that no crime occurred for those reasons.

[4] eg, in the 75 most populous American counties in 2006, 95% of convictions of felony defendants resulted from guilty pleas. T Cohen and T Kyckelhahn, *Felony Defendants in Large Urban Counties* (Washington, DC: US Bureau of Justice Statistics, 2010).

usually focus on double jeopardy concerns, unfairness, and threats to the integrity of the process.

The second section dips shallowly into the literature on moral luck to see whether it offers insight. It doesn't, except in one not unimportant respect: many writers believe and argue that some offenders who took the last step to commit a crime—but did not succeed—should be punished less severely than their culpability would warrant. Under-punished criminality is precisely the 'problem' that changes in double jeopardy and sentence appeal laws are meant to solve.

The third section presents a series of arguments concerning why wrongful acquittals and unduly lenient sentences should be allowed to rest where they fall, why policies should not be adopted to remedy them, and why conventional arguments in favour of remedies are unpersuasive.

1. The Discovery of Wrongful Acquittals and Unduly Lenient Sentences

In 1970 there was no great worry about wrongful acquittals, unduly lenient sentences, or insufficiently severe punishments. The prevailing view was that no one should be punished any more than was absolutely, minimally necessary. In the *Model Penal Code*,[5] drafted over a 13-year period ending in 1962, judges were authorized to impose probation in any case including homicide and were to be guided by a presumption against imprisonment. Parole boards were instructed to presume that prisoners should be released at first eligibility.

In England and Wales, the double jeopardy doctrine was uncontroversial and a well-established system for appellate review of sentences allowed defendants—but not prosecutors—to file appeals. In the United States, the Double Jeopardy Clause was similarly uncontroversial and appellate sentence review was unavailable to defendants or prosecutors. The National Commission on Reform of Federal Criminal Law[6] proposed authorization of sentence appeals by defendants, but not by the state. Similar proposals were made in the American Bar Association's *Standards Relating to Appellate Review of Sentences*[7] and by the President's Commission on Law Enforcement and Administration of Justice.[8]

Criminal justice reform was in the air in the 1960s and 1970s. Punishing blameworthy people in the retributively right amounts, however, was not a matter that received much attention. The American commitment to individualized, consequentialist thinking remained almost as much in vogue as in 1940 when Herbert

[5] American Law Institute, *Model Penal Code* (Proposed Official draft) (Philadelphia, PA: American Law Institute, 1962).

[6] National Commission on Reform of Federal Criminal Law, *Study Draft of a Proposed New Federal Criminal Code* (Washington, DC: US Government Printing Office, 1970).

[7] American Bar Association, *Standards Relating to Appellate Review of Sentences* (Chicago, IL: American Bar Association, 1968).

[8] President's Commission on Law Enforcement and Administration of Justice, *The Challenge of Crime in a Free Society* (Washington, DC: US Government Printing Office, 1967).

Wechsler and Jerome Michael explained that retribution may represent 'the unstudied belief of most men' but concluded, 'no legal provision can be justified merely because it calls for the punishment of the morally guilty by penalties proportioned to their guilt, or criticized merely because it fails to do so'.[9] In England and Wales, HLA Hart's 1959 lecture 'Prolegomenon to the Principles of Punishment'[10] was in significant part a reply to the Social Defence movement of the 1950s[11] in general and Barbara Wootton's related proposals[12] for shifting consideration of *mens rea* from the trial to the sentencing phase of a criminal case.

The situation in 2012 is different. Punishment has long been in the air. In England and Wales, the Criminal Justice Act 1988 authorized the Attorney General to refer cases to the Court of Appeal if it 'appear[ed] ... that the sentencing of a person in a proceeding in the Crown Court ha[d] been unduly lenient'. The Criminal Justice Act 2003 abrogated the double jeopardy rule. Application to the Court of Appeal to quash an acquittal was authorized in cases in which the Director of Public Prosecutions believes that a retrial is in the public interest and that new evidence was not reasonably available at the initial trial.

In the United States, the Double Jeopardy Clause is entrenched in the Fifth Amendment to the US Constitution and survives, but has been narrowed over the past 40 years in a series of relatively arcane US Supreme Court decisions concerning precisely when jeopardy 'attaches' and whether an individual can be punished both for a substantive offence and an inchoate offence relating to it (such as conspiracy). Few informed observers would disagree that the underlying rationale for the narrowing changes has been animus by the conservative courts of the past 40 years to the idea that the double jeopardy rule protects (factually) guilty offenders.[13]

The United States has gone much further than England and Wales concerning prosecutorial sentence appeals. The Crime Control Act of 1970[14] authorized prosecutors to appeal sentences imposed on 'dangerous special offenders'. Ten years later, the US Supreme Court in *US v DiFrancesco*[15] rejected constitutional due process and double jeopardy objections. Presumptive sentencing guidelines systems, dating from 1980 or later, authorize both defence and prosecution appeals. So would the recommendations of establishmentarian law reform documents such as the third edition of the American Bar Association's *Standards Relating to Sentencing Alternatives and Procedures*.[16]

[9] J Michael and H Wechsler, *Criminal Law and its Administration; Cases, Statutes, and Commentaries* (Chicago, IL: Foundation Press, 1940), 7, 11.

[10] HLA Hart, *Punishment and Responsibility: Essays in the Philosophy of Law* (Oxford: Oxford University Press, 1968).

[11] M Ancel, *Social Defence: A Modern Approach to Criminal Problems* (London: Routledge Kegan Paul, 1965).

[12] B Wootton, *Social Science and Social Pathology* (London: Allen Unwin, 1959); B Wootton, *Crime and the Criminal Law* (London: Stevens, 1963).

[13] eg, A Amar, 'Double Jeopardy Law Made Simple' (1997) 106 Yale Law Journal 1807.

[14] 18 USC §3576.

[15] 449 US 117 (1980).

[16] American Bar Association, *Standards Relating to Sentencing Alternatives and Procedures* (Chicago, IL: American Bar Association, 1994).

The reasons commonly given for these changes were significantly different in the two countries. Public opinion, politicians' worries about media reactions, and rhetorical concerns about the legitimacy of and public confidence in the legal system loomed larger in England. Inter-party jockeying to be seen as tough on crime was a recurring theme.[17] In the United States, where prosecutorial sentence appeals were authorized earlier, the process was less openly politically partisan and much less predicated on concerns about media reactions and public opinion.

Two primary rationales for prosecutorial sentence appeals of 'unduly lenient sentence' were given in England. The first was a concern, Conservative Party spokesmen regularly averred, to 'restore public confidence'.[18] Here are typical statements by leading Conservative Party figures:

> [Lenient sentences are one] problem too important to ignore [because of the] harm to public confidence which the occasional over-lenient sentence can cause. (Noble Earl);
>
> [In] serious cases where public emotions can be understandably engaged [unduly lenient sentences arouse] widespread concern . . . [and] govern the confidence of the citizen of the machinery for his protection. (Lord Elwyn-Jones);
>
> When a manifestly over-lenient sentence is passed, the damage to public confidence in the system is out of all proportion to the significance of the case . . . That is why the problem, though small in scale, is of great importance. (Douglas Hurd [Home Secretary]);
>
> An over-lenient sentence is a matter of great public concern. (John Patten).

Tabloid media pressures were the other most cited reasons:

> Hysterical headlines in the tabloid press . . . complain bitterly about a lenient sentence (Lord Wigoner);
>
> When the media criticize judges and sentences in that way it affects the confidence of the people in our system of justice and judges; . . . it shakes the confidence of the ordinary public; . . . if the media can make these allegations against the judges and they go uncontradicted and unchallenged' (Lord Denning [MR]);
>
> Each and every attack becomes more strident and their cumulative effect is . . . to undermine public confidence; [the aim of the bill is] lessening the hue and cry among the media. (Michael Irvine [later LCJ]

Passing mention was made of the need for symmetry in appeal rights between prosecution and defence and of concern about sentencing disparities, but public opinion and media reactions received much more prominent attention.

The principal arguments against allowing prosecutorial sentence appeals concerned fairness to offenders and two worries about unintended side-effects. The first was that judges might become risk averse about possible appeals and increase sentences beyond levels they believed appropriate in order to lessen risk of embarrassment if a sentence was overturned. The second was that the model of the prosecutor as an independent advocate, seeking to establish the truth, rather than as

[17] D Downes and R Morgan, 'No Turning Back: the Politics of Law and Order into the Millennium' in M Maguire, R Morgan, and R Reiner (eds), *The Oxford Handbook of Criminology* (4th edn, Oxford: Oxford University Press, 2007).

[18] D Windlesham, *Responses to Crime* (Oxford: Oxford University Press, 1993–2001), vols 2–4.

a partisan seeking to win a case, would be undermined. That is one reason why English prosecutors until recently did not make sentence recommendations.[19]

Many people attributed the double jeopardy provisions in the Criminal Justice Act 2003 to the Labour government's cynical efforts to harness 'populist punitiveness' to its electoral ambitions.[20] Rod Morgan, sometime head of the Youth Justice Board and later Her Majesty's Inspector of Probation, attributed Labour's policies to a tendency to seek 'short-term electoral gain rather than effectiveness in changing behaviour or creating a safer world'.[21]

Because prosecutorial sentence appeals subject defendants to anxieties equivalent to those double jeopardy doctrine was meant to avoid, appellate judges declared that 'there should be some regard to the element of double jeopardy' in resentencing offenders whose original sentences were adjudged unduly lenient.[22] Tabloid newspapers and populist politicians were affronted by the idea of solicitude for offenders. The Labour government responded in the Criminal Justice Act 2003 and the Criminal Justice and Immigration Act 2008 by forbidding appellate judges to take into account in designated cases that offenders were being 'sentenced for the second time'. Maria Eagle, a junior government minister, explained: 'It seems strange to an ordinary member of the public that when a sentence is increased because it has been unduly lenient, the offender should then get a discount . . . on the grounds of their distress.'[23]

The President's Commission on Law Enforcement and Administration of Justice, the National Commission on Reform of Federal Criminal Law, and the American Bar Association[24] called for sentence appeals for defendants but not prosecutors. The principal objections to defence appeals centred on deference to trial court judges and caseload concerns in over-burdened appellate courts. The principal objections to prosecution appeal were that it was inconsistent with double jeopardy doctrine and would give the prosecutor another weapon, thereby unfairly shifting the adversary balance of power toward the state.

Prosecution appeals, however, were soon authorized as a by-product of general sentencing reform efforts. Sentencing reform initiatives in the period from 1975 to 1985 were seen as aimed primarily at reducing racial and other disparities. Symmetrical rights of appeal were seen as commonsensically appropriate.[25] Otherwise, it was said, case law would develop asymmetrically, concerned only with sentences

[19] Windlesham, n 18 above.

[20] M Tonry, 'The Costly Consequences of Populist Posturing: ASBOs, Victims, "Rebalancing", and Diminution of Support for Civil Liberties' (2010) 12 Punishment & Society 387.

[21] R Morgan, 'With Respect to Order, The Rules of the Game Have Changed: New Labour's Dominance of the "Law and Order" Agenda' in T Newburn and P Rock (eds), *The Politics of Crime Control: Essays in Honour of David Downes* (Oxford: Oxford University Press, 2006), 111.

[22] *Attorney General's Reference (No 6 of 2000) (Goldsmith)* [2001] 1 Cr App R (S) 20 (CA).

[23] Hansard, HC, *General Committee, Criminal Justice and Immigration Bill, Clause 28*, statement of Maria Eagle, 21 November 2007.

[24] nn 6–8 above.

[25] A Blumstein, J Cohen, S Martin, and M Tonry (eds), *Sentencing Reform: The Search for Reform* (Washington, DC: National Academy Press, 1983).

more severe than applicable guidelines prescribed, and providing no appellate guidance concerning sentences less severe than guidelines prescribed.

2. Moral, Legal, and Plain Luck

When I realized that my instinctual reaction to wrongful acquittals—'he lucked out that time; so be it'—differs from those of many others, not unnaturally I looked for conceptual tools that might help me understand the different reactions. Other people, including Andrew Ashworth,[26] have consulted the often arcane philosophical literature on moral luck in trying to understand or explain situations in which legal doctrine or practice commonly produce results incompatible with conventional attributions of culpability.

The moral luck literature was catalysed by Thomas Nagel[27] and Bernard Williams.[28] The central question is whether assessments of people's willed behaviour should be affected by fortuities in their lives or in the outcomes of their behaviours. Nagel created a taxonomy of varieties of moral luck (resultant: things turn out other than as intended; circumstantial: incipient blameworthy character or aim has no occasion for fruition; constitutive: genes, care-givers, peers, and other environmental influences make some people likely to act in circumstances where others would not; luck in 'how one is determined by antecedent circumstances').[29] The fundamental insight is that luck often determines whether good or bad will or character produce bad results. Nagel begins with a quotation from Kant that a good will, even if ineffectual in achieving good things, 'would sparkle like a jewel in its own right'. Perhaps a bit quickly, Nagel posits: 'He would presumably have said the same thing about a bad will: whether it accomplishes its evil purposes is morally irrelevant.'[30] Nagel disagrees, accepting the legitimacy of the emotional intuition that consequences matter. He gives several examples to demonstrate that we blame ourselves and others do also when, after we behave wrongly, harms occur that are causally related to our wrongdoing (the minor auto repair not made; drunk driving). From this he concludes that people may fairly be deemed more blameworthy when harm results than when it does not. More recent articles by Jeremy Waldron[31] and David Enoch[32] deconstruct legal treatments of moral luck in far more detail, distinguishing among moral, legal, and plain luck, but like Nagel accept as morally germane the widely held intuition that resulting harms matter.

[26] See n 1 above.

[27] T Nagel, *Mortal Questions* (Cambridge: Cambridge University Press, 1979).

[28] B Williams, *Moral Luck: Philosophical Papers 1973–1980* (Cambridge: Cambridge University Press,1981).

[29] Nagel, n 27 above, 60.

[30] Ibid, 24.

[31] J Waldron, 'Lucky in Your Judge' (2008) 9 Theoretical Inquiries in Law 185.

[32] D Enoch, 'Luck between Morality, Law, and Justice' (2008) 9 Theoretical Inquiries in Law 23.

Ashworth[33] focused on offence classification and sentencing practice concerning completed but unsuccessful attempts. A completed but unsuccessful attempt is one in which the actor has tried her utmost, done everything believed necessary, but failed to accomplish an intended crime. A standard example is the shooter who misses or whose intended victim moves at the critical micro-second. In most common law jurisdictions, an individual can be convicted for an 'incomplete' attempt before that point is reached, and need not take the 'last step'. Concerning incomplete attempts, which by definition are not successful, plausible arguments can be made for lower offence classifications and lesser punishments: attempters should be given incentives to change their minds; without incentives, the actor may as well complete the crime as the punishment will not be affected; failure to complete an attempt may signify that the offender did not *really* want to complete it. Limiting attention to completed but unsuccessful attempts eliminates the relevance of those considerations, leaving only this: should it matter that a culpable actor, who did everything within his or her power to complete a crime, failed?

Notwithstanding that perpetrators of completed attempts, whether or not successful, are equally culpable, most common law jurisdictions classify and punish successful attempts as more serious offences. Ashworth disagreed. After canvassing retributivist and consequentialist ways of thinking, he argued that neither provided persuasive reasons for rejecting the—to him—persuasive proposition that equally culpable people ought in principle to suffer equally severe punishments. Thus, he concluded, neither classification systems nor punishment practice should distinguish between successful and unsuccessful completed attempts.

The philosophical literature on moral luck examines this kind of problem, including explicitly the criminal law of attempts. The moral luck literature does not help resolve the wrongful acquittal problem. Contributors to it and the parallel criminal law attempts literature are nearly equally divided in their conclusions. Some conclude that luck in the outcome should matter,[34] and others that it should not.[35]

Precisely, however, because contributors to it are fundamentally divided, the moral luck literature provided at least the solace that many serious theorists believe that offenders may sometimes appropriately be dealt with in ways that do not result in their suffering the penal consequences their wrongdoing might otherwise justify. This has implications for thinking about 'unduly lenient' sentences. If luck in the outcome of an attempt may appropriately affect how much an offender should be punished, it is not obvious why luck in the identity of the sentencing judge may not. Moreover, once the idea of an iron-clad, defining relationship between culpability and punishment is broken, the door is opened to consideration of policy

[33] Ashworth, 'Criminal Attempts', n 1 above.

[34] T Bittner, 'Punishment for Criminal Attempts: A Legal Perspective on the Problem of Moral Luck' (2008) 38 Canadian Journal of Philosophy 51; A Ripstein, 'Moral and Legal Luck: Closing the Gap' (2008) 9 Theoretical Inquiries in Law 61.

[35] SH Kadish, 'The Criminal Law and the Luck of the Draw' (1994) 84 Journal of Criminal Law and Criminology 679; J Feinberg, 'Equal Punishment for Failed Attempts' (1995) 37 Arizona Law Review 117.

and prudential reasons why equally culpable offenders may be treated differently. If the argument is as offered above—that sentences imposed after trials should be considered to be the normally appropriate sentence—most offenders are treated less severely than they deserve.

Life abounds with occasions in which the chance consequences of culpable acts lead to different outcomes legally and in conventional understanding. The drunk driver is a converse example to the unsuccessful completed attempt. Many people, after drinking, drive with blood alcohol content above the legal limit. Most get home safely, a few are involved in accidents, and a very few accidents result in serious injuries or deaths. Assuming there are no circumstances other than excess alcohol consumption that could be characterized as intentional or reckless, the likelihood of death, controlling for blood alcohol content, is probabilistic: it happens in X per cent of cases. Whether it occurs depends on the numerous circumstances that determine outcomes in any traffic accident—speed, driving skills, road conditions, non-alcohol-related negligence, driving behaviours of other people, use of seat belts, functioning of airbags. Is the death-or-injury-causing driver's moral responsibility different from that of the vast majority of comparably inebriated drivers who took the same risks but got home safely? A culpability-and-control analysis would conclude that all the drivers who knowingly ingested alcohol in amounts above legal blood alcohol content limits are equally culpable and should be judged and punished, if at all, in the same way. Argument could be made, paralleling unsuccessful-attempters-may-have-been-less-resolute arguments, that inebriated drivers involved in fatal accidents are a systematically distinguishable subset (Subset Z) of all inebriated drivers. That, however, only shrinks the reference group. Among inebriated drivers in the subset, some do and some do not experience situations in which alcohol-related impairment causally contributes to the occurrence of harms: children do or do not run into the road, the roads are or are not slippery, other drivers do or do not turn without signalling. Of drivers in Subset Z, some are involved in accidents whilst driving home. Others are not.

No one to my knowledge argues that everyone driving with illegal blood alcohol content levels, or possessing characteristics qualifying for Subset Z, should be charged with attempted homicide irrespective of whether an accident occurs or that all drivers in Subset Z who are involved in accidents should be charged with attempted homicide, irrespective of whether an injury (or a death) occurs. Nonetheless, conventional emotional responses and intuitions are that death is different and that the 'drunken' driver is criminally blameworthy. The drunken driver involved in a fatal accident may be charged with homicide and punished for it. The vast majority of his luckier brothers and sisters arrive home safely and are punished if at all only by a morning hangover—parallelling the conventional common law differentiation between successful and unsuccessful completed attempts. Dispassionate rational analysis points in one direction, emotional intuition in another.

Conflicts between reason and emotion occur in many criminal law contexts. One is the question whether previous convictions should be taken into account to increase punishments for a subsequent offence above that appropriately imposed for a first offence. A retributivist analysis suggests not: for the first offence the offender should have been punished as much as he deserved; the same thing should happen for each subsequent offence. However, Roberts[36] convincingly demonstrates the existence of a powerful and widely held intuition among citizens, judges, and offenders that supports additional punishment for the new offence because of the previous ones. There has been a number of efforts to explain in principle why a 'recidivist premium' is justified. Chris Bennett,[37] Andrew von Hirsch,[38] and others make retributivist attempts. To my mind none of them has developed a persuasive retributivist argument for why prior convictions should be relevant to amounts of punishment imposed for new offences (plausible consequentialist arguments can be made about recidivism as a predictor of later offending and about the effects of contravening widely shared intuitions on public perceptions of the legal system).

Norval Morris posed the underlying conflict in a short story, 'The Brothel Boy'. A mentally handicapped boy, who lived in a Burmese brothel observing men pay women for—sometimes violent—sex, attempts to have sexual relations with a young girl. In resisting, she falls, hits her head on a rock, and a few days later dies from the combined effects of the injury and septicaemia. The magistrate, Eric Blair, a fictionalized 1920s version of the writer better known as George Orwell, must decide whether the boy will be executed. From a moral perspective, he is doubtful. The boy did not intend to kill, the fatal injury was inadvertent, adequate medical care would have saved the victim, and in the boy's weak mind he may have thought what he wanted to do was all right. 'I paid her,' he repeats again and again. Blair has little doubt that in the eye of God, the boy is an innocent. From other perspectives Blair feels pressured. The planter community, his primary constituency, thinks the boy should be executed ('just another over-sexed native'). So do the indigenous Burmese people ('he tried to rape her and she died'). Blair has to worry about maintaining his personal authority and credibility in both communities, and about his institutional authority as a representative of the British colonial administration.

Morris describes the story as a conflict between guilt and blame. 'Guilt' is moral culpability. What did the boy intend? How knowingly culpable was he? Did he have sufficient maturity and capacity for moral reasoning fairly to be held accountable? 'Blame' is the community construction. How upset and angry are people? What do they think should be done? What are the likely consequences of doing something else? The law must deal with both guilt and blame, Morris counsels, and sometimes blame takes precedence:

[36] JV Roberts, *Punishing Persistent Offenders: Exploring Community and Offender Perspectives* (Oxford: Oxford University Press, 2008).

[37] C Bennett, '"More to Apologize For": Can We Find a Basis for the Recidivist Premium in a Communicative Theory of Punishment?' in JV Roberts and A von Hirsch (eds), *Previous Convictions at Sentencing: Theoretical and Applied Perspectives* (Oxford: Hart, 2010).

[38] A von Hirsch, 'Proportionality and the Progressive Loss of Mitigation: Some Further Reflections' in Roberts and von Hirsch, n 37 above.

> The criminal law is a dependent system, very reliant on culture, morals, values, custom, and the texture of all the interwoven rules of law. If you are compromised morally and chance to violate any of those rules, and the dice roll against you, then you may lose badly.[39]

Some philosophers, such as Susan Wolf, have tried to come up with 'happy mediums' between rejecting moral luck outright and accepting it wholesale. Wolf developed rationalist and irrationalist positions as part of such a reconciliation. The rationalist position is that equal fault deserves equal blame. Imagine two drivers, both of whom failed to check their brakes before driving. One hits a pedestrian only because he cannot stop in time; otherwise he is not negligent. The other hits no one.

The rationalist would say that the two drivers were equally at fault and it should make no difference that one was lucky in not hitting a pedestrian and the other was unlucky. Because moral fault is independent of consequences, the drivers should be treated in the same way. The irrationalist position argues that equal fault need not lead to equal blame, as blame should depend on the consequences: the lucky driver deserves less blame than the unlucky one.

Wolf tries to reconcile these views by introducing the concept of a virtuous agent who would accept that he has a special connection with the consequences of his actions, even when they result from luck. She retains the rationalist claim that equal fault is prima facie equally deserving of blame while accepting the irrationalist claim that different outcomes should cause moral agents to feel and act differently:

> One must recognize the considerable truth in both the rationalist and the irrationalist positions. It is that a morally conscientious approach to life, as well as a humanly conscientious approach to morality, must strike a balance between an interest, on the one hand, in attaining the kind of justice that comes from limiting the significance of that which is independent of the power and the quality of our wills with an interest, on the other hand, in acknowledging our earthly character and maintaining our connection to the social and physical world. The paradoxical quality of the phenomenon of moral luck comes from the fact that this latter interest can only be served if we affirm the significance that the former interest seeks to limit.[40]

Virtuous agents in Wolf's scheme would thus feel responsibility for, guilty about, harms resulting from their actions in ways that were outside their control, but that does not address the question whether we may or must be held legally accountable for such consequences.

Other philosophers have attempted other reconciliations. Arthur Ripstein argues that the gravamen of criminal punishment is not offenders' wickedness or the harm they cause but that they knowingly use 'means prohibited by law . . . The rationale for punishing them . . . [is] that they violate the legal system's entitlement to

[39] N Morris, *The Brothel Boy and Other Parables of the Law* (New York: Oxford University Press, 1992), 152.

[40] S Wolf, 'The Moral of Moral Luck' (2001) 31 Philosophic Exchange 5.

prohibit the use of certain means.'[41] The rationale for punishment thus comes from the underlying prohibition:

> The completed crime must also be the object of the punishment, because the punishment is merely the enforcement of the prohibition... an attempted crime is a deficient version of the completed one... a lesser included offence... Because [the attempt] is a derivative version, it is coherent (though not mandatory) to treat it differently.[42]

Thomas Bittner, for another example, distinguishes between 'strong' and 'weak' asymmetric and symmetric principles about responsibility for outcomes based on luck. Under the strong asymmetric principle, the man with a good will is protected from blame for bad consequences; the man with a bad will is responsible for all consequences. Under the weak symmetrical principle, the good man is not responsible for bad consequences; the bad man is. Thus while the successful attempted killer can fairly be held responsible for murder, the unsuccessful (but complete) murder attempter may not be: 'We can hold him responsible for endangering his victim in trying to kill him, but not for harming his victim, since his victim was not harmed.'[43]

All very interesting but none of it advances resolution of divergent views about moral luck generally or my narrower interest in wrongful acquittals and unduly lenient sentences. The difficulty in the moral luck literature is the existence of widely held incompatible intuitions—that control matters morally and limits responsibility, and that harm matters morally and aggravates responsibility—about people who behave wrongly. My only solace is that many who have wrestled with problems of moral luck have concluded that it justifies treating equally culpable offenders in different ways. That view justifies stigmatizing and punishing equally culpable offenders differently on the basis of the harms their wrongful actions do and do not cause. The preponderant view about attempts supports classifying and punishing successful and unsuccessful completed attempts differently.

Consistently with those views about moral luck and the law and sentencing of attempts, I see no good reason why equally culpable actors should not be treated differently if some are lucky in receiving a wrongful acquittal or an unduly lenient sentence, and others are not. The difficulty for my argument, however, is that the intuition that results matter in classifying and punishing crimes is widely held but that, inconsistently—in our time but not as recently as two generations ago—many, perhaps most, people believe that an offender's luck in seemingly being wrongly acquitted or sentenced unduly leniently are problems that need fixing.

3. Arguments For and Against

The moral luck literature indicates that many thoughtful people believe it appropriate and justifiable that some offenders receive punishments less severe than their

[41] Ripstein, n 34 above, 87. [42] Ibid, 93. [43] Bittner, n 34 above, 79.

relative culpability or blameworthiness would justify. There are numerous persuasive reasons why wrongful acquittals and unduly lenient sentences also should be allowed to lie where by happenstance they fall.

First, the process by which cases are selected for further proceedings will inevitably be arbitrary and will often be influenced by political or invidious considerations. It is not merely coincidence that England's recent Labour government, notorious for its effort to gain political advantage from being seen by voters to be tough on crime, abrogated the double jeopardy doctrine and initiated new prosecutions in notorious media-nominated cases of defendants who had been acquitted. Likewise, it was not merely coincidence that both the Home Secretary and the Lord Chief Justice in John Major's Conservative government successively, but thanks to the European Court of Human rights unsuccessfully, attempted to increase the prison sentences received by the killers of James Bulger. Former US Supreme Court Justice Oliver Wendell Holmes's aphorism that hard cases make bad law applies. When emotions are raw, media attention is great, and political considerations are salient, it is naïve to suppose that politicians' decisions about retrials of acquitted offenders and appeals of seemingly lenient sentences will be made dispassionately and impartially.

Prosecutorial appeals of sentence are everywhere comparatively rare and it is unlikely that cases will be comprehensively screened to assure that equivalently wrongful acquittals and unduly lenient outcomes will be treated similarly. Cases for further consideration will most likely be those that are identified by the media coverage or public notoriety they provoke and by the degree to which officials want to demonstrate that they are responsive to one or both. The increased use of pre-trial confinement and increased severity of punishment experienced by people arrested for offences during the August 2011 urban disorders in England and Wales offer recent examples. Public emotions are in many cases likely to be predicated on stereotyped and often inaccurate characterizations of cases.

Secondly, the impetus for English abrogation of the double jeopardy doctrine and authorization of prosecutorial sentence appeals prominently included concerns about sensational media coverage of selected cases and public emotionalism (some presumably naturally arising and some stimulated by media sensationalism). Those are good reasons not to take extraordinary measures, as the folk wisdom not to act under the influence of overwrought emotion instructs ('Don't take it out on your child'). Especially in England where concerns about public confidence are regularly expressed by judges and politicians, there is a serious risk that the double jeopardy rule will be set aside or sentences be appealed as unduly lenient in individual cases because *those* cases receive heavy media attention, and not because they are in important respects exceptional. There is substantial evidence that punishment policies are comparatively less severe in countries in which public perceptions of the legitimacy of state institutions are high.[44] There is no evidence that severe criminal justice policies foster increased levels of legitimacy.

[44] T Lappi-Seppälä, 'Trust, Welfare, and Political Culture—Explaining Differences in National Penal Policies' in M Tonry (ed), *Crime and Justice: A Review of Research* (Chicago, IL: University of Chicago Press, 2008), vol 37.

Thirdly, there is a fundamental empirical question of whether perceptions of wrongful acquittals or lenience in individual cases are correct. Research on public knowledge and opinion regularly shows that members of the general public are woefully uninformed and misinformed about the workings of the criminal justice system, and obtain most of such knowledge as they have from the mass news and entertainment media.[45] Media coverage of controversial cases focuses on a few factors and sensational details. The judges and lawyers immediately involved in a particular case may have valid reasons to believe that allegations reported in the media cannot be proven, that an offence was less awful or an offender less responsible than observers suppose, or that extenuating circumstances not evident to observers justify seemingly aberrant decisions. These are among the reasons why appellate judges typically defer to trial judges' and juries' findings of fact concerning matters they have considered much more closely than bystanders or appellate judges possibly could.

Fourthly, to focus on wrongful acquittals and lenient sentences is inherently arbitrary. In God's eye everyone who commits wrongful act A under circumstances B is equally culpable and deserving of equal punishment, but life is not like that. Crimes go unsolved, malefactors go unidentified or apprehended or charged, cases are dismissed for many reasons, evidentiary problems preclude convictions, and countless other contingencies intervene between wrongful acts and deserved punishments.

Fifthly, even though appellate courts reiterate that the double jeopardy rule historically applied to convictions and not to sentences, there is no reason why the underlying rationales should not encompass both. The affected defendant's interests are substantially the same in both cases. A defendant who learns after protracted post-conviction procedures that he is to be retried or resentenced suffers unwarranted material hardships and psychic injuries not attributable to his own failings but to those of the judge or jury that did not convict when conviction might have been justified or of the judge who sentenced less severely than others might have. The proceedings concluded and, arguably, the defendant had a lucky break. Then, because of decisions judges and juries made in good faith, but with which more distant and often politically motivated observers disagree, he is to be subjected to a limbo in which he does not know what will happen.[46] If the request for a second opportunity to subject the defendant to a new trial or a new sentencing proceeding succeeds, the defendant must again face the awesome power of the state. That is rather a lot to impose on an individual human being because outsiders disagree with a judge's or jury's good faith decision.

The major arguments in favour of retrials of acquitted defendants and resentencing of arguably insufficiently punished ones are insubstantial. One, a favourite of

[45] J Roberts, LJ Stalans, D Indermaur, and M Hough (eds), *Penal Populism and Public Opinion: Lessons from Five Countries* (New York: Oxford University Press, 2002).

[46] Sometimes, of course, judges may act in bad faith. When that seems to have happened, the proper redress is to initiate disciplinary proceedings against the judge. If a defendant was complicit, eg through bribery or witness intimidation, the proper redress is to initiate new criminal proceedings in respect of those new and additional alleged offences.

recent English governments, is that failure to respond to strong public or media sentiment concerning notorious cases will undermine the legitimacy of the legal system. There is no empirical evidence that this is true. There is some evidence to the contrary, that policies aimed at enhancing public confidence by enacting and implementing expressive or symbolic laws treating offenders harshly backfire and undermine confidence. British Crime Survey data show that citizens' concern about particular forms of antisocial behaviour *increased* during the period when antisocial behaviour orders were most extensively promoted, obtained, and enforced.[47] Research designs to test the legitimacy hypotheses (that is all they are despite more than a decade's English experience with expressive crime policies) can be imagined, but would be difficult to carry out. What would be needed are measures of general perceptions of legitimacy, and the effects on them of decisions in individual cases. Simply asking whether respondents approve or disapprove particular acquittals or sentences would not constitute such a measure. In any case, in the English-speaking countries, at least, 70 to 80 per cent of survey respondents typically say that they believe judges' sentences are too lenient; finding an additional effect attributable specifically to apparently wrongful acquittals or unduly lenient sentences would be exceedingly difficult. A second, zero-sum-game argument is that treating offenders more harshly somehow benefits victims. This is a nonsense. Victims do have needs—for respect, for sympathy, sometimes for counselling or material assistance—but those needs must be addressed in their own right. Nothing done, or not done, to particular offenders will address them. In so far as victims want vindication through the suffering or debasement of offenders, they are in the same position as any other observer. The parties to a criminal prosecution are the state and the defendant. It is the defendant whose liberty and other interests are at stake. In societies operating under the rule of law, decisions are to be made by impartial fact-finders and rule-appliers. The opinions and emotions of bystanders are not supposed to matter.

A third argument is that concerns for justice, for horizontal equity, for treating like cases alike, justify abrogation of the double jeopardy rule and prosecution sentence appeals. In our or any other imaginable world, the aims of arguments like these for cosmic justice are impossible to achieve because of the many reasons why most offenders do not receive their just deserts. To ignore the effects of divergent charging, prosecution, dismissal, plea bargaining, and case processing decisions on the dispositions of cases against people who commit comparable crimes while fixing and fixating on the tiny number of cases of apparently wrongful acquittals and unduly lenient sentences is inherently arbitrary, and for that reason alone unjust.

At the end of the day there are many reasons why abrogation of the double jeopardy rule and allowance of prosecutorial appeals of sentence are bad ideas. In the rhetoric of their promoters, those recently adopted diminutions of centuries-old protections of citizens against an overreaching state, aim only to assure that factually guilty offenders be convicted and that offenders be punished no less

[47] Tonry, n 20 above.

severely than they deserve. Promoters' motives are usually much more multi-faceted and self-interested than that. In practice, vast numbers of factually guilty offenders go unconvicted and most offenders, including convicted ones, receive punishments less severe than they deserve. The cruel and repressive laws discussed in this essay are unsound and unjust. They should not be enacted and where they have been, they should be repealed.

Index